Elvis Music FAQ

All That's Left to Know About the King's Recorded Works

Mike Eder

Backbeat
Books

An Imprint of Hal Leonard Corporation

Published in 2013 by Backbeat Books
An Imprint of Hal Leonard Corporation
7777 West Bluemound Road
Milwaukee, WI 53213

Trade Book Division Editorial Offices
33 Plymouth St., Montclair, NJ 07042

All photos are from the personal collection of the author except where otherwise specified.

The FAQ series was conceived by Robert Rodriguez and developed with Stuart Shea.

Printed in the United States of America

Book design by Snow Creative Services

Library of Congress Cataloging-in-Publication Data

Eder, Mike.
   Elvis music FAQ : all that's left to know about the King's recorded works / by Mike Eder. — 1st paperback edition.
      pages cm
   Includes bibliographical references and index.
   ISBN 978-1-61713-049-6
1. Presley, Elvis, 1935–1977—Criticism and interpretation. 2. Rock music—United States—History and criticism. I. Title.
   ML420.P96E27 2013
   782.42166—dc23

                                                                              2013019284

www.backbeatbooks.com

To my late mother, Suzy, who taught me to be myself,
not to limit what I think I can achieve

Also to my late grandpa Sam, who always made me laugh
as much as he made me proud

Contents

Foreword

Elvis Presley has been wearing the crown of "King of Rock and Roll" for more than five decades, and yet rock-and-roll recordings only make up a small part of the body of work he left for us. Elvis oozed talent. He had an amazingly capable voice, and he was by no means just a "rock and roll" singer; he also sang rockabilly, country, blues, ballads, and pop—and on occasion his voice was almost operatic. So how do you pigeonhole a man with that amount of talent and versatility in his voice?

There have been tens of thousands of books written about Elvis over the years, and they've all taken a look, or tried to take a look, at Elvis' life. The media and the public focus on Elvis' personal life, and the very thing that launched Elvis on his worldwide journey of fame—his amazing voice—is all but last when it comes to how Elvis the icon is examined.

Elvis has had more #1 and Top 10, Top 20, and Top 40 hits on the pop music charts than any other recording artist. On my Internet show, *Elvis Express Radio*, we've been calling Elvis the original and true King of Pop for some time now, and it really is the title he deserves when you take the time to examine the music he left us and his awards and chart positions around the world.

Presenting on *Elvis Express Radio* is an absolute pleasure, because sometimes as I listen to a particular song, it can almost be like hearing it for the first time. Before I began this show, I'd never really listened to Elvis under headphones, and in doing so today, what with the wonderful remastering for projects like the complete masters collection, I find that listening carefully to these songs really is like rediscovering them.

One day I received an e-mail from Backbeat Books, which was looking for the right person to author a book focusing on the music . . . yes, the music. At last, a book that would bring a detailed look at Elvis' music, at his record releases and his varying styles. There were a few writers that I knew of who could have done a good job looking at Elvis the artist and not the image, but one stood out to me. Mike Eder had been the author of several articles in some of the best Elvis publications, such as the acclaimed Elvis Files book series and the *Elvis Files* magazine, among others.

I am one fan who is really looking forward to reading this book, which takes a look at the King through his musical legacy. I invite you to join me in putting on those headphones as we take in the deep sounds of Elvis' music and enjoy the journey.

Lee Dawson
Host, *Elvis Express Radio*
May 2013

Acknowledgments

A book of this type cannot be written without the help of others, and I would like to try to thank them all. Lee Dawson, who does the *Elvis Express* radio show, literally made this book happen. I can't thank him enough, but I will recommend his show and his website: www.elvis-express.com. Also, a special thank-you is in order for Jeremy Roberts, who has done more to promote my work than anyone; thank you, my friend. Erik Lorentzen has been a great support, and I am very proud to have contributed to his excellent publications.

All those whom I have worked with at Backbeat have been terrific. Series editor Robert Rodriguez reached out to me first and really helped me get this off the ground. Project editor Jessica Burr has done a lot to make the book as attractive as I think it is, and proved invaluable in the production of it. Copy editor Tom Seabrook has made sure that my work came off as well as can be. Jaime Nelson in marketing was very encouraging, and it was fun sharing ideas. John Cerullo has been a great publisher to work for, and I hope our association will be long and rewarding. Finally, associate editor Bernadette Malavarca has helped me keep on track, encouraged my ideas, and basically made this one of the most enjoyable experiences in my career. Fellow FAQ author Jon Stebbins gave me a lot of tips when I started, and has been supportive over the years.

As far as researching the book, I could not have done without the help of all the websites listed. I would like to especially thank the members of www.elvis-collectors.com. Their informative and challenging message board has helped me refine and back up my individual point of view.

Family and friends have been very special in my life, and I just hope you all enjoy this book. Please take a moment to read the list below.

Special thanks to my wife, Debra Stock, my mother-in-law, Susanne, and my sister-in-law, Lisa (plus family); Larry Eder, Evelyn Eder, and the late Sam Eder; the late Suzy Behan; Barney Behan (plus his entire huge family); Edna Eder (and family, especially Henia); Brian Rabinowitz; Amanda, Tali, Bekira, and Jocelyn Rabinowitz ("the girls"); Marcus Eder (and family), Lilly Eder, Stuart Eder, and Marilynne Sprecht (plus family); Ricky Eder and Cleo Eder; David Richman (and family); Ron Smith; Michael and John Butchki; Bill Cappello; Sean and Aleks Neely (plus family); Terry Williams (and family); Gene Senibaldi (and family); Mike Settle (and family); Mary Arnold Miller (and family); Mickey Jones (and family); Thelma Camacho Ivie (and family); John Carpenter; Gary Lassin, Paul Dowling, and Joe Tunzi (for my start); Karen Powell; Garth Shaw;

Charlene Pollack; Barb Klein; Jim Shoemakersafe; Andrew Hearn; Barry McLean; Tom Macroy Frankie and Karla Wolsfeld; Leif Rocker; David and Lauren Levin; Billy Castillo; Dawn Kiefler; and Meikel Jungner. And finally, Elvis Presley should be thanked for making all of our lives a lot more fun.

Introduction

Do You Know Who I Am?

W hy is Elvis Presley's body of recorded work still so relevant, nearly sixty years after he first entered the studio?

I would like to think it's because his talent and career covered such a wide range. Whichever of the multiple images the name Elvis Presley evokes, they are all a reflection of the Americana of his era. Elvis appeals to the masses because most can find a little of him in themselves. Yet there are so many different Elvises. There was the "Hillbilly Cat" of his Sun Records period. This Elvis completely redefined the relationship of rhythm and blues to country by destroying both the racial and musical barriers between them. Then there was the "King of Rock and Roll." This was the gold lamé–wearing superstar who became the worldwide ambassador of early rock and roll, and of the inherent rebellion and fun that went along with that. There is the Hollywood idol, a reflection of a man who got what he wanted, then lost what he had. There was the more mature yet even more intense Elvis of his comeback era, who some would argue managed creatively—if not culturally—to top his record-breaking early achievements. Finally, there was the seventies Elvis, who started out so promisingly but went into a gradual personal decline before his death in 1977.

Certainly, Elvis is still remembered most as an entertainer, but it seems that with rare exception, Elvis the icon has overshadowed Elvis the artist. There have been literally thousands of books on Elvis Presley, but so few offer anything of value on his music. Most of those that do are dry reference books, and many of the others let Elvis' personal story intrude far too much on the authors' assessments of his creative work. As happens so often, a critical consensus is formed, and few bother to challenge it. Sadly, this has the effect of having the public—and even long-term fans—not only underestimate Elvis Presley, but also fail to form their own thoughts about his inherent value as a performer.

That's where *Elvis Music FAQ* comes in. While my personal opinions may be just as subjective, my goal is to get people thinking about Elvis' songs as more than just one aspect of why he is important. In short, this book hopes to convey that the music is the vital—if not sole—reason why Elvis Presley remains as famous today as he was at the height of his career. While the recorded catalogues of acts such as the Beatles, the Rolling Stones, and Bob Dylan have been preserved through the years, Elvis' original vision for his work has been all but lost. And although the comeback of vinyl and the establishing of Elvis' own official collector's label have clarified things to an extent, the records Elvis himself sanctioned for release are still largely lost to the ages. Today, too much time is spent focusing on an endless stream of hits packages, concert recordings, and alternate takes, which often muddy the waters on what Elvis was trying to convey personally. These "new" recordings have their place, but the trajectory of Elvis' career can be really misconstrued by present-day knowledge of his personal issues.

Unquestionably, Elvis had ups and downs in his music career, but many listeners, from John Lennon on down, tended to stick to the Elvis they were most comfortable with. The result is that much of his work has been ignored or dismissed unfairly. Like Bob Dylan after him, Elvis refused to be categorized. Elvis loved rock and roll, but he also loved pop ballads, folk songs, blues, gospel, and country. Elvis had a vision of music bigger than any genre. From blues wailer Arthur Crudup to crooner Dean Martin, from the gospel sounds of the Blackwood Brothers to the country-bluegrass of Bill Monroe, Elvis loved it all.

On his official 1958 interview EP *Elvis Sails*, Presley had this to say: "Rock-and-roll music, if you like it, if you feel it, you can't help but move to it. That's what happens to me. I can't help it. I mean, I have to move around. I can't stand still. I've tried, and I can't do it." In a rare 1956 TV interview with Wink Martindale, he added: "Rock and roll is real hot right now. I like it. It's very good. It has feeling and people enjoy it. People enjoy dancing to it and there's some very beautiful records made in rock and roll style. Stuff like 'The Magic Touch,' 'The Great Pretender,' and stuff like that. They don't make any prettier songs than that."

While undoubtedly excelling as rock and roll's first real spokesman, Presley was equally passionate when discussing other influences. In 1970, at a Houston press conference, he noted: "Country music was always a part of the influence on my type of music. It's a combination of country music and gospel, and rhythm and blues. I liked all different types of music as a child. Of course, the *Grand Ole Opry* is the first thing I ever heard, probably. But I like the blues, and I liked the gospel quartets and all that."

In 1972, Elvis granted several interviews to the producers of the documentary *Elvis on Tour*. It was here that you really got a sense of what made him tick musically. "I liked all types of music, you know. When I was in high school, I had records by Mario Lanza and the Metropolitan Opera. I just loved music. The Spanish—I liked the Mexican flavored songs. But the gospel thing is just . . . gospel is what we grew up with more than anything else. We do two shows a night for five weeks a lot of times, and we will go upstairs and sing until daylight, you know, gospel songs. It more or less puts your mind at ease—it does mine."

Elvis was obviously a man with a unique and intelligent view of music, but even many of those who do realize his talent put forth the myth that Presley went on instinct rather than intellect. *Elvis Music FAQ* will attempt to extinguish the misguided view of Presley as a malleable or opportunistic entertainer. When I spoke in 1996 to the most controversial—but perhaps most gifted—Elvis soundalike, Jimmy "Orion" Ellis, I gained insight from a performer who clearly got the essence of where Elvis was coming from creatively. "Elvis was an artist, and he carried himself as an artist. He took what he did very seriously, and that's why he was the best." Going back to Elvis' original records reveals the pure intent of his musical vision in a way that most compilers or latter-day critics cannot seem to grasp. He truly was an artist: one who even at his most compromised managed to put a little bit of his soul into everything he did.

Elvis Music FAQ has been designed for anyone who has been moved by Elvis Presley's recordings. Following the tradition of the FAQ series, it brings a lot of information together for the first time in one concise, entertaining package. Hardcore fans may know all the dates, or the basics found within, but they will get a fresh perspective that will breathe new life into the recordings they have long treasured. Casual fans will get all the important data on Elvis' oeuvre without any of the aridity or tedium found in countless other tomes. Those new to the Elvis world will find out why this man who began recording a full six decades ago still has such a grip on the world's imagination. Most importantly, the personal artistic vision of Elvis Presley will be restored, as will his creative reputation.

There are chapters on every year of Elvis' career and the music released and recorded therein. In addition, one will find a wide array of topics supplementing the basic commentary. There is a look at his pioneering original record label, Sun; insight into his management; the continued importance of television in his career; the amusing musical oddities created by those trying to ride the Elvis success train; the contentious role drugs played in his performances; and much more. All of these subjects are covered, not with lightweight trivia or gross speculation, but with a measured effort to give a substantial account of the truth behind the legend of Elvis Presley. One might say that the only truths about Elvis Presley can be found in the grooves of his records. *Elvis Music FAQ* aims to be the one essential companion to explain the reason why the voice heard over the speakers still carries such resonance.

Elvis Music
FAQ

Have You Heard the News?

Elvis' early career has been endlessly discussed over the years, and with good reason. Elvis was not the first rock-and-roll artist, but without him, rock and roll would likely not have lasted past the fifties. Elvis gave rock and roll an image—a persona—and from the start he was very serious about making good music. He didn't always maintain the high standards he initially set for himself, but at his best he was indeed "The King."

The story of Elvis' rise to fame is part of twentieth-century history as much as any political or social occurrence. Timing was part of it, but mainly it was down to talent and ambition. When Elvis first came to Sun Records at 706 Union, in his adopted hometown of Memphis, he was fresh out of high school. He was also exceedingly poor, to the point where he only allowed close friends into his home.

Elvis was born in 1935, the only living child of Gladys and Vernon Presley; a twin, Jesse, had died at birth. The family moved to Memphis from Tupelo, Mississippi, in 1948, hoping to better their yearly income. More money was not fast in coming, but Elvis already had big dreams. He wanted to be an actor, and music had been almost an obsession since early childhood. Liking the way Tony Curtis looked, Elvis grew his hair long in the era of crew cuts. Emulating his favorite blues and country artists, he was also dressing quite loudly by his junior year. He was quiet, even shy, but he stood out, which was likely his goal.

By the time Elvis graduated Humes High in June 1953, he seems already to have had his eye on the Memphis Recording Service owned by Sam Phillips. Today, multitudes of people visit the site of the facility now known as Sun Studios, and Elvis is a large reason why. If nothing else, the musical and social revolution that was to follow wouldn't have had the same impact without Elvis being there to lead the way.

Perhaps the most crucial thing Elvis and Sam had in common was a lack of racial prejudice. In the South of 1953, this wasn't exactly a common trait. Like his son, Vernon Presley has been accused of being a racist, but in an article for *Good Housekeeping* in late 1977, the elder Presley made a point of saying that he and Gladys made sure that Elvis was raised to treat everybody equally. Because of this, Elvis was open to all types of music. He was exposed as much to blues as he was to country. Once again, it should be pointed out that this was not an everyday thing among white teenagers of the early fifties.

Studio Work

Being a fan of Sam Phillips' work, and knowing Sam offered a service of cutting acetate records, Elvis had been eyeing 706 Union for several months before he finally summoned up the nerve to go in. He cut at least two discs there: "My Happiness"/"That's When Your Heartaches Began" in mid-1953 and "It Wouldn't Be the Same Without You"/"I'll Never Stand in Your Way" in early 1954. Both Sam and his secretary/assistant Marion Keisker heard something special in Elvis and kept his name on file.

Hearing these recordings today, one is struck by the fact that Elvis initially wanted to be a straight ballad singer. His voice wasn't yet suited for that sort of thing, but there was something in his phrasing that was already unique. You can almost hear the yearning quality of someone desperate to make a go of a singing career. Elvis may have told Marion that the records were for his mother, but he was unquestionably looking to be discovered.

Sam called Elvis on June 26, 1954, asking him to come down and try out a song that he had acquired in demo form. The song was called "Without You" (not to be confused with "It Wouldn't Be the Same Without You"). Try as he might, Elvis just couldn't master it. In early July, Sam talked with the guitar player from a group he had signed called the Starlite Wranglers. His name was Scotty Moore, and he agreed to have Elvis come over to his house to try out. Fellow Wrangler Bill Black stopped by during the informal audition, and although neither man was unduly impressed, they thought Sam might be able to help Presley out.

On July 5th, Elvis had his first recording session with Moore on lead guitar and Black on bass. Moore would stay with Elvis right through to the 1968 NBC TV special, while Black would remain until the *King Creole* sessions in 1958. At first, Elvis stuck to ballads, but the mood changed when he and the band (soon to be known as the Blue Moon Boys) started messing around with Arthur Crudup's "That's All Right Mama." Elvis completely reimagined the song, partly by including elements of other Crudup records, such as "If I Get Lucky" and "Dirt Road Blues" (as noted by Elvis collector George Smith). Sam heard something different in it and told them to do it over for a master take. Sam had been looking for a white artist who sang with the passion of a black performer, and in Elvis Presley he had unexpectedly found one.

That night, rockabilly—as it would come to be known—was born. Essentially a stripped-down, country-infused version of rock and roll, it had an inherent quality that many artists would soon try to emulate. It was big from 1954 to 1956, and by the late sixties, listeners worldwide would be collecting rockabilly records with a passion. Even today, there are young musicians who play rockabilly, and the original records are still heavily collectable—the Sun catalogue especially.

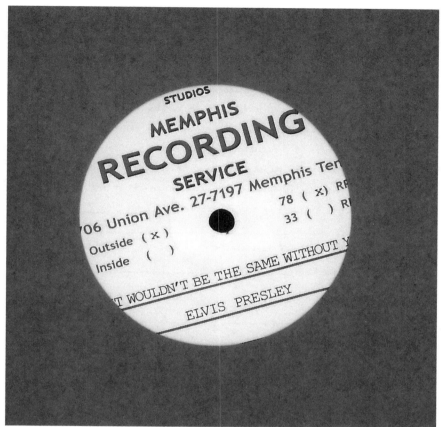

A very faithful boot of Elvis' second demo recording, featuring "It Wouldn't Be the Same Without You," from early 1954. The talent was obvious, but he had yet to cultivate a unique style.

Keen to encourage Elvis to keep going with what they discovered that night, on July 7th the guys came in and recorded "Blue Moon of Kentucky," a bluegrass standard by Bill Monroe. They played it straight country at first, and it sounded good, but then Sam encouraged them to make it more like "That's All Right" in feel. Over the course of three days, Elvis, Scotty, and Bill made a record that would change the course of country, blues, and rock and roll forever.

Elvis cut a lot of music during August and September, but of the seven known cuts, Sam opted to put out only two: "Good Rockin' Tonight" and "I Don't Care If the Sun Don't Shine," the most creative and forward looking of the bunch. Sam still didn't want to put out any slow songs, but these sessions saw Elvis developing his voice into something really special. With the blues of "Tomorrow Night," the (sadly lost) gospel of "Satisfied," and the balladry of "I'll Never Let You Go," the foundations of Elvis' career were already being set in place. Not

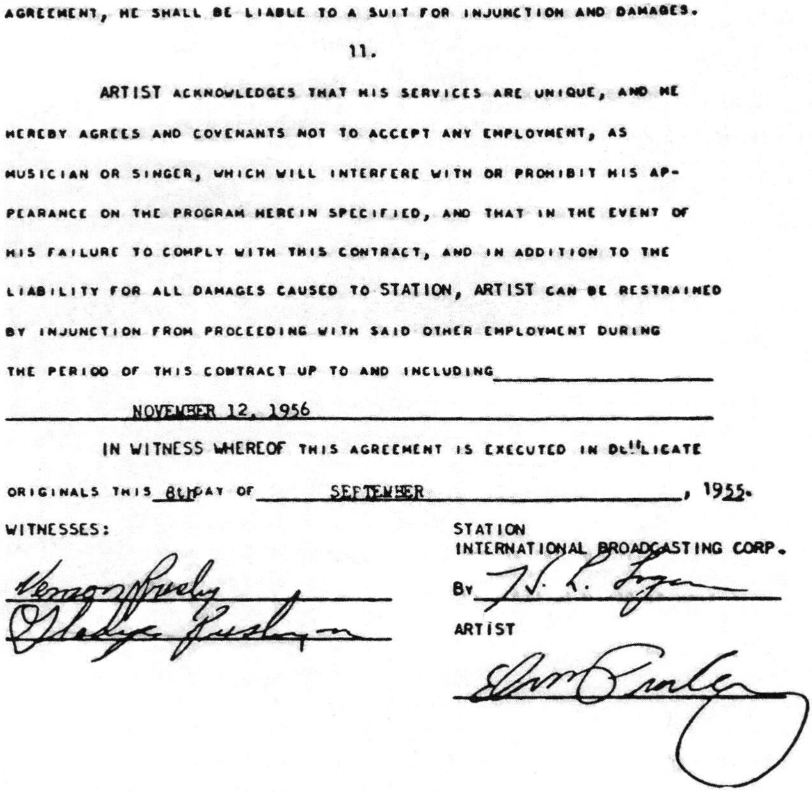

AGREEMENT, HE SHALL BE LIABLE TO A SUIT FOR INJUNCTION AND DAMAGES.

11.

ARTIST ACKNOWLEDGES THAT HIS SERVICES ARE UNIQUE, AND HE HEREBY AGREES AND COVENANTS NOT TO ACCEPT ANY EMPLOYMENT, AS MUSICIAN OR SINGER, WHICH WILL INTERFERE WITH OR PROHIBIT HIS AP- PEARANCE ON THE PROGRAM HEREIN SPECIFIED, AND THAT IN THE EVENT OF HIS FAILURE TO COMPLY WITH THIS CONTRACT, AND IN ADDITION TO THE LIABILITY FOR ALL DAMAGES CAUSED TO STATION, ARTIST CAN BE RESTRAINED BY INJUNCTION FROM PROCEEDING WITH SAID OTHER EMPLOYMENT DURING THE PERIOD OF THIS CONTRACT UP TO AND INCLUDING_____

_____NOVEMBER 12, 1956_____

IN WITNESS WHEREOF THIS AGREEMENT IS EXECUTED IN DUPLICATE ORIGINALS THIS 8th DAY OF_____SEPTEMBER_____, 1955.

WITNESSES:

STATION
INTERNATIONAL BROADCASTING CORP.
BY_____

ARTIST

This facsimile contract included in the LP *The Beginning Years* is the one Elvis signed to appear on *Louisiana Hayride*. His stint with the program was the most crucial exposure of his early career.

everything worked, but the eerie version of "Blue Moon" alone showed Presley already to be more inventive and unique than the majority of those that influenced him.

Elvis cut and released his third single late in the year, but "Milkcow Blues Boogie"/"You're a Heartbreaker" failed to make much of an impact. That's not to say they weren't great performances. The former is one of Elvis' most rollicking recordings, the latter one of his finest and purest in the country field.

Live Performance

Elvis didn't get into music full time until mid-October, but he started doing live shows with Scotty and Bill around Memphis soon after they cut their first record. He played the Bon Air club for a few months. Once or twice, he was backed up by the entire Starlite Wranglers band, but it wasn't a good fit. Scotty and Bill soon turned their energies toward Elvis, and gigs started to pick up. Perhaps the first major gig they played was at the bottom of the bill at the Overton Park Shell on July 30th. Shaking partly from nerves and partly from the example set by some of his favorite gospel and R&B singers, Elvis was still able to make an impression, even outshining the established Slim Whitman. That he was able to get the crowd to react favorably so early in his career must have been very encouraging.

On October 2nd, Elvis' played his first gig outside of Memphis on none other than the *Grand Ole Opry*. Nashville wasn't quite ready for him yet, however, and he received only polite applause. Nonetheless, to get on the stage of the Ryman a little less than three months after cutting your first record was a big achievement. After the *Opry* gig, Elvis made another radio broadcast from the legendary Ernest Tubb's Record Shop.

While Elvis never played the *Opry* again, he did catch the attention of its main rival, the somewhat less conservative *Louisiana Hayride*. This syndicated show out of Shreveport aired every Saturday night and had given Hank Williams one of his first big breaks. Elvis' first Hayride performance on October 16th has survived, and it reveals a crowd that was not quite hysterical but was nonetheless open. He is understandably somewhat awkward in his dialogue with host Frank Page, but he sings like a true professional when performing both sides of his debut. As it had for Williams before him, the *Hayride* would give a big boost to Elvis, who was quickly offered a contract to appear every weekend.

With his *Hayride* debut being the only 1954 Elvis live recording that exists today, it's hard to judge his early stage development in detail. On the evidence we have in photos, reviews, and this recording, Elvis was already having a strong effect on the limited audience he had been exposed to. Back in the summer of 1953, when he first went into Sun, Marion Keisker asked Elvis who he sounded like. He replied that he didn't sound like nobody. A year later, he showed that this was demonstrably true on vinyl, and there's little doubt he was any less distinctive onstage.

By November, Elvis was landing gigs in Louisiana, as well as Arkansas, but it was in Texas that he really first took off outside of Memphis. These were relatively small gigs, mainly in the Houston area, yet it was an important step in the right direction. As much as the *Hayride* or Memphis, the success Elvis enjoyed in Texas played a crucial role in his rise to superstardom. That he was already cultivating a fan base in a major region would prove invaluable in spreading his name nationally over the coming year.

Popularity and Impact

Elvis wasn't a household name by any means in 1954. He was becoming well known in certain Southern markets, but only his first record got any real chart action—and even then it was solely on a local level. Iconic Memphis DJ Dewey Phillips got "That's All Right" on his *Red, Hot & Blue* show within days of its being recorded, and he conducted Elvis' first interview on air. (Though Dewey was not related to Sam Phillips, he often played and premiered the recordings Sam produced.)

But something was happening almost from the start. The young demographic Elvis was playing to, and the level of their enthusiasm for his music and performances, was rather remarkable. When he joined the *Hayride* in October, the people that attended were mostly well into adulthood veering into middle age. By the end of the year, teenage girls—and a fair number of boys—were heading to the Municipal Auditorium to see Elvis perform.

Elvis already had hardcore fans like Joyce Railsback keeping track of what he performed every week in their diaries. Joyce's notes are invaluable in judging the way Elvis presented himself week to week and can be found in the late Frank Page's book (co-written with Joey Kent) *Elvis: The Hayride Years 54–56*. In addition to his singles, Elvis covered other proto-rock-and-roll hits of the day, like "Shake, Rattle and Roll" and "Fool, Fool, Fool." He even performed things like "Blue Moon," demonstrating that while Sam called the shots in the studio, Elvis was already following his own instincts onstage. Elvis had a long year ahead of him. He would go on to play around 300 sets in 1955, and it would pay off big time.

2

706 Union

The Birthplace of Rock and Roll

I t is the subject of endless debate, but a good case can be made that Sam Phillips and Sun were *the* catalysts for the rock-and-roll revolution that took place in the fifties. The biggest part of this was the lack of racial prejudice from Sam, plus his feeling that music didn't have to fit into a stilted set category.

Astonishingly, nearly all of the music issued on Sun or Phillips International (Sam's second major label) is worth pursuing. This is less the case after Sam moved the studios in 1960 and started to have less involvement with the sessions, yet even after Shelby Singleton took over the label in 1969, Sun still made some fascinating music, all the way to its last new release in 1983. For the purposes of this book, we will examine a half-dozen rock-and-roll artists (aside from Elvis) who first had a record issued or leased by Sam in the fifties.

Ike Turner

Ike Turner's successful and innovative career went far beyond his work with Sam Phillips, but his first and most historically important record was cut with Phillips before the dawn of Sun Records itself. Ike's band the Kings of Rhythm had many featured vocalists aside from Turner himself. One of these was Jackie Brenston, who would be inadvertently credited with Ike's first hit.

In early 1951, the band traveled to Memphis, having heard good things about Sam from a new blues artist named B. B. King. On the way over, Ike wrote a song called "Rocket 88." It differed from much of the R&B that came before it for three distinct reasons. The most obvious thing was the lyrics, which were teen-oriented and talked exclusively of a young man and his friends' adventures in his souped-up auto. The second reason was that Ike was into country music on a far deeper level than most of the blues artists that came before him. While this influence was more evident on songs where Ike played guitar rather than piano, country artist Bill Haley would shortly reinvent himself upon hearing "Rocket 88," and he and his Saddlemen duly became the very first white rock-and-roll act.

The third reason was a happy accident. On their way over to the studio, Ike and his band had to strap their amp to the top of their car so they had enough room to bring everyone. During the trip, the amp fell off the roof and sustained some damage, resulting in a pleasingly distortion sound that would set the

Elvis' debut opened the door for other white artists to record on the
Sun label. None of the original Elvis singles came in the custom Sun
sleeve first used in 1956. Legal and illegal reissues have utilized them
ever since the late sixties to add period appeal.

Courtesy of Robert Rodriguez

record apart from other popular songs of the day. In short, this was rock and
roll in its most fully developed form to date.

Sam liked the individuality of "Rocket 88" and encouraged Ike and the
Kings of Rhythm to be a little different and more modern. In the early fifties,
Sam leased his recordings to various labels, and "Rocket 88" was sent to Chess
Records in Chicago for distribution. Somebody at the label renamed the band
after lead singer Jackie Brenston and called the Kings of Rhythm the "Delta
Cats." When "Rocket 88" zoomed to #1 on the R&B charts, Jackie quickly left the
band to strike it solo. This left Ike and Sam holding the bag, but Turner would
occasionally return to Sun to play sessions over the next several years. Sam would
also find success with several of Ike's other singers, most notably Billy Emerson.

In the meantime, "Rocket 88" started a whole new trend, and the more hip
white teenagers like Elvis Presley took careful note of the sounds coming out of
Sam's studio. Ike would even hide Elvis behind his piano so Presley could watch
the Kings of Rhythm in the all-black over-twenty-one clubs. Clearly, the sounds of
Memphis were already becoming a big part of Elvis' life, years before he became
the city's most famous artist.

Johnny Cash

Calling Johnny Cash a rock-and-roll pioneer may seem odd to some, but he was the first country singer to have a rock-and-roll attitude. He also had a very elemental sound that helped set the foundation for rockabilly as much as anything else did. Cash had been writing for several years when he and his little band, soon known as the Tennessee Two (Luther Perkins and Marshall Grant), first showed up at Sun in late 1954. Elvis wasn't an outward influence on Cash, but his success admittedly caused Johnny to take making music a lot more seriously.

Cash would have a very long career, and is easily one of the top five figures in the history of country music, but the records he made at Sun through 1958 remain his most influential and consistent. Numbered among them are "Cry! Cry! Cry!," "Folsom Prison Blues," "I Walk the Line," "Get Rhythm," "Ballad of a Teenage Queen," "Big River," "Guess Things Happen That Way," and "The Ways of a Woman in Love," all of which redefined what country music was. Like Ike Turner before him, Cash brought an established genre to the attention of teens.

Being on the same label as Presley and sharing a manager with him in Bob Neal, Johnny would tour with Elvis quite a bit in 1955. Cash took part in the "Million Dollar Quartet" jam of December 4, 1956, although he is inaudible on the known recordings. Still, Johnny insisted he was there in the harmonies, singing higher than usual in order to accommodate Elvis.

One thing that should be squashed is the assertion in the film *I Walk the Line* that Elvis introduced Cash to drugs. Cash is on record as saying he never saw Elvis take a pill in those days, nor did Cash have a notable drug habit while he was on Sun. Elvis and Cash would continue to enjoy each others' music; Elvis would occasionally perform a humorous medley of "Folsom Prison" and "I Walk the Line" in his 1970 live set.

Carl Perkins

Carl Perkins may have enjoyed only fleeting chart success, but his talent and influence were just as notable as those of his labelmates. Arriving at 706 Union at roughly the same time as Cash, he recorded one single on Sam's short-lived country label, Flip, before becoming an official Sun Records artist. Elvis' influence on Perkins was due more to the fact that when Carl first heard him he realized that other artists were having success with music that was similar to his own.

Carl's music resonates with many rockabilly aficionados, as he cut some of the most hard-hitting and biting records of the idiom. Among these are "Gone, Gone, Gone," "Honey Don't," the then-unreleased "Put Your Cat Clothes On," "Sure to Fall," "Boppin' the Blues," "Dixie Fried" (which depicted a knife fight), "Matchbox," "Your True Love," "Glad All Over," and "Lend Me Your Comb." The Beatles were to become one of Perkins' major proponents, and over the years they would record and/or perform nearly all of the aforementioned tracks.

For all that wonderful music, Carl is still best known for his fantastic hit record and composition "Blue Suede Shoes." Along with early Elvis singles like "Heartbreak Hotel" and "Hound Dog," it was one of the defining songs of fifties rock and roll. Elvis ended up becoming associated with the song after his early A&R man at RCA, Steve Sholes, realized he didn't have enough new material to fill Elvis' first LP. Sholes asked Sam for permission to cut "Blue Suede Shoes," which Phillips granted on the condition that it wouldn't be released as a competing single. True to his word, Sholes didn't issue Elvis' version on 45 until the Perkins version had enjoyed a full chart run.

While Perkins' recording was indisputably a bigger hit, Elvis' version is arguably better known because of its inclusion on his iconic first LP and in many concert and television performances. It even made the background of one of his movies. Perkins never had any long-term hard feelings toward Elvis, largely because Presley's various studio and live recordings of the song made Carl a small fortune. In fact, when Carl had a car crash in the wake of "Blue Suede Shoes'" success, Elvis was one of the first people to get in contact. Having toured with Elvis in 1955, Carl was another member of the "Million Dollar Quartet," and Elvis seemed to have a ball harmonizing with him. Perkins spoke very fondly of Elvis over the years, and they maintained a distant but enduring friendship.

Roy Orbison

The Sun Records material Roy Orbison recorded with his fifties band the Teen Kings isn't nearly as well known as his work on the Monument label, but it stands as some of his best. Roy got his start with Sun in 1956. He had known Presley for nearly a year and had even had him on his local television show in Texas. Roy's early work was heavily influenced by Elvis, and is mostly hard rockabilly. His best-known song of the era was "Ooby Dooby," a song Elvis joked about onstage at his May 6, 1956, show in Little Rock, Arkansas, after it was shouted as a request.

Roy wasn't on Sun at the same time as Elvis, but he chose the label largely because of Presley's Sun Records connection. Sam didn't really share Roy's penchant for ballads, so Orbison departed after little over a year. Roy's breakthrough on Monument occurred in 1960 with the seminal "Only the Lonely." Roy wrote the song for Elvis, but Elvis was asleep when Orbison came to Graceland to play it. Roy decided to do it himself and the rest was history. Orbison saw Elvis perform in Las Vegas in 1976, when Elvis introduced him from the stage as the best singer in the industry.

Jerry Lee Lewis

For sheer charisma and impact, Jerry Lee was one of Elvis' biggest competitors in the fifties. His style is entirely dissimilar to Presley's, and, in a rare move for a white rock-and-roller in the mid-to-late fifties, he took great pains to be original in the wake of Elvis' success. That's not to say that "The Killer" didn't love Elvis' early records, but—like everything else—he sang them in his own inimitable style.

Jerry Lee first tried to make it in Nashville, but was told he should put away the piano and play guitar like Elvis. Though Lewis could play a credible guitar, he already had a vision for his music and decided to go try out for Sam. Phillips began recording him in late 1956, both as a solo artist and a session man. Jerry Lee was playing the Carl Perkins session that morphed into the "Million Dollar Quartet" jam, and he more than held his own with the two stars. Elvis was duly impressed and told the reporters present how great and unique he felt Jerry Lee to be.

Jerry Lee became one of the hottest new stars of 1957 with his mega-hits "Whole Lotta Shakin' Going On" and "Great Balls of Fire." Because of the scandal involving his marriage to his underage second cousin, Lewis never quite matched the success of those early hits, but he recorded one of the most consistently excellent bodies of work in music history. Elvis was one of the few to speak up for Lewis in the wake of the scandal, and though Jerry Lee was quite competitive, he and Elvis hung out together in Memphis throughout the fifties and sixties.

Before the story of his marriage hit in the early summer of 1958, Jerry Lee had already marked up two more classic hits in "Breathless" and "High School Confidential." Although all of his Sun recordings maintained his early standards, he only really scored again with Sun in the U.S. with an incendiary cover of Ray Charles' "What'd I Say" in 1961. This was to be Sun's last major hit. Though Jerry Lee has expressed his dismay at the way Colonel Tom Parker bossed Elvis around, Presley is one of the few artists Lewis greatly respects (aside from himself).

Charlie Rich

Of all of the performers Phillips recorded, Charlie Rich was the most vocally similar to Elvis, but like Lewis he was a piano player—albeit one with a decidedly more jazzy bent. Except for an instrumental under another name, Rich recorded exclusively for Sam's more adult-oriented Phillips International label. He didn't know Elvis as well as the other artists mentioned here, as he didn't become a hit maker until late in 1959, with "Lonely Weekends." Rich only achieved consistent success when he became a middle-of-the-road country singer in the early seventies. Still, the work he did on Phillips, RCA, Smash, and Hi make up some of the most intense Memphis rock and roll ever cut.

Elvis was an early fan and recorded Rich's "I'm Comin' Home" in 1961. When Elvis was hospitalized in 1973, he had his turntable brought in and would constantly play Charlie's *Behind Closed Doors* LP on it. The Beatles also noted that when they met Elvis in 1965, Rich's "Mohair Sam" was one of their and Presley's favorite current hits. In 1975, Elvis cut a version of "Pieces of My Life," which had featured on Rich's partial return to rock, *The Silver Fox*, the year before. Like so many others, Rich had originally sought Sam out in light of Elvis' success.

3

Nothing That Could Hold Me

T he Boppin' Hillbilly," "The Hillbilly Cat," "The King of Western Bop," and a plethora of other nicknames surfaced in 1955 as commentators made wild attempts to categorize Elvis. Driven to make it big, Elvis performed more shows than he ever would again. Granted, many of these were short appearances, but taking into consideration all the traveling involved and the sheer total of performances (over 300), one is overwhelmed by his determination to succeed.

The arrival of Colonel Tom Parker and RCA Victor changed Elvis' life for good. Both his label and his manager would let him down in years to come, but in 1955, Elvis felt on top of the world. His phenomenal growth was not just as a moneymaker. Experimenting with his sound, he used *Hayride* pianist Leon Post and steel guitarist Sunny Trammell on some of his January dates. Recorded evidence shows the additions to be more cute than organic, but it was important to Elvis to build a bigger band around him.

Two more *Hayride* veterans joined the troupe on and off for the remainder of the year. Jimmy Day would play steel guitar and Floyd Cramer, who would go on to work a lot of studio dates with Elvis, played the piano. A much more permanent addition came on August 8th with the arrival of *Hayride* drummer D. J. Fontana. Though he missed much of September due to illness, Fontana would become an essential part of the Blue Moon Boys, staying with Elvis all the way through to the 1968 NBC television special.

Studio Work

Elvis was on the road so often he managed only four brief sessions in 1955. Nevertheless, the resulting music is some of the most seminal rockabilly or rock and roll ever recorded. The first session was held at some point between January 31st and the first few days of February. Early versions of "I Got a Woman" and "Tryin' to Get to You" were recorded but haven't been heard since, as the tapes are lost. The sole surviving recording from this date was "Baby Let's Play House."

There may have been a session sometime in March, but the next confirmed studio date took place in mid-April, when "How Do You Think I Feel" and a remake of "You're a Heartbreaker" failed to get finished. The latter has since disappeared. Elvis did however get a final cut of "I'm Left, You're Right, She's Gone," a song he may have been working on for as long as six months.

On July 21st, Elvis held his most productive sessions since the previous fall. In fact, it was one of the most stunning he ever held. The apex of his creativity on Sun, "Mystery Train" and "Tryin' to Get to You" are both epic performances. "I Forgot to Remember to Forget" was also pretty darn good, and it gave Elvis his first #1 record when it hit the top of the country charts on February 25, 1956.

This beautiful 1955 photograph came with the 1984 six-LP set *A Golden Celebration*.

Sometime in early November, Elvis wanted to cut a flip side for his next intended single, "Tryin' to Get to You." He worked on an arrangement of fellow Sun artist Billy "The Kid" Emerson's "When It Rains, It Pours," which on most Elvis releases is given the more exacting title "When It Rains, It Really Pours." The sessions came to an abrupt stop when Elvis was informed that he was no longer able to record for Sun in the wake of negotiations with RCA.

It's kind of sad in retrospect that Elvis would no longer record with Sam Phillips. Few were able to offer the kind of guidance Sam had provided, and nobody could replicate his sound. On the other hand, Elvis probably would have outgrown the studio within several years, as his musical horizons quickly began to expand. It would now be up to Elvis to provide the creative vision required, as he certainly wasn't going to get any help from the staid RCA production team.

Live Performance

Though there's far less surviving recorded material, and next to no video, working through the details of Elvis' early appearances isn't quite as daunting a task as it once was. As the most eagerly chronicled period of his career, a picture can be painted of Elvis' early stage appearances with some accuracy. Though it's impossible to examine the changes from tour to tour, or to confirm his exact set on many nights, there's still a lot of information available due to the feverish work of Elvis researchers like Ger Ryff and Ernst Jorgensen.

With Elvis working as much as he did, it was almost inevitable that tapes, acetates (demo records made to be played a limited number of times), and wire recordings would surface. Excerpts from nine shows, mostly from the *Hayride*, have surfaced in varying quality. Together, they give us a pretty good idea of what Elvis was like as a performer, pre-superstardom. As spontaneous here in 1955 as he would be later on in his career, he was apt to do any given early rock-and-roll or R&B song along with his own records. The sheer raw energy of Elvis as a live performer through 1970 is something to behold, and the honest reason for his stunning success onstage was that he did give something extra, visually and vocally, when he performed before an audience.

From a chronological standpoint, some dates are notable. After promoting an Elvis show on January 11th, DJ and promoter Ernest Hackworth (a.k.a. Uncle Dudley) from New Boston, Texas, told Colonel Parker about the crowd's intense reaction to Elvis. Later that week, on the 15th, Parker went down to watch Elvis' weekly *Louisiana Hayride* performance. The Colonel first put Elvis on some of his package shows in mid-February, and on the 26th, Elvis' current manager, Bob Neal, booked him to play his first show outside the South in Cleveland, Ohio.

Elvis took his first airplane flight on March 23rd to audition for Arthur Godfrey's talent scouts, but he was rejected. On a happier note, April 16th saw Elvis headline the first of four *Big "D" Jamboree* broadcasts on KRLD radio in Dallas. The station had an especially strong signal and did a lot to cement Elvis'

ELVIS PRESLEY TOMORROW NIGHT   MONO

This 2000 mock Sun EP used a nice shot from February 6, 1955. It looks far more like the British reissue it is than anything Sam would have put out.

popularity throughout the region. By the 25th, he had begun his first headlining tour, which lasted for five days and took in various cities in Texas and New Mexico.

May 13th was a real turning point, as fans ran riot after Elvis' show at New Baseball Park (which was to become the Gator Bowl) in Jacksonville, Florida. As he left the stage, Elvis jokingly suggested the girls in the audience meet him backstage—and most in attendance tried to do just that. When they got to Elvis, they tore off most of his clothes and even some of his skin.

On July 4th, Elvis was scheduled to play three shows. His first show that day, at Hodges Park in De Leon, Texas, stands out for out for being his one and only full gospel set. Elvis was inspired by playing on the same bill as his gospel idols the Statesmen and the Blackwood Brothers, but was not well received by the teens that came to see him rock. Though a gospel tour would have yielded fantastic results in the early seventies, it was something Elvis never tried again after the failure in De Leon. It didn't matter, however, as by now nothing could get in the way of his rapid ascent.

On Celluloid

No professional footage has surfaced from Elvis' Sun period, but his October 20th set at Brooklyn High in Cleveland, Ohio, opening for Pat Boone and Bill Haley (both of whom already had national pop hits), was filmed along with the rest of the show, with excerpts set to be included in a movie short about local disc jockey Bill Randle, *The Pied Piper of Cleveland*. Along with Alan Freed (before both moved to New York), Randle had put Cleveland on the map as the first Northern city to take to rock and roll in a big way. It's likely that Elvis would have been shown only briefly, as film shorts usually ran from fifteen to twenty minutes, and he wasn't the biggest name included at the time. Many rumors have circulated about the footage over the years, but as of 2013 there's still no sign of it.

Popularity and Impact

Elvis hadn't yet become a national or international phenomenon, but both of his 1955 records hit the country charts hard. In his wake, dozens of new (and even a handful of established) country artists decided to give rock and roll a try. To show just how much he grew over the year, on a date in San Angelo, Texas, on January 5th, he had been erroneously billed as "Alvis." By July, *Cash Box* magazine had named him the #1 up-and-coming country male vocalist.

On November 10th, Elvis appeared at the country music disc jockeys' convention in Nashville for promotional purposes, where he made important contacts and spoke about his upcoming deal with RCA Victor. Later that night, songwriter and DJ Mae Boren Axton played Elvis the demo of "Heartbreak Hotel." By November 21st, Elvis was under contract to RCA, which paid Sam Phillips a record-breaking $35,000 for Elvis' contract, plus a $5,000 personal bonus. It was a dizzying ride, but this would be only the tip of the iceberg.

4

I Forgot to Remember to Forget

A Guide to the Sun Years

The music Elvis recorded at Sun is so overwhelmingly iconic that it's somewhat hard to have an objective view on it. It's fair to say that the Sun material was heard far more in the years that followed, but the impact it had on those who heard it in 1954–55 is immeasurable. This holds particularly true for the musicians who caught on to Elvis' individuality long before he became a national—let alone international—phenomenon. Anybody who has ever recorded rockabilly, or even country-rock, owes some debt to what Elvis did in the Sun studio.

The setup for this and the record review chapters to follow is simple. All albums presented as a full-price new release are given a full review. Every 45 side not issued on one of Elvis' forty-six regular LP releases is reviewed as part of its separate original release. Cuts premiering on EPs are all to be found in chapter 12 or 19, and everything else is examined in chapter 15. Compilations are not fully reviewed, except for the essential *Elvis at Sun*. All the others are detailed in the chapter covering the respective year of release; on the occasion that they provide new material, they are also covered in chapter 15.

What follows is a review of all the original Sun singles. Heard today, what is so refreshing is how natural Elvis' Sun recordings sound. To the end of his days, Elvis preferred to record his vocals simultaneously with the band. Of course, back in 1954, doing so was a necessity, but even later in his career he continued to feel his records benefited from having him play off his musicians on the basic track.

"That's All Right"/"Blue Moon of Kentucky" (Released July 19, 1954)

This is what started it all. Elvis' first record may not have been the debut of rock-and-roll music, but it was the catalyst for much of the subsequent upheaval in the youth culture of the fifties. There was a new kind of freedom to be found in the performances—an element of joyously breaking the restrictions of what was then the norm. If it was decided on spontaneously, "That's All Right" carries with it a sense of purpose. I doubt Elvis, Scotty, and Bill knew exactly how to classify what they were doing, yet they did realize that it was worth pursuing in that it was different.

The main difference between Elvis circa 1954 and how he would sound on RCA has a lot to do with arrangement and production. Other than the slap-back echo, which was never quite matched elsewhere, there are no drums or backing vocals. "That's All Right" also has Elvis' acoustic guitar playing high in the mix. Elvis was never excessively secure as a guitar player, but he had an effective sense of rhythm that worked in its simplicity. Scotty and Bill weren't technically brilliant either, but they shared with Elvis an innate sense of what would and wouldn't work. Their playing tends to be economical, but therein lays the beauty. The truism "less is more" was what made rock and roll so irresistible for kids to either learn from or make their own.

"Blue Moon of Kentucky" is seen rightly as the B-side, but local charts reveal that it was the more popular of the two songs in Memphis. The energy in Elvis' voice is infectious—he sounds elated to be recording, to have found something to invest his creativity in. He first tried to sing it with a slower tempo in a more traditional country fashion, but ultimately that just wasn't him. For one thing, he sounded too young and happy, the mood in the studio too jocular to convey pain.

On the master, Elvis sounded defiant, almost glad to be rid of the girl who'd gone and made him blue. This isn't conveyed by any sense of the world-weariness that had served for so long as the foundation of blues and country, but rather by the self-confidence of a youth who knows things will work out for him. Call it arrogance if you will, but really it was just breaking the mold of what was then considered an acceptable public persona.

Though he has been dogged by spurious accusations since the day he reached the top, Elvis never stole or copied his style from anyone. Frankly, anyone who has ever argued otherwise isn't basing this on anything but their own reservations over a poor white Southerner making something uniquely his own. "That's All Right" was originally a blues record by Arthur Crudup, "Blue Moon of Kentucky" a heavy country record by Bill Monroe; neither sounded anything like Elvis Presley. Sure, Elvis had influences, but there wasn't one musician who sounded even remotely like "Elvis Presley" before he made his debut. Elvis may not have turned out to be the purist some wished he were, but there was nobody else who interpreted music the same way.

"Good Rockin' Tonight"/"I Don't Care If the Sun Don't Shine" (Released September 25, 1954)

The biggest difference between Elvis' first and second records is the level of poise on display. Elvis hadn't in any way compromised his music, but here he sounds much more certain about who he is and what he's trying to get across. His playful sexuality is first displayed here, and it was his refusal to take himself seriously as a lady-killer that made his ability to seduce so effective. He doesn't come across like he's lording over anyone with how cool he is; rather, he's acting as a messenger. In effect, he's saying there's nothing wrong with having fun with the opposite sex—an attitude he conveyed through a delivery far earthier than those of the white performers that came before him. This doesn't mean "Good Rockin' Tonight" is solely about the act of sex, but what it does say is that being young and carefree is allowed—an almost radical sentiment to families of lower-to-middle-class income in 1954.

"Good Rockin' Tonight" had been recorded as a jump blues by Wynonie Harris and its author, Roy Brown, in 1947. The biggest change Elvis made to the song was to take out a segment that revolved around fictional characters' names (many taken from song titles) and make the line "we're gonna rock" sound like a command. With the phrase "rock and roll" just beginning to enter the lexicon, this was an early call to arms for all who loved it. Elvis was among the first to loudly trumpet the arrival of this new music, and soon he would become the embodiment of its outlook and culture.

"I Don't Care If the Sun Don't Shine" was first included on an American LP when the *Sun Sessions* album was released in 1976. Prior to Elvis' recording of it, the song had been popularized by Patti Page, though Elvis probably was more personally impressed by Dean Martin's 1953 rendition. Though the song didn't come from a country or blues background, Elvis, Scotty, and Bill turned it to a rockabilly romp. For percussion, Elvis beat on his guitar—something he would continue to do on select titles through the end of the fifties. "I Don't Care If the Sun Don't Shine" wasn't as definitive a performance as many of the other Sun rockers, but it is a lot of fun. Elvis had an infectious laugh, and you can hear it coming out in his voice over the course of the song. He never lost his sense of humor, but he would seldom sound so carefree in the years to come.

"Milkcow Blues Boogie"/"You're a Heartbreaker" (Released December 28, 1954)

Though Kokomo Arnold wrote and recorded "Milkcow Blues Boogie" first, Elvis' version is almost unrecognizable from the original. It was the least successful of the Sun singles, probably because the staged false start would have been a little off-putting to disc jockeys. Heard away from the confines of mid-fifties radio, however, it is another amazing record. The slow beginning is abruptly stopped by Elvis, who tells his band to get "real real gone for a change." From there, Elvis and his Blue Moon Boys take the number at a frantic pace, leaving the listener breathless. The riff Scotty plays has motion to it—the same traveling ambience that would soon be used to great effect on "Mystery Train."

Elvis continued to show confidence in his vocals, giving off the same sneering attitude toward his missing woman that transformed "Blue Moon of Kentucky" into something quite different from the original. The original version of "Milkcow" was also something of a lament for the protagonist's girl to come home, but Elvis once again seems to revel in the fact that she will miss him. Rock and roll never was about being gracious!

"You're a Heartbreaker" wasn't Elvis' first country song, but it was the first record he made that could be termed as such. The performance is as playful as those found on his first two records, just cast within a different genre. It's got a very nice bare and elemental feel, and it is most notable for marking the first time Sam allowed Elvis a change of pace. The attitude Elvis has toward his unfaithful woman is no different than what came before, but there is a certain eagerness in his phrasing. Though informed by the music he had made previously, "You're a Heartbreaker" was inherently a nod to tradition. Despite the mixed reaction Elvis had with his remake of "Blue Moon of Kentucky," it's doubtful that "You're a Heartbreaker" would have raised many eyebrows on the *Grand Ole Opry*.

"Baby Let's Play House"/"I'm Left, You're Right, She's Gone" (Released April 10, 1955)

Records like "Baby Let's Play House" usually come along once in a career. It is the sound of an artist fully realizing his potential and running all the way with it. That it was only the first of many Elvis Presley songs that can only be defined as "epic" is an achievement in itself; that Presley was only twenty years young when he made it takes his feat to a whole other level. Easily his best recording to date, "Baby Let's Play House" has it all. There's the thumping slap bass; the succulent guitar solo, which climaxes in a series of rhythmic notes for Elvis to visually convey onstage; and the masterful yet mischievous vocal. Rock and roll—nay, music—doesn't get better than this. It also has the bonus of adding the pink Cadillac to the list of fifties iconography, once a flip religious reference was replaced by one addressing the grandiose vehicle.

There's a fairly common clip circulating of a fifties preacher railing against rock and roll because of the beat. While there was indeed a sexual aspect to it, the main effect of the beat on a record like "Baby Let's Play House" is that it makes the listener feel alive. One of the most lasting qualities of Elvis Presley's early music is that it makes you feel good. Because he put so much heart into his music, the joy he was so obviously feeling when recording is transferred over to the audience. By this point, the music industry was waking up to rock and roll, and with "Baby Let's Play House," Elvis finally made the national charts (albeit only as a #5 hit on the Country Singles chart).

"I'm Left, You're Right, She's Gone" was fairly gimmicky by comparison. It's a fine rockabilly ballad, but it comes across far more seriously in the blues arrangement Elvis had tried originally. The released version, being something of a novelty, was more in line with the commercial considerations of the day, and admittedly it does have a kind of galloping snap to it missing from "My Baby's Gone" (the name by which fans refer to the blues arrangement). Artistically,

"Mystery Train"—simply one of the finest pieces of recorded music there ever has been.

however, it's far less revealing as far as displaying the colossal depth of Elvis' talent. Elvis never had the missionary zeal of bringing blues to the general public that possessed British bands like the Rolling Stones. It was simply that he refused to be defined by genre. For Elvis, good music was good music; if he enjoyed it, he would record or perform any style of song without a second thought.

For now, Elvis would have to wait before he could reveal all the aspects of his musical persona on vinyl. Sam Phillips was a pioneer in music, but he did have a personal vision for his artists. While he often let sessions act as an open forum to try out anything his performers wished, he was also very selective as to what he would put out on record. In Elvis' case, this usually worked to his benefit, as sometimes his lack of musical or personal prejudice would lead to a lack of direction.

On the other hand, in the case of "I'm Left, You're Right, She's Gone," the rough edges should perhaps have been left on. It's unwise to place the blame for this totally on Sam, since Elvis did after all willingly work on the completed master. Yet it's almost uncanny how close this flip side sounded, mood-wise, to "You're a Heartbreaker" before it and "I Forgot to Remember to Forget" after. That "I'm Left, You're Right, She's Gone" has more of a sparkle to it than the other two titles shouldn't be overlooked, but upon hearing the out-take, one can't help but feel that some of the life was ultimately polished out of it.

"Mystery Train"/"I Forgot to Remember to Forget" (Released August 6, 1955)

"I Forgot to Remember to Forget" was Elvis Presley's first #1 record. It took quite a few months to get there, by which time RCA Victor had taken over distribution of the single, but in late February of 1956, this ballad did indeed top the country charts. For all that, the song is almost forgotten today, having been overshadowed greatly by its intended A-side. It's not that "I Forgot to Remember" is a bad song. It's a rollicking country tune, and Elvis would never sound quite this Southern again. Had it been his inclination, Elvis could have made a career out of rhythmic country ballads, yet "I Forgot to Remember to Forget" is stylistically more of a semi-farewell than the start of something new.

"Mystery Train," on the other hand, was a stunner. While music is in many ways subjective, there are a select few records that are so well made that even those who don't rank the artist or genre must at least acknowledge the pure quality. "Mystery Train" is one of those special songs—one that just makes you stand back in admiration. As much as anything, this is American music at its most pure. Scotty's hypnotic guitar line (adapted from Little Junior's Blue Flames' Sun recording "Love My Baby") generates a distinct visual image of a train going down the track, while Bill Black holds the beat steady; the tempo itself is brilliantly evocative.

Yet as good as the band were, it was Elvis who really outdid himself. He sounds as playful as ever, but there is insight on display here. His phrasing, his breath control, his pure delight in making this recording—all speak to Presley already being a seasoned artist. There's a palpable feeling of the basic pleasures one can get from singing, from creating something lasting, from just being alive. The vibrancy of the twenty-year-old Elvis Presley is something to behold.

Though it is unfair to the wonderful work that was to follow, a contingent of rockabilly purists insist "Mystery Train" was the moment where Elvis peaked. Certainly, Elvis' RCA material would be different—and yes, the Sun years feel somewhat fresher as they haven't been over exposed—but this certainly wasn't the last Elvis song to offer insight into his life and times. Some say these records are more serious than those that immediately followed, but in reality they just come from a different perspective.

The voice heard on all of Elvis' Sun records is one of an artist not yet hardened by fame or its attendant phoniness. I would agree that Elvis never sounded quite as carefree again, but the course his life was to take couldn't help but change how he performed. While no one stays a kid forever, the young Elvis provided a most romantic visage that some listeners would never let go of. It may have become dim at the end, and the songs it would tackle would be variable to say the least, but that voice never ceased being very special indeed.

Elvis at Sun (Vinyl Released June 22, 2004)

Though it has a collector's premium that is part and parcel of nearly all post-1989 records, the Sun records catalogue is the most glaringly obvious example of music that should be played only with a needle. The book-and-three-CD package *A Boy from Tupelo*, issued on Elvis' own FTD (Follow That Dream) collector's label, is extremely well done, but it still doesn't feel the same as seeing the yellow Sun label spin around a turntable. There are easier albums of Sun material to find, but this one trumps them all. Some master tapes were lost as early as late 1955; some have until now had an invasive layer of echo upon them. On this LP, the Sun recordings sound (nearly) pristine.

This LP of nineteen songs, arranged by recording date, is truly seminal. "That's All Right" and "Blue Moon of Kentucky" still betray a small hint of echo not found on the original Sun 45, but otherwise this is a perfect album. It has the long ending of "Mystery Train," a beautifully remastered "When It Rains, It

This 2004 compilation is the best official Sun LP to date. If anything deserves to be heard on vinyl, it is Elvis' Sun sessions, but this album only saw a brief release in that format.

Really Pours," and the master of "Tomorrow Night" sounding smoother than ever before.

Elvis at Sun is a vinyl album that should be reissued and kept in print indefinitely. If a new transfer is redone with analog methods, so much the better. Still, this album sounds terrific as it is, and is the one modern vinyl reissue that should be sought out no matter what the price. It is indispensable.

5

One for the Money

Colonel Tom Parker

olonel Tom Parker's life was certainly eventful, but he remains a largely inscrutable character. He has become a figure for all that is shady in the music business, yet you can count on one hand all the acts that became as famous as Elvis Presley. How Parker managed Elvis has been portrayed as either the work of the genius who made Elvis an international phenomenon, or the villain who took Presley and his fans for everything they were worth. Because he has historically drawn such strong reactions, much remains unanswered. Only Parker or Elvis could have provided a definitive account, but there's room for some rationale to the issues surrounding their relationship.

My Name Should Be Trouble?

Parker never discussed his life at length and took great pains to hide his ancestry. His real name was Andreas Cornelis van Kuijk, and he was born in 1909 in Breda, Holland. Speculation is rife as to what he did before coming to America, but we do know he somehow managed to join the U.S. Army. He took the name "Tom Parker" from the officer that interviewed him, but he was eventually discharged for having mental issues.

After leaving the military, Parker effectively erased his past. Telling people he was an orphan from West Virginia, he soon joined the carnival circuit. In the late thirties, finding that his carny background prepared him for a life in business, he began managing singers. His first client was Gene Austin, and in 1945 he became the manager of country crooner Eddy Arnold, who would later reluctantly credit Parker for helping his rise to stardom. After being made an honorary Colonel by Louisiana governor (and Parker crony) Jimmie Davis in 1948, he insisted from that point on that he be addressed by all as "The Colonel."

Arnold and Parker parted ways acrimoniously in 1953 because Arnold felt the Colonel was devoting too much of his time to country-music legend Hank Snow. It's been said that Parker was shaken by this termination, and it's notable that he took on no other clients after signing Elvis. By the time he had first become aware of Elvis in early 1955, he and Snow had formed a company together called Jamboree Productions. For now, it acted as a booking agency and management firm, but things would change fast after the Colonel signed Presley to be an opener on one of their tours.

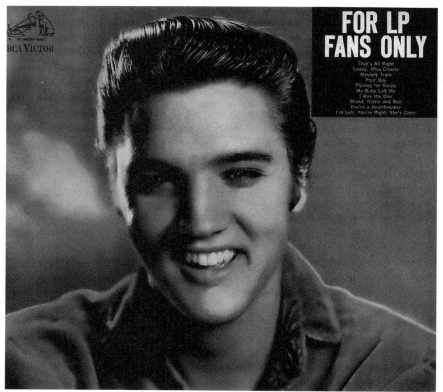

RCA VICTOR

FOR LP FANS ONLY

That's All Right
Lawdy, Miss Clawdy
Mystery Train
Poor Boy
Playing for Keeps
My Baby Left Me
I Was the One
Shake, Rattle and Roll
You're a Heartbreaker
I'm Left, You're Right, She's Gone

This LP was issued while Elvis was in Germany for his army stint, with an intrusive layer of echo slathered over some of the selections. It was an early sign that Parker had no concept of artistic integrity. This rare cover variation was used for the second pressing.

Riding the Rainbow

Parker quickly tried to make himself indispensable to Elvis. He wanted Elvis on a big label, to have his own publishing interests, to be seen on TV and in the cinema. As Presley wanted those same things, he let the Colonel systematically gain control over his career. By the time Elvis was signed to RCA Victor in November 1955, his manager, Bob Neal, was being pushed out of the picture, as was Hank Snow. For Neal, this almost came as a relief, as he felt he didn't have the ability to handle Elvis' rapid ascent to fame, but this was not the case for Snow. Hank had helped talk Elvis' parents into letting Parker take the reins and was under the impression that he would be part of Elvis' management team. Parker cut Hank out as soon as he became non-essential to proceedings, however, and in March 1956, the Colonel became Presley's sole manager.

From 1955 to 1958, Elvis had the most enthralling rise to stardom of just about anybody. Parker did a lot of things right during this period. First, he got Elvis a deal with RCA—and a concurrent publishing deal with Hill &

Range—that was very generous, considering that Elvis was only really known in parts of the South. He was also able to get Elvis on TV, which was still a relatively new medium. Back in 1956, network television was a far more powerful means of exposure, and Elvis came along just as TV sets were becoming a firm fixture in American homes. Parker knew that, in addition to being a good recording artist, Elvis had great looks and a riveting stage presence. Being that there were very few choices for the viewer in those pre-cable, pre–home video days, by the spring of 1956, Elvis had suddenly become the hottest act in music.

Parker seemed to thrive on the ensuing controversy Elvis created. He was able to secure multi-film deals with Paramount and 20th Century Fox and then license a truckload of merchandise bearing Elvis' name and face. Never before had teens been catered to in such a way, and these trinkets raked in serious dollars. In the early years, Elvis had a good balance of TV, recording sessions, films, and touring. It was only when Parker stopped diversifying his career direction that Elvis fell victim to boredom and routine. The essential thing the Colonel didn't ever realize is that Elvis needed to go in a lot of different areas to keep things fresh for himself. One can fault Elvis to some extent for getting lazy, but one wonders why the blueprint laid down in the fifties was subsequently ignored.

G.I. Blues

The first small cracks began to appear in Parker's game plan when Elvis went into the army. On the day of his induction, on March 24, 1958, Elvis was shown an already-released LP called *Elvis' Golden Records*. It was a fine collection, but Elvis had had no input into it. Parker had already started to overreach when he started discouraging Elvis from keeping his original band together, feeling they had begun to get too involved with Elvis' sessions. He also worked to prevent Elvis from getting close to the songwriting team of Jerry Leiber and Mike Stoller.

This, however, was a new low. Colonel Tom hadn't consulted with his client on the LP whatsoever. This was common in those days, but Elvis wasn't a common artist, and he had so far enjoyed a sense of artistic control.

Sure, Parker had let RCA flood the market in 1956, but it seems as though Elvis was aware of what was being done. Perhaps the worst thing Colonel had allowed RCA to do was to add echo to their reissue of "That's All Right" and prematurely cut off the ending to "Mystery Train." That was something Elvis never would have consented to, as he was always very precise how he wanted his music to sound. Yet whom do we point the finger at? It's unlikely that Elvis ever played the RCA versions of his Sun singles, as he was probably told they were straight reissues. Parker had to have given his consent on the "remix" as he was zealous about having control over what "his boy" put out.

In any case, after Elvis was inducted into the army, Parker continued to supervise the reissues. Parker may have run these ideas by Elvis, but would Presley have consented to the excessive echo that all but ruined his compilation albums *For LP Fans Only* and *A Date with Elvis*, which were already too short?

Would Elvis have allowed the wrong take of "Doncha' Think It's Time" to appear on *Gold Records Volume 2*? Later on, it was obvious Elvis didn't care about what was being done with his catalogue, but this certainly didn't apply to him in the fifties. Maybe Elvis did complain, only to be told they couldn't change the records. The question remains, did Parker let the interference with the music happen, or was he privy to it? Sadly, it's likely he either didn't know the records well enough to notice the mistakes, or simply didn't care.

Steppin' out of Line

In the sixties, Parker gradually fell out of step with what an increasingly sophisticated audience wanted from Elvis. When Elvis first came home from the army in 1960, Parker handled his first "comeback," so to speak, with aplomb. There were only three high-quality singles that year, two terrific LPs, and, in *G.I. Blues*, one fairly decent soundtrack album and film. Elvis also shot *Flaming Star* and *Wild in the Country* later in the year, and both were worthy dramas. To top it off, he set up a TV special with Frank Sinatra that exposed a more sophisticated Elvis to a new a new audience.

If *G.I. Blues* and the soundtracks for *Flaming Star* and *Wild in the Country* weren't quite up to Elvis' normal standards, they merely seemed like mild aberrations. The only problem at this point was that, with three pictures being filmed, Elvis couldn't go back on the road.

Nineteen sixty-one is where Parker's plan began to grow questionable. Elvis never did TV as a guest again. Parker had now priced him so high that nobody wanted to pay up. This was due mainly to the Colonel wanting people to go to theatres and not see Elvis for free. Elvis was so hot at this point that his singles sold themselves for a few years, but after the early sixties, Elvis released many great singles that would have fared far better, had he appeared on television to promote them. Videos never even seemed to cross Parker's mind, even though most big names were shooting them by the mid-sixties so that they didn't have to go on TV too often.

There was a huge demand for Elvis to tour, and he wanted to get back onstage. Parker set up a few charity concerts early in 1961, and the lo-fi recording of the USS *Arizona* Memorial Benefit gives ample evidence that Elvis sounded as good as ever. Yet Parker had booked so many movies that Elvis couldn't even consider touring until late 1962. That Parker then botched that scheme by insisting RCA foot too much of the bill should have served as a loud warning sign. Elvis had so far put his faith in his manager, but it is probably no coincidence that he adopted a slightly jaundiced view of the Colonel after the tour fell through.

In the end, Elvis would make no live appearances of any sort from April 1961 to May 1968—this despite the fact that huge offers were coming in, especially from Europe. Yet Elvis was never permitted to tour outside North America, and one wonders if it's because Parker didn't want his ancestry to be discovered.

Parker had acquaintances in high places, so it seems logical that a wheeler-dealer like him could have arranged something if his citizenship was an issue. Yet once he became Tom Parker, the Colonel never did leave the country, except for during Elvis' brief 1957 tours of Canada and Hawaii (which was then still a couple of years away from becoming a U.S. state). Quite why is simply a mystery, and Parker's various excuses make no sense. He didn't even go to Germany the whole time Elvis was stationed there. Elvis was forbidden even to shoot movies set in Mexico, Germany, or England on location. Was Parker that scared about Elvis and RCA finding out who he really was? Rumors of a hidden past are only rumors, and we will likely never understand completely why Parker insisted that Elvis stay in the States. But it would eventually limit Elvis to a great degree, and cause him to grow bored of performing.

The year 1961 also marked the point where Elvis' songs took a dive. To be fair, his obsession with Latin/Italian-styled ballads (which never again matched the highs of "It's Now or Never") hurt his regular studio recordings from late 1960 through early 1964 to a certain extent, but that was nothing compared to what happened with his film soundtracks. After the tremendous commercial—if not artistic—success of *Blue Hawaii* in late 1961, Elvis' soundtracks became less about good music and more about moving along the plot. Instead of simply having to write the best song possible, composers were now told they had to pen songs that served to fit the script. Eventually, this even extended to the composers being given a song title to write to order. It's not that a film's locale wasn't taken into consideration before, but by 1962 it was becoming all too formulaic. While Parker had always tried to get publishing on everything Elvis recorded, in time Presley's best writers stopped submitting songs for him. Most simply wouldn't go through the demeaning creative process that Parker now called for. Once the regular sessions became rare, and the big hits stopped coming, they began to look elsewhere for work.

Even worse is that Parker turned down many excellent movie roles for Elvis simply because "his boy" had to be the star. Not only did this stop Elvis from growing as an actor, it also caused a lot of ill will in those who could have helped Elvis reach his silver screen goals. To name but three, Parker turned down *The Defiant Ones*, *West Side Story*, and *A Star Is Born*, even though Elvis would have been perfect for the roles. From 1962 to 1967, Elvis shot sixteen lightly comedic musicals in a row. A few were worthy, but by the end of that period, the casts, the scripts, and the songs had deeply declined in quality.

Parker didn't even put out an album for the best movie and soundtrack of the era, *Viva Las Vegas*, because he didn't want Ann-Margret getting any more attention than she already had. The Colonel was furious that she had equal billing, and despite *Viva* having a higher gross than any other Elvis film, he also balked when it went slightly over budget. Until the very late sixties, the movies that came after that were made very cheaply, which showed painfully in every frame.

By 1964, the Colonel's formerly careful record-release schedule was in tatters. Reissues and soundtrack fodder now made up most of the singles (of which there were now way too many), and a solid studio LP Elvis had cut in the summer of 1963 was left on the shelf. With not one regular session scheduled, and with the worst music and films Elvis ever made on release, 1965 was rock bottom. The films would not improve for several years, but Elvis finally began to speak out, and even the Colonel was horrified when he saw the final cut of *Harum Scarum*.

From 1966 onward, things began to improve, but that was only due to Elvis' tenacity. Parker had long interfered with Elvis' personal life. He encouraged Elvis to get rid of friends he didn't like, and he even tried to break up several relationships. The turning point came when the Colonel arranged Elvis and Priscilla's wedding in Las Vegas in May 1967. It was a rushed affair—one that the couple had no input in—and in the process many of Elvis' close friends were snubbed. Parker's weak excuse was that there wasn't enough room in the hotel suite where it took place. Elvis, it seemed, had had enough. When Parker tried to cut greedy publishing deals for some new quality material, Elvis stood up to him.

Presley had to fight hard to cut songs like "Guitar Man" or "Suspicious Minds," and even the 1968 TV special was almost ruined by Parker's almost pathetically old-fashioned vision. The Colonel had wanted Elvis to sing Christmas carols for an hour; he railed against producer Steve Binder's modern ideas, and tried to dissuade Elvis from cutting the socially conscious "If I Can Dream." Parker eventually gave in, but he didn't learn. By having his cronies harangue producer Chips Moman about publishing, he almost put a premature end to Elvis' groundbreaking (and hit-making) 1969 Memphis sessions. That Elvis didn't pay attention to the business side of things is well known, but by this point he had to have realized that Parker was increasingly getting in the way of his creative progress.

Carny Town

Though some have put Parker down for taking Elvis to Las Vegas for his 1969 return to the stage, it wasn't actually a bad idea. Much of Elvis' fan base was getting older, and the town was opening itself up to rock-and-roll musicians—or at least those who appealed to audiences over twenty-one. Yet once Parker was there on a regular basis, the town changed him. He became severely addicted to gambling, and Elvis' profit margins entered a sharp decline. As the gambling worsened, it is said that Parker began to cut deals to benefit himself rather than Elvis. This certainly appears to be true when it came to merchandising, where, for example, Parker would charge RCA for the rights to use the Elvis pictures he provided for photo book and LP covers. Elvis never saw a dime.

After Elvis' 1969 opening night proved to be a major success, the Colonel negotiated long-term contracts that kept Elvis in Las Vegas for a month at a time, doing two shows a night, without a single day off. Maybe this worked for the crooners who went before him, but for Elvis, putting on a highly physical show up to sixty-four times in thirty days took its toll. The money started off good, but by the mid-seventies Elvis was no longer even close to being the highest-paid

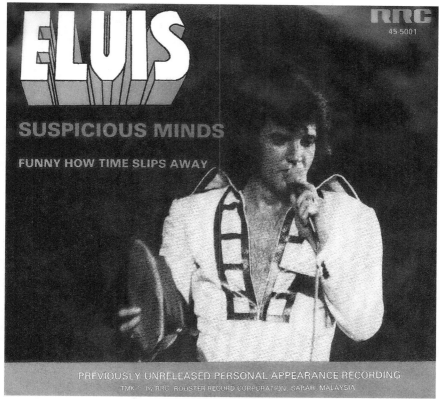

ELVIS
RRC
45-5001

SUSPICIOUS MINDS

FUNNY HOW TIME SLIPS AWAY

PREVIOUSLY UNRELEASED PERSONAL APPEARANCE RECORDING
TMK ® by RRC ROOSTER RECORD CORPORATION, SABAH, MALAYSIA

"Suspicious Minds" brought Elvis back to the top of the charts, but Parker's publishing cronies almost derailed the session. This boot 45 features a stunning live version from early 1970.

star on the strip. He gave his musicians the top dollar they deserved once he returned to the stage, but he had to fight Parker on that as well.

During the seventies, Parker continued to flood the market with record releases that were often ill thought-out. In 1973, he ended up selling all of Elvis' back catalogue to RCA for a lump sum. Both Parker and Elvis needed a quick cash infusion, but this short-term fix meant that they now had no say on how the old music was presented, nor did they make any money from it.

In any case, Parker had long ago given up any restraint with how Elvis was marketed. When "Burning Love" became a huge hit in 1972, Parker canceled the planned new album it was to appear on and instead used it to head up a truly awful compilation on RCA's budget Camden label. RCA and Parker bragged about it being the best-selling budget album ever, but Elvis was made to look like a joke. He would never again break the Top 10 pop singles charts.

Elvis' early seventies tours were wildly successful, but after a while the towns began to get smaller, and it became clear that he was falling into another stifling pattern. He was doing no movies, the record dates began to get further apart, and once boredom reared its ugly head, the shows began to suffer. Parker did do a good job of putting together the *Aloha from Hawaii Via Satellite* TV special in early 1973, but its motivation was mainly to satiate Elvis and his fans, who were demanding that he tour overseas. Actually, the success worked against the Colonel, as demand for Elvis in Europe and Japan was now higher than ever. The sad thing is that Parker should have already seen that Elvis couldn't sustain his interest without variety. The lessons of the movie years should still have been fresh in his mind, but Parker seemed neither to care nor to realize that his client tended to wither without a challenge.

I Want to Be Free

After *Aloha*, Elvis returned to Vegas and the road, but his drug use and depression were getting out of control. At the end of his summer 1973 Vegas engagement, Elvis made some remarks onstage about how his favorite waiter was being fired, coming down hard on the Hilton management for it. He and Parker got into a big argument about it afterward, resulting in Elvis finally firing his manager. Yet with a divorce looming, his health going into decline, and his father being scared by the large (yet bogus) bill Parker hit them with for services rendered, Elvis soon took the Colonel back.

The rest of Elvis' career offered no real challenges, and Parker continued to fight against anything that deviated from the norm. The strong, healthy Elvis who fought for his career in the late sixties was gone, replaced with an artist whose personal problems caused him to become complacent. Elvis' records never again sank to the low of the soundtracks, and Parker gradually interfered less with them, but even the best ones got buried in the pop market. The times had changed, but Parker's style of promotion hadn't. The main problem was that the albums, like the compilations, now mostly featured a succession of live shots, and the titles all seemed to blend together.

It's been said by several of Elvis' friends that Presley's personal decline only bothered Parker when Elvis was too sick to get onstage. That Parker signed Elvis up for a TV special, on what would prove to be his final tour, seems to back up the fact that he no longer cared how Elvis looked or performed as long as they made a profit. When Elvis died, Parker's first call was to a merchandiser to set up a new spate of memorabilia.

After Vernon Presley's death in 1979, Parker was finally removed from the scene by Elvis' ex-wife, Priscilla, who watched over the estate until her and Elvis' daughter Lisa Marie came of age. The Colonel lived the rest of his life quietly, mostly in Las Vegas with his second wife, and died in 1997, aged 87. Today, he is looked at with a mix of scorn and grudging respect. There was certainly no one else like him, but though his unusual methods initially helped Elvis achieve a stunning level of fame, he quickly wore out his welcome after that fame had been established. That Elvis managed to grow creatively after 1960 seems to be largely in spite of the Colonel's actions. It would be wrong to blame Parker for the bad choices Elvis made offstage, but had Presley had a manager that cared about him and his music as much as what could be made off of him, things might have worked out very differently.

Some say Parker held Vernon's brief prison spell (for passing a bad check) over the Presleys' head, and that Elvis stayed with Parker to protect his father. One thing that is for certain is that early on, Elvis was loyal to Parker and feared that he would fail without him. By the time Elvis realized that Parker was holding him back, he was too immersed in his own troubles and had become complacent in almost every area of his life.

6

It All Happened So Fast

1956

Elvis' career went through the roof in 1956. Fulfilling all of his promise, he became the most famous singer in the entire Western world during these twelve months. Except Sinatra, nothing had happened quite on this scale before, and only the Beatles and Michael Jackson would hit as hard in the future. In this one year, Elvis went from being a hardworking rockabilly performer to *the* icon of his generation.

The biggest and most lasting contributions Elvis made in 1956 were his recordings. With the move to RCA, he began to change his sound. He wanted more instruments, and he also wanted to make use of backing vocalists. He requested his favorites, the Jordanaires, but only Gordon Stoker was available for the first few sessions. By July, the remaining members of the quartet had begun their fifteen years association with Elvis, and before long they were all out on the road together.

Though traces of country or rockabilly could be heard, there was a definite shift to hard rock and roll and rhythmic ballads. The music Elvis released this year connected with the public in an enormous way. Even more than fifty-five years later, this material is considered some of the best rock and roll ever recorded. These records changed the way people thought of music, opening numerous avenues for experimentation and self-expression that would have otherwise remained shut. Though it had been going on for a good five years, the tremendous reception to Elvis this year is what put rock and roll on the map for good.

Aside from his records, it was television that put Elvis across. The medium had reached the right saturation point by 1956 to where it had become an essential part of Western culture. It had already made icons out of Milton Berle, Ed Sullivan, Lucille Ball, and George "Superman" Reeves. Elvis was the first singer to make full use of the technology in terms of riding its popularity to his own stardom. That the shows Elvis appeared on in the fifties aired live only added an additional level of immediacy and excitement.

Being stunningly good-looking and a kinetic stage performer, Elvis created controversy and havoc. Most youths and less rigid adults found a lot to like, but for many less forward-thinking individuals, Elvis' sexual energy (playful as it was) seemed shocking. Supporters and detractors alike were riveted, and by the time Elvis played his first *Ed Sullivan Show* in September, he drew 82 percent of the viewing audience.

Elvis toured heavily through the first half of the year, and in August he even got to fulfill his goal of being an actor when he began shooting the western film *The Reno Brothers*. After he previewed the ballad from the score, "Love Me Tender," on the initial *Ed Sullivan Show*, the song was rush-released, zoomed to #1, and quickly became the title of the feature. It was an ominous portent of Elvis' future in Hollywood.

Studio Work

The best of Elvis' 1956 recordings are the stuff on which legends are made. The energy, good nature, and sheer quality of these records galvanized the burgeoning rock-and-roll movement all over the world. These records both transcend their era and also stand as the most influential of the period. Anyone with even a rudimentary knowledge of early rock and roll will know at least one of these songs. That stands not only for America but almost any civilized country across the entire globe.

Elvis' earliest sessions for RCA were held in Nashville and New York over January and February. These selections comprised the new material for Elvis' first LP, a few EP cuts, plus both sides of Elvis' debut RCA single, "Heartbreak Hotel"/"I Was the One."

With "My Baby Left Me" Elvis recorded a new pure rockabilly track, but most of the songs here are hard rock and roll that had fuller instrumentation and less of a connection to the country and swing music that had been popular in the forties. The few ballads yielded mixed results, but Elvis now sounds more grown-up and assured. With "Heartbreak Hotel," a case can be made that Presley was now an even better artist than before. Certainly, he couldn't have carried off the macabre fascination of the track eighteen months earlier.

After a very frightening flight to Nashville, during which the plane almost crashed, Elvis' April session resulted only in "I Want You, I Need You, I Love You." Nonetheless, it was a big hit, and the quality was outstanding. The only problem was that RCA wanted to strike while the iron was hot, and Elvis' nominal producer Steve Sholes was greatly disappointed that more couldn't be finished. In reality, Elvis was now his own producer, but the idea of a self-produced artist in the fifties was unheard of. (Amazingly, Elvis didn't get credit for his crucial input in arrangement and mixing preferences until 1974!)

Elvis' next recording engagement was a one-day session in New York on July 2nd. One of Elvis' most successful day's work on both a critical and commercial level, it resulted in three songs being cut: "Hound Dog," "Don't Be Cruel," and "Any Way You Want Me." This didn't come about by serendipity. Elvis worked very hard to get each song right. He went a full thirty-one takes on "Hound Dog" before he felt it was up to his standard, and insisted on twenty-eight takes for "Don't Be Cruel." The two songs made for a tremendous single that sold over thirteen million records worldwide. Today, the record is still one of the cornerstones of rock and roll.

Elvis began cutting the soundtrack for *Love Me Tender* on August 24th, on the 20th Century Fox soundstage, finishing up on September 5th. He found the atmosphere clinical and the sound less easy to balance, and as a result would use soundstages as little as possible in the future. Not letting him use his own band after they auditioned was an early indication of how little the movie companies understood Elvis' creativity. Seemingly unaware that this was a period piece with ersatz country and folk numbers, Scotty, Bill, and D. J. thought the executives wanted to hear their normal rock-and-roll show. Ironically, country was the type of music Presley's band knew best. Elvis vowed that he would use his own people on any films he made in the future.

Ken Darby wrote the songs used in *Love Me Tender*, but for publishing purposes they were credited to Elvis and to Darby's wife, Vera Matson. Elvis didn't like getting credit he didn't deserve, so he put a stop to the practice within the next year. Even so, it's interesting that the classic 1958 LP, *Elvis' Golden Records*, talks of Elvis' songwriting talents in the liner notes. Again, this was not something Elvis himself promoted, but from early 1956 to early 1957, a handful of songs—particularly the lucrative single cuts—would bear his name in the credits.

Sandwiched between the two soundtrack dates were the early September sessions for Elvis' second LP and a new 45. This was the first time Elvis cut tracks at Radio Recorders in Hollywood, and he was very pleased with engineer Thorne Nogar and the clarity of the results. Whenever he could over the next eleven years, Elvis used Radio Recorders for his West Coast recording dates. The results were comparable to the previous RCA recordings both in sound and sales. A fine blend of rock, ballads, and country, the songs included classics like "Love Me" and "Too Much."

On December 4th, Elvis stopped by Sun Studios and found Carl Perkins cutting some new sides. Among the musicians Perkins was using that day was an up-and-coming piano player named Jerry Lee Lewis. They quickly fell into a jam, with Jerry Lee not at all shy in front of his famous companions. Johnny Cash was called in to join them for a photo shoot, and the four were dubbed "the Million Dollar Quartet" by the *Memphis Press-Scimitar*.

Johnny left quickly to go shopping with his wife, Vivian, and careful study of the material proves there were no vocals by anyone but Elvis, Jerry Lee, and Carl. It is likely Cash did sing a few numbers with the others that have been lost over time, however, and he must have misremembered when he claimed to feature on the archival releases later in life.

Either way, the recordings are priceless in capturing the good-natured atmosphere of a Sun session, not to mention the camaraderie felt among these Sam Phillips protégés—all of whom were in the process of changing the course of music history. The material they played was a mix of the type of gospel tunes they all treasured from boyhood on, a few of their own songs, and some of their favorite current music.

Elvis shines on a version of Pat Boone's "Don't Forbid Me" that he mentions he had been sent first. They all seem to love Chuck Berry's new song "Brown Eyed Handsome Man," and "Keeper of the Key" has some truly wondrous harmonies. Another cool moment comes when Elvis talks about having recently seen Billy Ward and His Dominos perform in Las Vegas. Though Elvis doesn't mention him by name, the singer that so impressed him was a young Jackie Wilson singing "Don't Be Cruel." After telling a skeptical Perkins and Lewis that Wilson's version was better than his own, Elvis proceeds to run through the song in Wilson's style. This was something Presley also took to doing live, most notably on his January 6, 1957, *Ed Sullivan* appearance.

Segments of the tapes were released a few times in the eighties, semi-legally, by Charly Records, which owned the Sun catalogue in the U.K. RCA put out a version in 1990, and in 2006 an even longer LP/CD was issued. Though lacking the polish of regular studio material, it remains one of the most essential artifacts of early rock and roll. Nothing else is as illuminating in exploring the roots and influences of three of the genre's most important artists.

Live Performance

Because Elvis did so much television, and because five entire concerts have survived, Elvis' set this year is a little easier to put together. Gradually gaining confidence, by the time of his last performance of the year, a charity farewell performance for the *Hayride*, Elvis came off as a seasoned (though no less exciting) pro.

For the first six months of 1956, Elvis maintained a hectic schedule. After playing St. Louis on New Year's Day, he undertook his last dates as a supporting act on a six-day Hank Snow tour of Texas that began on the 15th. After touring nonstop, Elvis collapsed from exhaustion following a show in Jacksonville, Florida, on February 23rd. He had so much energy that he was able to go on the next day, but the doctor warned him to slow down. It was advice Elvis would heed as soon as he could, but there was no slowing down the momentum of his career.

During the first three months of the year, Elvis made six appearances on Tommy and Jimmy Dorsey's *Stage Show*. Though the program wasn't popular enough to create the stir of Elvis' later television dates, it did provide his first coast-to-coast exposure to a national audience. Funnily enough, he never performed "I Forgot to Remember to Forget" on the show, instead choosing to do various selections from his early RCA sessions, including his new single "Heartbreak Hotel," plus the Sun cut "Baby Let's Play House."

Film survives of each of the six weeks and presents Elvis at his most raw. He wasn't extraordinarily famous yet, but he already had a good-humored approach to himself and his music. With Scotty and (especially) Bill getting a fair amount

June 8, 1956, Los Angeles. This series of musically outstanding bootlegs also features artwork that perfectly conveys the potency of early Elvis.

of screen time, this is the closest one can get to visually assessing their exciting early act.

By April, Elvis was becoming a very big name. He had now stopped performing on the *Louisiana Hayride*, but to thank them for letting him out of his contract, Elvis promised to return for a special concert. His next television appearance came on April 3rd, on *The Milton Berle Show*, shot aboard the USS *Hancock*. Berle let Elvis be more natural in his performance than other hosts would in the future, and Elvis comes across more viscerally exciting than ever. He has a more professional air about him, having now perfected his look of slick hair and sideburns.

Elvis played his first formal California show the next night, in San Diego, and over the next three weeks he toured Texas, Denver, New Mexico, and Oklahoma. It was then that the real mania for Elvis started, and a crowd that wasn't driven out of control became a rare thing indeed. Elvis did have something of a setback, though, when he was booked to play two weeks from April 23rd at the New Frontier hotel in Las Vegas. He still only had Scotty, Bill, and D. J. with him at this point, and the crowds in Vegas at the time where mostly older and conservative. Other than a few matinee performances, Elvis didn't go over all that well. A recording in excellent quality exists of his final show on May 6th. Elvis and the band play superbly, but the crowd is only polite; his cornball jokes go down particularly poorly. Elvis didn't brood too much, however, since the day before both his debut LP and "Heartbreak Hotel" had reached the top of the charts. Though it would take Las Vegas years to catch up, Elvis had well and truly arrived.

On May 13th, Elvis began a two-week tour, taking in dates in Memphis, Wisconsin, Minnesota, Kansas, Arkansas, Nebraska, Iowa, Kansas City, Detroit, Columbus, and Dayton, Ohio. From here on, Elvis would never have an opening act of note, except for his backing vocalists. Before this, he had toured with many singers, including Sun labelmates Johnny Cash and Carl Perkins. Now more than ever, the show rested upon Elvis' shoulders. This held particularly true after Bill Black was told to tone it down by Parker. The Little Rock performance from this tour has been released various times over the years, and is a less inhibited version of the act in Vegas. Again, all the participants are as sharp as a tack, delivering performances that were very comparable to their classic studio counterparts.

Elvis started a weeklong tour of major California cities and Arizona on June 3rd. On June 5th, he took a day off to appear on *The Milton Berle Show*. This was the performance that caused all the controversy that surrounded Elvis over the next eighteen months. Along with a performance of his latest hit, "I Want You, I Need You, I Love You," Elvis introduced a song he had heard Freddie Bell and the Bellboys perform in Las Vegas. "Hound Dog" was recorded by Big Mama Thornton in 1952, shortly after it was written by two young R&B fans, Jerry Leiber and Mike Stoller. Not knowing of Freddie Bell's version, they were somewhat shocked to hear Elvis change gender perspectives and make the song less obviously about an angry female.

Aired almost a full month before the song was cut in the studio, the performance showed Elvis and his band rocking their hearts out. Shaking his legs frantically to Fontana's drumbeats, Elvis slows the rhythm down near the conclusion. He and the girls in the audience were only having a bit of sexy fun, yet it caused moral outrage across the nation. Elvis barely had time to think over—let alone respond to—the controversy; later in June, he went out on a new tour through Atlanta and the Carolinas, ending it, after eight days, in Richmond, Virginia. Then he went up to New York.

On July 1st, Elvis appeared on *The Steve Allen Show*, and later on the New York talk show *Hy Gardner Calling*. Steve Allen looked at Elvis, and rock and roll, as something of a joke. He had Elvis appear in a degrading hillbilly sketch and then dressed him in a tux to sing "Hound Dog" to a real hound dog. On top of all that, Elvis wasn't allowed to move, which made his performances considerably tamer than normal.

Talking with Gardner later that night, Elvis sounded tired and bewildered by the sensation he is causing. He comes across as a sincere individual—one who is more than ready to speak up for himself and his family. The next day, Elvis had a recording session in New York before heading home to Memphis to play a July 4th charity homecoming performance in Memphis at Russwood Park. By all accounts, he gave one of his best performances to date. After that, Elvis finally took a month off—his first since becoming a professional entertainer. Still only

To some, Elvis seemed like he arrived from another planet. This 1957 magazine suggests that he came straight from hell!

twenty-one, it was only his youthful energy that had allowed him to tour as much as he did. Though he kept up a pretty brutal pace in the seventies, he would never again have to—or choose to—work so incessantly. With movies now on the horizon, touring would become merely one part of his career, not the near sole focus.

On August 3rd, Elvis began a tour of Florida that only ventured out of the state for two shows in New Orleans nine days later. After taking a month off to shoot *Love Me Tender*, he played another charity homecoming show, this time in Tupelo on September 26th. He performed as the headline attraction at the same Mississippi-Alabama Fair and Dairy Show that he had played as a ten-year-old, when he placed fifth in the amateur contest. Now, eleven years later, Elvis and his folks came home as conquering heroes. Both shows Elvis gave that day (for which he performed a slew of hits) have since been issued, and considerable film material has turned up in recent years. Probably the most informative footage of how he paced and ran his show in the fifties, it shows Elvis and his group (now including the Jordanaires) tearing up the town, with the audience literally in hysterics.

While shooting *Love Me Tender*, Elvis made his first appearance on *The Ed Sullivan Show*. Sullivan had been injured in a car crash, so guest host Charles Laughton took on the job of introducing Elvis to the masses, marking the moment he became "The King." Elvis was filmed singing four songs on a remote broadcast from Hollywood. The best of the songs, from a visual standpoint, is a rip-roaring performance of Little Richard's "Ready Teddy." Even though he was several thousand miles away from the audience in New York, he completely mesmerized both them and America.

After taking a couple of weeks off, Elvis went on a four-day tour of Texas on October 11th, followed by two more weeks of down time. He then flew to New York on October 28th to appear in person with Ed Sullivan himself. For his second appearance, a newly black-haired Elvis nearly repeated his set of the previous month, removing "Ready Teddy" and putting in a theatrical performance of "Love Me" in its place. After shooting a new ending for *Love Me Tender* the next day, Elvis then took a nearly monthlong sabbatical.

Elvis' last tour dates of the year were focused on Ohio and Kentucky, including a trip back to Cleveland. Closing out the year was his December 15th return to the *Hayride*. It would prove to be his final performance for the show, but *Hayride* personnel would later remember it as the wildest night in the show's history. The full recording of this surfaced recently, and as noted earlier, Elvis had gained poise without being any less vibrant.

On Celluloid

Becoming a good actor was as important to Elvis as anything else in his life, rivaling even his love of music. His enthusiasm for being on the set of his debut film manifested itself in him memorizing not only his lines, but also the entire script.

Publicly, Elvis did his first acting on television. For both of his appearances on *The Milton Berle Show*, plus his lone episode of *The Steve Allen Show*, he took part in silly but amusing live sketches. They weren't as earth-shattering as his music, but they do reveal a natural charisma and decent comic timing.

By the time of the first *Berle* appearance, in April 1956, Elvis was already well on his way to being a star of the silver screen. As early as January of that year, the Colonel was putting out feelers for a movie deal. On February 24th, William Morris liaison Henry Kalcheim confirmed to Parker that a screen test was being arranged with noted producer Hal Wallis. From March 26th to the 28th, Elvis had a three-day test that saw him doing scenes from the upcoming Burt Lancaster film *The Rainmaker*. He was also filmed in color, miming to "Blue Suede Shoes."

Directed by Frank Tashlin, the performance footage has survived the years, and has much of the bright colors and kinetic energy Tashlin applied later in the year to his rock-and-roll cinema classic *The Girl Can't Help It*. Still, it came down to Elvis, who is visibly excited to be on a movie set. With his natural hair color on display, he looks amazing youthful and vibrant. He puts so much into his performance that one can easily miss the fact that the prop guitar he is playing has no strings!

By April 2nd, Wallis was offering a seven-picture deal to Elvis—one that was signed on the 25th. Elvis' popularity ensured that his movies would be a financial success, but the question remained as to whether he could match the standard of his as-yet flawless recording and stage career on a movie set.

Originally, Elvis had hoped not to sing in the movies. In fact, he even made a statement to reporter Charlie Walker, on April 15, 1956, that as far as he knew he wouldn't be doing so. In an interview in Wisconsin, on May 14th, he said that he had been offered a part in *The Rainmaker* but turned it down, as he didn't think he could do it justice.

This change of plan meant that Hal Wallis needed time to come up with another role that Elvis felt more comfortable with. Part of their deal was that Elvis could make movies for rival studios as long as they weren't released at the same time as anything he did for Wallis. Elvis then signed a contract for three pictures with 20th Century Fox, which already had a project called *The Reno Brothers* ready for its new young talent.

It's been said that the film was initially intended not to include any songs, but the fact that Elvis recorded the soundtrack very early in the production seems to indicate that this changed as soon as he took on the role. *Love Me Tender* is the one anomalous Elvis Presley film that doesn't star Elvis Presley. He was clearly the reason for the film's existence, from a promotional standpoint, but at heart it is a fairly typical period western. Taken on those terms, *Love Me Tender* holds up rather well, yet the fact remains that most who have viewed it aren't that interested in the plot points that don't concern Elvis. It's not that the film isn't music-based so much as that Elvis doesn't appear in roughly half of it.

Love Me Tender was shot principally from August 22nd to September 21st, and Elvis is indeed different in it than in any other film. His hair is still dark blond (instead of black), he doesn't carry the whole film, and his acting is much less refined than it would be later. Also noticeable is the fact that Elvis' moves were quite similar to what he was doing onstage at the time. These aren't his wildest performances on celluloid, but they are the least choreographed.

Not only did many of Elvis' devoted fans attend the film multiple times, they treated his appearance as if he was there in person. As would happen nearly a decade later, with the Beatles' first few films, girls screamed every time he spoke, sang, or moved. Yet there was something of a sense of disappointment, because it took approximately eighteen and a half minutes for him to first show his face. That may not seem too long to those few that actually wanted to see the movie for what it had to offer, but most were there to see Elvis and only Elvis. The people were soon given what they wanted, but this proved to be problematical later, when Elvis' audience matured and did indeed want to see their hero go beyond his established image.

The importance of *Love Me Tender* can be measured on what it made possible, if not so much on the quality of what was captured on film. The title song is still one of Elvis' most popular hits, but to the more critical ear it can be seen as more of a door-opener in the ballad field than anything remarkable in and of itself. Critics of the day weren't too kind, but the money the film and soundtrack generated made their harping fairly immaterial. This would one day make for a stifling situation for Elvis the movie star, but early on he cared too much to let money stunt his creative growth. He had decided he was going to be a good actor, and that's exactly what he would (all too fleetingly) become.

Popularity and Impact

In 1956, Elvis became one of the most important figures in music history. Both of his first two LPs hit the top of the charts, his EPs were top sellers, and his singles of new material were smashes as well. "Heartbreak Hotel," "Don't Be Cruel," and "Love Me Tender" all hit #1. "Hound Dog" made it to #2, "I Want You, I Need You, I Love You" got to #3, and the EP-only cut "Love Me" got all the way to #6. That doesn't even count the three flip sides and additional three EP cuts that hit the Top 40.

Looking back, Elvis played a huge part of mid-twentieth-century societal history as well. There simply was no other individual with the same level of influence. Though he was an unfailingly polite young man, he wasn't afraid to defend rock and roll when it was accused of corrupting the youth. He also wasn't afraid to list his influences, both white and black, and attended events like the otherwise "negro only" WDIA radio event fundraiser for black youths. Without being self-aggrandizing, Elvis made his feelings known on racial equality well known in a time and region where this was still anything but commonplace.

Finally, Elvis had no qualms about displaying his attraction to the opposite sex in a realistic, adult manner. He wasn't in any way lewd, but he made it known he enjoyed playing the field. Despite the fact that he had decidedly modern ideas on certain issues, he still had basic, all-American values. He loved his mom and dad, he was religious, and he also proved to have a charitable nature very early into his success. He was fifties America in a nutshell, and by being an original, he became a part of millions of people's lives.

7

I Want to Be Free

1957

Nineteen fifty-seven was a fantastic year in Elvis' career. The most popular singer in the world, he was making music, movies, and concerts that were commercially and creatively satisfying. It was possibly the best year ever for rock and roll as it was originally conceived, and Elvis was absolutely the King. In April, Elvis bought the home of his dreams, Graceland, in Memphis. He would buy bigger places in years to come, but he always came back to Graceland—it was home.

While he continued to scale back his touring engagements, Elvis' 1957 shows had become events, with much ballyhoo and press coverage surrounding them. He only did one national television show in 1957, but being that it was again *Ed Sullivan,* he certainly picked the one that would give him the best exposure. His two movies that year were both well made, with excellent casts, and his music continued to be most innovative and influential.

The only clouds on the horizon were Elvis' imminent draft and some discord among his original band. Both of these developments would change the course of his life and career. The long-lasting results were not totally for the worse, but the great balance found here of TV, films, recording, and touring was puzzlingly never repeated. Under direction from his management, in the future Elvis would focus on one or two of the four outlets for his talents and completely ignore the others. He was someone who thrived on variety, yet the rest of his career would be defined by a quickly stifling routine.

Studio Work

Elvis' sound continued to evolve over the course of the year. His voice gradually took on more of a gentle harmonious quality on his ballads, and he was now filling out most of his records with the piano stylings of Dudley Brooks. Elvis tried to record as much as he could at his preferred studio, Radio Recorders in Hollywood, but he was forced at times, during the filming of *Loving You,* to cut tracks on the Paramount soundstage. He rightly felt that the latter's poor acoustics and generally mediocre working conditions were hurting his sound. Eventually, the company relented and allowed Elvis to go back to Radio Recorders.

The recordings that took place during the first two months of the year were plentiful and varied. Still extremely involved with his music, Elvis insisted on proper Radio Recorders sessions for all but the most bare of arrangements of the *Loving You* material. Enough tracks were recorded for a full twelve-track album, a gospel EP, and three non-LP singles, although some were not released until years later. The gospel cuts and ballads have a nice simplicity to them, yet Elvis still sounds a mite timid. On the rock and blues, he excels just as consistently as he had before—even more so if you consider that he had a larger quotient of original material during this period.

The *Jailhouse Rock* sessions were a lot neater and more compact. The entire album was recorded at Radio Recorders, except for one vocal overdub and several things for the movie only, which were done on the MGM soundstage. Elvis again made it known he didn't like the sound but seemed satisfied that the record itself was recorded under optimal circumstances.

The songs were the strongest he ever had for a film, and near enough the best he ever had, period. More than half of them were written by Jerry Leiber and Mike Stoller, who also took part in co-producing the sessions with Elvis. The fast friendship they all struck up infuriated Parker, who didn't want Elvis to favor Leiber and Stoller over the other songwriters in his roster—and heaven forbid Elvis doing something creative that the Colonel wasn't able to control.

In the early part of September, Elvis made it back to Hollywood for a three-day Radio Recorders session. Elvis mostly focused on songs for a Christmas LP. He also re-cut "Treat Me Nice" from *Jailhouse Rock* in a fuller arrangement, which he preferred to the film version, and laid down two sides for two separate 45s. Though a few things didn't work perfectly, Elvis and his crew performed at the top of their game. Yet here is where Scotty and Bill were finally pushed too far. After a spin-off instrumental LP featuring them with Elvis as part of the lineup was postponed indefinitely, Scotty Moore and Bill Black resigned from Elvis' band. They would soon return on a per diem basis, but things were never quite the same.

Live Performance

Elvis started off the year with his third and final *Ed Sullivan Show* appearance. The longest television showcase for Elvis to date, this was the notorious appearance where he was only allowed to be filmed from the waist up. Elvis handled this with some levity by moving his hands a lot more than normal. His version of "Don't Be Cruel" was heavily influenced by the version he saw performed by Billy Ward and His Dominos, whose lead singer, Jackie Wilson, would soon go solo and become a legend of R&B.

Elvis also performed several more hits, including his new single "Too Much" and "When My Blue Moon Turns to Gold Again," and previewed "Peace in the Valley," after which Sullivan came out to declare him as "a decent fine boy." For someone as "establishment" as Sullivan to speak positively about Elvis in public was a major step in having Elvis be taken more seriously as an artist and less as a freaky flash in the pan.

On March 28, 1957, Elvis began his first tour for four months. The Colonel hired Australian-based American promoter Lee Gordon, and together they set up a series of shows that set a new standard, even for Elvis. With his new gold-lamé outfit on display, and a longer, more varied set-list, Presley's presentation was more professional than ever. The Blue Moon Boys and the Jordanaires were all there to provide expert backup. The tour lasted until April 6th, taking in Chicago, St. Louis, Buffalo, Toronto, Ottawa, and Philadelphia. Most notable among these dates were the shows in Canada, which, along with a return appearance later in the year, would mark the only time (outside of an appearance in Hawaii in 1957) that Elvis formally played outside of the fifty States.

Elvis spent the rest of his time over the spring shooting *Jailhouse Rock*. During the summer, he had two months off—his longest period of downtime since turning professional three years earlier. Then, at the end of August, it was time to go back to work. The Colonel booked Elvis on a five-city Labor Day weekend tour, including stops in Seattle, Portland, and Vancouver. The gold-lamé coat was worn on every date of this jaunt, which musically was even more diverse than his last.

When audiences were somewhat under control, Elvis played up to eighteen selections. Inevitably, security problems plagued several of the venues. Due to inadequate acoustics, as well as the inability for all patrons to see him clearly, outdoor stadiums were not the ideal place for an Elvis Presley show. Though even Parker would have preferred indoor venues, stadiums were the only places that could afford to pay the kind of dollars the Colonel sought this time out.

For his second charity gig at the Mississippi-Alabama Fair in Tupelo, which took place on September 27th during the brief period when Scotty and Bill were gone, Elvis needed to find a replacement guitarist and bass player. He recruited session-guitarist extraordinaire Hank Garland and bassist Chuck Wiginton, an acquaintance of D. J. Fontana's. Ten thousand seats were sold that evening, with 2,000 more attendees paying to stand or sit on the ground and watch. Elvis was not remunerated for the concert; he intended the proceeds to go to building a youth center in East Tupelo.

Being that Elvis was a hometown boy intent on helping the community, Tupelo gave him easily his best write-ups of the year. Elvis was on stage at 8:00 that night, and due to the special nature of the show there do not seem to have been any opening acts. Silent newsreel cameras captured a portion of Elvis' performance and press conference. It is among the most exciting footage of a live performer ever shot. Wearing his dazzling gold jacket, Elvis is on fire, delivering expertly executed gyrations to his ecstatic fans. Unwittingly, it served as his farewell performance to the city of his birth.

Though outwardly satisfied with the concert, Elvis confided to D. J. that he missed Scotty and Bill. Indeed, Elvis saw to it that they were back for what would be his final tour of the fifties, which was set to commence a month later, in

California. Having bought an array of new stage apparel, Elvis didn't wear his gold-lamé coat for most of his short California jaunt, bringing it out only for the most high profile date of the tour, an October 28th booking at the Los Angeles Pan-Pacific Auditorium.

This 1988 calendar uses a wonderful still from the 1957 film *Loving You*.

For what was among the most celebrated and reviled performances of his career, Elvis was by all accounts at his wildest. Ricky Nelson attended the show, and was pleased to find out afterward that Elvis admired him as much as he admired Elvis. Conversely, actor Alan Ladd was seen heatedly leading his children out of the door well before Elvis finished his set. Including both sides of the single from his exceptional new movie, *Jailhouse Rock*, Elvis outdid himself in front of an audience of 9,000. The band was in top form, too, with Scotty's playing even rating a rare mention in a newspaper review.

Fundamentally, it was just another great 1957 Elvis concert, but certain critics who were gunning for Presley tried to make one part of the act sound lewd. During the tour, Elvis used a large replica of the RCA Victor mascot, Nipper, as a prop. As he belted out "Hound Dog," Elvis sang to the toy and dragged it to the floor during his climatic drop to the stage. Falling to his knees and lying down during "Hound Dog" was a normal part of the act, but openly hostile critics like *Los Angles Mirror-News* entertainment editor Dick Williams twisted it into a depiction of simulated sex. It was innocent fun, but Williams' hysterical column the next day caused police to come and film that night's show, just to be sure nothing obscene was taking place. To stay on the good side of the law, a somewhat mocking Elvis kept Nipper off the stage.

Los Angeles had been set to mark the end of the tour, but Lee Gordon had something else in mind. Arguing that Elvis had a lot of free time in his schedule, he convinced Parker to add three shows in Hawaii. Wanting to avoid air travel, Elvis made a four-and-a-half-day journey by boat on the USS *Matsonia*, arriving on November 9th. On the 10th, Elvis performed twice in his gold-lamé coat at the Honolulu Stadium, with shows at 3:00 and 8:15. All told, almost 15,000 islanders attended the two shows. Interestingly, a review of the evening show noted that Elvis played more piano than guitar. It's hard to ascertain exactly what numbers he played on, but going on their structure, "Blueberry Hill," "Treat Me Nice," and "Mean Woman Blues" are strong possibilities.

Elvis finished his visit and tour with a performance at the Schofield Barracks, near Pearl Harbor, the next evening. With Elvis soon to be drafted, this was his last show of the fifties, as well as his final concert with Bill Black. The Hawaiian press and public proved to have a kindly disposition toward Elvis, particularly by 1957 standards. Appreciating that they didn't rush to judge him, Elvis developed a lifelong affinity for the islands. Over the following two decades, he would return many times for both work and leisure purposes.

On Celluloid

Filmed from January 22nd to March 10th, Elvis' second feature, *Loving You*, was a discernible improvement over his debut in every conceivable fashion. Everything—from the cinematography to the cast to Elvis' acting, and especially the songs—was immeasurably better than what had been seen in *Love Me Tender*. The basic reason for this is that, instead of shoving him into a somewhat nondescript role, *Loving You* was created with Elvis and his career in mind. There was no question in this or any of his future films that Elvis was the star.

Loving You set a number of other precedents in Elvis' film career, both good and bad. Firstly, the movie revolved around the songs. Here, it's not a bad thing, as the songs were, all in all, excellent. Secondly, it was the first of three movies that concerned the life of a musician (in this case one by the name of Deke Rivers) and the unique situations that thusly presented themselves. Finally, it was the first film where Elvis attempted some light comedy. This would yield mixed results later on, but there is a subtlety here compared with what was to come.

If one goes from Elvis' visible unease in his first movie to the confidence of his third, his command of the screen is a shock. By catching him in between these two stages, *Loving You* proves his evolution to be quite natural. It was the best movie for him at the time because it didn't make great demands, but it did push him far enough that he could go on to better things. While somewhat less gritty than the films that follow, it is valuable in that it captured the more joyous side of rock and roll.

The fairly open subtext of *Loving You* is to legitimize rock and roll as a quality form of music. It's not preachy in this message, but Deke's music is shown to ultimately win over audiences young and old—and, more significantly, black and white. That rock and roll appealed to different races is handled subtly, but it is there, and it does make a statement.

In the sense that it is more of a rock-and-roll vehicle than a dramatic story, *Loving You* may not be the greatest movie Elvis filmed. Yet it is an indispensable filmed document of Elvis at his most raw and sexual. In *Loving You*, Elvis *is* rock and roll personified, rendering the film one of the most important documents of the medium's first decade.

Filming on *Jailhouse Rock* started on May 13th and ended June 14th. Not only is it among the best Elvis Presley movies, but it also may just be one of the most potent films of its era. Is there any other film that so succinctly captures the rebellion of early rock and roll? Right before your eyes, you can see the changing of the guard.

Unlike most cinematic ventures from the fifties and sixties to address the rock-and-roll phenomenon, *Jailhouse Rock* wasn't a teen movie. Sure, Elvis' name on the marquee was going to bring in his young fan base, but this was a movie made for a mature audience. The thematic sensuality and violence wasn't watered down—this was an intelligent movie that never took on the condescending tone of most Presley films.

Not once is Elvis' accent or Southern manner attacked. His character, Vince Everett, was not a sophisticate, but he was nobody's fool either. Everett was not some kid but a fully grown man who drank and bedded women. Being that this was shot in 1957, the sexual chemistry between Vince and the various females he came across wasn't handled in a tawdry way, but neither was sex presented as something that would lead to instant ruin.

Vince wasn't a romanticized character; he has a streak in him that's down-right cruel, but this is realistic. An ex-con who killed a man in a bar fight is not going to be genteel. *Jailhouse Rock* proves that Elvis Presley had legitimate skills. It wasn't merely looks or charisma that he brought to the table. If it were as simple as that, his other film characterizations would be a lot more memorable. When Elvis was given something meaty, he could grippingly bring a scene to life. He was able to get into Vince's brain, give him layers, and relay how the events taking place affected his psyche.

Treating Elvis like a creative entity whose input mattered, choreographer Alex Romero didn't make Presley conform to his vision of how the music would be presented. Instead, he created the dance routines around Elvis' real style. With the possible exception of *Loving You*, none of his other films presented him with such a proper showcase for his music. The musical numbers have a touch of the traditional Hollywood musical, while also setting a blueprint for perfor-mance-oriented music videos.

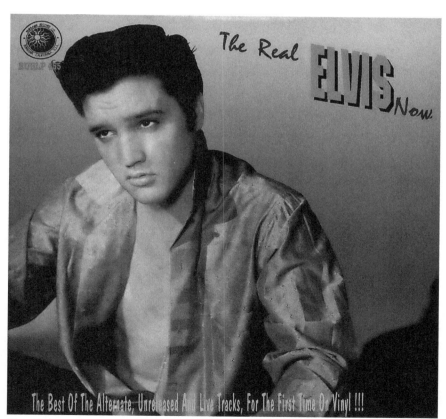

This 1997 bootleg was the highlight of several mid-nineties 10-inch bootleg releases. This shot was a bit too earthy for an actual 1957 LP.

Jailhouse Rock continues to be relevant because it took chances in an era where conformity was the norm. The sordid environment below the glossy surface of celebrity is something that continues to fascinate us. The script provides some real insight into what can happen to someone when his connection with everyday reality is severed. The way this film both defines and transcends the time it was made is remarkable.

Elvis Presley may not have had a movie career that was personally or artistically fulfilling as a whole, but with *Jailhouse Rock* he did achieve his goal of becoming an accomplished actor. In 2004, *Jailhouse Rock* was added to the Library of Congress' Film Registry. Bearing in mind how badly Elvis wanted to make his mark in Hollywood, this honor would likely have been among his proudest achievements.

Popularity and Impact

Now firmly established as the biggest star in the world, Elvis was at the very height of his fame. "Too Much" went to #2, and "All Shook Up," "Teddy Bear," and "Jailhouse Rock" all topped the charts. Elvis' EPs all sold extremely well, and both of his 1957 LPs, *Loving You* and *Elvis' Christmas Album*, hit #1. Artistically, there were a few experiments that didn't work, but overall this music was as strong and influential as any Elvis ever made.

When you are on the top, however, there is always someone to come and try to knock you. Perhaps the most unfortunate rumor Elvis ever had to deal with was the one that suggested he was a racist. This was untrue, but even now you hear occasionally among the black community that Elvis once said that the only thing a black person could do for him was buy his records and shine his shoes. Yet this is patently untrue. Elvis spoke out about the value of black music and, as noted before, he attended events where he broke the segregation line.

When Louie Robinson interviewed Elvis for the August issue of *Jet Magazine*, Presley spoke out strongly. "I never said anything like that, and people who know me know that I wouldn't have said it." The article made clear that, while Elvis ignored most rumors, this was something he had to make clear had no basis in fact.

8

I'm Not Asking Much of You

W ith Elvis' army induction set for March 24th, the year 1958 marked the end of an era by default. He didn't do anything in the studio between June 1958 and March 1960, which by today's standards seems quite normal. Yet, when you consider how prolific recording artists were in the fifties and sixties, it must have felt like a very long time for Elvis and his fans.

Elvis did his level best throughout the early part of the year to deliver in quality what he couldn't in quantity. He filmed the outstanding *King Creole*, which had the bonus of a soundtrack that held its own with almost anything he ever recorded. He also cut some classic singles that contain some of the wildest rock and roll he ever attempted. RCA complained to Parker that they wanted more, but the Colonel had yet to lose his edge, and he kept anticipation high for Elvis' return by not flooding the market. There was some talk that Elvis could do some recording at his home off-base for a special EP, but he didn't consider the idea seriously.

The course of the rest of Elvis' life was determined by many of the events that took place while he was in the army. The biggest tragedy of his life occurred on August 14, 1958, when his mother, Gladys, passed away. She was Elvis' best friend—his link to reality. Had she lived, one wonders whether Elvis' world would have become so insular. He left for Germany a few weeks later, and he met his future wife Priscilla in the early fall of 1959. Elvis also began to take pills regularly after one of his commanding officers gave him some Dexedrine to stay awake during maneuvers.

Musically, Elvis kept abreast of things and made it a goal to expand his vocal range. In a way, he relished having an everyday schedule, and was proud of his military achievements. On the other hand, he missed his work greatly, and was quite worried that he would have no career to return to. This may seem to be an unreasonable case of self-doubt in retrospect, but rock and roll was still less than a decade old, and nobody knew if it would have longevity. While it was likely that he had a bright future ahead of him, he was acutely aware that it wasn't a given until he actually resumed his career.

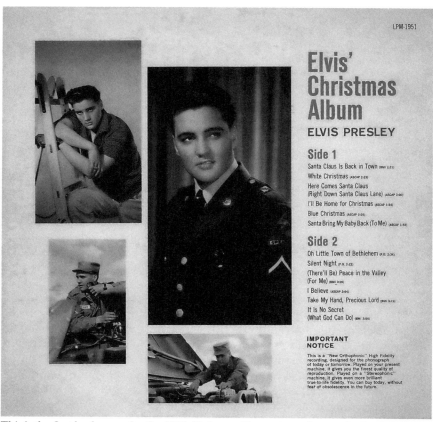

This is the first back cover for the 1959 *Christmas Album* reissue. It was mistakenly believed to be from 1958, until the discoveries of several Elvis experts proved otherwise.

Studio Work

Elvis managed to cut twenty new songs before he set sail for Europe, and they maintain the high standards of his earlier work. The *King Creole* soundtrack takes advantage of the film's New Orleans setting, and most of the cuts were very tastefully arranged. If a few of the songs on the *King Creole* LP have elements of artifice, everything Elvis recorded in 1958 was fundamentally strong.

Elvis' ballad voice was developing nicely, and the five rock-oriented tunes that were the focus of his June 1958 session in Nashville rank among his finest achievements. Of the five songs cut that evening, four went Top 10, with the other one hitting the Top 20. For reasons that remain murky, Scotty and Bill didn't attend the session. A February date at Radio Recorders had been hard going, and there may have been a feeling upon Elvis' first Nashville Studio B outing for two years that he should take advantage of the excellent players that made up what were known as the "A-Team." Even with all the troubles he had in getting good masters in February, the "Wear My Ring Around Your Neck"/"Doncha' Think It's Time" single that resulted was another big hit.

Due to his army stint, the only recordings Elvis made during 1959 were done at home for his personal use. Being inherently loose and of somewhat compromised fidelity, these aren't songs one would play casually. From a historical standpoint, these are interesting mainly for Elvis' first attempts at operatic-styled ballads. Certainly, as the precursor to "It's Now or Never," "There's No Tomorrow" provides much insight into where Elvis was heading musically.

On Celluloid

King Creole is the last of the four movies Elvis made in the fifties, and it's surprisingly the last in which his character's career as a musician fits naturally into the plot. There would be many films in the future that featured Elvis as a working musician, but never again would there be any insights into fame or the inherent struggle to achieve success. *King Creole* was decidedly not a film aimed solely at young teens. If anything, the story revolved around sex and violence, but these issues weren't exploited for their own sake. Instead, they were major story points, handled with much sensitivity.

The film is set in New Orleans, but Elvis' Southernness is not made an issue. While it would have been nice if other major characters in the movie also had accents, the feel of the town is captured well by the sets and background players. The songs are, by and large, very entertaining, but with some tweaks the movie could still have had legs without them. Music is central to the plot, but unlike in Presley's previous two films, it is not *the* most important aspect.

King Creole ended an era. Elvis' post-army work has been unfairly slammed, but it is fair to say he never rose to this level as an actor again. It will always be a mystery as to why his sixties films were never made with the same level of care, but because of his first four movies, Elvis not only became a Hollywood legend but also was able to contribute to the field some classic moments of cinema.

Popularity and Impact

Elvis going into the army was major news, yet because he couldn't make movies, appear on television, or go on tour, he was faintly less omnipresent than he had been in 1956–57. The six singles he put out during this period were still huge hits, but the most popular music he cut in the fifties was all contained on the classic 1958 compilation *Elvis' Golden Records*. The fourteen tracks formed an extremely well chosen selection of all of Elvis' 1956–57 Top 10 hits, along with a smattering of flip sides. It is still astounding how much he had accomplished in such a short amount of time.

King Creole was Elvis' only new LP release during this period, and much of it had already been out on EP. Though it still did well on the strength of the (considerable) attraction of offering the whole soundtrack in one place, none

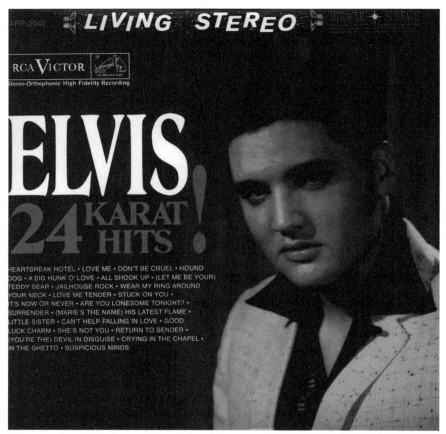

This stunning 1959 photo accompanies *the* best-sounding Elvis LP of all time. This 1997 release was a two-record set, and it has recently been reissued as a 45 rpm three-LP set.

of the three 1959 LP comps that followed made the Top 10. The first two LP releases combined Sun singles, EP tracks, and flip sides in skimpy ten-track lineups that didn't utilize all of Elvis' non-album cuts. *For LP Fans Only* and *A Date with Elvis* both had excellent jackets, but they didn't have any sense of respect for the music within. Astonishingly, all of the Sun cuts—as well as some of the RCA masters—had a heavy layer of echo laid on them, which ruined their sparse, natural charm.

One LP that came closer to being a product of quality was *50,000,000 Elvis Fans Can't Be Wrong—Elvis' Gold Records Volume 2.* The cover artwork of Elvis in his gold-lamé outfit is an iconic classic, but the record itself had problems. While the single from *King Creole* ("Hard Headed Woman"/"Don't Ask Me Why") was probably excised because it had already appeared on that LP, it served only to make this short, ten-song album less definitive. Another problem was the mistaken inclusion of an inferior alternate take of "Doncha' Think It's Time." Sure, this made things interesting for collectors, but it also meant that the alternate was invariably used on future comps, despite it not being the hit version.

Despite the diminishing LP returns, the lack of new material only served to whet the appetite of Elvis' fans. As the two years of his military service went by, the buildup to what would amount to his first comeback was escalating. Elvis had a valid concern over what would be waiting for him back home, but little did he know that his absence only made him seem that much more special.

9

The Music Really Sends Me

Fifties Elvis on RCA

I
f the Sun singles contained the most musically influential recordings Elvis
ever made, most critics and fans agree that his fifties recordings for RCA
Victor represent a truly golden era. While some have argued that his early
RCA records were not as "pure" as those he cut at Sun, this is fundamentally
unfair. These records did sound different than what came before, but that
doesn't mean that Elvis had sold out to commercial interests. He was still developing his style, and he happened to be making music that defined the era in
which it was recorded. In other words, he was starting a trend, not following one.

Not every song cut during this period was a watershed moment in music
history—not all of them are even good—but the best of the following records
shaped and redefined how young society looked at itself worldwide. Musically,
Elvis was a constant pioneer simply by doing what came naturally to him. This
period saw the introduction of new sounds and different ways of performing, all
of which would soon become an essential part of the fabric of modern music.

"Heartbreak Hotel"/"I Was the One" (Released January 27, 1956)

A record that altered the path of so many people and things, "Heartbreak Hotel"
is the song that put Elvis on the map. It was written by Mae Boren Axton, who
was inspired by a story her friend Tommy Durden told her about a John Doe
who left a suicide note reading, "I walk a lonely street." Axton gave Tommy and
Elvis a third of the credit and royalties on the song, the latter because Axton felt
sorry for the kid from Memphis who just escaped from poverty.

"Heartbreak Hotel" stands out as a composition because of Axton's use of
imagery. The hotel is at the end of "Lonely Street"; there's a crying bellhop, and
a desk clerk dressed in black. The music matches the glum mood of the lyric,
with the piano of Shorty Long sounding, in the immortal words of author Robert
Matthew-Walker, like "sad rain." Elvis sings with distress in his voice and a newly
honed sense of the dramatic. Still mysterious and alluring, "Heartbreak Hotel"

HEARTBREAK HOTEL · I WAS THE ONE · MONEY
HONEY · I FORGOT TO REMEMBER TO FORGET

EPA-821

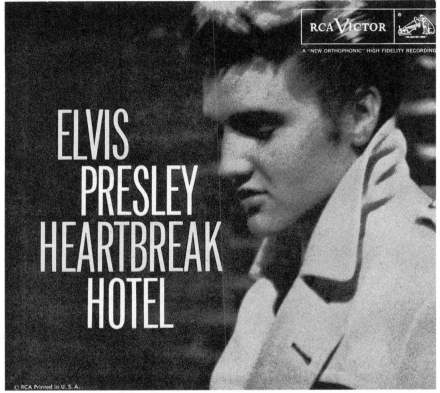

RCA VICTOR

A "NEW ORTHOPHONIC" HIGH FIDELITY RECORDING

ELVIS PRESLEY HEARTBREAK HOTEL

© RCA Printed in U. S. A.

"Heartbreak Hotel" changed both social and musical history. This EP was released to capitalize on the success of the single.   *Courtesy of Robert Rodriguez*

is an incredibly unusual song. Teens could relate to the feeling of bottomless despair, and moreover Elvis made anguish sound cool.

As "Heartbreak Hotel" slowly became a phenomenon, it gave young people something of their own to hold on to. Elvis launched the whole rock-and-roll image—he talked the talk and walked the walk. He wasn't going into this thinking he was going to change things in society; he just wanted be good at what he did, make enough money to give his parents the things they wanted, and, most of all, find some personal redemption. After all, how many people who are considered outcasts actually bend society to their way of thinking?

"I Was the One" was another leap forward in an unexpected direction. Elvis' attachment to romantic love songs had not been on public display before, and his use of backing singers (makeshift though they were) was also something new for him. Until now, Elvis had never sounded even close to this self-assured when dealing with a slow beat, nor had he issued a ballad that modern teens could relate to so personally. Backed by a good rhythm, and coming across far less country than the slow songs he had cut up until now, it was the prototype of the Elvis "beat ballads" to come over the next several years.

Elvis cited "I Was the One" often in his interviews of the period as being a favorite, and like its top side, it put him in a new role of authority. The lyric concerns a male protagonist bemoaning all the things he taught his younger ex-girlfriend about love and passion. That Elvis sounds more seasoned vocally than he had at Sun helps his credibility in getting the theme across. Only eighteen months into his career, the growth in Elvis is staggering.

Elvis Presley (Released March 23, 1956)

As the first #1 rock-and-roll LP, a format previously considered the province of adults, *Elvis Presley* brought a new cachet to the genre and formally announced that it had well and truly arrived. Though the EPs taken from the fifties albums all outsold their LP counterpoints, this was RCA's all-time best seller since the arrival of the 12-inch 33⅓ format seven years earlier. Fresh and vivacious as the day it was issued, *Elvis Presley* remains one of Elvis' top LPs. First time out, and only a mere quarter of the albums he issued later can match or better it.

The original cover is a perfect fifties graphic—one that has been altered to ill effect on vinyl since the second, early-sixties pressing, with the contrast of pink and green lost in the record company logo and the picture zoomed in. The notes on the back briefly try to make sense of who Elvis is and what he has to offer.

As RCA had bought the unused Sun masters as part of their deal, Steve Sholes picked out five he considered releasable to augment seven recent RCA numbers. The blend is a hodge-podge, but the high points of the album are so good, they nullify the fact that a couple of the early out-takes weren't all that impressive. Elvis' creative growth and improved self-confidence meant that most of the new songs are spectacular.

Let's start with the Sun numbers. "Blue Moon" is a haunting experiment from August 1954. Elvis sounds ghostly and very young. He sings this Rodgers and Hart ballad over a very spare backing. The individualism Elvis told himself he had is present, even this early on. There's a warmth and calmness in Elvis' voice not heard before; a hint that he might have the ability to innovate in more than solely rockabilly. Wailing in falsetto, Elvis sounds vulnerable, with a level of candor unlike any interpreter who came before him. Long on dark atmosphere, "Blue Moon" is a bizarre and chilling recording. If perhaps a grower that only comes alive after repeated plays, it is inspirational once you connect to it.

"I Love You Because" is interesting mainly because it shows what Elvis was shooting for before coming up with "That's All Right." It was recorded at Elvis' very first professional session, and his voice sounds cleaner than it had on his demo recordings. Yet despite the basic attractiveness of his voice, he's not yet assured at this type of song. Besides, it was much closer to what music had been before—rather than what it would become after—Elvis exploded.

Also none too perfect was the monotonous "I'll Never Let You Go (Little Darlin')," recorded in September 1954. Elvis doesn't have enough expression in his voice, only coming alive on the mid-tempo pick-up at the end, or when uttering the phrase "baby doll." All of the Sun masters elicit a historical fascination, but "I'll Never Let You Go" is a terribly ordinary recording.

"Just Because" also dates from the September session, and is a cute rockabilly revival of a song that had been a hit in a number of different genres since the late twenties. It doesn't have the menace Elvis would have imparted later, but the self-mocking flirtatiousness is firmly in place. Listen closely to the solo, and it is instructive on how solidly Elvis, Scotty, and Bill coalesced together.

"Tryin' to Get to You" comes from July 1955, and it makes sense that it is a bridge between the early Sun and 1956 selections. A standout among Presley's entire output, the depth of feeling Elvis puts into his blues singing is startling, especially coming from a man of only twenty. He also does a fine job on piano, hitting some resonant low notes. This was the only cut on the album Sam Phillips was willing to issue, but the sale of Elvis' contract canceled that notion.

"Tryin' to Get to You" came from the same session as "Mystery Train," and few evenings in history can match the ingenuity or zeal on display. The sound is thicker than it had been a year ago, Elvis' voice having slightly filled out. Musically, the heavy drumming of Johnny Bernero made clear that Elvis' rockabilly sound was already evolving into a harder rock and roll. There is no hint of contrivance—Elvis seems born to sing this. The unfiltered power of Presley on his best Sun-era recordings was staggering then, is still astonishing now, and will for the infinite future be a source of enthrallment to all sorts of music lovers.

Moving on to the RCA recordings, the lone low point comes with "I'm Counting on You." It's too heavy a ballad for Elvis in 1956, and he couldn't put it over without straining his adenoids. In another ball game entirely is Elvis' thrash through Clyde McPhatter and the Drifters' "Money Honey." Elvis sounds impossibly young and vibrant, so very much alive.

The early 1956 RCA sessions were the first with D. J. Fontana, who was already acting as a more natural part of the band than those who had come before. Booming out loud and crisp, his playing on "Money Honey" is some of his best stick work. This would be one of several songs Elvis did through 1960 that had a beat suitable for a mid-twentieth-century stripper. Of course, that was all done in good-natured fun—a tip to Fontana's experience playing behind actual exotic (or "burlesque," in fifties terminology) dancers. Scotty's remark about being in the only band in the world led by an ass applies more to Fontana than anyone. Since it was hard to hear his bandmates over the barrage of female screams, D. J. memorized Elvis' stage movements in order to keep up.

"Tutti Frutti" was Little Richard's first hit, and among the best covers Elvis ever attempted. Every bit as crazed as Richard himself, Elvis rocks with all his might. The band add a distinct spark of their own, and should be applauded most of all for keeping up with him. At the time this album came out, Elvis' "Tutti Frutti" was a candidate for being the heaviest rock-and-roll cut to date. As with so much else happening in music, Presley was leading the way. Listen for his heavily echoed "boom" on the fade!

One of Elvis' favorite secular artists was the unique R&B crooner Roy Hamilton. For the album, Presley selected Hamilton's debonair "I'm Gonna Sit Right Down and Cry (Over You)." Elvis' cover is a little wilder than the original, but the piano playing of Shorty Long helps it match the swing of Hamilton's rendition. Otherwise, it shares the raucous feel of the majority of Elvis' fifties rockers. He is still unrefined, and some wouldn't want him any other way.

"I Got a Woman" rocks up Ray Charles' hit R&B record, and over the years it would become as synonymous with Elvis as it was with Charles. Despite happily taking the money Presley's covers earned, Charles was bitter about this, and about Elvis' success in general. In the end it doesn't matter, because to the impartial observer, Elvis' Ray Charles covers are noteworthy, even enlightening.

Where Elvis adds most to "I Got a Woman" is in the way he uses the pauses to heighten the lyrical tension. The first song Elvis cut for RCA, by now his fifties rock-and-roll sound is solidly in place and thoroughly entertaining. Though the post-1972 performances lack power and focus, from 1955 to the very end, Elvis kept the song as a regular part of his live set.

The jaunty "One-Sided Love Affair" was Elvis' favorite song on the album. He liked the philosophy it had on the give-and-take between the sexes, and he was still quoting the lyric in conversation two decades later. Shorty Long's piano playing had a good-time barroom atmosphere, more tinkly in technique than the people Elvis used in Nashville or Los Angeles. Including an array of jovial hiccups in every line, Presley has the air of a strutting (if harmless) peacock.

"Blue Suede Shoes" is a fantastic reinvention of Carl Perkins' classic rocka-billy hit. Elvis had begun performing this strident rock-and-roll version of the song soon after Carl's came out. With a promise kept to not release it as a single until Carl's 45 peaked, Elvis' "Blue Suede Shoes" did hit the Top 30 as a track from one of this LP's EP releases. Perkins still had the bigger hit, and also enjoyed the remarkable supplementary songwriting royalties Presley's version generated.

"Blue Suede Shoes" will always be Carl's signature song, but Elvis did it so well that it is also one of his. The energy of the performance was captured perfectly on tape. It is amazing to think that some of Elvis' 1956 recordings sound better than much of what he recorded in the decades to come. There was a very clean, shimmering sound at the 1956 New York sessions. The mixes jump out at you, flaunting superb, crunchy rock and roll.

"I Want You, I Need You, I Love You"/"My Baby Left Me" (Released May 4, 1956)

Though not quite as big a landmark as Elvis' other 1956 singles, "I Want You, I Need You, I Love You" is a marvelous recording. Taking the sound of "I Was the One" a step further, the melody has better changes, and Elvis is at his most vital. It is also immediately evocative of its time. In one of his last interviews, John Lennon raved about hearing it on the radio, and how it brought back the whole period for him.

"I Want You, I Need You, I Love You" puts the focus on Elvis' voice. He had such an individualistic take on singing, in the syllables he stressed or in any given inflection he was prepared to take on. The tongue-twisting title presented a big challenge for Elvis and his band, all of whom had narrowly missed being involved in a potentially fatal airplane crash on the way to the studio. The applied echo adds a lower resonance to Presley's bottom end, and as the song required full use of his range you can hear his higher nasal tones are intact, if further refined.

Though the fifteenth take (first released in 1976 on *Legendary Performer Volume 2*) has Elvis singing with an ease missing from the spliced master, he had a major problem remembering the order "I Want You, I Need You, I Love You" should go in. To keep the title in proper order, two takes had to be edited together, neither of which had the breeziness of the fine alternate. Still, the original is a first-rate record, suffering only slightly from being comparatively mannered.

"My Baby Left Me" is the first Elvis flip side to be in the same rank as its better-known companion. Marking the only time RCA came close to the feel of a Sun master, this Arthur Crudup blues was given a full-on rockabilly arrangement. Scotty plays a wicked, short riff; Bill pummels the slap bass; and D. J. beats his snare with an unconventionally melodic cacophony. It remains bewildering how Elvis recorded so much spectacular material in such a brief window of time.

Elvis was still able to sound like his 1954 self—albeit in a deservedly more self-assured incarnation. "My Baby Left Me" was enjoyable the few times he sang it in the seventies, but Elvis didn't differentiate it enough from his concurrent arrangement(s) of "That's All Right." The story is different on record, as the two do have some core differences. The sound is bigger, and the playing of Bill Black has developed. In fact, Black's quick bass run at the beginning has him making almost like a jazzman straight out of a Scott Bradley–scored *Tom & Jerry* cartoon.

"Don't Be Cruel"/"Hound Dog" (Released July 13, 1956)

From the start, people knew this was a special record. Neither cut took a backseat, as they were both enormously successful and creative. Each song accounted for multi-million sales (four million within the first five months of release), and there are few singles in history that live up to the standards it set. If one record had to be selected to represent what fifties music was all about, this wouldn't be a bad choice.

Boasting an incredible repeating guitar intro, "Don't Be Cruel" was a captivating illustration of Otis Blackwell's genius for penning exceptional mid-paced pop. The Jordanaires join in for the first time, and their "bop bops" give the record an affable quality—a little sugar coating for wider appeal. That they happen to spur Elvis on as an artist, going on to mold with Presley a major part of his sound, is a tremendous bonus.

Elvis was at the height of his fame and powers. Everything about him has this aura of perfection in 1956. Every utterance he made was lapped up rabidly, but who can argue with success when it's based on substance? On "Don't Be Cruel," Elvis sounds supernaturally perfect, hitting all the right marks in what he is trying to communicate. There's a mischievous sense of humor, a bit of contrition, and an overwhelming amount of assurance. This is not only important from the viewpoint of a historian. "Don't Be Cruel" is among the most entertaining high points in all recorded music.

"Hound Dog" breathes the same rarefied air of prestige as "Don't Be Cruel." An iconic recording of the first order, there was some truth to the gag when Elvis took to introducing it as the national anthem. It is a magical record, one that grabs the listeners from the first note and doesn't let go until it's finished. There's so much for the ears to indulge in: take, for example, the Jordanaires' long "aws" over their synchronized hand claps. Scotty's multiple solos are incrementally more wild and metallic. The defining work of his entire career, it's no hyperbole to call this an important part of the evolution of hard-rock guitar. Booming and echoing around the ear canal, D. J.'s drums sound like machine gun fire.

Then there's Elvis. In cutting one of the defining recordings of American culture, he goes all-out. Displaying his feverish passion for his work, the growl of his voice perfectly fits the storming music. "Hound Dog" may be lighthearted, but he sounds deadly serious. Being the expert performer he was, Elvis had the natural instinct and self-taught knowledge to grasp the way his audience would best respond to him. He knew when to play the clown, and he knew to take a clownish situation and turn it into something with meat on its bones. Because of his efforts to put out records with durability, "Hound Dog" continues to be one of the songs most closely identified with Elvis, the fifties, and rock and roll itself.

"Love Me Tender"/"Any Way You Want Me (That's How I Will Be)" (Released September 28, 1956)

With Elvis' premiere of it on *The Ed Sullivan Show* popular enough to justify a rush release, "Love Me Tender" was Elvis' first heavily promoted straight ballad. Showing an attention to detail that his later film music sorely lacked, the melody was appropriately taken from the public domain Civil War–era ballad "Aura Lee."

Elvis had been singing ballads in the studio ever since he started, but Sam Phillips for one wasn't interested in issuing them. The RCA Victor releases before this time did include some balladry, but they either were plaintive Sun-era material or had a slow rock-and-roll beat. This track has a stark beauty mostly coming from the sincerity of Presley's voice, but compared to what he could do even a year or two later, it sounds tentative. Still, it was one of Elvis' biggest hits, and did reveal another side of his talent to the masses.

A prime example of the romantic side of fifties rock and roll, "Any Way You Want Me" has all the innocent yearning one associates with the period. Because Elvis is in his element—as opposed to cautiously trying to broaden his style—this is actually the better song of the two sides. It's not nearly as recognizable to the public at large, but it was included on quite a few hits collections, and reached the Top 30. It dates from the July sessions that saw Elvis use the Jordanaires for the first time, and their backup gives it a rich sound.

Elvis (Released October 19, 1956)

Elvis captures the singer at the very peak of his fame and going through an intensely creative streak. It continues the high standards set by his debut, despite not having quite as many first-rate songs. The benefit of being creatively unified accounted for the basic strength of the album. One advantage was that there were no jarring shifts stemming from the use of both Sun and RCA recordings. "So Glad You're Mine" numbered among the selections recorded for RCA back in January, but the rest of this LP was recorded as a solid entity in September.

Elvis presented a somewhat more diverse performer than heard before. There is a touch of a rhumba beat on "How Do You Think I Feel"; "Old Shep" was in effect arranged as a folk song, with Elvis playing the piano himself; and "Anyplace Is Paradise" has a slight leaning toward jazz. Throw in the usual liberal doses of country, rock and roll, and R&B, and you have yourself another milestone-setting fifties masterpiece. The cover is interesting, for the pose with the acoustic guitar and striped shirt makes Elvis look like something of a folk singer.

Another of Elvis' many 1956 masterworks, "Love Me" was the big hit off the album, getting to #6 off the first volume of this LP's EP counterpart. Leiber and Stoller wrote the ballad several years before as a parody of country music; to the credit of his fertile creativity, Elvis heard something else in it. Milking every line like it was the most important song ever written, Elvis makes it over into something soulful and genuine. The rhythm is slow, with a steady beat behind it, and the harmonies of the Jordanaires and Elvis on the closing "Oh yes" are bright and velvety.

"When My Blue Moon Turns to Gold Again" had been a popular country song in the forties, and it is one of the last pure rockabilly records Elvis came up with. The lyrics are clever, and the overall mood of happy optimism is catching. There's a winning sense of ease in Presley's approach, and the melody stands up well to the modernization. Scotty plays a worthwhile crisp solo and Elvis blends in well with the Jordanaires backing. After Elvis performed the song on his final *Ed Sullivan Show* appearance on January 6, 1957, it got to #29 from airplay as an excerpt from the *Elvis Volume 1* EP.

"Paralyzed" was another of Elvis' infrequent RCA rockabilly cuts, and has the most happy-go-lucky attitude imaginable. There's an agreeably uncomplicated feel to the track—it rocks, but gently so. Otis Blackwell was a conversational lyricist. His songs tell a little story, are well versed in fifties slang, and most of his stuff was pretty chipper to boot. Elvis was great at these bouncy tunes, and the music is nicely executed.

An interesting note is that, after hearing Jackie Wilson sing in Las Vegas after this LP came out, Elvis changed "Paralyzed" into a slower and more enunciated song. His new arrangement can be heard on the "Million Dollar Quartet" releases and on the December 1956 *Hayride* show.

Cut during the sessions of the first album, "So Glad You're Mine" is a slinky blues belter with a burlesque beat. It was an Arthur Crudup cut from the mid-forties, reconfigured as an ideal adjunct to Elvis' teasing sex appeal. The zeal with which Elvis imparts the straightforwardly sensual lyrics creates a great randy atmosphere, and D. J.'s drumming caters strongly to the gyrations in Elvis' stage act. This fits in impeccably with the September recordings, from which it is set apart only by the ringing tones of Shorty Long's ivory plunking.

"Anyplace Is Paradise" is the same type of mid-paced R&B, but is—daringly—even more erotically charged. Using his full array of vocal tricks, Elvis has fun with his phrasing. Layered in a thick echo, the song has a mysterious and intriguingly murky tone. This is Elvis at his least compromising. There's no softening of the edges, no subtly to the biting vocals, just plain out-and-out rocking and wailing, the way his wildest fans loved him.

The three Little Richard cuts may not be the most original part of the album, but they showcase it at its rocking best. Appearing so youthful and full of life, Elvis opened the LP with an uninhibited bash through "Rip It Up." Elvis chose fast, raucous songs as the first cut on each of his first six original albums, and this raver served notice that *Elvis* was going to rock just as hard as his debut. Listen to the terrific syncopation between Elvis and D. J.'s bright drums. Scotty takes a killer solo, and Black keeps the beat going on slap bass. It's tremendous.

The second of these is "Long Tall Sally." In Elvis' set throughout 1956–57, and again on and off through the seventies, it loses nothing in the transition from stage to studio. Though swaggering with cocky energy, Elvis' arrangement is less frantic than the Beatles' or Little Richard's own. The rhythm has a beaty shuffle to it, and Scotty essays his solo in the fashion of Danny Cedrone's on the Bill Haley classic "Rock Around the Clock."

The third and final component of this Richard Penniman trilogy was an edgy "Ready Teddy." Elvis is untamed and electric, not one bit less focused than he was with his songs chosen for singles. Showing off how tight-knit Elvis and his band had become, the guitar is lively and agreeably trebly, and Fontana pounds away with expert power. As it was performed on the high-profile *Ed Sullivan* debut, "Ready Teddy" became one of Presley's best-known early album cuts. Later, the *Sullivan* performance reached a whole new set of people when it was included as part of the 1972 documentary *Elvis on Tour*.

"Old Shep" has importance in being the first song Elvis sang in public as a child. The Red Foley song had been popular in both country and folk circles, and Elvis' version subsequently drew from both fields. Elvis is sincere enough, and his piano work adds some of its usual soul. On the other hand, the ballad is languid, lengthy, and fairly maudlin. It's not bad, but it doesn't lend itself well to its more sprightly surroundings. It's a curiosity appealing to a certain taste, but what it stands for is far more interesting than what it is.

"How's the World Treating You" is dreary, self-pitying nonsense that seems to drag on forever. It is one of the few early Elvis cuts that are outright crummy. It has a fuzzy relation to the typical fifties ballad but was missing the commitment Elvis usually imparted in 1956. It wasn't just that he wasn't yet vocally up for the challenge; this is a poor arrangement of an undistinguished number.

The peculiarly off-pitch ballad "First in Line" was underwhelming for many of the same reasons. Drenched in far too much echo, Elvis' voice is unattractively nasal. The song has a paint-by-numbers mediocrity, is overlong, and almost stops the momentum of the first side entirely. Maybe there was a minor attempt at some interesting chord changes, but it fails to come close to Elvis' preeminent fifties love songs.

"How Do You Think I Feel" was a revival of a song Elvis had run through but not cut formally while at Sun. His friend singer Jimmie Rodgers Snow had a hit with it in 1954, and Elvis probably recorded it as a tip of the hat to him. It's decent enough, but the verbiage seems stuck in the previous decade. It boils down to Elvis doing an innocuous rhumba dance-craze number of the kind that offered the timid, or old-fashioned, an alternative to authentic rock and roll.

"Too Much"/"Playing for Keeps" (Released January 4, 1957)

"Too Much" was one of Elvis' biggest hits, but because he never performed it live after 1957, it is considerably more obscure than it deserves to be. In tempo and atmosphere, it comes off like something for a burlesque dancer to strip to. Elvis and the Jordanaires play it all for fun, though there is more than a hint of Presley's patented sneer. Scotty has called his pinched and slightly improvised solo "ancient psychedelia," and his lead guitar does sound ten years ahead of its time in being heavier and more distorted than usual. Beyond any of that, "Too Much" is an energetic, tough rocker, with Elvis at his early peak.

"Playing for Keeps" is one of the few early Elvis single sides that wasn't worthy of the spotlight it was given. He tries too hard at putting feeling into the track, pushing his voice into an awkward whine. Elvis didn't yet possess the kind of big voice he wanted for ballads like this, but you can't blame him for trying to go beyond his comfort zone. The song was written by Stan Kesler, who had been a friend of Elvis' when they both worked for Sun Records. Kesler had co-composed early single sides "I'm Left, You're Right, She's Gone," and "I Forgot to Remember to Forget," and Elvis may have recorded this somewhat dreary ballad partially as a favor to him.

"All Shook Up"/"That's When Your Heartaches Begin" (Released March 22, 1957)

"All Shook Up" belongs in that very select group of songs that have an impact to the point that they belong among the eternal symbols of the era. The phrase "all shook up" caught on strongly as this record headed to #1. The strolling beat engraves itself into your memory bank, feeling at once like it had existed for all time. Elvis is transcendently cool, shining center stage with an expressive intelligence in his performance. Vocally, his upbeat attitude is what makes his singing on "All Shook Up" so effective. There's no air of superiority; it's more like someone being on top of the world and wanting all who like him to join in the fun.

This was to be the last time Elvis was credited as a co-writer for purely cosmetic reasons. Not feeling it was right to have his name appear where it didn't deserve to be, he would subsequently be credited on only two other tracks, both which had some level of genuine input from him. "All Shook Up" author Otis Blackwell didn't seem to hold any kind of grudge, however, and pointed out that he made more money with an Elvis cut than with anyone else as the sales made up for his loss in full publishing or authorship.

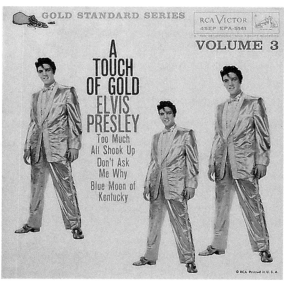

Elvis always rushed the tempo when singing "All Shook Up" live in his later years. The only time he got the cool groove of the record correct onstage was during his 1957 and 1961 shows. His 1968–70 performances had a high-octane energy to them that is almost as fascinating. Particularly cool was the early-1970 version with the long Bob Lanning drum pattern, which Elvis used to open his shows that winter. Sadly, this was one of the songs Elvis tired of, and none of the renditions from mid-1971 onward added anything worthy to the show.

Elvis' striking gold suit was used on the cover of three EPs and one LP. This 1960 EP was the last of the bunch.

Courtesy of Robert Rodriguez

Even without the attendant history it carried, "That's When

Your Heartaches Begin" was an effective (if sentimental) record. Elvis' supremacy and poise alone ensured it left a lasting impression, but since his first 1953 demo became available it is hard not to make comparisons. The very fact that Elvis returned to the ballad is evidence that he enjoyed his first experience at Sam Phillips' Memphis Recording Service, and there is no doubt he cut this as something of a salute to the occasion.

The gains Elvis had made in every way over the last four years were astronomical. Besides the obvious detail that he was now a professional, his voice was more mature, he knew what range was best for him, and he was able to make the spoken part believable without taking it too seriously. In listening to the starkness present in the 1953 recording, the value of having a strong band and fine singers like the Jordanaires also make themselves evident.

Loving You (Released July 1, 1957)

Elvis' third album is an embryonic version of the soundtrack LPs that would one day dominate the sixties Presley catalogue. In a reversal of what would be, here it is the movie songs that are the standouts, with the ones cut strictly for record not of quite the same caliber. The seven movie songs are on side one, while the five regular cuts comprise side two.

Elvis' hectic early-1957 recording schedule meant that he was in and out of Radio Recorders and the Paramount soundstage, recording singles, a gospel EP, the actual soundtrack for the movie, and this LP, which often used different arrangements and performances. The quality varied a bit more than it had in 1956, but that came down to experimentation, not inertia.

The LP's opening cut is the smoking, R&B-flavored hand-clapper "Mean Woman Blues." One of the standout songs in the film and on this record, Elvis has a tough snarl in his voice softened only by the merest hint of irony. The track exudes fifties cool, even in little details like the Jordanaires' evident fun with the brief improvised talking section. Elvis sounds halfway between a strutting peacock and a revved-up preacher. Certainly, his performance is riveting enough to demand the listener's full attention. To break it down simply, "Mean Woman Blues" is among the many fifties Elvis recordings that define their era and excel at doing so.

"(Let Me Be Your) Teddy Bear" is more pop than most of Elvis' fifties chart-toppers. Indeed, one may be excused for believing it to be "Don't Be Cruel"–lite. What gives it classic status is the arrestingly cool vocal. The inflections speak to the fun Elvis had with the tune. In the seventies, Elvis often performed "Teddy Bear" in a medley with "Don't Be Cruel." As with so many of his timeless fifties hits, he started off the decade performing them with enthusiasm and ended up audibly loathing the material by the time of his death seven and a half years later.

"Lonesome Cowboy" was considered as the LP's title track at some point, but "Loving You" was much stronger single material, so the switch was made. Still, this slow, western-themed song is quite interesting in how it combines the style of Elvis' Sun Records balladry (the rhythm sounds uncannily like "Blue Moon") with the Jordanaires and a fuller backing. It makes clear that even if the song is less illustrious, Elvis' voice is far more practiced. What it lost in vulnerability is gained in pure ability.

Leiber and Stoller land the first of three consecutive movie title songs with their unusually heartfelt love song "Loving You." To suit the needs of the film, it was sung many different ways over the course of two months of sessions. For the record release, Elvis ultimately decided on a slow arrangement led by the piano playing of Dudley Brooks. Elvis still wasn't a consummate ballad singer at this stage, but he shows a marked improvement to the halting approach he used on "Love Me Tender." Smooth as silk, "Loving You" became very popular over the years due to its inclusion on high-profile hits packages.

"Hot Dog" isn't in the top echelon of Leiber and Stoller songs Elvis tackled, but his liking for the slang-laden rocker can be plainly heard. A little jerky in transition, the rhythm tapped into the traveling vibe of "Mystery Train." Just your basic, short, durable rock-and-roll filler.

"Party" is another short, rocking cut, but a somewhat more substantial one. The words are oddly phrased, but the song benefits from the gospel intonation Elvis used throughout this album for the fast selections. The song itself was good enough to be a rockabilly hit for Wanda Jackson in 1960, but unflagging enthusiasm throughout these sessions makes Elvis' more rock-and-roll-oriented arrangement even more memorable. In England, his version got all the way to #2 in the charts.

A highlight of Elvis' early RCA years, "Got a Lot o' Livin' to Do!" is tremendous, jubilee-influenced rock and roll. What leaves the most lasting impression is the buoyant feeling of being young and having so much ahead of you. The youthful enthusiasm Elvis exhibits on this cut is in itself captivating, never mind how great he sounds. With an increased emphasis on piano adding a new boogie-woogie undertone to the collective sound, this isn't dissimilar to the hard-rocking piano style soon to be popularized by Jerry Lee Lewis.

Taken track by track, all of side two has certain merit. Perhaps it's just the polite nature of the performances that makes them pale as a whole next to the movie songs on side one. Take "Don't Leave Me Now." The version heard on the LP of this melancholic lament is pretty, but it never gets out of first gear. Elvis seems to be holding back for some reason, likely due to uncertainty about where he wanted the song to go. It would take until the *Jailhouse Rock* sessions several months later for Elvis to bring the song to its full potential.

"Blueberry Hill" also comes across a little sluggish. Elvis' voice and the piano (played by either Hoyt Hawkins of the Jordanaires or Dudley Brooks) are right on target, but the ambience is missing the sprightly spirit of Fats Domino's hit version. Elvis tried several times to get it down the way he felt it, and an even more careful recording on the soundstage was replaced with this Radio Recorders master the next day. Despite the effort put forth, this is still one of the least interesting R&B covers Elvis attempted.

Bing Crosby's recent hit "True Love" was a pretty square number for Elvis to try out. While there are moments of beautiful harmony between Elvis and the Jordanaires, the overall pre-rock ethos of the cut stands out like a sore thumb. Other than Elvis sounding a little young for it, there's nothing particularly wrong with this performance. The bigger issue is one of there being so many other hits of the day that would have been more exciting for Elvis to interpret.

Strangely, "Have I Told You Lately That I Love You" had also been a hit for Crosby. This ballad isn't nearly as awkward for Elvis because of its roots in country. Set to a mild, loping beat, it has more of a modern spin—done convincingly enough for Ricky Nelson and Eddie Cochran to swiftly record covers based on this arrangement. Neither below par nor a standout track, this is one to file under the category of "agreeable and adept."

R&B hit-maker Ivory Joe Hunter penned the fine rhythm-ballad "I Need You So." During this period, these kinds of self-recriminatory songs, begging for the forgiveness of a girl hurt by the protagonist, were part of Elvis' bread and butter. If in a more adolescent fashion, "I Need You So" acts as proof that Elvis was drawn to tales of love being lost long before the seventies. The difference here is that he sounds more persuasive than desolate. If "I Need You So" wasn't the very best of what the album had to offer, it is better than the rest of the side in that Elvis and his players don't seem at all inhibited. Of special note are the dulcet tones from the piano of Dudley Brooks.

"Jailhouse Rock"/"Treat Me Nice" (Released September 24, 1957)

This pairing may well be the coolest 45 ever released. In "Jailhouse Rock," Leiber and Stoller wrote a masterpiece of early rock that possesses the lyrical humor, rhythmic vitality, and lascivious tone that set the genre apart from everything that came before it. Of course, Elvis and his band deserve an equal share of the credit for turning a clever song into a classic rock-and-roll recording. From D. J.'s rock-breaking beat to Scotty's out-of-control solo, this is an invigorating listen. Holding nothing back, Elvis sings in a sandpapery rasp that comes across tough and uncompromising.

"Treat Me Nice" is a cool Leiber and Stoller mid-tempo rocker. The fluidity of the melody was always in place, but Elvis tried the song many different ways until he was happy with it. The final version dating from September has a fuller band sound, as typified by Dudley Brooks' masterful boogie-woogie piano. Elvis' instincts as to what would make a better record were correct, but the early version with the handclaps and finger-snaps had an unassuming warmth missing on the final master. What the record version did have to spare was attitude. Celebrating the delights of fifties-style flirting, Elvis' approach was swaggering, surly, and exuberant.

Elvis' Christmas Album (Released October 15, 1957)

Elvis took a somewhat unexpected turn with his Christmas recordings. For more hardcore rockers, it must have seemed like Elvis was conforming, but to listeners who were conformist, Elvis' vocals seemed raucous—even blasphemous. Legendary Chicago disc jockey Dick Biondi got fired from his job when he dared to play the whole LP. In retrospect, it all seems very silly. The seasonal theme was somewhat creatively limiting at times, but within the confines of the genre, *Elvis' Christmas Album* is a classic. While somewhat lessened by the somewhat incongruous gospel EP tracks at the end of it, overall this is a very satisfying release.

That goes for the eyes as well as the ears. Original copies came in gatefold sleeves with full portrait booklets from the *Jailhouse Rock* publicity sessions. Some shots were garishly doctored with paint, but, all in all, it was extraordinary packaging. To top it off, a gold holiday "To" and "From" sticker was attached to the outer plastic of the sleeve.

Elvis recorded the eight new songs required for the holiday offering over three early-September 1957 evenings at Radio Recorders. Though several of the compositions would have benefited from the maturity in his post-army voice, he was in as fine form as ever. There were several songs written fresh for the album, plus an array of covers—some performed in a surprisingly straightforward fashion. It would be wrong to suggest that this LP carries the same artistic weight as Elvis' other 1956–58 albums, but it is easily the best known. In various configurations, *Elvis' Christmas Album* has sold a whopping thirteen million copies in the U.S. alone.

"Blue Christmas" is easily the most popular Elvis Christmas song. It had been a country hit for Ernest Tubb in 1949, and hints of the country flavor are maintained here. Elvis' acoustic guitar can be heard nicely in the mix, and his vocals are tongue-in-cheek fun. The Jordanaires do a fine job on harmony, and Millie Kirkham's soprano line almost steals the show. Elvis being Elvis, when he felt like performing the song in his last three years he would do so, holiday season or not.

"Silent Night" and "O Little Town of Bethlehem" have some of the same drawbacks as Elvis' 1957 gospel cuts. Though pretty, they are a bit over-pronounced in parts, almost as if he is trying too consciously to put his own mannerisms on them. Very conservatively arranged, these tracks act more as agreeable background music than anything that invites close attention. "I'll Be Home for Christmas" invites much the same comments, because it too is restrained by a traditional, albeit beautiful, arrangement. What differentiates it from the other two recordings is that Elvis puts forth a more considered vocal performance.

"White Christmas" is more like it. The Drifters had done a version that turned the morose song into a lively affair. Elvis liked their sharp R&B phrasing and harmonies, and his version was influenced directly by what they had done. He did add a few of his own touches, giving the song a slightly more rocking feel and adapting it vocally to his own style. What was kept was the playful phrasing and general bright air. Ignorant of the Drifters record, composer Irving Berlin found Elvis' recording to be in bad taste and tried to get it pulled from the airwaves. After all, how dare Elvis make his masterpiece groove? This is what generated most of the controversy over the LP's release at the time, but now it sounds only like Christmas music, fortified by ingenuity and good cheer.

"Here Comes Santa Claus (Right Down Santa Claus Lane)" is one of the few kids' songs Elvis pulled off. Maybe it's better because, unlike his sixties soundtrack fare for tykes, he was aiming here at the whole family. Likely the big difference is Elvis actually wanting to sing the song and make the album. Whatever the circumstance, there aren't too many versions that better the mix of joyousness and youthful excitement of this one. Elvis could have taken it further in a rockabilly or hard-rock-and-roll direction, but the sincerity of his performance makes it worthwhile.

"Santa Claus Is Back in Town" is the pièce de résistance of the collection. Written by Leiber and Stoller, their good-natured humor shines as Elvis sings about being Santa Claus fifties-style. He isn't riding a sleigh; he's coming to town in a big black Cadillac. Rocking as hard as any of Elvis' fifties singles, it perfectly encapsulates the sexy, rebellious attitude of the period. No doubt he is speaking in metaphor about coming down a chimney tonight. Scotty Moore plays a searing guitar solo that fits together impeccably with Dudley Brooks' pumpin' piano. The Jordanaires also make their mark on the simple and suitably hip introduction and fade.

"Santa Bring My Baby Back to Me" was a number in the happy, pop "Teddy Bear" tradition. It typifies the era in which it was recorded by having a jolly sense of humor about itself. Elvis uses a full array of his unique hiccups and mannerisms to splendid effect, and along with the Jordanaires he seems to be having a great time making the vocals sparkle and pop.

"Don't"/"I Beg of You" (Released January 7, 1958)

"Don't" was recorded during the *Christmas Album* sessions in September 1957. Leiber and Stoller sustained their hot streak when this melodic ballad zoomed to the top of the charts. There are a number of factors at play that make it a bona fide gem. "Don't" thoughtfully discusses the frustration many young men feel when their girlfriends want to wait for sex. Though the subject of sex is presented fairly directly, with no watering down of Elvis' message, there's no titillation or distaste contained within.

You can also hear Elvis' continually improving tonal quality and greater control over his voice—clear progress attributable only to his dedication and drive. Because Elvis was never happy staying in one creative spot, he tried to top himself each time he made a record in any given style. "Don't" has an inherent sincerity. There's honesty in Elvis' singing—a sense that he's expressing his actual feelings. That he can convey such emotion with his voice came purely from his willingness to practice his craft as often as possible.

First taped at the January 13th Radio Recorders session, "I Beg of You" initially had a completely different arrangement. The direct variances include a repeating guitar pattern and a harder-edged, echoing vocal attack. Though the final version, taped back at Radio Records on February 23rd, is less passionate, it does have a more bubbly flow. Adding color, the Jordanaires come off terrifically with their background "bum-ba-bum bum-bums." Elvis' gruff note on the word "hold" sends chills down the spine by virtue of its sheer audacity. Another prime example of the era Elvis dominated, it's fifties to the core.

"Wear My Ring Around Your Neck"/"Doncha' Think It's Time" (Released April 1, 1958)

Totally belying the stress of recording it, "Wear My Ring Around Your Neck" is one of Elvis' most peppy, good-natured rockers. Though the date it was recorded at was fraught with frustration, Elvis tried his best to make it sound right. He even took the extra step of going back later to overdub more guitar, percussion played on the back of his guitar, and piano. It is aimed at pulling on the heart-strings of any female teen that considered Elvis "fantasy boyfriend" material, but the raunchy good fun heard in the music and voices sees that it goes beyond that initial demographic. If not what can be termed innovative or choice, "Wear My Ring" has lasted the years as a fundamentally entertaining pre-army rocker. It also was very successful, reaching #3 just over a month after release.

"Doncha' Think It's Time" is a smooth, mid-paced song with a mellow, easygoing vibe. There's even a small hint of the incipient folk boom in the prominently featured bongos. Ironically, it was from the arduous February 1, 1958, session, and required forty-eight takes. To be fair, that count may have started the previous week, when Elvis attempted to cut the song as an adjunct non-soundtrack master at a *King Creole* session. Despite the two nights of work, several versions had to be spliced together for the single master. By mistake, what became known as the "album" version used a different set of splices when issued on *Elvis' Gold Records Volume 2*.

The single is more playful, with Elvis accentuating the ending more stridently. By working hard to blend the very best parts of the track for release, the trickery puts forth a deceptive ease. The Blue Moon Boys were coming apart, but you would never know it from the finished product. No matter: this is a classic cut despite it all, in what seems like a clear-cut example of serendipity.

King Creole (September 19, 1958)

King Creole was Elvis' last new LP of the fifties, and it demonstrates considerable creative growth. With the movie set in New Orleans, Elvis adapts the style of

Dixieland to his own sound, with some fascinating results. It was the last project Leiber and Stoller would contribute to directly, and the songs were a generally strong lot. With only a faint hint of the artifice that would plague Elvis' future film scores, *King Creole* stands proudly amongst the best Elvis albums.

Listening to the album makes one wonder what might have been had Elvis not been drafted. When you hear this record, you realize that Elvis' evolution over the fifties was gradual, and his music never lost its toughness. Though initially he would be as creative as ever, the two-year pause changed his image and sound drastically. The questions that remain are whether Elvis' career would have continued to follow the 1957 model of variety, and whether his music would have gone in the same direction it did. A crystal-clear answer is not provided here, but Elvis was singing better than ever, and he was obviously into trying new things. Thus it can be said with some certainty that a change was going to happen, one way or another, albeit maybe not at the same pace.

The sultry "Crawfish" was sung on film and in the studio as something of a duet between Elvis and Kitty White. Why she was only heard on backing vocals on the LP may come down to the racial sensibilities of the era. If so, it had nothing to do with Elvis, as he openly enjoyed performing the song with her in the movie, and never liked his singers to be marginalized. "Crawfish" feels authentic, both geographically and lyrically. Elvis has an unusually thick tone of voice, and a vague New Orleans inflection can be detected. The tone on this cut is murky and dark—you can feel a sort of raw sensuality or threat beneath the tuneful surface.

"Hard Headed Woman" was the hit single off the LP, and it is a weird but wonderful amalgamation of rock and Dixieland. Tempo-wise, it is the fastest song on an album packed full of rock and roll. There's a boundless energy coming from the ensemble, and Elvis' machine-gun vocal delivery brings genuine delight. It's loud, brash, and in-your-face, and that's why it is terrific. The only shame is that the scene of Elvis performing it was cut out of the final film.

Because it worked so well in the context of both *King Creole* and the 1968 NBC TV special, "Trouble" became an iconic fifties "tough guy" anthem. It's another great composition by Leiber and Stoller, who had a genuine feel and love for blues and also put across a healthy dose of self-mocking. Full of their usual sharp wit and strong hooks, it was a missed opportunity on what would have made for a surefire hit single. What made Elvis so great an interpreter on "Trouble" was that he delivered a passionate, R&B-drenched performance, fully aware of the humor intended. Up until the final section, where the satiric nature of the song becomes a smidgen too obvious, the balance he strikes between menace and mockery is faultless.

With Elvis sounding better on a ballad than ever before, "As Long as I Have You" is an absolutely beautiful song. He had obviously kept himself in practice over the previous seven weeks off, for here his voice had better control, deeper pitch, and a more emotive tone. The melody is simple and pretty, the guitars all strummed with delicacy. The cumulative effect is marvelous.

The frantic "King Creole" is a classic. Going all the way to #2 in England, this rocker has often been revived, most notably by the Max Weinberg 7 on Conan O'Brien's late-night NBC show. Here, Scotty takes the spotlight in playing a repeating riff and a nimble-fingered solo. The band had tried a Dixieland jazz arrangement at first, but eventually settled on straight rock and roll with a sinister atmosphere.

"Lover Doll" is a pop confection through and through, a bouncy acoustic charmer that succeeds on lack of pretense. As well being a cute album cut, it worked as a realistic song within the framework of the movie. You didn't have to work hard to imagine a talented amateur like Presley's Danny Fisher singing it precisely the same way.

"Dixieland Rock" can be called a pastiche of its title, but it was brilliantly arranged and performed. This makes one speculate whether more of Elvis' sixties soundtracks would have been salvageable, had they featured tasteful arrangements to spur on the artist. Elvis spits out the lyric with a melodic rapidity and a laughing snarl. Though not seamless, the jazz-styled horns—particularly the trombone blowing of Elmer Schneider—form an interesting fusion with the main band's tight rock backing.

"New Orleans" is plastic Dixieland, but Elvis, the Jordanaires, and the Blue Moon Boys make it come alive. A fitting showcase for their sense of teamwork, this sequence in the film is the last footage of them all together. If the song is stylistically little more than a substandard "Trouble," all involved perform it with guts. Elvis' vocal contains a sense of wit and comic timing that infuses the song with more charm than might have been there to begin with.

An insubstantial ballad, "Young Dreams" is another cut saved by tongue-in-cheek humor. It doesn't quite ignite, but it benefits from Elvis being on his game. "Don't Ask Me Why" has a coolly typical fifties melody, but is run of the mill as a whole. Elvis' voice had filled out a lot, but still lacked the control to carry a grandiose ballad of this nature. There's a whining tone that results from Elvis pitching himself too high in his register to come off without strain. It didn't make for a very convincing flip side to "Hard Headed Woman."

"Steadfast, Loyal and True" is the first Elvis song to exist only because of a movie plot. It is a short school song written for Danny Fisher to quickly improvise. To keep his new friend Ronnie (played by Carolyn Jones) from getting beaten, Fisher had to prove on the spot to Walter Matthau's Maxie Fields that he could sing. Sounding suitably youthful and sincere, Elvis gamely performs the slight ditty to the best of his ability.

"One Night"/"I Got Stung" (Released October 21, 1958)

"One Night" was a Smiley Lewis song from 1955 that had considerably racier lyrics than the version that became a hit for Elvis. Initially, Elvis had recorded this sexy blues during the *Loving You* soundstage sessions. It was never intended to be in the film, but was viewed as a possible single. Word came down that Elvis' version would not be released as it was, so he remade it during a February 23rd LP and single session at Radio Recorders. Though Elvis would soon add it to his live set, he wasn't satisfied with the results and wanted to record it again. Not getting the chance to do so before he sailed to Germany, he relented and allowed it to be released.

It's very hard to hear what Elvis could have done better. Throughout his career, Elvis' unique lead-handed guitar parts always added some soul into the blend. Elvis is miked high in the mix, playing in tandem with Scotty's sharp electric lead. Perhaps to make up for the words being tamer than usual, Elvis sings his tail off. You can tell sex is on his brain, and there is no element of humor to soften the lust driving his approach.

"I Got Stung" set the pattern of all the June 1958 recordings in that all were sizable hits no matter what side of a single they appeared on. Getting up to #8, this was the first cut released from the session, and a fine sample of the enthusiastic performances that made up the date. Over Elvis' hiccupping lead, the band puts forth a fast boogie beat that is hard to sit still for. The likable "Uh uh huh yeah!" catchphrase that Elvis sings between more formal lines gives the cut a distinct hook. The lyrics are hard to catch unless you are listening closely, yet Elvis sounds cool singing them.

"(Now and Then There's) A Fool Such as I"/"I Need Your Love Tonight" (Released March 10, 1959)

An extremely strong duo from the June 1958 sessions, both sides of this single raced up the Top 5. Though neither would be performed live again, they also received excellent performances as part of Elvis' 1961 Pearl Harbor benefit show.

"A Fool Such as I" is a delightful mid-tempo rocker, with a hint of doo-wop thanks to the Jordanaires. It had a country origin, having been a 1952 hit for Hank Snow. While keeping the lyrics and basic chord changes, Elvis fundamentally reinvented this staid ballad in his own image. There's a freewheeling sense of enjoyment running through it, and it is one of the Presley songs that provide a brief summary of what fifties rock and roll was all about.

"I Need Your Love Tonight" doesn't have the same kind of artistry to it, but is instead an amusing, hard-rocking novelty number that Elvis breathes a lot of life into. The new band members do their part as well. Showing himself to have all the fire of Scotty Moore, Hank Garland plays an uninhibited guitar solo, and new Jordanaire Ray Walker made his presence felt by contributing some ace bass vocals. Most important was the enthusiasm Elvis brought to the table. Knowing that rock and roll doesn't have to be weighty to be effective, his vocal conveys a carefree outlook that in time would become increasingly difficult for him to recapture.

"A Big Hunk o' Love"/"My Wish Came True" (Released June 23, 1959)

"A Big Hunk o' Love" was the last of the June 1958 recordings to be issued while Elvis was in the army and is a choice moment. One of Elvis' wildest cuts, this out-of-control rocker finds him and the Nashville crew turning up the heat. Never losing the smirk in his voice, Elvis comes on strong and direct. There is definitely a leering sexuality present—something similar to what Jerry Lee Lewis became renowned for. In capturing the party vibe going down in the studio, "A Big Hunk o' Love" is an ideal song for any enjoyable occasion. Performing it live from early 1972 through early 1974, Elvis always treated it with reverence.

"My Wish Came True" was an Ivory Joe Hunter ballad that doesn't come off so well. Ruining any sense of delicately, Millie Kirkham's ghostly backing vocal is screechy. Though his singing is pretty, Elvis doesn't sound at all certain. In fact, he wasn't happy with it, having tried unsuccessfully to remake the September 1957 master during both the *King Creole* and "Wear My Ring Around Your Neck" sessions. It did very well to get to #12.

10

Doin' the Best That I Can

1960

When Elvis came back from the army, nobody—himself especially—was sure just how things would work out. Certainly, he was going to be busy. He had a TV special, two albums, three singles, and three movies with attendant soundtracks to make. Though the lack of live shows was slightly troubling, 1960 would prove to be as artistically and commercially potent as what came before.

Even though he displayed more expertise than ever before, it's at this point that Elvis' career begins to get controversial. Until recently, most critics dismissed Elvis' early-sixties music as being too tame. Because Elvis began to record a wider variety of material, many hardcore rockers claim that Elvis lost relevance after the army. This, of course, is pure malarkey.

One could argue that both his voice and the recordings themselves were less raw, but this does not indicate that Elvis had lost his edge. Yes, Elvis had changed during his two years away, but he should be lauded for his legitimate creative maturation. After all, Elvis took a calculated risk by differing his approach. In short, he did not want to make 1955-styled records in 1960—something a certain faction of his audience never forgave him for. In reality, Elvis' new sound was an extension (rather than a desertion) of his past.

Studio Work

Elvis' non-soundtrack recordings of 1960 stand out in that they are uniformly solid. Not everything he cut was a masterpiece, but I cannot single out anything as being mundane or uninspired. Recorded in Nashville at RCA's Studio B in March and April 1960, *Elvis Is Back!* was the first Elvis album that had no weak spots. Extremely versatile in its explorations of rock, gospel-infused harmony, teen-pop, and blues, it has a great production that brings together everything as one.

With sophisticated singles such as "It's Now or Never" and "Are You Lonesome Tonight?," Elvis expanded his audience as well as his creativity. Having already proved himself on blues and rockers, Elvis had now become a ballad singer with few genuine peers. His voice had improved to the point that even

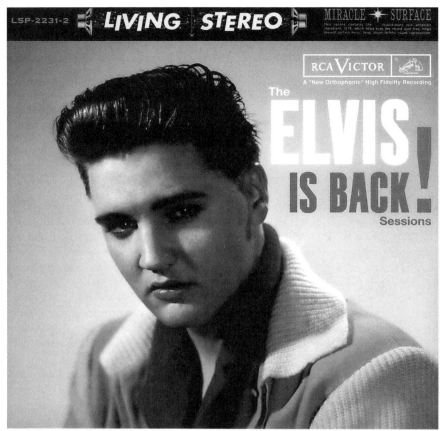

Elvis' spring 1960 sessions benefited from him being able to pick out the best songs waiting for him over nearly a two-year period. This 2011 FTD two-record set offers further proof of the consistent excellence achieved.

adults began to acknowledge that he was an entertainer of considerable ability.

Recorded in Nashville in October, Elvis' first gospel LP, *His Hand in Mine*, was also groundbreaking. It put gospel music in the Top 20 and allowed Elvis to pay tribute to the music he held closest to his heart. It was a real risk for a mainstream artist to do this type of material, and unlike the sacred material from 1957, Elvis did put his personal stamp on the recordings.

Sadly, the quality was not maintained on the music he was cutting for his movies. The first set of sessions for *G.I. Blues* took place at the end of April at RCA Studios in Hollywood. Dissatisfied with the sound, Elvis switched to Radio Recorders in May to finish the album. Though it can be seen now as a warning of what was to come, overall *G.I. Blues* was much better than what came later.

The *Flaming Star* soundtrack was laid down at Radio Recorders in August and finished in October, when the title of the movie was changed from *Black Star*. The two western-flavored ballads were all right, but "Britches" and "A Cane and a High Starched Collar" were the worst songs Elvis had tackled to date.

Elvis returned to Radio Recorders in November to cut the score for *Wild in the Country*. Consisting mostly of lilting acoustic ballads, the results were better. Maybe these weren't the most striking items in the Elvis catalogue, but with a sound akin to folk, they were a departure from his previous work. It showed Elvis growing adept at yet another vein of American music, as his vocal prowess grew and creative ambitions broadened.

Live Performance

Though Frank Sinatra had been an outspoken opponent of rock, he now needed a boost in ratings for his Timex TV specials, so he signed Elvis for a whopping $125,000 to appear in eight minutes of an hour-long broadcast. Elvis was joined by the Rat Pack, minus Dean Martin, who was ironically Elvis' biggest influence among the quartet (which also included Frank, Sammy Davis Jr., and comedian Joey Bishop). Frank's daughter Nancy Sinatra also appeared, and for publicity had met Elvis at the airport upon his return to the States earlier in March. Shooting took place at the Fontainebleau Hotel in Miami on March 26th, and the special aired May 8th on the ABC network. Though most critics were still snooty when it came to Elvis and rock and roll, more than 67 percent of the American television audience watched the program.

Elvis appeared in his army dress as a brief part of the "It's Very Nice to Go Traveling" intro. Looking slimmer than ever, he had his haired dyed black again, and had decided not to regrow his sideburns. When Elvis wore a tuxedo for the main portion of his performance, it no longer seemed ironic—not that he wasn't as cool as ever when he began to sing. "Stuck on You" and "Fame and Fortune" each get one-time-only live performances, and both are infused with passion and energy. The footage provides a tantalizing glimpse of the live artist that could have been.

As good as Elvis could have been onscreen with the right material, he absolutely owned any stage he walked out onto. This is made abundantly clear during his duet with Sinatra. Frank comes across as cute and hammy singing Elvis' "Love Me Tender," but Elvis positively smolders on his interjections during Sinatra's "Witchcraft." They end with some nice harmony on "Love Me Tender," and with that, Elvis' only stage performance of 1960 was over.

On Celluloid

With Elvis' army duty providing a good angle to exploit on film, *G.I. Blues* was every bit the financial success that was predicted. A fair comedy with a sizable budget, it still seemed a step backward for Elvis as an actor. Unlike his previous

THE **REAL** ALTERNATE ALBUM

Elvis Presley

Heavy &
Coloured
Virgin Vinyl
3 LP'S
Plus all Tracks on 2 CD's
PIN UP
RECORDS
Limited And Numbered
13 / 500

Wonderful World Of Christmas

This fine 2010 boxed set mainly focuses on the erratic 1971 Christmas selections. The 3-D version of the 1960 *His Hand in Mine* jacket was a nice touch.

roles there was nothing demanded of him dramatically except to sing frequently, fight the bad guys, and romance his leading lady.

If this had been Presley's sole diversion into family-friendly musicals, *G.I. Blues* would be more than acceptable. As the prototype of a formula to be copied countless times—with a steady creative decline in nearly every successive project—it takes on a more depressing feel. Indeed, seeing Elvis croon "Wooden Heart" to a puppet or "Big Boots" to a baby were cringe-worthy moments. Yet because Elvis is still making an effort, and the songs were decent, *G.I. Blues* is enjoyable, in a light, vacuous fashion.

Coming well before Elvis was boxed into his string of musicals, *Flaming Star* and *Wild in the Country* are worthy (if not exceptional) dramatic films. *Flaming Star* was a western that found Elvis playing a half-white, half–Native American character. Though the nineteenth-century setting allowed for less controversy, the film was a muddled treatise on racial equality. Getting the opportunity to work with fine actors like Dolores del Rio and Steve Forrest, Elvis gives a thoughtful and effective performance. Sadly, his role as Pacer Burton wasn't as multifaceted or fleshed out as Vince Everett, Danny Fisher, or even Deke Rivers.

Wild in the Country was a little bit too close to soap opera to be top cinema, but as the last time Elvis got to play a confused rebel, it has appeal. Millie Perkins and Hope Lange were two of the finest young actresses of the period, and Tuesday Weld held a sexual charisma as potent as Presley's. The plot gave Elvis plenty of chances to emote, and the songs were fairly inconspicuous overall. Elvis would have several chances to truly act in the future, but the quiet grace of *Wild in the Country* was not recaptured.

Popularity and Impact

The influence and sales of Elvis' records continued to run very high in 1960. Diversity was the order of the day, and with every LP and single release, Elvis found himself with a slew of new admirers. "Stuck on You," "It's Now or Never," and "Are You Lonesome Tonight?" all raced to the top of the charts and sold in the millions. Elvis remained the most popular recording artist in rock and roll, and these recordings ushered in further sophistication in the genre. With Phil Spector and Berry Gordy on the brink of setting new standards as far as what could be done in the use of the studio itself as an instrument of creativity, Elvis' records not only matched them in clarity but also led the way in pushing the boundaries of what could be done in the rock-and-roll medium.

Elvis Is Back! did very well in hitting #2, but with no singles included, and Elvis not immediately performing the songs on television or film, sales were lower than they could have been. By contrast, despite being half the album that *Elvis Is Back!* was creatively, *G.I. Blues* sold twice as many copies, the accompanying film acting as a terrific promotional tool. *His Hand in Mine* also did well for a gospel LP, peaking just outside the pop Top 10. Like the Christmas releases, Elvis' gospel recordings sold more slowly but more steadily than his secular albums.

11

Dreams Come True?

Elvis had firmly re-established himself in 1960 by continuing to make the best music in the rock-and-roll field. As the new year dawned, all he had left to do was go back onstage. In February, Elvis played two charity shows in Memphis, and in March he played a date in Hawaii to raise funds for the USS *Arizona* Memorial. With Elvis wearing his gold-lamé outfit in Hawaii, and using most of his original band for the last time in a regular concert setting, these performances marked the end of his most sociologically significant era.

Touring remained a part of the Colonel's long-term plans, but for now he told Elvis that he had to keep his movie commitments. Acting was still something Elvis wanted to master, so he didn't complain at first, but upon getting the script for *Blue Hawaii*, he wondered whether he would actually be allowed to act. Anne Fulchino was a publicity director at RCA who had written liner notes for several Elvis LPs. During her visit to the set of *Blue Hawaii*, Elvis commented that this wasn't what he had envisioned back in 1955.

It was a bit hard to quantify or articulate as of yet, but things had begun to slip slightly, compared to the past. The music in the studio sessions was good overall, but only a portion of it reached the high standards Elvis had previously set for himself. The soundtracks and the movies were still decent, too, but Elvis felt wary of the direction family-friendly films like *Blue Hawaii* were leading him in. Most of the problems are only glaring in retrospect. Elvis was still the biggest rock-and-roll artist out there, and the new trends that would change music so radically over the decade were still in their infancy. It looked like smooth sailing ahead, but it wasn't to be.

Studio Work

The year 1961 was the only one, post-fifties, when Elvis' soundtracks more or less equaled his regular studio recordings. This only happened because the film scores had yet to fully decline, while the studio cuts weren't as uniformly well chosen. That doesn't mean there wasn't good Elvis music recorded in 1961, but you now had to pick through a degree of dross to find the gold.

Elvis' first session of the year was in March at the celebrated Studio B in Nashville, where he recorded his LP *Something for Everybody*, plus the "I Feel So Bad" 45. Elvis sang well, the players were on, and respectable work was done.

What seemed to be missing at times was the attitude. With his hair short and sideburns gone, Elvis didn't seem quite the same anymore. "Judy" was lighter pop than anything he had done outside of *G.I. Blues*, and even on some of the rockers he sounded polite and nonthreatening. Nothing raised a red flag, but some of the fizz had left the cola. The sneer was there for "I Feel So Bad" and "I Want You with Me," both of which offered tough rock and roll done the old-fashioned way. Most ballads were also good, with "There's Always Me" possessing Elvis' most considered vocal to date.

The *Blue Hawaii* sessions, held later that month at Radio Recorders, were by turns lovely and ridiculous. Fifteen songs were recorded for the movie, which itself presented a problem. Simply put, there was a paucity of great songs available. Elvis tried to make the rock numbers groove, but was told to be more mellow. He was able to excel on the ballads, but even some of these got repetitive. The novelty songs shouldn't have been there in the first place. It was still early enough that everyone worked hard, and the LP was one of Elvis' most successful, but this should have been as bad as things got.

Elvis came back to Nashville in June to cut a new single and a few cuts for his next regular LP. The single "(Marie's the Name) His Latest Flame"/"Little Sister" was Elvis rock and roll at its finest. The LP cuts didn't measure up, however, and were rather bland and overwrought by contrast. A week later, in early July, Elvis returned to cut his soundtrack for *Follow That Dream*. By later standards, it was passable, but at the time it felt distressingly flimsy. The title song is a fine rocker with a good message; the rest is average or worse.

Elvis came back to Nashville in October to do more work on the album and cut another 45. The "Good Luck Charm"/"Anything That's Part of You" single again stood out greatly compared to the rest of the songs, but it was somewhat mild. One could point to the loss of the terrific guitarist Hank Garland (who was injured in a car crash and would never play again) as one reason why all the songs sounded so tame, but with Elvis now infatuated with Latin cha-cha songs, his own artistic inclinations were also to blame.

Elvis finished up the year with his best movie session since returning from the army. *Kid Galahad* had six solid tracks that have stood the test of time. "King of the Whole Wide World" was sturdy rock and roll, "I Got Lucky" is superb pop, and the rest are all pleasant and respectable. It sounded right for the period, being a bit softer than what Elvis may have cut in the fifties. Rendering that irrelevant was the strength of the performances, and the tunes themselves.

Live Performance

Revealing Elvis to have all the raw power of before, plus a new level of poise and diversity in his set, the 1961 concerts were rapturously received. The Hawaiian show on March 25th has survived the years, and despite being so low-fidelity it remains one of the most fascinating Elvis performances ever documented. Presenting a perfect cross-section of 1954–60 masterpieces, Elvis makes every

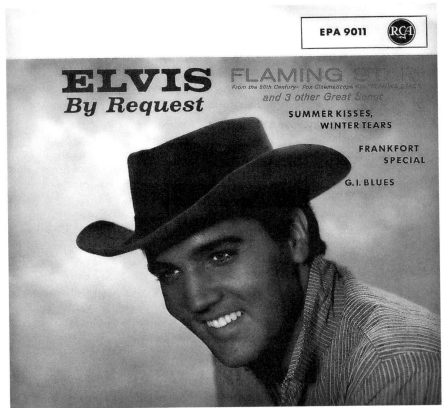

Elvis hesitated to put out any of the songs from *Flaming Star*, but due to bootleg copies being played on the radio, he eventually sanctioned the release of the best two songs on this 1961 EP. This U.K. version uses two album cuts from *G.I. Blues* for the other selections.

song sound as important as the record. On "Reconsider Baby," he even goes above and beyond his studio master by getting caught up in the frenzy of the crowd. With Boots Randolph on sax and Hank Garland doubling Scotty Moore on lead, Elvis was also playing with a crack band who performed their hearts out. Officially issued on the 1980 eight-record *Elvis Aron Presley* set, this is the best example of what a young Elvis was capable of in concert.

On Celluloid

Blue Hawaii had corny moments (like the spanking) that made Elvis look square, but it was carried out smoothly. It succeeds in showing off the beauty of the 50th state and its music. The actors, such as Angela Lansbury, are well chosen, and Elvis proved himself to be adept at light humor. He is allowed to rebel to a point, but underlying that is a responsible young lad straight out of *Leave It to Beaver*.

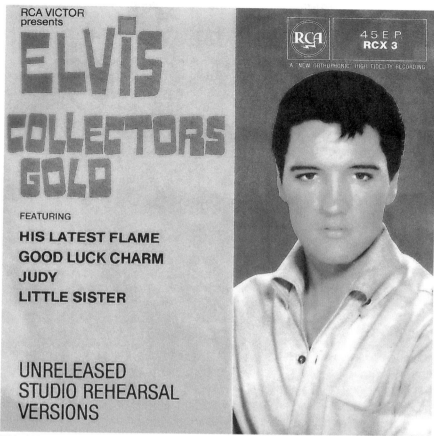

RCA VICTOR
presents

ELVIS COLLECTORS GOLD

RCA
45 E.P.
RCX 3

A "NEW ORTHOPHONIC" HIGH FIDELITY RECORDING

FEATURING

HIS LATEST FLAME

GOOD LUCK CHARM

JUDY

LITTLE SISTER

UNRELEASED
STUDIO REHEARSAL
VERSIONS

This 1982 U.K. EP offered then-exclusive alternate takes from 1961. The cover had been used with a different background for the *Easy Come, Easy Go* EP in 1967.

Rock and roll and Elvis Presley are supposed to be badass, but that's one thing *Blue Hawaii* most assuredly isn't. A semi-decent family film that was never really right for Elvis, it became the template for most of his future roles solely because of its runaway success.

Follow That Dream was a somewhat condescending comedy, but as it and *Kid Galahad* were filmed before the *Blue Hawaii* clone program began, they are actual movies. They have good actors, interesting scripts, and few unctuous moments, and, in the case of *Kid Galahad*, there are even some cool songs. These films for United Artists gave Elvis his last chance to do anything like real acting for six years.

Follow That Dream also gave Elvis a chance to display his onscreen humor to its best advantage. Elvis was probably funnier in real life, judging by his live and private recordings, but he did have a well-timed naivety that generated laughs.

The story about a quasi-family of beach homesteaders was moderately entertaining, but Elvis' Toby Kwimper is a dumb Southern stereotype that likely embarrassed him at some level. Overall, *Follow That Dream* is a good watch, though, in that Presley is given something different to do. The courtroom speech at the end was another example of how well Elvis could handle drama when given the infrequent chance. It's interesting to note that Elvis had gained some weight by this time, and had his first potbelly in this flick. He still looked pretty good, though, with his hair briefly allowed to return to its natural shade of blond.

Kid Galahad was one of the few Elvis movies that had the right blend of music and storyline. This is not just a good Elvis movie—it is a solid film by any standard. Charles Bronson, Gig Young, and Lola Albright made up a fine lineup of co-stars, and Elvis turns in a grown-up performance that seems tailor-made for his actual age of twenty-six. Having received training from champion fighter Mushy Callahan, Elvis was believable as a boxer, while the singing is staged informally enough to be only slightly incongruous.

Kid Galahad wasn't going to win any awards, but it showed that nothing had been lost as far as Elvis' acting talent goes. It was sadly becoming rare for Elvis to get the chance to nurture his dramatic chops, but *Kid Galahad* give him one last chance to do something semi-serious of quality.

Popularity and Impact

Nineteen sixty-one was Elvis' last year of almost omnipresent success, and some impressive music was waxed. Though they didn't present Elvis at his very best, *Something for Everybody* and *Blue Hawaii* both hit #1. He also had a #14 EP, *Elvis by Request*, plus a stunning five Top 10 single hits. "Surrender" was well performed, but not quite as good as "It's Now or Never," the hit it cloned. "I Feel So Bad" was a welcome return to R&B, and one that felt more authentic than "Mess of Blues." "Little Sister" rocked hard and unforgiving, "His Latest Flame" was wonderfully confident pop, and "Can't Help Falling in Love" was the glorious *Blue Hawaii* ballad that Elvis would make his signature farewell when he finally got back onstage.

Wild in the Country was fairly well received, but it was a quieter movie that generated a quieter level of success. It wouldn't have hurt for Elvis to have low-key dramas continue to alternate with the light musicals, but that ended after *Blue Hawaii* came out.

Blue Hawaii is one of Elvis' more iconic roles, but it wasn't nearly his best. It's not a bad movie, but predictable elements had begun to appear. Elvis kisses girls, has trouble with a girl, makes up with a girl, sings, fights, and plays with children. Hal Wallis' sixties Elvis films stand in direct contrast to their fifties collaborations. While Wallis seemed to have his finger on the pulse of fifties youth, his and Parker's idea to turn Elvis into some sort of family entertainer came from an outmoded perspective. *Blue Hawaii* did do very well, but most of Elvis' sixteen-to-twenty-five-year-old male fans wouldn't stick around much longer.

12

For EP Fans Only

E. P. on EP

The Extended Play 45, or EP, was a single that had three to six songs on it, and was for the most part marketed as a cheaper way to acquire album cuts. This didn't always hold true, however, and artists ranging from Elvis and Ricky Nelson to the Beatles, the Rolling Stones, and the Kinks all issued original EPs with tracks that didn't necessarily fit into their regular 45 or album releases. The sleeves were thicker, like LP covers, and the record came out of the side. Though the format remained popular in Europe through the sixties (and is still occasionally used on both vinyl and CD), in America the EP's heyday had come to an end by the early sixties.

Despite this—and the subsequent decline in sales—Elvis continued issuing EPs through 1967 for some of his shorter soundtracks. All in all, Elvis issued twenty-nine American EPs from 1956–67 that are highly coveted today. Some of them are as good as any of his records, and others are oddly compiled or conceptualized; all are of interest. Except in the case of material first released in this format, the following reviews aren't extensive. Releases that previewed a forthcoming album (or ended up being used on LP shortly thereafter) are also touched upon briefly. Still, this should give readers a good overview of some of Elvis' most obscure and interesting releases.

Elvis Presley (Released March 23, 1956)

This EP was released simultaneously with Elvis' first LP and replicates the front cover. All four songs are rock-oriented, with "Blue Suede Shoes" taking prominence. Getting to #24 on the charts, it was the first of many hits Elvis had off his EPs. It was an extreme rarity for EP cuts to hit the singles charts, but this was something Elvis did with regularity.

The four tracks were all found on the debut album, though many first heard them on EP. Some of the less expensive record players at the time were 45-only, selling mostly to teenagers on a budget. Because of this, RCA saw to it that nearly every fifties Elvis LP track was also issued on EPs that would fit the speed and size of these players. Incredibly, RCA would subsequently release the first album as a series of six 45s that served mostly as catalogue items. The EPs, however, seemed to have a shelf life of their own.

Elvis Presley (Released March 23, 1956)

No, that isn't a typo; there was a second EP release drawn from the first album in an altogether more lavish package. This double-EP, housed in a gatefold sleeve, featured eight cuts from the first LP, three of which also featured on its sister EP. It didn't sell particularly well—most fans either bought the one-record EP or went ahead and bought the album. It was an experiment that wasn't repeated.

Heartbreak Hotel (Released April 20, 1956)

This EP had a striking cover that captured Elvis in a serious, brooding pose. It featured both sides of the title single, Elvis' big country hit "I Forgot to Remember to Forget," and a cut from the first album not used on previous EPs. The use of the Sun side is interesting, as it would be sorely neglected in Elvis' future hit packages. "Money Honey" got to #76.

The Real Elvis (Released August 17, 1956)

A truly strong cover graces this classic EP, with a black-and-white action photo of Elvis live on *Stage Show* put against a bright pink background. The Alfred Wertheimer photo from Elvis' July 1956 recording session on the back is also very cool. *The Real Elvis* contains his excellent second and third 45s of 1956, its title taken from signs that fans made to protest Elvis' appearance on *The Steve Allen Show* in a tuxedo.

Elvis Presley (Released September 1956)

Here, for the first and last time, Scotty and Bill join Elvis on an original record cover. Though their faces are shadowed, this was the only time RCA gave them any sort of acknowledgment, although Bill had also been partially seen on the debut album and excerpted EPs. This record comprises two Sun songs from the debut, plus two unreleased selections from the late-January session.

"Shake, Rattle and Roll" was a hit for Joe Turner and Bill Haley that Elvis had performed on his first *Stage Show* appearance. An alternate take released in 1992 showed how Elvis had initially patterned his version after the lascivious Turner original, but he toned it down here to where it ended up somewhere between the cleaned-up Haley lyric and the set Charles Calhoun wrote for Joe. It was the wildest version out of these three, and is a piece of fifties gold. In keeping with the EP cover, Scotty, Bill, and D. J. overdubbed the backing vocals along with Elvis.

"Lawdy, Miss Clawdy" was another rhythm-and-blues cut, first issued and written by Lloyd Price. With Shorty Long's piano to the fore, Elvis knocks out another great record. His delivery is both sexy and playful, and not a solitary word is wasted. Price sounded pleading and angry, but Elvis seems to view Miss Clawdy's behavior with bemusement. A timeless moment from his early catalogue,

Elvis here shows himself to be not a copyist of rhythm and blues but rather a proponent who created something wholly original out of an existing form.

Anyway You Want Me (Released September 21, 1956)

This EP is a little odd in that it pairs three random Sun cuts with the title ballad. "Any Way You Want Me" was also released one week later as the flip of "Love Me Tender." The Wertheimer photo on the front is quite nice, and "I Don't Care If the Sun Don't Shine" hit #74.

Elvis Volume 1 (Released October 19, 1956)

The first of three EPs that would see Elvis' entire second LP released on 45-speed records, this was easily the most popular. "Love Me" went all the way to #6 on the singles charts on the strength of the tremendous sales and airplay this EP generated. Elvis also enjoyed a #29 hit with "When My Blue Moon Turns to Gold Again," and a #59 hit with "Paralyzed."

Elvis Volume 2 (Released October 19, 1956)

This is the companion volume to the above EP. They share the same cover and notes with the LP they were taken from. "Old Shep" hit #47.

Love Me Tender (Released November 21, 1956)

This EP was the first in what would be a long line of soundtrack releases, and like most to follow it paled along side Elvis' usual records. The best song included was "We're Gonna Move," a track based on an old public domain gospel tune entitled "There's a Leak in This Old Building." While this secular version was diluted, and was the first of many Elvis film songs that lyrically pertain too directly to the scene, it is fun. Elvis clearly enjoyed singing this type of material, and would return to sacred music throughout his entire career.

The accordion-laden country pastiches "Let Me" and "Poor Boy" were somewhat harmless in and of themselves, but ominously they are the worst songs Presley had recorded to date. This should have acted as a forewarning that more thought needed to be put into how Elvis' music translated to celluloid, yet you can't fault Presley himself at this point. His vocals are committed, and he got a kick out of doing his routines for the camera. "Poor Boy" peaked at #35.

Strictly Elvis (Released January 25, 1957)

This release saw the four remaining songs from the *Elvis* LP issued as an EP. The back cover still uses the same notes, but RCA did use an attractive alternate from the front cover photo session.

Just for You (Released March 1957)

This EP was made up of new material, but the release of three of the four songs on Elvis' third LP four months later would dim its importance. The cover is another shot from the *Elvis* LP shoot, and the title seems to have been chosen by Elvis for his estranged girlfriend, June Juanico. June clamed Elvis cut the dramatic ballad "Is It So Strange" in an effort at reconciliation. Elvis had been fooling around with the Faron Young song for a few months, and had played it at the "Million Dollar Quartet" jam the previous December. He mentioned something about wanting to get a publishing deal on it, and by the time he cut it the following month, he undoubtedly had one. An assured, confident delivery meant that this was Elvis' best ballad thus far, yet it didn't get promoted very well. It was a shame when it didn't join the three inferior cuts that were soon included on the *Loving You* LP.

Peace in the Valley (Released April 11, 1957)

Elvis' first gospel release, this EP is covered in full in chapter 19. "(There'll Be) Peace in the Valley (for Me)" hit #39.

Loving You Vol. 1 (Released July 1957)

This EP contained four of the songs from the new *Loving You* album. Considering that the LP used the same front cover, the only thing of interest was that some different photos were used on the reverse.

Loving You Vol. 2 (Released July 1957)

The comments above can be applied again here. This volume seemed to focus on the harder-edged songs.

Elvis Sings Christmas Songs (Released October 16, 1957)

This EP presented some of the best material from Elvis' first Christmas LP. Both were top sellers.

Jailhouse Rock (Released October 30, 1957)

If any Elvis movie fully captured the mood, the music, and the mores of its era, it was *Jailhouse Rock*. The soundtrack was no less potent, and can be numbered among Elvis' best releases. "Treat Me Nice" was only included on a UK early-eighties reissue, so this isn't the complete score, but "Jailhouse Rock" and the four exclusive songs are enough to make this a classic. Jerry Leiber and Mike Stoller wrote four out of the six songs for the film, and helped out on the sessions.

The duo's "I Want to Be Free" was a particularly clever lament that worked as well on film as it did on vinyl. Obviously, it can be construed as a love song, but the idea of freedom seems to carry more meaning when sung by a prisoner. Like many of the songs used in the film, Elvis re-recorded it for record release. This was necessary because his character Vince doesn't have a distinct style until halfway through the picture. Ironically, when performed in the more typical Presley style, "I Want to Be Free" lost a lot of the plaintive qualities that made it work in the movie. That said, the record does have a stronger rhythm and arrangement, with Mike Stoller's piano to the forefront.

"Young and Beautiful" serves as the movie's informal theme, becoming something more personal at the film's climax. This too had a more melancholic intimacy in the movie, but the record was a nice showcase for Elvis' developing balladry, and Dudley Brooks' piano playing is exemplary.

A moderately dull version of "Don't Leave Me Now" had featured on Elvis' last album, *Loving You*, and he apparently thought he could improve on it. Indeed he did, giving this rendition a sneering attitude and a nice, greasy appeal. The arrangement was tightened, and again the piano playing by Brooks brings it all together.

"(You're So Square) Baby I Don't Care" is rock and roll in its purest form. Leiber and Stoller's song is icy cool on all possible levels. Elvis gives off an impression of casual ease while being completely in command of his every nuance. There is a measure of rebellion or aggression, but there is also a degree of good-humored charm. Bill Black was still getting used to electric bass, and when he threw his instrument down in frustration, Elvis simply picked it up and played the part. That the bass line is the song's most striking feature says a lot for Presley's ability to improvise—and come up with the goods.

King Creole Vol. 1 (Released July 1, 1958)

King Creole was initially only going to have its soundtrack appear on two EPs and a 45. This decision was then wisely reconsidered, but for a few months, fans had to buy the music on three separate releases. The front cover was eventually reused (reversed) on the LP jacket, and this EP does present "Lover Doll" without the later overdubs by the Jordanaires.

King Creole Vol. 2 (Released July 29, 1958)

Of all of the *King Creole* releases, this one had the nicest artwork. The stark blue backup and excellent color portrait of Elvis would have made a better jacket for the LP.

Elvis Sails (Released November 18, 1958)

This EP of interviews, recorded shortly before Elvis set sail to Germany, was something of a pacifier to RCA. The label wanted to keep the flow of Elvis' record releases going while he was in the army—as opposed to Parker, who felt that restraint was needed to keep the fans interested. *Elvis Sails* made both sides happy. RCA had new product to sell, and Parker was able to use Elvis' status as a soldier to garner good will. The cover was nicely executed, with Elvis bursting out of a newspaper on the front, while the back is a 1959 calendar. The sleeve even had a hole punched in it so one could hang it up.

Elvis had lost his mother only weeks before, and sounded somewhat solemn throughout the interview. Still, he fielded the questions with aplomb, giving the impression that he was an articulate, good-natured young man. Most of the talk is centered on Elvis being stationed in Germany, and he expresses how much he is looking forward to his first trip to Europe. Although only of interest to historians today, *Elvis Sails* neatly preserves an interesting moment in Presley's life, without any element of hindsight to blur it.

A Touch of Gold Volume 1 (Released April 21, 1959)

The *Touch of Gold* series was a somewhat halfhearted attempt to make a greatest-hits EP series. Other than the fact that they hadn't been on EP before, there was no rhyme or reason to the tracks chosen. Because Elvis' style had shifted so much over the past few years, "Good Rockin' Tonight" stood out awkwardly alongside a trio of Elvis' 1958 hits. The jacket was the first to show Elvis in his gold-lamé outfit, but the same shot was used to better effect seven months later on the second *Gold Records* LP.

A Touch of Gold Volume 2 (Released September 2, 1959)

This EP repeats the format of the first volume: three recent hits joined with a Sun single. The cover has two images of the gold-suited Elvis and an ad for *50,000,000 Elvis Fans Can't Be Wrong* on the back.

Christmas with Elvis (Released October 13, 1959)

To promote their repackaging of *Elvis' Christmas Album* in a standard cover, RCA released this EP, which also showcased the new artwork. Containing the four tracks from the album not issued in this format before, it would be the last time an American EP was issued straight off any particular album. As with the LP reissue, only recent research by Internet Elvis scholars Dr. John Carpenter and Keith Flynn has proven this to be a 1959 release.

A Touch of Gold Volume 3 (Released February 23, 1960)

Elvis' first release of the sixties was an ersatz farewell to his fifties music and imagery. Again, these songs were singles that had not previously been on EP, with another Sun side thrown in too. The cover simply repeats the familiar gold-suit image in triplicate.

Elvis by Request (Released February 11, 1961)

Elvis felt the *Flaming Star* soundtrack was of too poor quality to release, but disc jockeys began to play the title track from recordings made straight off the movie screen. A full soundtrack EP was mooted, but Elvis wouldn't permit the weaker songs to be issued. To compromise, he allowed "Flaming Star" and "Summer Kisses, Winter Tears," a song cut from the film, to be issued, along with "It's Now or Never" and "Are You Lonesome Tonight?"

The cowboy-styled ballad "Flaming Star" became a fair-sized hit on the strength of this release, getting up to #14. It is singularly contrived, but the rhythm moves along spiritedly. "Summer Kisses, Winter Tears" was minor next to Elvis' non-soundtrack ballads of the period, but the vaguely Asian sound has allure. Both new songs are sung superbly. The notes are fairly straightforward, and the photo used from the film *Flaming Star* was quite nice. The record played at 33⅓ as part of a short-lived attempt to set this speed as the industry standard.

Follow That Dream (Released April 17, 1962)

Follow That Dream came early enough in Elvis' film career to be made without any set formula. Alas, the music wasn't as good as the script, and this EP was his weakest release to date. It's far more credible than many of the soundtracks to follow, but it has a plastic feel to it that came to define Elvis' movie music.

Elvis had the worst song from the film, "Sound Advice," removed from the EP, but the only song truly worthy of release was the title track. "Follow That Dream" was a bit short, but it became a #15 hit for good reason. It's a rollicking slice of up-tempo pop with a strong performance and an upbeat message. Maybe calling it philosophical is taking things too far, but Bruce Springsteen liked the meaning of it enough to revamp it as part of his early-eighties live set.

The other songs didn't come close to being significant. The ballad "Angel" is sung very well, but the arrangement was terrible. With Millie Kirkham's "angelic" interludes and Boots Randolph's claves, "Angel" appears to be nothing more than juvenile kiddie music. "I'm Not the Marrying Kind" didn't even try to hide the fact that it was merely adolescent pimple-cream, truthfully better suited to a young Paul Anka than the King. "What a Wonderful Life" tried to rock, but the lyrics are clumsy, and the melody generic. It's not unpleasant, but there's nothing to it.

Bettering the bland U.S. artwork, this is the attractive U.K. back sleeve of the *Follow That Dream* EP.

G.I. Blues and *Blue Hawaii* may have cost Elvis some of his old fans, but the quality of the work won him many new ones. *Follow That Dream* (the EP, not the film) had nothing going for it outside of the title song, and must have given some pause for thought as to whether they would buy Elvis' music as readily in the future.

Kid Galahad (Released August 28, 1962)

Now this was more like it. *Kid Galahad* may not be as carefully constructed as Elvis' fifties films, but it was a genuinely worthy project that had the bonus of a great soundtrack. This EP didn't do quite as well as *Follow That Dream*, but this can be explained by two factors. First, the quality of the previous release wasn't good enough to sustain interest, and secondly, the American EP market was going into decline. Regardless, *Kid Galahad* was one of Elvis' best records of the early-to-mid-sixties, and the last soundtrack that stood completely apart from its accompanying film. It is Elvis' happiest-sounding music, and therein lays its appeal.

"King of the Whole Wide World" endures as one of Elvis' finest rockers from any period. The lyrics are witty, the sax-infused arrangement sounds like it came right off the *Elvis Is Back!* LP, and Presley wails on the lead. His technique didn't have the raw grit found on his fifties recordings, but this was replaced with an unerring sense of timing and polish. It would have made a hell of a single—and reaffirmed Elvis' rocker credentials in the process. It got to #30.

Nothing else is quite that stunning, but all of the material is likeable. "This Is Living" is a cheerful pop/rock song with the Jordanaires brought to the forefront. Playing off of Elvis' lead, their combined pep is convivial and charming. It's the closest Elvis came to doing a full duet with them on a secular recording.

The piano playing of Dudley Brooks took center stage on "Riding the Rainbow." The mood of light frivolity is maintained, and the Jordanaires blend splendidly with Elvis. The optimism of the times is felt all the way through this EP. Out-takes reveal the hard work involved, but on the finished product, Elvis sounds positively elated. Listen for the mastery of his phrasing on the chorus.

"Home Is Where the Heart Is" may not be the most arresting ballad Elvis ever attempted, but its unassuming nature is attractive. Elvis sings this warmly, without any sign of the Mediterranean affectation plaguing most of his current love songs. The mood is quiet and reflective, with a level of personal maturity Elvis couldn't previously have brought to a song.

"I Got Lucky" was stronger than any of Elvis' 1962 singles. The bouncy melody is infectious, the words are thought-out and clever, and Elvis sounds on top of the world. The pure pop sensibilities of "I Got Lucky" may not have sat well with the hardcore rockers in Elvis' fan base, but that's only a reflection of their own conceits. This is an exceptional illustration of the best in early-sixties rock and roll.

"A Whistling Tune" was a moderately artificial ballad already recorded for (and rejected from) *Follow That Dream*. Elvis sings his lead with assurance and composure, but on the whole "A Whistling Tune" feels vanilla. It's not bad enough to bring down the rest of the EP, but it is only acceptable.

Viva Las Vegas (Released May 13, 1964)

After *Kid Galahad*, the quality of Elvis' movies and their soundtracks nose-dived. The soundtrack recordings made from 1962 to 1967 (with rare exceptions) represent some of the most embarrassing work ever done by an otherwise great artist. *Viva Las Vegas* proved to be the one film from this period that had lasting value. It may seem painfully obvious today that the movies should have reflected Presley's musical instincts, but outside of the old studio cuts used for *Tickle Me*, *Viva Las Vegas* was the sole mid-sixties soundtrack that had any relation to what Elvis was doing in his regular studio sessions.

As the music was more appropriate, it is unfortunate that its commercial potential wasn't fully exploited. "What'd I Say" and "Viva Las Vegas" were issued as a single, and this EP of "If You Think I Don't Need You," "I Need Somebody to Lean On," "C'mon Everybody," and "Today, Tomorrow and Forever" came out soon after. The other six songs Elvis recorded during the sessions were first released on four different collections spanning 1965–91.

A glance at the chart positions of the soundtrack releases reveals that RCA misjudged the current market by not issuing a proper LP. The single was admirable musically, but the selections may have been too even a match. With disc jockeys seeming unsure of what side to plug, "What'd I Say" and "Viva Las Vegas" only got to #21 and #29 respectively. Further diluting sales was a 45 released the same month consisting of the 1962 album cuts "Kiss Me Quick" and "Suspicion." Saturation marketing may have worked in 1956, but by 1964, Elvis had a new generation of hit-makers to compete against.

It was also a fact that the EP format was by now nearly obsolete in the American market. Despite being extremely strong, this soundtrack EP only made it to #92. In spite of this, and the fact that the title tune wasn't included, *Viva Las Vegas* was a delightful EP. Joy Byers' "C'mon Everybody" was one of the best

This iconic July 31, 1955, image was used on Elvis' first LP and EPs for RCA. It was also used extensively for promotion. This early-eighties U.K. reissue is one of the only ones to get the original colors of the jacket correct.

rock-and-roll numbers Elvis cut for any of his sixties movies. It's a catchy dance tune that was fairly different on vinyl than onscreen, and Elvis sounds like he's having a blast singing something appropriate, for once.

Bill Giant, Bernie Baum, and Florence Kaye based their ballad "Today, Tomorrow and Forever" melodically on "Liebestraum" by Franz Liszt. Originally intended to be a duet between Elvis and Ann-Margret, the version chosen on record and on celluloid had Presley taking the sole lead. It is a lovely adaptation, sung with delicacy. The production was fairly simple, but it should have been pared back even more to eliminate a pair of distracting maracas. Nevertheless, "Today, Tomorrow and Forever" was effective in creating an intimate mood.

The slick Red West and Joe Cooper rocker "If You Think I Don't Need You" was a solid selection. It lacks some of the daring Elvis might have given it during the fifties or late sixties, but the restraint in this case adds a nice bit of tension. Though missing the requisite funky keyboard line, Red thought going for a Ray Charles type of song would yield better results than writing something stereotypically "Elvis." Elvis in turn seemed to have more fun stretching out than sticking to a more predictable formula.

Doc Pomus and Mort Shuman contributed the moody ballad "I Need Somebody to Lean On." The atmosphere is desolate, and jazzier than Elvis normally went for. One can almost picture a young Charlie Rich doodling away with it late at night in a smoky nightclub. As he was wont to do when presented with a challenge, Elvis pushed himself into this new area with seamless precision. In years to come, a fair number of Elvis' slower songs would become big productions with attendant larger-than-life vocalizing. Many of these songs had their own charm, but the appealing intimacy displayed on songs like "I Need Somebody to Lean On" was all but abandoned.

Tickle Me (Released June 15, 1965)

With there being no budget for new songs, old album cuts made up the attendant *Tickle Me* soundtrack. The choices ranged from 1960 to 1963, and they naturally put Elvis' other mid-sixties soundtracks to shame. What were deemed more commercial choices were set aside for single release, and the rest were included here. It's not a bad EP musically, but it was just a re-release of common songs in a dead format. Other than providing a questionable amount of promotion for the movie, it had no reason to exist.

Easy Come, Easy Go (Released March 10, 1967)

By 1967, the EP format was long considered domestically obsolete. Elvis' movie career was still sinking, and this record proved to be his worst selling. Obviously these two factors played a role, but the quality of the music and the movie would have killed it alone. It isn't the worst soundtrack Elvis did, but in light of all the fantastic music coming out in this era (including his own *How Great Thou Art*), this seemed to be nothing but an unfunny joke. The songs are poorly mixed, and an atrocious horn section ruins even the better moments.

"Easy Come, Easy Go" was a faux rocker that sounded hopelessly out of date. In the film, Elvis plays the guitar solo by picking up and strumming an oar. Still, it's more tolerable than "The Love Machine." Initially, it had a bit more of a groove to it, but the final arrangement was annoyingly shrill. It's about—I kid you not—a wheel of fortune with girls' pictures on it, which sailors spin for dates. Moronic isn't even the word. "I'll Take Love" is just as bad. A calypso number in 1967 was not what the doctor ordered. The words are wretched, and Elvis sounds like he's just trying to get it over with as fast as possible.

"Sing You Children" even makes gospel music sound hackneyed. Other than the blaring horns being as irritating as a fly buzzing in your ear, the problem is that it sounds so contrived. I would say it's ineptitude, but one has to work hard to sound that bad. Yet nothing but incompetence can explain "Yoga Is as Yoga Does." It's hard to express how stupid this song is. Elvis did a duet of it in the film with co-star Elsa Lanchester, which was surreal in itself, but this led to a huge blunder on the EP. Because no one bothered to change the lyric for the solo version, Presley sounds as if he's arguing with himself about the merits of yoga! According to his friend Larry Geller, Elvis took this song as an insult to his own interest in yoga and felt that it was a dig from Parker.

Somehow, as if by a miracle, a song worth hearing made it into the film. "You Gotta Stop" wasn't vintage Presley, and certainly it was not relevant to contemporary music, but is infinitely better than its surroundings. Given a crumb of a catchy tune, and the hint of lyrical inspiration, Elvis ran with it. There's a guitar line that resembles rock and roll, the vocal doesn't sound completely perfunctory, and is that a chorus that doesn't make you wince? In all seriousness, "You Gotta Stop" was decent, but only to the level of light filler. It certainly shouldn't have been the highlight of the score, but that's how low standards had fallen.

13

I Don't Want to Be Tied

1962

As the year began, *Blue Hawaii* looked like it might be Elvis' most commercially successful project to date. In retrospect, it's rather sad that it took off so well, as the next sixteen movies shot after its release were basically cookie-cutter retreads of the same formula. Granted, a couple of these films were to better *Blue Hawaii* in concept or execution, but Elvis was stuck in an image that didn't echo himself or anything that was going on in the music business. With 1962 being the only year during this period that saw his popularity remain undimmed, all but his most diehard fans caught on to the lowered creative standards pretty quickly. Sadly, those who had Elvis under contract did not grasp this in time, and his catalogue was soon filled with substandard films and records he never quite lived down.

Elvis should have spoken up early on about his dissatisfaction, but he made the mistake of letting others guide him creatively in the thought that they knew how to market him. He later admitted that it was only in 1965 that he knew his career needed to change direction in favor of live shows, but that didn't mean that he wasn't already alarmed by the declining quality of his scripts and music. True, he continued to choose his own songs, but he was being actively encouraged to stick to compositions his music publishers Hill & Range had either a full or partial cut on. This was fine in the early days. However, as the sixties progressed, and Elvis' sales declined, fewer writers allowed Hill & Range to take a piece of the pie. This meant that they mostly stuck to their staff writers, and as years went by, the best of them left to greener pastures. Those that did remain openly admit to losing inspiration when having to write to suit specific moments in vapid storylines.

Elvis' lack of exposure to better songs, and the way he was discouraged from looking outside his publishing catalogue, continued to dog him for the rest of his career. Things improved quite a bit after the movie years, but it's hard to escape the fact that the worst songs he cut from 1969 to 1976 tended to be those that were in-house. In retrospect, the material Elvis got in 1962 (especially for the movies) should have led to this restrictive regime's abandonment, but sadly this was not to be.

six big hits from Elvis' latest screen smash!

Side One	Side Two
1. KING OF THE WHOLE WIDE WORLD (Batchlor, Roberts)	1. HOME IS WHERE THE HEART IS (Edwards, David)
2. THIS IS LIVING (Weisman, Wise)	2. I GOT LUCKY (Fuller, Weisman, Wise)
3. RIDING THE RAINBOW (Weisman, Wise)	3. A WHISTLING TUNE (Edwards, David)

Colour by Deluxe: Released by UNITED ARTISTS
A MIRSCH COMPANY PRODUCTION

RCA VICTOR

Printed in England
by Robert Stace.

PRODUCT OF THE DECCA RECORD COMPANY LIMITED, LONDON.
MADE FROM A MASTER RECORDING OF RCA VICTOR.

Kid Galahad was one of Elvis' best films and soundtracks. Once again, RCA in the U.K. improved the rear graphics.

Studio Work

Elvis held only one regular recording session this year, in March. Overall, the songs were respectable, though only a few depart from what went before. He finished up his *Pot Luck* LP as well as cutting two more singles. Rock was basically off the menu, except for a remake of "Night Rider" that was so similar to the original that the 1961 master ended up being used instead. Though many of the ballads stuck to the decidedly Italian sound Elvis favored at the time, the melodies were a bit more varied than they had been in some time. "Suspicion" was the clear standout of the session, but it was surprisingly passed over for single release in favor of the lightweight (if attractive) pop of "She's Not You."

"(Such an) Easy Question" was quite a commercial selection, and a fairly big hit for Elvis when it was issued on 45 in 1965. "Just Tell Her Jim Said Hello" was another single contender, but it ended up being a flip that hovered just outside the Top 50. Along with the beautiful, mature "Something Blue," "You'll Be Gone" seemed to be the most personal of the songs recorded—and no wonder, considering the latter was the one and only track Elvis took a real hand in writing. His friends Red West and Charlie Hodge handled the lion's share of the work, but the fact that he was even attempting to compose showed a desire on Presley's part to expand his horizons.

Sadly, the two soundtrack sessions held for *Girls! Girls! Girls!* and *It Happened at the World's Fair* gave Elvis little opportunity to grow. There were a few excellent songs, such as "Plantation Rock" (which for some reason wasn't used), "Return to Sender," and "They Remind Me Too Much of You," but upon release these were Elvis' worst albums yet. *Girls! Girls! Girls!* at least had a full thirteen cuts, but *It Happened at the World's Fair* was a scant ten selections that ran to a little over twenty minutes. Elvis still sounded like he cared, but there's only so much one can do with bizarre ditties like "Cotton Candy Land" or "Song of the Shrimp." The LPs sold well, yet they undoubtedly encouraged many to not purchase further movie albums.

On Celluloid

Elvis was giving energetic performances, but *Girls! Girls! Girls!* and *It Happened at the World's Fair* weren't worthy of him. As an actor, Elvis proved most adept at playing a rebel. After all, the idea that Elvis was slightly dangerous was part of his initial appeal. Those who grew up on "Mystery Train" and "Jailhouse Rock"—or even recent fans who enjoyed *Elvis Is Back!* or *Wild in the Country*—were in for a shock upon seeing what these films had to offer.

Girls! Girls! Girls! had Elvis play a shrimp boat captain and (big surprise) a part-time singer. "Return to Sender" has endured, and all of the choreography was high-spirited, but there were far too many mediocre songs. The plot was wafer thin, and even a return to Hawaii for part of the action failed to impress. Much worse was to follow, but there wasn't enough comedy or drama to lift it beyond the level of humdrum.

It Happened at the World's Fair wasn't bad for a family movie, but the wisdom of Elvis taking such roles is highly questionable. The music was fairly bad, but the location of the Seattle 1962 World's Fair was an interesting one. With a few tweaks—having Elvis be an entertainer at the fair without singing songs about the fair, say—it could have been better than average. As it stands, too much of it is implausible, and the most exciting part is watching for Kurt Russell (who revived his career playing Elvis in a 1979 TV movie) as the kid who kicks Elvis in the shin.

Popularity and Impact

This was the last year that Elvis was considered the world's top rock-and-roll artist, and it was also the last year that all of his singles went Top 10. With Motown, Phil Spector, the Beach Boys, Bob Dylan, and the Beatles emerging, by 1963 teenagers began to elsewhere for new sounds. Its doubtful Elvis could have continued to be the top fad for much longer—he was hardly a teen idol at

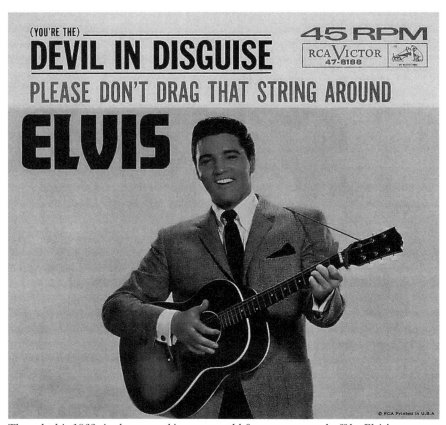

Though this 1963 single was rocking, many old fans were turned off by Elvis' conservative clothes and hair. This all-too-cheerful photo was taken during the 1962 shoot for *It
Happened at the World's Fair.*   *Courtesy of Robert Rodriguez*

27—but he could have retained his credibility and continued to be a leading
artistic light. *Follow That Dream* and *Kid Galahad* were fine movies that must have
given some hope that Elvis would continue to make real films alongside his more
lavish musicals. Unfortunately, as with all of Elvis' strongest efforts in the early
sixties, the dross outsold the gold. With "Return to Sender" acting as a constant
commercial, *Girls! Girls! Girls!* was what most people went to see.

Elvis' records continued to sell extremely well, if not to the level they had
previously. *Pot Luck* was a solid if unspectacular album, but it failed to top the
charts. Without concerts or television to support them, the pure studio albums
weren't getting real promotion. That these were far better than the soundtrack
LPs didn't matter, in light of the kind of advertising the films provided. Because
of this, *Girls! Girls! Girls!* outsold its superior counterparts in theaters and record
stores. The *Follow That Dream* EP wasn't all that much better, but the *Kid Galahad*
EP was excellent.

With "Good Luck Charm" getting all the way to #1, as a singles artist Elvis was literally still on top. It was innocuous, but it fit the current marketplace. "She's Not You" was even less daring, and for that it only made it to #5. Several of the songs saved for *Pot Luck* were better, but it was good and kept Elvis' streak of Top 10s going. "Return to Sender" shot all the way to #2. Though it was poppy, some of the old Elvis was there in the growl in which he delivered it.

Elvis shot only two films in 1962, and held only one set of studio sessions. Clearly, a tour or a few television guest spots would have been easy enough to do, but Parker had priced Elvis out of range on the latter, and he canceled a planned tour when RCA wouldn't put up enough money for it. If it hadn't been clear before, dollars now took precedence over intelligent management, and Parker's ego was now at a level where he turned down many rewarding projects (both creative and financial) if he didn't get to "advise" (or, to be more blunt, interfere) with how they turned out. In other words, Elvis' incipient decline was being set in motion.

14

Just Three Words and No More

W ith the 1962 tour canceled, Elvis was now to focus strictly on Hollywood. Three movies were shot this year, and an LP was recorded. The mismanagement of the best of his music should have been a clear warning to Elvis that things had to change, but he didn't realize that he was the one who held all the winning cards, and Parker made sure it remained that way.

It was around the time Elvis shot his third movie of the year, the ghastly *Kissin' Cousins*, that he started to get physically ill from reading his scripts. He hated what was happening to his career and his music, but he was led to think by Parker that he couldn't do anything about it. Elvis misplaced his trust in his manager because he felt the Colonel had got him where he was—which was sadly all too accurate.

Studio Work

Elvis headed back to Radio Recorders to cut the *Fun in Acapulco* LP. It was a poor collection, with "Bossa Nova Baby" being the only good song, and "Guadalajara" the sole authentic representation of Mexican music. Otherwise, it was distressingly bad, coming only three years after the brilliance of the *Elvis Is Back!* recordings. Elvis sang well enough, but he couldn't save the album or the movie.

In May, Elvis went to Nashville to record a new studio LP and a few singles. The sessions weren't completely devoid of the quality issues plaguing the 1961–62 non-soundtrack recordings, but on the whole the results were better than almost anything he had cut since 1960. There was less Latin-style crooning, and even those numbers were more restrained. A lot of rock and roll was cut, and there was even an R&B flavor to some of the masters. Top that with a few remarkably well-sung ballads and you have yourself a fine LP.

Sadly, Colonel Parker didn't see it the same way, and the music was to be parceled off as soundtrack LP filler, a few singles, and the 1965 *Elvis for Everyone* compilation. The soundtracks were selling more, and that's the only thing he or RCA cared about. It took until 1968 for each title to be issued, 1990 for an LP/CD to be released, and 1991 until the original masters of "Ask Me" and

"Memphis, Tennessee" saw the light of day. This album would have put to rest the rumors the Elvis had now largely forsaken rock and roll, and it took decades before this period of his career could be evaluated properly.

The *Viva Las Vegas* soundtrack, laid down in July at Radio Recorders, was nearly as rewarding. These, unbelievably, wouldn't see LP release either, but at least in this instance the film gave a good idea of what had been accomplished.

This ad for the *Gold Records* series was included in a booklet sometimes given away with the third volume. The main picture dates from 1957, with Elvis in his famous gold outfit.

There are a few songs Elvis wouldn't have considered for a normal recording date, but in general the music held up to the May session in Nashville. The blend of styles was similar, and Elvis' performance level was maintained.

Just when things seemed to be turning around on the record and movie front, the bottom fell out. *Kissin' Cousins* was an awful movie with a rural setting. It was thought that recording the songs for the film in Nashville might give them a country flavor, but the sophisticated sounds coming out of the area at the time didn't consist of blowing on a jug while singing about kissing your cousin! Elvis showed up briefly, but his throat was sore. Having to overdub his vocals later in California, he couldn't fake the excitement anymore, only pushing himself the few times where he was given a crumb of something to work with. The cupboard was mostly bare.

On Celluloid

Fun in Acapulco was somewhat scenic, although Parker refused to let Elvis film in Mexico. The film suffered for it, but it wasn't all that good to begin with. With a few exceptions, Elvis sings some silly songs that have no feel for Mexican music or culture. He was now being dragged to the level of singing novelty pieces like "There's No Room to Rhumba in a Sports Car." Ursula Andress, popular at the time for appearing the James Bond flick *Dr. No*, was Elvis' leading lady, but they didn't have much to go on. The basic plot involves Elvis dating two girls—trying to figure out which one he likes more—while trying to conquer his fear of heights. The films would drop even further from here.

One exception was *Viva Las Vegas*. On the face of it, *Viva Las Vegas* shouldn't have stood out from the pack. Plot-wise, it stuck strictly to the proven formula. For the first of three outings, Elvis is a singing race-car driver who romances his leading lady. Yet the finished product delivers so much more than any other musical Elvis attempted in the sixties. A lot of the success of the film is due to a great choice for Elvis' leading lady. Ann-Margret was the current "it" girl in Hollywood, having made a name for herself starring in the Presley-inspired musical *Bye Bye Birdie*. She shares top billing with Elvis, and the chemistry between the stars sizzled both on- and offscreen.

The one word that describes *Viva Las Vegas* best is "entertainment." There's no message, no deep meaning, no real attempt to convey humdrum reality. The point of *Viva Las Vegas* was to cinematically offer up the same kind of escapism provided by the city it celebrates. *Viva Las Vegas* was significant in that it gave the city a more youthful identity. Elvis' films have (for good reason) been dismissively called travelogues, but *Viva Las Vegas* remains as vibrant as the location it depicts.

In being one of the few Elvis movies where music and plot intertwine comfortably, it was fortuitous that *Viva Las Vegas* also had a solid soundtrack. While there was some filler that doesn't work outside of the context of the film, we also have examples of real rock and rhythm and blues. It may seem like a no-brainer

This enormous poster, taken during the shooting of *Fun in Acapulco*, was included in the *Gold Records Volume 3* promo booklet.

to let Elvis perform the styles he excelled at, but his other movies during this period didn't give him the chance. It's the last time a scripted Elvis movie was worthy of its star.

Kissin' Cousins sure wasn't. Parker, angry at how much *Viva Las Vegas* had cost (never mind that it was to become Elvis' most successful movie), now hooked Elvis up with penny-pinching producer Sam Katzman. The low budget made its mark in the ridiculous sets, lack of name co-stars, and truly awful trick photography. Elvis plays a twin set of cousins, and in one scene Elvis' double looks straight into the camera. The songs managed to be the worst Elvis had received to date, and the plot was ridiculous and insulting to Southerners.

Kissin' Cousins marked the point where Elvis more or less gave up trying to act. Before, he had always made an effort to turn in respectable work, but with the only criteria now being to get the movie in the can, he didn't have the chance to do anything but run through his lines. Not every Elvis picture to follow was this cheap-looking, but his acting wouldn't recover until his parts became a challenge again. There are laughs aplenty in the film, but not one of them is intentional.

Popularity and Impact

Elvis' popularity was starting to take a hit. Most of his records were still Top 10, but "One Broken Heart for Sale" broke an amazing string of twenty-four Top 10 singles in a row when it came in at #11. The only Elvis singles from 1956 to 1962 that hadn't had a major chart impact were a series of reissues off the first LP.

Things picked up briefly. "(You're the) Devil in Disguise" got all the way to #3 and was an excellent choice for a single. "Bossa Nova Baby" was the strongest song in *Fun in Acapulco*, and it got up to #8.

On the LP front, all three 1963 releases made it into the Top 5. However, there were serious concerns raised about quality. *It Happened at the World's Fair* and *Fun in Acapulco* were Elvis' first downright bad albums. They each have two songs apiece that are excellent, but that was far too low a number to ensure that the same level of interest in Elvis would be maintained. *It Happened at the World's Fair* was also criticized for having only ten selections. That practice wouldn't become acceptable for a new full-priced album until track lengths became longer in the late sixties.

To make up for this, Parker began to put "bonus songs" on the soundtracks if the movie recordings numbered less than twelve. These were usually the best tracks, as they weren't always from the movie session, but using them in this way meant that Elvis' 1963 LP was canceled. It would be 1969 before a secular LP of all new, non-movie songs would appear. Yes, the initial sixties soundtracks had outsold the regular studio albums, but this was only due to Elvis wanting to give his fans value for their money by not putting his singles on them.

In that it was clear that Elvis' best music was no longer going to come from his films, one has to point the finger squarely at Parker and RCA for not giving

In 1963, Elvis' planned studio album was inanely canceled. Finally put out in 1990, the cover of the newly titled *For the Asking* successfully captured the period.

a damn about anything but how much money they made off Presley. Elvis was the best artist of his generation, but he was saddled with the least creative team in music history. It was an appalling state of affairs that not only ended up costing everyone money but also killed Elvis' credibility. Even the fine *Elvis' Golden Records Volume 3* compilation, released in the summer, could have been better timed and compiled. Continuing the 1959 volume's practice of not including album songs meant that both "Can't Help Falling in Love" and "Return to Sender" were ignored. This time, it was a full twelve-track release, but the first volume in the series had showed that a fourteen-cut LP could be done. Still, in including each a side of Elvis' 1960–62 non-soundtrack singles, plus a good number of the flips, the music itself can't be faulted. It would be the last time that this could be said about an Elvis Presley album for many years.

15

Come Along with Me

The Discards

Although RCA often complained of not having enough to release, there were several Elvis songs that didn't make the cut of any regular LP, EP, or 45. In the following chapter are songs that never made it to a contemporary release. Some of these weren't intended for public consumption, others fell through the cracks, but it should be stressed that Elvis only once asked for a song not to come out due to quality concerns.

The Rules

To keep this section from being unwieldy, I have set six ground rules for inclusion:

1. When a previously unreleased song is issued on a new, pre-1978 collection—such as the Camden titles, the *Legendary Performer* LPs, or the *Elvis for Everyone* album—they are automatic inclusions. All these compilations are given a brief overview in the year they are issued, but here you will find a more detailed description of their contents.
2. No alternate takes allowed! Some of the final masters differ greatly from how they initially sounded, but even radical re-workings aren't new songs. Exceptions include rewrites, or the rare occasion when a song was recorded before or after a finished master in a completely different era.
3. There are no home recordings. Some of these are very good, and all are interesting to a historian, but they aren't professional recordings done for commercial purposes.
4. Only studio recordings and songs first issued live officially are considered. A book with a song-by-song commentary on each live selection over the years has yet to be written. For concert recordings, what is reviewed isn't the first version chronologically but the first issued version.
5. Each song must be more than a one-liner. Elvis goofed around with many songs in the studio and onstage, but if he ever did full versions of these, they weren't attempted professionally. Thus this list covers only songs Elvis recorded that were set aside indefinitely until they were put out on lifetime compilations or postmortem archival releases.
6. Studio jams and rehearsals are included if they have songs never done otherwise professionally. Thus "I Shall Be Released" is included, while tracks

like "Tiger Man" (the mid-tempo 1975 version) or "Johnny B. Goode" (1972 *On Tour* studio rehearsal) aren't. The reason for this is that, whereas the otherwise unknown songs give an insight into what Elvis may have done with them, we know what Elvis did with the common cut. The rough jams found here each give us an idea of Elvis' artistic instincts at the time in that one can imagine how a complete version would have sounded.

"My Happiness" (Recorded July 1953)

The story behind this record has been told many times, including in this book's first chapter. Because of the historical significance of Elvis' first several visits to a studio, rating his amateur demos is a challenge. The question of how developed he was before his first real session isn't easy to qualify, as we only hear him singing straight ballads. Unlike blues or country, ballad singing was something Elvis only grew into with practice. That's not to say the potential in his voice isn't present. There's a good-natured sensuality in the way Elvis returns to the verse after the chorus, but he's raw, unformed, not well pitched. The Ink Spots' recording was Elvis' inspiration for "My Happiness," but like he told Marion Keisker, he already doesn't sound like anyone else. It's not remarkable, but it is unique, and that's probably why Marion made note of him.

Its not being a masterpiece strictly as music takes nothing away from "My Happiness" being among the most historically important recordings of all time. A full quarter-century hasn't dimmed the excitement around its discovery. Elvis gave it to his friend Ed Leek to hold onto for him, and never took it back. Leek eventually decided to sell it to RCA, and fans anxiously awaited its release after it was authenticated in 1988. Sadly, at that point RCA was only just beginning to treat Elvis' work with sensitivity, and it ended up on a nondescript 1990 LP/CD called *The Great Performances*. It is heard in much better context on future titles, such as *The King of Rock 'n' Roll* or *A Boy from Tupelo*.

"That's When Your Heartaches Begin" (Recorded July 1953)

The 1992 LP/CD boxed set *The King of Rock 'n' Roll* also featured the second side of Elvis' first demo, "That's When Your Heartaches Begin." In that Elvis recorded it for RCA three and a half years later, this is the most interesting track Elvis attempted before "That's All Right." His voice wavers more than it would later, but it does possess a rough beauty. Most odd is how much he overacts during the spoken section. He doesn't seem to know where to go from there, sheepishly emphasizing his abrupt last line, "That's the end."

"I'll Never Stand in Your Way" (Recorded January 1954)

Elvis' second demo session was only slightly different than the first. The songs are crooning ballads, and the only accompaniment is his own guitar, but Elvis does seem to have been practicing. His voice is more consistent, he sounds less hesitant, and you can more readily discern that this is a young Elvis Presley. This track was a minor country hit for a fellow named Ernie Lee in 1953, but there isn't any trace of country in Elvis' rendition, so he probably based it on Joni James' more successful pop cover.

It was first released on the 1997 *Platinum* CD boxed set, but it is heard in a better setting on releases like *Sunrise* or *A Boy from Tupelo*. Vinyl fans can acquire it on the excellent two-LP 2004 U.K. public-domain set, *The King of Western Bop*.

"It Wouldn't Be the Same Without You" (Recorded January 1954)

A more country-flavored number, this song had been a hit for singer Al Rogers in 1951. Elvis researcher "Dr. John Carpenter" pointed out on the FECC message board that Elvis actually based his vocals more on the pop cover by Lily Ann Carol. Being quite practiced this time out, Elvis' strides over the last six months are even more noticeable here. Though he lacks polish, he's slowly gaining more focus over these formative months. This fascinating recording can be found on CD releases such as *Sunrise* (where it debuted) and *A Boy from Tupelo*, and on the LP *The King of Western Bop*.

"Harbor Lights" (Recorded July 5, 1954)

This appears to be the first song Elvis did at his very first session. It's a standard ballad of the pre-rock era that doesn't hint at what was to come later that night. Elvis had an interesting voice in 1954, but it wasn't yet suited to straight pop. It's the only Sun master that can be called downright lifeless, and it likely wasn't released on the debut album because it's frankly not good. It took until 1976 for "Harbor Lights" to be issued on the *Legendary Performer Volume 2* LP. It wasn't until 1984's *Golden Celebration* boxed set that it was heard without a layer of RCA-added echo. As a historical artifact, "Harbor Lights" can't be beaten, but it's not musically anything to get excited over.

"Tomorrow Night" (Recorded September 12–16, 1954)

"Tomorrow Night" used to be the odd one out when it came to Elvis' Sun period. It went unreleased until 1965, a time where the historical implications of Elvis' early work were not yet clear to those who should have already realized them. Horrible, distorted fake stereo was being applied to Elvis' fifties recordings in the early-to-mid-sixties, and from 1968 to 1983 the mono originals were (with a few exceptions) disregarded by RCA—particularly in the States. The song that suffered most, even in mono, was "Tomorrow Night."

Recorded sometime between September 12 and 16, 1954, the song was stripped of all its music when it was released on the LP *Elvis for Everyone*, the vocal laid across a "modern" re-recording. Elvis had nothing to do with the new session, which had been spearheaded by Chet Atkins. The results weren't bad, but they only hinted at Elvis' artistic intentions. The original "Tomorrow Night" master wasn't unearthed until 1985, and even then it wasn't until 1992 that it was released with the minimalist guitar solo intact.

It's a basic but wonderful blues on which Elvis, for the first time, sounds at ease singing a slow tempo. "Blue Moon" was a pointer in the right direction, but there is a new level of self-assurance here. All of the gawky phrasing heard on "I Love You Because" or "Harbor Lights" is gone, replaced with hints of the baritone Elvis was to use extensively on his early RCA love songs. Why this splendid song was passed over in favor of some of the more dreary selections found on Elvis' debut album is inexplicable.

"Fool, Fool, Fool" (Recorded January 6, 1955)

Recorded as a concert promo for a radio station in Lubbock, Texas, "Fool, Fool, Fool" is one of the coolest "found" artifacts of the Sun era. By this point, Elvis had his persona perfectly worked out, and he gasps, hiccups, and rocks his way through this 1951 hit for the Clovers. Elvis doesn't water it down—if anything he makes it wilder. What other white performer dared to do that in early 1955? It premiered on the 1992 LP/CD boxed set *The King of Rock 'n' Roll*, strangely without much comment.

"Hearts of Stone" (Recorded January 15, 1955)

A nice glimpse of what Elvis was doing at his early shows, this recording from the *Louisiana Hayride* first appeared legally on *Sunrise* in 1999. This R&B cut was first recorded by the Jewels and then quickly surpassed on that chart category by a version by the Charms. Soon enough, the pop charts were topped by a tame rendition by the Fontaine Sisters. With his wide palate, Elvis probably enjoyed all the recordings of the song that passed his radar, but unlike the Fontaines', his version is as gritty and raucous as any other. Due to the fine steel-guitar playing of *Hayride* musician Jimmy Day, there's a unique element of country here that blends perfectly with Elvis' R&B-styled vocal.

"How Do You Think I Feel" (Recorded early 1955)

For his first session with a drummer, Jimmie Lott, Elvis took the opportunity to rehearse the rhumba-inspired "How Do You Think I Feel." It isn't known whether a formal take was attempted, since all that survives is a tape of Scotty

Moore practicing his guitar part and Elvis singing off-mic. Though it obviously would have had a different ambience, what can be heard here isn't all that different from how this track ended up sounding on the eventual master from 1956. First heard on the eleven-LP Sun Records boxed set *The Rocking Years*, issued by Bear Family Records in 1986, it was not included on an official Elvis LP or CD until *A Boy from Tupelo* in 2012. All of the Sun material is worth hearing, but "How Do You Think I Feel" wasn't particularly stirring in any form.

"Little Mama" (Recorded March 5, 1955)

Elvis has had his own collector's label since 1999. Covering his entire career in depth, more than 100 books, CDs, and LPs have been issued, and it's still going strong. Despite the lack of vinyl on a set that cries out for it, *A Boy from Tupelo* is one of their most definitive releases. Detailing the Sun years in both print and CD form, the coolest item in the set was a "new" song Elvis sang on the *Louisiana Hayride* called "Little Mama." It's got all the hallmarks of Elvis' Sun era in execution and sound, and it sounds superb. It had been first recorded by one of Elvis' favorite R&B vocal groups, the Clovers, in 1953.

"Tweedlee Dee" (Recorded April 20, 1955)

Elvis' version of LaVern Baker's hit is exceptionally good. It's got that mix of country that steel guitarist Jimmy Day provides, and Elvis' playful, gutsy singing is full-out R&B. Recorded in Gladewater, Texas, for broadcast on the *Hayride*, this went around on bootlegs for a few years before being officially released on the 1983 LP *The Beginning Years*.

"Maybellene" (Recorded August 20, 1955)

First heard on *The Beginning Years*, this ranks among the top live Elvis recordings. Recorded on the *Hayride*, barely a month after Chuck Berry released "Maybellene" as his debut record, this must be one of the earliest Berry covers in existence. It's comparable to "Mystery Train" in rhythm and excitement. Elvis fast-talks his way through the lead, Scotty plays some wild electric guitar lines, and Bill Black brutally strikes his bass and hollers along enthusiastically. Almost every rock-and-roll artist in existence has done a Chuck Berry song. Elvis was one of the few able to give Berry's work a markedly individualistic interpretation.

"When It Rains, It Really Pours" (Recorded November 1955)

This cover of Billy Emerson's great 1954 Sun 45 turned out to be the last thing Elvis ever did for Sam. The session wasn't finished; Elvis was called during the recording and told to stop, as he was being signed by RCA. Elvis promised to record the song later, as Sam owned the publishing on it, and he eventually did. Funny that publishing concerns entered the picture even during the Sun period. This version is slower, and only Elvis and his guitar are heard distinctly. A final mix doesn't seem to have been done, and the feed from the other instruments hasn't surfaced, though they are distinctly present.

Despite Scotty, Bill, and session drummer Johnny Bernero's parts sounding muddy, this performance is full of humor and passion. Elvis was in good spirits, and Carl Perkins was an observer. This was first released, with a few false starts, in 1983, on the *Legendary Performer Volume 4* record. As with all of the Sun material, the vinyl version of *Elvis at Sun* is the best way to hear what is now considered the master.

"One Night of Sin" (Recorded January 18, 1957)

Though recorded during the *Loving You* session, this song wasn't intended for the film. This is an early version of Elvis' classic "One Night," with the original lyrics as performed by Smiley Lewis. The line "one night of sin" was replaced by "one night with you" in the remake, and represented a general toning-down to get the song released without controversy. Maybe it is a stretch to call this a completely unreleased track, but this was the only time a song had to be completely rewritten due to the pressures of censorship. For that reason alone, this initial run at "One Night" stands on its own. First released on the fourth *Legendary Performer* compilation in 1983, this has been a popular track with compilers and fans ever since.

"When It Rains, It Really Pours" (Recorded February 24, 1957)

Little over a year after his aborted last session for Sun, Elvis finally got around to recording this. With Elvis sounding gritty and uncompromising, it had a generally tougher sound. Because what survives of the Sun session is a bit muffled, it's not really fair to say this is better. Yet with Dudley Brooks on piano, and a harder groove all around, it is hard to imagine the 1957 version being topped. It closed the 1965 *Elvis for Everyone* LP.

"Your Cheatin' Heart" (Recorded February 1, 1958)

Other than traces of it in the guitar work, this is possibly the least country-sounding version of this Hank Williams standard ever cut. Elvis turns the song into fairly hard rock, growling out the lyric with a trace of vengeance. It's not the most extraordinary track Elvis cut at the time, but with the Jordanaires providing their trademark backing, it is solid.

"Danny" (Recorded February 11, 1958)

One of Elvis' best cuts of the era, this was supposed to be the title track of the film *King Creole* when it was still being called *A Stone for Danny Fisher*. This ballad shows the tremendous growth Presley had made vocally, only three and a half years after turning professional. "Danny" has a nice beat behind it, and the U.K.'s number-one rock star of the fifties, Cliff Richard, covered it (likely off a demo) on his first LP soon after. In 1959, Conway Twitty (who sounded uncannily like Elvis in his early career) had a huge hit with the song after the specific name of Danny was altered, with "Lonely Blue Boy" becoming the new title. If any song in this chapter would likely have been a sizeable hit for Elvis, "Danny" is the one that got away.

"Tonight's All Right for Love" (Recorded May 6, 1960)

This song exists because Hill & Range didn't realize that Jacques Offenbach's *The Tales of Hoffmann* wasn't copyright free in Europe. They didn't want to spend the extra money, so something had to be substituted for "Tonight Is So Right for Love"—the "European"-sounding track composed by staff writers Abner Silver and Sid Wayne. With the help of Joe Lilly, they adapted Johann Strauss Jr.'s "Tales from the Vienna Woods" for the melody, and mildly rewrote the lyrics, calling it "Tonight's All Right for Love."

The reworking is slightly better, but like so many times during the *G.I. Blues* sessions, a blander take was used over a number of more energetic run-throughs. This was first released in America on the *Legendary Performer Volume 1* LP in 1974. A single version from Germany artificially lengthened the running time with a bad edit.

"Black Star" (Recorded August 8, 1960)

This technically isn't an unreleased song, but it didn't come out in this configuration. Until this recording surfaced in the eighties, only hardcore fans knew that the movie *Flaming Star* had undergone a major last-minute title change that altered the title song and its chorus. Even those aware that the name *Black Star* was being used had no way of knowing that it didn't disappear until the film was well into production. "Black Star" is identical to "Flaming Star," so comparing the two only reveals that the latter name flows better when sung. For record collectors, the best place to find it is on the 1991 three-LP version of the *Collectors Gold* boxed set. CD fans can find it on *The Complete Masters* boxed set. It can also be found—alongside many of the film out-takes to follow—in the *Double Features* CD series.

"Britches" (Recorded August 8, 1960)

As early as 1956, Elvis was recording some lesser songs for his movies. The 1957–58 soundtracks were as good as anything he did, but in 1960, *G.I. Blues* had a few mediocre cuts that pointed toward the future. For *Flaming Star*, Elvis wasn't required to sing much, and only five songs (counting both "Flaming Star and "Black Star") were recorded. Three (again counting "Black Star") were edited out of the final print, and Elvis didn't think any of the five numbers were good enough to release on record. Because radio stations were playing versions of the two featured tracks recorded off the screen, Elvis was persuaded to allow "Flaming Star" and a ballad cut from the final print, "Summer Kisses, Winter Tears," to be released on an EP. The other two songs were of such poor quality that they didn't come out until selections from the archives began to appear.

"Britches" made history as the first thoroughly bad song Elvis cut. It's square, silly, and downright stupid. If hearing Elvis yodel gets your heart pumping, then this is for you. It was deleted from the film, and only came out in 1978, on the *Legendary Performer Volume 3* LP.

"A Cane and a High Starched Collar" (Recorded August 8, 1960)

When Elvis needed a happy little tune to begin *Flaming Star*, "A Cane and a High Starched Collar" fit the bill. Like the songs from *Love Me Tender*, the *Flaming Star* cuts had to sound archaic in order to fit the time period of the story. This is a square dance–oriented ditty that Elvis does all he can with. It's not as bad as "Britches," but only by a small margin. "Cane" did make the film, but it too had to wait for a *Legendary Performer* LP (*Volume 2* in 1976) before it saw the light of day on RCA. A few false starts were included, featuring Elvis laughing at the cornball lyrics.

"In My Way" (Recorded November 7, 1960)

This beautiful little love song is just Elvis and an acoustic guitar. It's taken from *Wild in the Country*, the rural low-key setting allowing Elvis to record some well-crafted quiet tracks for the soundtrack. His voice is tender, and the lyric has a degree of maturity to it that was appropriate for Elvis at age 25. Sadly, there is a low buzz heard throughout its original release, on *Elvis for Everyone*.

"Forget Me Never" (Recorded November 7, 1960)

One of the numerous Latin-styled ballads Elvis recorded from 1960 to 1964, this is OK, but they all kind of blend together. It doesn't have much in common with the other songs recorded for *Wild in the Country*, and it's not surprising it was cut. It was among the cuts on *Elvis for Everyone*.

"Sound Advice" (Recorded July 2, 1961)

A silly acoustic ditty, Elvis asked for this to be taken off the *Follow That Dream* EP for reasons of quality. His wishes were granted, but that didn't stop it from being in the film, nor on the 1965 *Elvis for Everyone* collection. In all fairness, it was meant as a kids' song and works well under that description. The issue is Elvis recording kids' songs in the first place.

"For the Millionth and the Last Time" (Recorded October 15, 1961)

Elvis the Latin-styled crooner strikes again. The fact that the lyric is unimaginative, and that the song had nothing new to say musically, led to it being excluded from the *Pot Luck* LP. *Elvis for Everyone* eventually gave it a home, but even among the other out-takes it was still pretty weak. Elvis sang his 1961 tracks with good focus, but a worrying number of the songs didn't match the standards of years past.

"I Met Her Today" (Recorded October 16, 1961)

Another *Pot Luck* reject, this also first saw the light of day on *Elvis for Everyone*. Though Elvis' seventies work has been dragged through the mud for lacking guts, the truly wimpy material was the lesser early-sixties ballads. This has moments where Elvis' voice is lovely, but it seems to be a second-rate "Anything That's Part of You," which had been recorded the previous night. The harmonized intro and outro are a nice touch, but "I Met Her Today" plays things light and safe.

"Dainty Little Moonbeams" (Recorded March 28, 1962)

A lot of songs were recorded for *Girls! Girls! Girls!* Some were used in the film but not the LP, and there were also a few songs on the album but not in the movie. "Dainty Little Moonbeams" missed out on the LP as it was inserted into a reprise of the "Girls! Girls! Girls!" song that wouldn't have made sense on vinyl. Really just a Chinese stereotype of the title song, this short fragment is found with the "Girls! Girls! Girls!" reprise on the FTD version of the soundtrack. Vinyl fans should seek out the excellent *Elvis Rocks and the Girls Roll* bootleg.

"Plantation Rock" (Recorded March 28, 1962)

This is an excellent song that fell through the cracks. It has a hypnotic guitar line, an appealing smattering of drums backed with tambourine, and a premium performance from Elvis. If the lyrical attempt to start a new dance craze dates it slightly, by 1962 Elvis was rarely getting material this good on his regular sessions—let alone on a soundtrack. Despite rivaling "Return to Sender" as single material, "Plantation Rock" was unceremoniously dropped from *Girls! Girls! Girls!* It was a matter of too many songs being recorded for the movie, and whoever decided on the final edit making a poor judgment call.

Even after it was rejected, Elvis believed "Plantation Rock" was worth salvaging. He asked Red West to rewrite it as something a little less gimmicky, and West indeed went on to pen a lyrical remake called "We're Gonna Have a Good Time" for use on Elvis' next record date. Regrettably, by the time the next non-soundtrack session occurred, fourteen months later, "We're Gonna Have a Good Time" had been forgotten. The original "Plantation Rock" surfaced soon after Elvis' death on a bootleg LP of the same name. There was some surface noise, as their source was an acetate, and they also did a bad edit to lengthen it, but it was a standout new Elvis song that was all but unknown. RCA put it on the 1983 *Legendary Performer Volume 4* record, but they accidentally made a sloppy edit that shortened the track. The real edit surfaced, also in 1983, on the *Memphis, Tennessee* bootleg. For vinyl collectors, this is the recommended source; others should seek out the *Girls! Girls! Girls!* FTD CD.

"Mama" (Recorded March 28, 1962)

Replaced by "We'll Be Together" in *Girls! Girls! Girls!*, this is a decidedly old world–flavored cut, with an over-the-top intro and outro by the Amigos (who sang on the soundtrack) grafted uncomfortably onto Elvis' master. Though it's far less interesting than "Plantation Rock," it came out years earlier, on the 1970 *Let's Be Friends* LP.

"Finders Keepers, Losers Weepers" (Recorded May 26, 1963)

A victim of the canceled 1963 studio LP, this wasn't held back for reasons of quality. A pop/rock selection, "Finders Keepers, Losers Weepers" plays off a few common sayings in an inoffensive manner. It's not anything grand, but would have been a solid album cut—and still acted as such when released on *Elvis for Everyone.*

"Night Life" (Recorded July 9, 1963)

It's a huge compliment to the *Viva Las Vegas* sessions to say that they were as good as the regular studio recordings Elvis was doing at the time—and something that can't be said about any other soundtrack past 1961. "Night Life" was an out-take from the film, a fairly convincing rocker that is only lacking in that the lyrics cover much the same ground as the superior title track. This was likely the reason it first emerged in 1968, on an LP with the ungainly title *Singer Presents Elvis Singing Flaming Star and Others.*

"Do the Vega" (Recorded July 10, 1963)

This is yet another Latin-flavored song, but it provides a change of pace in that it's an up-tempo dance novelty. It's slight, but well executed. Excised from *Viva Las Vegas*, it was included on the *Singer Presents Elvis* collection.

"The Climb" (Recorded July 11, 1963)

Viva Las Vegas was a musical in the true sense of the word in that Elvis, as well as his co-stars Ann-Margret and the Jubilee Four, all got the opportunity to perform. For this number by the Jubilee Four, it turned out that three of them weren't miming to their own voices. With only lead singer George McFadden participating at the recording session, the backing vocals were handed off to the Jordanaires and Elvis himself. It is easily the finest song in an Elvis movie that Presley doesn't do the lead on. He and Ann dance to this slow, churning number about a third of the way into the film, on the "Swingers Club" set.

Despite the strength of this song—and almost the entire soundtrack—Parker decided against a *Viva Las Vegas* LP. It's likely that he didn't want to give another artist prominence on an Elvis Presley record (a rule he broke only once, in 1968, for Nancy Sinatra). What the Colonel didn't understand was that the inclusion of George McFadden and Ann-Margret would have added considerably to the sales appeal of the album, making for a truly authentic soundtrack. Yet with a few of Elvis' songs dropped from the movie, and Parker not wanting to take away the spotlight from "his boy" with the other singers, only six songs immediately surfaced.

Getting the entire soundtrack released in its intended form took some doing. A bootleg from 1978 looked great but was mainly just taped off the actual film. In 1983, the songs were grouped together on a picture disc that featured all of the previously released songs on one side and the *Jailhouse Rock* soundtrack on the other. In 2010, a proper *Viva Las Vegas* soundtrack LP was issued by the excellent Music on Vinyl label. "The Climb" wasn't included on that, but it was included on the FTD vinyl edition of *Viva Las Vegas* issued later that year. Both twenty-first-century records were first released on CD then remastered for LP, as vinyl began a resurgence.

"Santa Lucia" (Recorded July 11, 1963)

Only a minute long, this was seen in *Viva Las Vegas* but was considered too minor to be released on the EP. Fitting into the movie, Elvis does this traditional number in Italian. It's not a great record, but it obviously wasn't conceived as one. It helped pad out *Elvis for Everyone*.

"Yellow Rose of Texas"/"The Eyes of Texas" (Recorded July 11, 1963)

A strange choice for a movie set in Las Vegas, this medley was far more entertaining as part of a comedic scene than it is as a record. Being that it's obviously done with tongue planted solidly in cheek, it is excusable, if decidedly moronic. It first made it to vinyl on the *Singer Presents Elvis* LP.

"The Lady Loves Me" (Recorded July 11, 1963)

"The Lady Loves Me" is a puerile song, but in the context of *Viva Las Vegas* it worked visually, because Elvis and Ann had a great chemistry together. Sung as a duet, it was written as a lighthearted verbal spar between the duo. Despite not being too hot, "The Lady Loves Me" was the first *Viva Las Vegas* out-take that came out after Elvis' death. It was included on the *Legendary Performer Volume 4* album, and it now finds a home on both the Music on Vinyl and FTD soundtracks.

"You're the Boss" (Recorded July 11, 1963)

If the chemistry heard on "The Lady Loves Me" was tepid, "You're the Boss" sizzles. Elvis and Ann sound quite intimate on this slinky Leiber and Stoller rhythm-and-blues song, trading lines in an openly erotic fashion. Cut from the film, it didn't come out until the early nineties, presumably because it was too hot for the sensibilities of 1964. That's a bona fide indignity, as "You're the Boss" is one of Elvis' best film songs—and one of his most steamy studio performances. Ann sounds quite sexy herself.

"Memphis, Tennessee" (Recorded January 12, 1964)

Elvis first cut this during his 1963 non-soundtrack session in a slightly heavier manner. The 1964 cut for once took the Latin rhythm out, and Elvis voiced his lead in a slightly higher pitch than normal. With Elvis careful to hold the reveal that the subject of the song is his daughter (not his wife) until the very end of the track, the story comes across stronger here than in other renditions of this seminal Chuck Berry composition. It was gentler than one might expect, but that only makes this version of "Memphis" more unique. Had it been released in a timely fashion, it likely would have been the hit Elvis thought it could be. Instead, it had to settle for being a highlight of *Elvis for Everyone*.

"Roustabout" (Recorded March 3, 1964)

As Elvis' movies stopped reflecting his natural musical instincts, his regular teams of songwriters would get told to write a song of a specific title to fit into a particular scene. This meant that the songwriters were set against each other, in a contest of sorts, to get in on the action. Elvis was left to pick the best out of the demos, and record whatever version of a "title" he deemed best. Sometimes it was hard to decide what worked best for the movie and the album, and they weren't always the same thing. On the *Kissin' Cousins* project, Elvis simply used two songs as the title track, but when two versions of the title song for *Roustabout* came along, one got the axe.

The original "Roustabout" was surprising in that it's a great song for the period. Giving Elvis a chance to growl a little like the old days, the rock-and-roll beat was genuine. It was becoming distressingly predictable by 1964 that business took on far more importance to Elvis' management than quality. Two things caused its disappearance. First, it was very mildly rebellious lyrically, and somebody high-level might have taken offense. The second (more likely) scenario was that songwriters Otis Blackwell and Winfield Scott were being pushed out of the picture after a publishing split. Bernie Baum, Bill Giant, and Florence Kaye came up with the replacement, but it was a cotton candy–light piece of pop that Elvis seemed wary of. The Blackwell/Scott version didn't come out until 2003, as "I'm a Roustabout," on the *2nd to None* LP/CD.

"She's a Machine" (Recorded September 29, 1966)

Considering that it is an out-take from the wretched *Easy Come, Easy Go* sessions, this is a shockingly decent rocker. It's not particularly imaginative, and other than a reference to marijuana ("pot-taking machine"), it was hopelessly out of date. However, Elvis was hungry to cut anything resembling rock and roll, and his valiant attempt to bring this song to life lifts it out of the doldrums. It made its initial vinyl outing on *Singer Presents Elvis.*

"Leave My Woman Alone" (Recorded September 29, 1966)

Elvis planned at one point to include this Ray Charles song in his film *Easy Come, Easy Go,* but he ultimately picked "You Gotta Stop" in its place. Elvis never did his lead vocal, but he is among the backup singers on the surviving music track. It sounds like he is having fun with the gospel timing, but perhaps he realized that he couldn't do the song justice under the circumstances. It's a pity he didn't return to it at one of his regular recording dates, as this was the type of song Elvis could have put his stamp on. The FTD release of *Easy Come, Easy Go* was the first time this ever saw the light of day.

"All I Needed Was the Rain" (Recorded October 2, 1967)

Stay Away, Joe was a turning point for Elvis. It was the first movie to break the formulaic pattern of his films in six years. The sense of overall improvement can be felt in most of the songs, particularly the atmospheric "All I Needed Was the Rain." It's a nice piece of blues, with a wailing harmonica by Charlie McCoy and a tidy arrangement. Elvis sings this with the kind of commitment he gave his regular cuts, and he comes close to the quality he had achieved at his non-soundtrack date the month before.

"Dominic" (Recorded October 2, 1967)

This is also from the *Stay Away, Joe* soundtrack, and represents the one time Elvis actually asked a song not come out—even if he died! Sung to a bull that is impotent (you read right), the plopping sound effects make this one literally a stinker. Actually, the ambience reflects the improved conditions that began with this flick, but it still is intrinsically lame. At the turn of the century, Castle Music put out a series of Elvis soundtracks on vinyl and included bonus EPs of some of the shorter soundtracks with almost all of them. Check out their version of *Blue Hawaii* to hear the otherwise respectable *Stay Away, Joe* soundtrack in a way that would have fit right in with the times, had the American market not abandoned the EP format.

"Stay Away, Joe" (Recorded October 2, 1967)

Reflecting the loose ambience found in the film, "Stay Away, Joe" is a goofy hoedown that Elvis sings with a laugh in his voice. This isn't a quality offering in any shape or form, but at least it didn't resemble the bland movie songs of years past. First released on *Let's Be Friends*, an even looser alternate take was mistakenly issued on the first pressing of the 1970 Camden collection *Almost in Love*, in place of the intended "Stay Away."

"Too Much Monkey Business" (Recorded January 15, 1968)

Cut in the same vein as the "Big Boss Man" and "Guitar Man" 45s, this has Jerry Reed back and picking some fine acoustic guitar. A first-rate cover of Chuck Berry's 1956 single, Elvis' performance is gutsy and personable. A reference to Vietnam is thrown in, but the atmosphere is nothing less than exuberant. Possessing a fast-talking lead over a pounding, circular rhythm, that Elvis was recommitted to cutting premium Southern rock makes his comeback seem inevitable. It deserved to be placed on a better project than *Singer Presents Elvis*.

"Wonderful World" (Recorded March 7, 1968)

Sounding like something out of a children's musical, this waltz was the worst inclusion in the *Live a Little, Love a Little* score. Elvis tries his level best, but there wasn't much substance he could hold on to. It was a part of the *Singer Presents Elvis* LP.

"Tiger Man" (Recorded June 27, 1968)

This is a showstopper. Elvis sounds like he's going on pure adrenalin on this cut from the second "sit down" show, taped for what was to become known as Elvis' comeback performance. Only a handful Elvis recordings rock this feverishly hard, and it only takes the three-minute duration to understand how Elvis got himself back on top. "Tiger Man" remained a fine addition to Elvis' set, and he would usually combine it with "Mystery Train."

Intriguingly, on some of the occasions he performed it alone, Elvis would introduce "Tiger Man" as his second record that very few people ever heard. This was done more than once, and one has to wonder if it was first recorded during a Sun session. Sam didn't keep great records of songs that were ultimately rejected, and it could indeed have been what Elvis briefly considered for his second Sun single. There's very little hope that a session tape will turn up, but there could be an acetate waiting to be found.

"Tiger Man" was included in the original cut of the NBC special, but on Parker's mandate it was pushed aside on the initial airing by "Blue Christmas." This astounding recording didn't deserve to be relegated to the *Singer Presents Elvis* LP.

"Let's Forget About the Stars" (Recorded October 15, 1968)

It's hard to say where this would have fit into the movie *Charro!* Elvis had finished shooting the film by this point, and the lyrics point to a scene in the already released *Live a Little, Love a Little.* Despite Elvis' voice being strong on all his 1968 recordings, this is a poor excuse for a song. Most annoying is a percussion part (maracas?) that sounds like a cross between sandpaper and someone going "sit sit sit sit." The piano is off-key, too. It was unleashed to the world on the *Let's Be Friends* LP.

"Swing Down Sweet Chariot" (Recorded October 21, 1968)

This only gets onto this list as it was recorded a full eight years after the original was cut and issued. *The Trouble with Girls* was a perfectly serviceable Elvis movie, as was the soundtrack. It followed the recent pattern of fewer songs and more story, but with the EP format dead in America, most of the songs didn't come out until the eighties and nineties.

If anything, this improved on the original, as Elvis' voice had matured nicely. It begins and ends with a few seconds of fantastic harmony between Presley and the Mello Men. A magnificent hidden treasure, only the fact that the title had come out before stopped it being released at the time.

"Signs of the Zodiac" (Recorded October 21, 1968)

A silly duet with co-star Marlyn Mason, this is much more entertaining in the film than on record. RCA probably didn't issue it as Elvis only does about a third of the lead. It's dumb, but at least Elvis sounds in good humor.

"The Whiffenpoof Song"/"Violet" (Recorded October 21, 1968)

This medley fits the era the movie took place in quite well, but it wouldn't have made sense outside of a soundtrack album or EP. As there was no soundtrack, this didn't come out until the nineties. Musically, the only tie to Elvis' past is that "Violet" used the melody of "Aura Lee," a.k.a. "Love Me Tender." Once again, a Castle Music vinyl Elvis soundtrack (*Jailhouse Rock*) had a bonus EP that collected everything together in a fashion befitting the era. If one does not want to spring for a Complete Masters box, the EP is a sensible way to hear the *Trouble with Girls* soundtrack.

"Poor Man's Gold" (Recorded January 21, 1969)

Elvis had to stop midway through the American Sound Studio sessions due to a sore throat. When he came back, he had quite a few songs that had only guide vocals from either himself or studio pianist Bobby Wood. There were a few selections Elvis never took the time to repair, but this was not one of them. Elvis did indeed begin to record his lead, but he stopped after one line to laugh at a passing ambulance that ruined the take. Seemingly not totally behind the song, which was close in tone to some of the lesser adult-contemporary cuts from the period, he moved on and never returned to it. Surprisingly not used on an FTD release, it only officially appeared on the out-of-print CD *Suspicious Minds: The Memphis 1969 Anthology*.

"I'll Be There" (Recorded January 23, 1969)

Strangely overlooked when Elvis' Memphis albums were compiled, this gem was wasted on the *Let's Be Friends* collection. A Bobby Darin composition and record from 1960, Elvis' version is a nice blend of country and pop, held together with the soul-infused playing of the American Sound Studio musicians. It may not have been top-side single material, but it contains a markedly commercial element that would have made it perfect for a flip. A happy Elvis can't stop humming and scatting along during the instrumental passages.

"It's My Way (of Loving You)"/"This Time"/"I Can't Stop Loving You" (Recorded February 16, 1969)

This semi-random medley bursts with the good humor around the Memphis sessions. Webb Pierce had a hit with the first selection, which Elvis only touches on briefly. "This Time" was a composition by Chips Moman that Troy Shondell had a hit with, and which Elvis does here as a tribute to his producer. It's got a nice sound, but Elvis only really got going on "I Can't Stop Loving You," a song he would include a sizzling version of in his live shows. This impromptu take captures the same energy.

"If I'm a Fool (for Loving You)" (Recorded February 21, 1969)

Bobby Wood was part of the house band at American Sound and acted as Elvis' piano player during the session. Elvis' father liked Wood's 1964 minor hit 45 "If I'm a Fool (for Loving You)," and that played a role in Elvis cutting it. The presence of Wood doubtless spurred Presley on, and both turn in a beautiful performance. Elvis' guitar style was distinct, partly because of how hard he hit the chords, and it's one of the charms of this rendition. It's not the most stunning cut of the period, but this mellow country excursion was better than a few of the songs used on *Back in Memphis*. It wasn't on the album as Elvis didn't like how it turned out. It ended up on *Let's Be Friends*.

"Who Am I?" (Recorded February 22, 1969)

This is the song that brought the Memphis sessions to their conclusion. There's nothing wrong with this gospel ballad, but it isn't stunning. Bobby Emmons gets the sound of a church organ down well, the melody is fine, and Elvis sounds sincere enough. Other than the lyric being slightly wordy, it hard to pinpoint why it doesn't gel. Elvis' singing recalls the *His Hand in Mine* album, but by 1969 his voice had deepened to where a more powerful lower key would've given the song more sustenance. This recording can be found on the 1971 Camden LP *You'll Never Walk Alone*.

"Change of Habit" (Recorded March 5, 1969)

Change of Habit was Elvis' last acting role, and its recording sessions brought a long overdue end to the soundtracks. Elvis made some mediocre records after this, but not one is as banal as the worst of his sixties film recordings. The sessions specifically held for *Change of Habit* were all released on the budget RCA

Camden label LP *Let's Be Friends.* This title song wasn't up to Elvis' new standard, but self-consciously modern lyric aside, "Change of Habit" isn't bad. Funky, with a stinging bass line, you can actually picture Elvis doing his gyrations as the song speeds up at the close.

"Let's Be Friends" (Recorded March 5, 1969)

What a comedown from the Memphis sessions this is! In 1969, Elvis was so on top of things that he even gives this otherwise abysmal song a little heart. The piano doesn't sound like it has been tuned correctly, and the sentiments are right off a greeting card. It's easy to see why this was cut from the film. It is also to be found on—surprise—the *Let's Be Friends* LP.

"Have a Happy" (Recorded March 6, 1969)

If the rest of the *Change of Habit* sessions are redeemed to an extent by Elvis' strong performances, this is unbearable. Cutesy piano, wretched lyrics, and a forgettable melody make this the last complete out-and-out travesty Elvis cut. Even if it is meant as a kids' song, it didn't have to be appalling to appeal to children. It became the feeble closing track on *Let's Be Friends.*

"Happy Birthday" (Recorded August 21, 1969)

Once in a while, Elvis would sing "Happy Birthday" to one of his band members, or someone in the audience. The 1991 *Collectors Gold* LP/CD set captures Elvis dedicating it to James Burton. It isn't more than one verse, but it's mentioned here as it had long been a favorite on the bootleg circuit.

"Let Us Pray" (Recorded September 26, 1969)

Though Elvis had first recorded this song, along with the other songs from his film *Change of Habit,* back in March, he took the chance to redo his vocals at an overdubbing session, which mostly consisted of him replacing some recent leads that he felt he could do better. Lacking the excitement of Elvis' best gospel work, it was originally released on the *You'll Never Walk Alone* album.

"I Didn't Make It on Playing Guitar" (Recorded June 6, 1970)

In the midst of one of his most productive series of sessions, an invigorated Elvis led the band on this rocking improvised jam. The only lyrics that appear are Elvis' shouting out the title eventually given to it by BMG (the company that owned RCA for a period). This can currently be found on the FTD LP/CD *Elvis Country.*

"Ghost Riders in the Sky" (Recorded July 15, 1970)

Elvis sings a little off mic, but this selection from the *That's the Way It Is* rehearsals is a fun if sloppy jam. It gets a good Johnny Cash–styled groove going, though funnily enough Cash wasn't to record it for nearly a decade. It was included on the CD that came with the FTD book *The Way It Was* in 2001.

"Alla En El Rancho Grande" (Recorded July 15, 1970)

How this made the 1995 *Walk a Mile in My Shoes* boxed set over the many superior songs Elvis ran through during the *T.T.W.I.I.* rehearsals can only be explained by the fact that it was a "new" selection. It's just Elvis goofing off, and not all that entertaining to hear more than once. On the other hand, it is indicative of just how wide Elvis' musical palate was that he even knew such an obscure Spanish song from the twenties.

"Cottonfields" (Recorded July 15, 1970)

Included on the thirtieth anniversary LP/CD boxed set of *That's the Way It Is*, Elvis' sprightly run-through of this Leadbelly classic is off the cuff but charming. A seasoned musician can pick up any song quickly, and these rehearsals document just how worthy the people Elvis had with him were. The song had recently been covered by the Beach Boys and Creedence Clearwater Revival, but Elvis' version is more souped-up country than a reflection of either of those contemporary recordings.

"Cattle Call" (Recorded July 29, 1970)

Elvis messed with this Eddy Arnold number a few times during the *T.T.W.I.I.* rehearsals. It's no more than a brief example of Elvis' humor, but it made for a fun moment on the 1992 *Lost Performances* VHS tape. The audio first came out on the *Platinum* CD set in 1997.

"Froggy Went a Courtin'" (Recorded July 29, 1970)

A minor jam, Elvis only fooled around with this old folk song. He mostly does it at double speed, but it seems to go on forever. It was another extremely odd addition to 1995's *Walk a Mile in My Shoes*, the CD boxed set supposed to represent the essential seventies Elvis recordings. That this and not "Early Morning Rain" was included proves the old axiom that one man's trash is one man's treasure. Essential it ain't!

"Oh Happy Day" (Recorded August 7, 1970)

Taken from an onstage rehearsal at the International, Elvis gives this gospel cut—a recent pop hit for the Edwin Hawkins Singers—a soulful spin. The Sweet Inspirations seem to enjoy their tight interplay with Elvis, especially during the passionate middle eight. This somewhat muddy recording was first officially heard on the *That's the Way It Is* thirtieth-anniversary vinyl and CD boxed set. It was done live at least once during the upcoming Vegas engagement. Most notably, a nearly identical recording from August 14th appeared on the *Command Performance* bootleg LP.

"Men with Broken Hearts" (Recorded August 11, 1970)

As far as can be ascertained, this is the only time Elvis performed this Hank Williams monologue onstage. It made for a moving introduction to "Walk a Mile in My Shoes," but it was also indicative of Elvis' roots and general worldview. It was an inspired choice to open the *Lost Performances* VHS release, and it finally made it onto record on the 2001 *Live in Las Vegas* LP/CD boxed set.

"When the Snow Is on the Roses" (Recorded August 24, 1970)

It was common for Elvis, when he was in Reno or Las Vegas, to introduce the celebrities that attended his show each night. Ed Ames was in the audience on this occasion, and Elvis quickly improvised a version of Ed's hit "When the Snow Is on the Roses." It came together quite well, and was captured on an audience tape. The fidelity isn't great, but it's an interesting, slightly country-tinged performance that first saw the light of day on the 1970 *Hillbilly Cat Live* double-LP bootleg. It was officially put out thirty-one years later on the LP/CD boxed set collection *Live in Las Vegas*.

"The Lord's Prayer" (Recorded May 16, 1971)

Elvis was in a jamming mood at his May 1971 sessions, and several finished tracks resulted from his spur of the moment inspirations. "The Lord's Prayer" finds Elvis singing a cappella. His voice sounds raw and uncertain, but he sings this with an amazing amount of depth and feeling. This isn't a polished performance, but, had it been worked on, it could have been terrific. This was cut in the middle of "I'll Be Home on Christmas Day" and retains some of its earthy feel. It is on both the *Wonderful World of Christmas* and *He Touched Me* FTD albums.

"Lady Madonna" (Recorded May 17, 1971)

Ringo Starr once attested that Paul McCartney was trying to sound like Elvis on this 1968 Beatles hit. Indeed, this old-fashioned rocker seems tailor made for

Presley, but based on the evidence here it was the Fats Domino cover that he connected with. This jam wasn't close to being a serious contender for release, though Elvis and the musicians sound wonderful playing it. Look for it on the *Elvis Now* FTD.

"I Shall Be Released" (Recorded May 20, 1971)

This shouldn't be seen as a fully fledged out-take, but it's remarkable how tuned-in to Bob Dylan Elvis was. Recorded between the takes of "It's Only Love," the potential shown here makes one mourn the fact that a proper folk album didn't result from these sessions. The way Elvis says the name "Dylan" at the end demonstrates a great reverence for his work. It is to be found on the *Elvis Now* FTD.

"My Way" (Recorded June 10, 1971)

Not as emotional as later live renditions, "My Way" still gave Elvis a chance to show off the maturation of his voice and music. This comparatively stiff studio rendition likely would have been used on the *Fool* LP, had Elvis not included it in his *Aloha* set—indeed, it is now included on the FTD version of the *Fool* album. Hearing this with a studio ambience is a nice change of pace, but as found here it was unlikely to become one of Elvis' signature tunes. Still, it didn't deserve to sit on a shelf for more than two decades.

"For the Good Times" (Recorded March 27, 1972)

This was the only studio track from the unreleased *Standing Room Only* album that didn't get reused in short order. Likely this is because Presley recorded a version for *Elvis as Recorded at Madison Square Garden* LP, which was performed and released that June. It's a pity, as this studio recording is definitive. "For the Good Times" reflects both the tasteful arrangements and Elvis' own strong engagement during this session. It's astounding that over twenty years passed before it saw the light of day. Today, "For the Good Times" is best heard on the FTD LP and CD release of what was most likely to be the original *Standing Room Only*.

"You Better Run" (Recorded March 31, 1972)

Performed as part of—but excised from—the gospel jam featured in *Elvis on Tour*, this is another delightful song in the jubilee tradition. It was done onstage a few times in tandem with "Bosom of Abraham," and Elvis' arrangements on both were basically identical. In light of this, "You Better Run" can be viewed as a fine variation on one of Elvis' best gospel recordings. It first came out on the

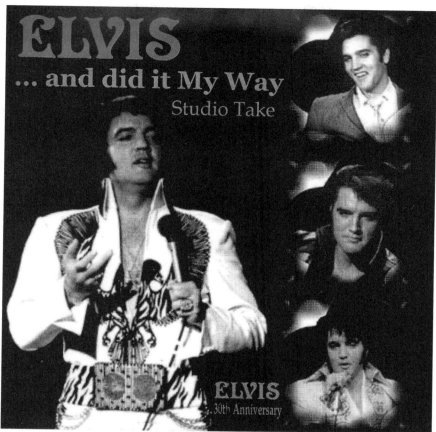

Elvis' stiff 1971 studio version of "My Way" didn't get a vinyl release until this bootleg 45 came out in 2007. Elvis left the session in a huff because the studio singers weren't paying attention; a few more takes would have made for a good record. The main photo was taken in June 1975.

CD *Amazing Grace* in 1994, and was later issued on the *Peace in the Valley* LP/CD boxed set in 2000.

"Turn Your Eyes upon Jesus"/"Nearer My God to Thee" (Recorded March 31, 1972)

Coming at the end of the gospel numbers loosely performed for the *Elvis on Tour* cameras, this beautiful medley has Elvis singing with tremendous volume and power. The official recording is edited to run a bit more smoothly, and the volume levels are brought down on Elvis' voice because it sounded distorted on the louder passages. This version debuted on the 1994 *Amazing Grace* CD, and was also included in the 2000 LP/CD boxed set *Peace in the Valley*. Oddly enough, a promo-only 45 of the unedited master was issued in 1989 by the legitimate Creative Radio Shows run by Elvis fan Jerry Osborne. It doesn't have any mention of RCA on it, so it must only have only been allowed because it wasn't released commercially. It was largely given away with a three-LP set of all the non-musical *Elvis on Tour* out-takes Osborne had access to.

"Portrait of My Love" (Recorded August 3, 1972)

Straight pop always had an influence on what Elvis sang, and here he tackles the 1961 Steve Lawrence hit "Portrait of My Love." There were plenty of fine singers in the pre-rock tradition that continued to sell records throughout the sixties, but a comparison between this and Lawrence's version makes a quiet point about why Elvis was so important to the overall development of music.

Before Elvis came along, all but the most inventive pop singers were focused on traditional technique, recording polished product. Elvis made it OK for pop to be more raw, and "Portrait of My Love" is but one of the many times he proved that emotion could elevate a song far beyond a performance with mere technical perfection. This short run-through isn't a major moment in Elvis' career, but it is an example of what his personal vision made possible. It was first issued on the 2011 FTD label CD *Stage Rehearsal*.

"I'm Leavin' It All Up to You" (Recorded January 25, 1973)

When Elvis wanted to add this R&B and pop standard to his early 1972 set, he requested a set of lyrics from his publishers Hill & Range. Proving to still be oblivious to their artist's tastes, longtime liaison Freddy Bienstock made a note on the delivered sheet music that Elvis couldn't possibly want this type of material.

Recorded the day before he opened his eighth monthlong Vegas run in three and a half years, it was—like much of what Elvis was doing at the time—a somewhat mild rendition. Despite that, he comes across as far more dedicated than during most of his shows in the month to follow. The title song of a popular 1978 bootleg, "I'm Leavin' It All Up to You" finally came out officially on the FTD CD from 2011, *Stage Rehearsal*.

"It's Diff'rent Now" (Recorded July 21, 1973)

Only a rehearsal of this exists, because Elvis decided not to do the song before recording formal takes. It does sound fairly finished as it stands, but "It's

Diff'rent Now" has little to recommend it. It's a dreary ballad that didn't fit in with most of the other recordings Elvis was doing at the session. It can be found in the best context on the FTD issue of *Raised on Rock*.

"You Can Have Her" (Recorded May 11, 1974)

Elvis' tour shows before the fall of 1974 were entertaining on the whole, and you never knew what he might do on any given appearance. One such one-off performance came during his matinee 1974 Los Angeles concert, when he pulled out Roy Hamilton's "You Can Have Her." Elvis had likely had the band rehearse this for the tour, and he turns in a nicely rocking rendition that should have been given more than one (known) airing. It was featured on the CD included with the FTD book *Live in L.A.*

"The Twelfth of Never" (Recorded August 16, 1974)

Nearly making the U.K. Top 20 when released as a 45 in 1995, this recording was taken from the *Walk a Mile in My Shoes* CD boxed set, which featured cuts from Elvis' seventies sessions and shows. Elvis was trying to change the format of his concerts at this time, and although that ultimately didn't work out, he did keep a number of new songs in his set. "The Twelfth of Never" didn't even make to the stage; this version stems from an interesting rehearsal Elvis held exactly three years before he died. It's not stunningly innovative, but Elvis' performance is melodic and pretty. Had he held a session that year, this would have been a decent choice for it.

"Aubrey" (Recorded September 2, 1974)

Taken from the infamous closing show of Elvis' summer 1974 Hilton engagement, this is a cover of a song by the group Bread. It's very similar to Presley's version of "Softly as I Leave You" in that Sherrill Nielsen sings lead while Elvis recites the lyrics. It's an oddity, but nothing amazing. A good example of Elvis' willingness to try out new things that summer, it was released on the FTD CD *From Sunset to Las Vegas* in 2010.

"You're the Reason I'm Living" (Recorded March 22, 1975)

Elvis liked Bobby Darin's work but recorded only a few of his songs. This is done fairly off the cuff, but Elvis and the band had rehearsed it for this Las Vegas engagement, so the arrangement is thought-out. It isn't extraordinary, but it is a good version that is refreshing in that it was only performed once (that we know of). It was issued on the LP/CD boxed set *Live in Las Vegas* in 2001.

"Jambalaya" (Recorded May 4, 1975)

At his evening show in Lake Charles, Louisiana, Elvis threw in about a minute of this Bayou-infused Hank Williams cut. It clearly wasn't rehearsed, but it's a fun moment that demonstrates Elvis' continued ability to improvise onstage. It was released on the FTD CD *Southern Nights* in 2006.

"School Days" (Recorded June 6, 1975)

Released on the eight-record set *Elvis Aron Presley* in 1980 under the title "Long Live Rock and Roll"—with the wrong author credited—Elvis sang this Chuck Berry song during his band introductions from 1975 up through his penultimate tour. With Elvis only singing the chorus, it can't be called any more than decent.

"Auld Lang Syne" (Recorded December 31, 1976)

Taken from Elvis' last landmark concert, this was sung to ring in 1977. The double-LP bootleg *Rockin' with Elvis New Year's Eve* is still a classic, but this recording can be obtained legally (with a few sound glitches) on the 2003 FTD CD *New Year's Eve*.

16

It Hurts Me

1964

I f Elvis already seemed behind the times, the arrival of the Beatles effectively made him irrelevant to teens. He still appealed enough to his original fans to make *Viva Las Vegas* a smash, but the poor marketing of the soundtrack meant that it wasn't on the radar for the majority of radio listeners and record buyers. His albums still charted high, but he would only hit the Top 10 singles chart a half-dozen more times. It didn't have to be this way. A short session at the beginning of the year showed that Elvis could have remained a contender, if not for his focus on films and soundtracks that were becoming garbage.

After his studio date in January, it would be over two years before Elvis recorded anything not connected to his movie career. In the face of new blood, Elvis all but surrendered. He had been put in a situation where he would have had to make a major stink not to do so. The defeated King was becoming less likely to rock the boat, and in a 1972 interview he took full blame for what happened. Elvis' own culpability isn't in doubt, but Presley would have never been offered these roles or songs in the first place had his management, his publishers, or Hollywood itself given a damn about him as an artist or a person.

Studio Work

Elvis' sole non-soundtrack session of the year consisted of only three songs. Since his last album hadn't been released, it seems that Elvis now felt that making another one wasn't worth his time. This didn't mean he didn't want to put out quality singles, however, and that was the point of booking this date. Arguably the least notable of the three cuts, "Ask Me" ended up being the only song put out as an A-side. It hovered around the Top 10, but an organ-based ballad wasn't what was needed to make inroads against the British Invasion the Beatles had initiated. It was pretty, but it didn't match up to the slower-paced singles Elvis put out from 1958 to 1962.

"It Hurts Me," on the other hand, may have bettered them all. Elvis had rarely sung with such authority or passion before, yet this song was put out on the flip side of the wretched "Kissin' Cousins." "Memphis, Tennessee" was the track Elvis really wanted to put out as a 45, but he was keen to hold it back until the right time. Johnny Rivers had a hit with it before Elvis could get his version out, Presley having played Rivers his version beforehand. Though some have accused Rivers of trying to kill Elvis' chance at a hit, Rivers strongly professes his innocence. Regardless of the circumstances, the Rivers record meant that Elvis' "Memphis" was relegated to the *Elvis for Everyone* LP the following year, where it sat without comment.

Elvis had only two more sessions this year, recording the *Roustabout* and *Girl Happy* soundtrack albums. *Roustabout* did very well to reach #1, likely on the strength of his cover of the Coasters' "Little Egypt." It isn't good, but it is somewhat less painful than most of Elvis' mid-sixties LPs. Along with the R&B-infused "Little Egypt," some decent pop appeared in the form of tracks like "One Track Heart," "Poison Ivy League," and "Big Love Big Heartache." Otherwise, it was as bad as usual, as typified by the fluff of "Carny Town" and "It's Carnival Time."

Girl Happy was another new low. Marking the point were his albums were no longer technically competent, Elvis' voice was sped up on several of the tracks, and all of them had his singing drowning out the band. Things like the title song fall into the category of "so bad it's good," but it would be much funnier if this album were a lone anomaly.

On Celluloid

Roustabout attempted to give Elvis a role with more of an edge, but the rebellion seems contrived. Story-wise, this tale of intrigue on the carnival circuit isn't much, but the (at times mildly racy) dialogue is decent, and the actors, including Barbara Stanwyck, give their characters some depth. It's a little old-fashioned-looking, as far as hair and style goes, but *Roustabout* is something that can be shown to casual fans without too much embarrassment. For an unintentional laugh, watch for the scene where Barbara Stanwyck passionately defends the carnival as not being a circus.

Considering how dire the music is, *Girl Happy* plays a lot better than it should. The colors are bright and very sixties, the actors are attractive and competent, and there were a few moments that are funny. Elvis looks good, and has a nice chemistry with Shelley Fabares, who does a sexy, G-rated striptease. Elvis gets to explore his sexuality, too, in a scene he does—for comedic effect—in drag. The electric guitars may be plugged into the sand, but for a Fort Lauderdale beach movie, this isn't a bad one.

Tickle Me has even less reason to work. Elvis has a developing belly, the production was cheap, and the premise of Elvis being an out-of-work rodeo rider moonlighting at a woman's health ranch is insane. Yet this is a funny—even lovable—movie. The songs were good, as they come from Elvis' early-sixties non-movie albums. The staging may often be poor, but it was nice to hear authentic Presley music for a change.

The clever script was written by Edward Bernds and Elwood Ullman, who were responsible for many of the best mid-period Three Stooges shorts and went on to do a few of their features. Taking its cue from Stooges films like *Out West*, the most amusing sequences have Elvis doing refurbished versions of their old routines with his co-star Jack Mullaney. Speaking of co-stars, Jocelyn Lane was one of Elvis' best-looking cinematic romantic interests, and she had personality as well.

Popularity and Impact

Commercially, Elvis was still a relative success, but he was no longer defining the times. *Kissin' Cousins* did decent business, but it was the very worst film one could release in the wake of the Beatles coming to America. Even fans were hard pressed to find any redeeming qualities in what they could no longer deny was a career in creative free fall. The stylish and appropriate *Viva Las Vegas* almost made up for it, but it was a shame that a *Viva Las Vegas* album was not issued until the twenty-first century.

It was a huge mistake to not release a *Viva Las Vegas* album. This bootleg is mainly a humdrum copy of the music from the actual film, but the cover is dynamite.

With *Viva Las Vegas* doing so well at the box office, one can surmise that the music from the film would have sold quite well, had there been a proper soundtrack album. All of Elvis' new LPs through 1965 went Top 10, and a mix of the songs used and rejected for the movie could have been very popular. Conceivably, the album didn't get issued because Elvis' manager Colonel Tom Parker felt that Ann-Margret was getting more attention than she was due. Certainly, RCA was in no hurry to issue any of the duets she and Elvis had recorded together, nor did they put out any of her solo numbers from the film.

Despite this, the songs gradually became well known as the movie remained popular over the years. It was Elvis' most successful box-office take ever. *Roustabout* did terrifically as an album, but it didn't quite match the accomplishment of *Viva Las Vegas* in sales or plaudits.

Elvis was still a looming presence on the LP charts, but his long run atop the singles chart was over. This is due to two factors, the first being RCA putting out too many records. A total of six 45s appeared in 1964—double the amount Elvis had put out on average. Presley was still hot enough to get them all in the Top 40, but only "Blue Christmas" hit the Top 10, when it topped *Billboard*'s Christmas chart.

The second major problem was the songs themselves. The "Kissin' Cousins" debacle is noted above; RCA strangely followed it with a single off the 1962 LP *Pot Luck*. If "Suspicion" was meant to cash in on Terry Stafford's hit cover, it failed, though admittedly it was only the flip of the dated "Kiss Me Quick." "What'd I Say" followed, but didn't get into the Top 20. It seems radio play was divided between "What'd I Say" and the almost equally successful flip "Viva Las Vegas." Though Elvis' cover of the Ray Charles tune was good, it was already an oldie that had charted several times for other artists. In retrospect, it's easy to see that "Viva Las Vegas" should have been the promoted side.

Somewhat desperate now, RCA Victor decided to issue "Such a Night" from 1960 as a single. Although it had already been on *Elvis Is Back!* (and the picture on the sleeve was from 1956!), it had a newly released and relatively modern flip in "Never Ending," and got Elvis back into the Top 20. "Ask Me" was the last single, and it did decently, though the unreleased 1958 flip side "Ain't That Loving You Baby" outshone it and got nearly as high on the charts. "Blue Christmas," backed by "Wooden Heart," ended the year on a high, but these were reissued masters that didn't help Elvis regain his contemporary footing.

17

Long Lonely Highway

A Guide to the Hollywood Years

In 1960, Elvis returned from the army ready to relaunch his career. He recorded two great studio albums, made a fine appearance on television, had a slew of chart-topping singles, and became a full-time movie star. Two of his three films gave him quality dramatic parts; the third was a runaway commercial success. By 1965, however, Elvis was reduced to appearing in ridiculously contrived musical comedies, where the only thing worse than the scripts was the songs.

Focusing on the movie scores from *G. I. Blues* to *Speedway* and Elvis' 1960–64 studio recordings, this chapter follows a curious decline that could have been avoided. There is a dual career that emerges as Elvis the recording artist and Elvis the movie star became two different creatures. Elvis flourished briefly in the studio, but the increasingly bad movies began to undermine his confidence, and some poor marketing choices brought this essential part of his career to a temporary standstill. As an actor, Elvis initially received a reasonable mix of parts, but the music became an almost immediate problem. When the more vacuous flicks outsold his more interesting roles, it instigated a free fall that had once seemed impossible.

"Stuck on You"/"Fame and Fortune" (Released March 23, 1960)

Somewhat lost in the wake of the phenomenal success of the two singles to follow, "Stuck on You" was a cool pop song that rocked along nicely. The sound and vocals were cleaner than they had been before the army, and if the song was a bit tame compared to Elvis' hardest rockers, a new poise made up for it. Indeed, Presley's performance was flawless. Now a consummate, seasoned professional, Elvis sang with more confidence, but he hadn't lost that touch of self-mocking humor that endeared him to his fans.

Artistically, "Fame and Fortune" was even better. It was a terrific beat ballad, with a fullness to Elvis' vocals that betrayed how hard he had worked on his singing while in the service. There was no hesitance, no flatting—for the first time, it could be said that Elvis was every bit as good at ballads as he was at rock or country. The breath control is astounding. When Elvis sings the line "I know that I'll have nothing," listen to how he hits the long "I" sounds. His voice goes up, stays on top, and goes back down in a split second. Having gone through many new experiences during his two years away, Elvis sounds no longer like a boy but like a fully grown man.

Elvis Is Back! (Released April 8, 1960)

Rock and roll doesn't get better than this. There are a multitude of reasons why *Elvis Is Back!* was Elvis' best LP. For starters, stereo recording had been perfected while Elvis was in the service. Not too many pop artists would use it properly until the end of the decade, but Presley's Nashville sessions of the early sixties utilized sound placement in a way that holds up extraordinarily well today. Then there

Elvis released many non-movie records in the sixties, some of which were superb. This set of stamps featured all of the studio-based record covers of the period. It was included in the 1993 LP version of *The Essential 60's Masters.*

was the band. Nothing can take away what Scotty Moore or Bill Black contributed in the early days: they helped Elvis shape his sound, they gave him confidence to build up an exciting stage act, and they alone fully shared his experiences as he rose to fame. Yet with Bill gone for good to head up his successful combo, and Elvis wanting to grow beyond the music he did before, he took the opportunity to tweak his studio lineup.

Liking the fuller sound he got on his last session in 1958, Elvis invited guitarist Hank Garland, bassist Bob Moore, and drummer Buddy Harmon to continue working with him. D. J. and Scotty remained with Elvis through early 1968, and joined him later that year for his NBC TV special, but (with occasional exception) they were to be part of the overall blend instead of acting as an organic band. This cost Elvis' music some of its earthier qualities, but there was a new level of expertise he could achieve by hiring musicians who were somewhat more versatile.

The material was also excellent. The twenty-one-month pause allowed Elvis' regular writers the time to stock up and submit only top-quality compositions. The covers were also well chosen, showing Elvis and the players to their best advantage. Yet it was Elvis himself who made the true difference. After such a long break, he felt the need to prove himself, and that—combined with the work he did to expand his octave range—allowed him to come forth with performances that reached a whole new level of superiority.

The entire album is a uniform masterpiece, so I'll review it in order. "Make Me Know It" starts things off with a bang. It was the first cut to be taped at the initial session in March, and Elvis sounds ecstatic to be recording again. There's an energy here that soon would be diluted. A bouncy rocker with a catchy refrain, the sound is crisp and the atmosphere jubilant.

"Fever" has a sexy sophistication not heard in Elvis' music before. Though informed slightly by Little Willie John's original, Peggy Lee's nightclub-soaked cover is the main influence. Using finger snapping and a smoldering vocal technique, Elvis puts his own stamp on what was already becoming a standard.

"The Girl of My Best Friend" is the strongest piece of early teen-idol pop one can find. The Jordanaires excel on the doo-wop vocal backing, and Elvis interacts beautifully with them. The words are well chosen, sounding pretty in structure. The melody is commercial in the best sense of the word—it was custom-made for radio airplay. This didn't escape Chicago-area fan Ral Donner, whose career as one of the best early Elvis soundalikes went into high gear with his hit cover.

"I Will Be Home Again" is a near duet with Elvis' friend Charlie Hodge. Hodge and Elvis had met while both were in the service, and they formed a musical kinship that lasted until Elvis' death. Though Charlie has been rightly described as a flunky of sorts, he did provide Elvis with input on the structuring of his later stage shows, and, more importantly, kept him upbeat during his performances. This was originally a secular hit for the Golden Gate Quartet, whom Elvis and Charlie had been to see perform while on leave in Paris. "I

Will Be Home Again" appealed to them both, being as they were so far away from home, and they perfected an interpretation that owed a lot to their tight harmonies. Charlie's voice would get nasal and creaky by the mid-seventies, but here his crooning is solid. The *Elvis Is Back!* sessions featured Elvis playing a lot of acoustic guitar, and his hard strumming fits this song like a glove.

"Dirty, Dirty Feeling" was a Leiber and Stoller cut that they had submitted for *King Creole*. Disgusted with Parker's treatment of them, they would no longer write anything directly for Elvis (with the exception of "She's Not You," written in collaboration with Doc Pomus). Their lack of participation would be acutely felt in years to come, but their music would remain a highlight of Elvis' early-sixties recordings, as he still cut as many of their songs as possible. "Dirty, Dirty Feeling" is filled with their usual blend of raunchy rock and roll and satirical humor. Saxophonist Boots Randolph was one of the new additions to the sessions, and his bright tones enhanced the sprightly mood. Hank Garland's guitar solo was biting, and the vocals recall the uninhibited sting and close harmonies of the exceptional June 1958 session.

Stan Kesler's "Thrill of Your Love" was one of the LP's most substantial compositions. There's a slight philosophical bent to the lyrics, as well as a maturation of romantic attitude. Musically sophisticated, Floyd Cramer's alternately delicate and strident piano playing was as soulful as Jerry Lee Lewis'. Now twenty-five, Elvis responded to the substance inherent in the song. His serious, emotional vocal phrasing foreshadows the way he would develop his gospel style later that year. A thrilling step forward in self-possession and confidence.

"Soldier Boy" is an obvious attempt to play off Elvis' military duty. That this was an element of the LP's marketing was obvious from the title, plus the LP cover was a gatefold, full of army shots inside. No matter, Elvis fully connects with the ballad, transcending any ploy to appeal to the girls that missed him. The strides Elvis had made as a singer are obvious from the ease with which he handles the key change in the chorus. Very few singers put that much power into their voice yet have it remain silky smooth. Easily justifying the change in personnel, the music is a perfect complement to Elvis' passion.

"Such a Night" was an R&B hit in 1954 for Clyde McPhatter and the Drifters, whom Elvis had already displayed an affinity for with "Money Honey." The former, with its depiction of sexual desire, was especially lascivious for the era. There's nothing lewd about it, but that it discussed sex even obliquely made it controversial. If anything, Elvis amps up the sex quotient, even groaning suggestively over the final thirty seconds. Probably the only reason he got away with it is because he played his appeal as something more teasing than coarse.

Boots' sax keeps things moving, the melody is effervescent, and Elvis has a total mastery over every vocal grunt and purr. Everyone's having a blast, right through the coda, which has a flashy bit of drumming by Fontana or Harmon. With mores changing rapidly, "Such a Night" became a decent-sized hit for Elvis four years later, when quality single material was desperately needed.

"It Feels So Right" spices things up even further. A bluesy stroll with sting-ing guitar and heavy drum fills, this time Elvis sounds like he isn't playing. The words are innocuous, but the way Presley sings them drips with suggestion. He had all the toughness in his voice from the fifties, but he displayed greater authority than before. This even is the case for the blues-based music he had always excelled at.

Showing off his true dichotomy as a polite bad boy, "The Girl Next Door" is a second nod to the Technicolor world of teen-idol worship. Elvis was just young enough to still make certain characteristics of innocence shine through. He essentially did the song as a favor to Scotty, who owned part of the publishing. It's not less potent than the other cuts, and only furthers what Elvis could do well. He and Ricky Nelson were big fans of one another, and for years Ricky had been doing some seriously good approximations of rockabilly. "The Girl Next Door" finds Elvis turning things around to pay something of a tribute to the rocking pop that made Nelson a star.

The final two cuts take us back to more earthy territory, where Elvis again injects everything with a worldly, carnal approach. "Like a Baby" was an R&B single by Vikki Nelson & the Sounds that Elvis had enjoyed several years earlier. He gives a riveting reading as both a singer and a musician, shadowing Hank Garland's electric fills with acoustic runs of his own. Fattening up the sound, Boots' sax gives further dimension to track. Putting out the air of the cat about to swallow the canary, the vocals are knowing and deliberate. Elvis isn't begging for one night here—he's already won more than the heart of his paramour. Notably, when James Brown covered the song several years later, Elvis' recording was something of an influence.

Ranking in the Top 10 of any Elvis performances, "Reconsider Baby" is a rock-solid classic. With this one song, Elvis goes down in history as one of the best blues performers of any race or era. Blues is a music you have to feel as much as study. There are some basic blues patterns taken up by most who attempt the genre, and there are also a lot of clichés that pop up often. Elvis was never predictable when he sang the blues, and he didn't attempt to emulate anybody else. It's the spontaneity he brings to the form that sets him apart. You can tell he doesn't map out where he's going to take the song—he knows, on the spot, the right thing to do. Presley was well versed in blues and its history, and his need to be original overrode all other desires.

"Reconsider Baby" rewards you with every play. Elvis' heavy acoustic guitar, Randolph's madly honking sax—everything reeks of expertise and cool. Elvis eggs Boots on to play a long, hardy solo. You can hear in Presley's asides that he is as entertained as anyone.

Elvis never felt the need to take the whole spotlight. He valued making good music over self-promotion, and this made him the perfect group leader. He knew that he was the vital cog in the machine, but that all the parts had to be well oiled for maximum impact.

With "Reconsider Baby," Elvis topped off an album that showed him at his most masterful. *Elvis Is Back!* has so much to it, yet the beauty lies in how it can speak to almost anyone. There have been more grandiose albums in rock and roll, but few hit the spot so succinctly and straightforwardly.

"It's Now or Never"/"A Mess of Blues" (Released July 5, 1960)

Elvis had always been musically open to different influences. As much as he enjoyed the blues of Arthur Crudup, or his rock-and-roll contemporaries like Little Richard, Elvis also immersed himself in the work of Mario Lanza, and the Metropolitan Opera. "It's Now or Never" was based on the Italian standard "O Sole Mio." A tremendous departure from his public image, if no less remarkable it wasn't surprising to those who knew Elvis personally. Elvis took a risk with this record, but it paid off handsomely, as another #1 hit and one of his all-time biggest sellers.

The romanticism of the lyric appealed to Elvis' usual audience, but the change in style saw his music played on radio stations that were previously closed off to him. People of different age groups or tastes who had previously ignored or disdained his work bought "It's Now or Never" in droves. It's not so much that Elvis had been tamed, more that his voice had gotten fuller to the point where no objective listener could deny its quality. Plus, by presenting himself in a traditional setting, he proved once and for all his inherent versatility as an artist.

Besides any of that, "It's Now or Never" was an excellent recording. The first time out, Elvis' Latin-tinged voice had a captivating freshness and individuality. The music, particularly the strummed mandolin intro, was brilliantly played, and the Jordanaires provided perfect backup. The only downside to the record is that Elvis tried to follow it up too many times. The overabundance of Latin crooning would be one of the few mistakes this early on that can be attributed to a lapse of taste on Elvis' part.

Equally as strong as the top side (and a sizable hit of its own in England), "A Mess of Blues" blends Elvis' grittier, fifties-styled vocal approach on the brief chorus with his recently honed croon on the verse. With Scotty Moore playing one of his soon-to-be-rare guitar leads, it bears a resemblance to Elvis' earlier rock but is more polished overall. One of Elvis' more salacious cuts, the fuller style works to the track's advantage. Floyd Cramer's piano playing is nice and slinky, and there's a striptease-styled backbeat over which Elvis and the Jordanaires get to emote.

The sensuality was (as usual) presented with tongue planted firmly in cheek. Elvis' being playful made his sexuality palatable to the sensibilities of the early sixties, but his basic magnetism was in no way watered down. "A Mess of Blues" is never less than classy, but it owes its very existence to the changes Elvis had made in the basic perception of what was seen as "proper" in popular culture.

G.I. Blues (Released October 1, 1960)

The first Elvis LP to represent the light musical comedies cluttering up his film and record catalogue, *G.I. Blues* is far better than most of the soundtracks to follow. Standing out from the later movie albums is the premium sound quality and care taken with the production. Elvis, the players, and the technicians worked as hard on this album as on anything else they did. Ultimately, solid effort is what makes *G.I. Blues* different. Elvis privately expressed unease over a number of selections that he worried were beneath the standards he had previously set. Overall, the songs seem to be a good fit for him, but there was cause for concern.

With Elvis now doing a more traditional musical, the plot began to play a bigger role in the songs. He still had quality material to choose from, but plot-driven songs were to prove inherently limiting for the writers and Elvis. Had it been a one-time experiment, *G.I. Blues* would be seen simply as the reasonable LP it is, but because most of the soundtracks to follow weren't solid, this record has had to answer for a lot.

For instance, "Blue Suede Shoes" might not have the animalistic energy of Elvis' 1956 cut, but the lighter, acoustic-based arrangement works as an interesting alternative. Elvis' guitar playing is up front, and he still had a rebellious attitude in his voice. Maybe the fact that Elvis didn't often remake his records has made this look like a cheap move, but the gag in the movie of an "Elvis Presley" record interrupting the music of Elvis' character was a witty one. It was different enough to come off as something new, and Elvis should be applauded for not trying to copy his original record.

Not that there aren't some moments that hint at what was to come. "Wooden Heart" was a very popular song in Europe—a given, considering its generic "Euro" feel, and the inclusion of a verse sung in German. It's a cute novelty, but there is something really off about it as an Elvis Presley cut. The man wasn't put on this earth to sing beer-hall polkas. Out-takes reveal this to be the first in a long line of movie cuts he just couldn't take seriously.

"Tonight Is So Right for Love" was another attempt at something of a stereotypical traditional German number, but it comes off lame. The Jordanaires are given goofy "lu-lu-lus" to sing, and Elvis seems encumbered by the style. Little did the producers realize that Elvis' German fans liked hard rockabilly even more than their American counterparts.

"G.I. Blues" also seems written for the wrong singer. There are hints of rock, but the song's formulaic nature keeps Elvis from letting loose. He tries to make the chorus sound sexy, but there's not enough grit. It works slightly as a parody of army life, but it could have been cool and funny, had there not been a keenness on the movie producers' part to appeal to all ages. "Didja' Ever" is more of the same, a song built around a mildly amusing army chant. The problem here is that it goes on far too long, and isn't as clever as it attempts to be.

"Big Boots" is a song Elvis would never have touched had the movie not called for it. It is a lullaby sung to an infant, with lyrics addressing the father's military nickname. As much as Parker may have wanted Elvis to cut a children's album (his notoriously bad compilation *Elvis Sings for Children and Grownups Too!* would be issued a year after Elvis' death), it simply wasn't what was called for when Presley was trying to prove himself again and stay relevant.

The rest of the album is quite good, if not stunning. "Shoppin' Around" is a sprightly pop song, with Elvis' acoustic guitar placed high up. Out-takes demonstrate that he envisioned it sounding more edgy at first, and though diluting movie music would be a continual problem, at this stage he was still allowed to infuse his masters with some sly fun. "What's She Really Like" is another nice bit of pop with a breezy air. The intro is juvenile, but the way Elvis puts it across is masterful.

"Frankfort Special" has been called a sanitized "Mystery Train," and there's truth in that. Being that it was written for a movie, with attendant references to being a soldier, how could it possibly carry the same weight? On its own terms, this is a perfectly catchy song, with a good rhythm and fine performances all around. Originally, it bore little resemblance to the Sun classic. Taken at the pace of a rocket, one can only imagine how strange Elvis and the extras would have looked trying to lip-synch it. The speedy version left on the shelf has more spirit to it, but slowing it to a medium shuffle brought out an untapped musicality.

"Pocketful of Rainbows" was watery in the movie, when sung as a duet of sorts with co-star Juliet Prowse. On record, it's a pleasant ballad, with Elvis in superb voice. Even the accordion is nicely incorporated. Used with subtlety, it added an interesting texture to the overall sound. "Pocketful of Rainbows" can easily exist without any consideration of the storyline. It goes to show that Elvis could have easily recorded music for all ages without having to sacrifice inherent quality.

"Doin' the Best That I Can" does suffer slightly for the accordion, but it was strong material that one could imagine Elvis wanting to record under any circumstance. A thoughtful plea from the heart, it's somewhat longer than most cuts of the period. Displaying vulnerability underneath his outward bravado, Elvis tellingly sings it without aping his past. His voice is pitched high in parts, with a delicacy he couldn't have mustered before 1960. He is very careful, putting a lot of thought into how he pronounces each vowel and consonant. Elvis does this type of material with a sense of ease and freedom. Pop balladry was as legitimate a part of his creative makeup as anything else. If only the standards had been maintained.

"Are You Lonesome Tonight?"/"I Gotta Know" (Released November 1, 1960)

Just when it seemed Elvis couldn't be further defined, along came "Are You Lonesome Tonight?," a fairly straightforward cover of a twenties-era ballad, with the sound itself modernized to 1960 standards. Other than being better recorded (or executed), it wasn't such a tremendous departure for Elvis, but coming in the wake of "It's Now or Never," it was construed by many to be a move away from rock and roll. Truthfully, "Are You Lonesome Tonight?" (spelled "To-Night" on the original 45) was more of an expansion of boundaries than anything resembling desertion.

The upfront acoustic-guitar playing sets a nice tone. There's a sense of stillness at the core of Elvis' performance. He had developed the skill to know where not to add something, to leave a bit of air and room. The spoken part is done seriously, which often wasn't the case live. The air of moroseness makes for interesting art, with a great atmosphere of late-night regret. It was one of the few times Parker asked Elvis to cut a song outside of the film soundtracks, as it was a favorite of the Colonel's wife Marie. It was a good suggestion, Parker for once helping to expand Elvis' horizons.

With the Jordanaires and Elvis playing off each other with ease, "I Gotta Know" is a fine doo-wop number. As much as it is of its era, there's an earnestness that keeps it fresh. It isn't the mature piece of reflection of the other side—it's just wonderfully executed rockin' pop. Fantastic and refreshing.

"Surrender"/"Lonely Man" (Released February 7, 1961)

Of all of Elvis' classic 1956–62 singles run, "Surrender" has fared the worst over time. There's nothing wrong with it, exactly, but it's one of his few singles of the period not to offer something new. Elvis' singing is technically brilliant, but he sounds affected. He takes the Latin tone of "It's Now or Never" and pumps it up to where it's overwhelming. Elvis was so popular at the time that it easily hit #1, and he admittedly was dedicated to the material.

"Lonely Man" is a second-tier ballad that ended up being cut from *Wild in the Country*. Elvis' performance is spot on, but the accordion played by Jimmie Haskell ruins the folk ambience. The solo version with just Elvis and an acoustic guitar is recommended as an alternative, and first appeared in 1991 on the three-LP/CD set *Collectors Gold*.

"I Feel So Bad"/"Wild in the Country" (Released May 2, 1961)

After three ballads and one soft-rocker, "I Feel So Bad" was a welcome return to hard-blues single material. Elvis' voice has a more refined tone than it would have before the army, but he's able to get more expression out of it. The piano playing by Floyd Cramer is pumpin', and Boots Randolph's sax is dirty. One of Elvis' best singles of the era, it oddly didn't sell as well as the records it preceded.

"Wild in the Country" was the title song of the motion picture of the same name. Like nearly all the cuts from the session, it is unassuming and acoustic-based. One of the qualities Elvis had gained over time was the ability to sing gently while retaining a sense of poise. "Wild in the Country" wasn't a significant

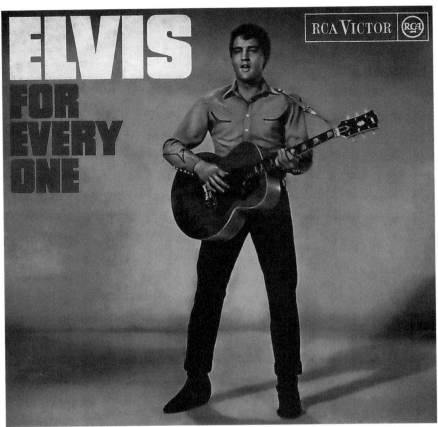

One of the most oddball releases in Elvis' catalogue, this U.K. stereo copy of *Elvis for Everyone* ups the ante by including "Wild in the Country" with a strange maraca overdub. Other than an early-seventies reissue of this lineup, it hasn't seen the (official) light of day since.

tune, but it was a change of pace in that it has elements of folk music previously undetectable in Elvis' records.

Something for Everybody (Released June 17, 1961)

Something for Everybody tried to be just that. It doesn't quite meet its goals with the same effectiveness as the past, but there are still a fair amount of successes on hand. Being an early example of a blatantly thematic rock-and-roll album, *Something for Everybody* set itself apart more in programming than in musical achievement. One half was called the "ballads" side, the other side "rhythm." The performances from all involved are excellent; it was the material that wasn't so universally strong.

On the plus side, the singing is marvelous. Elvis' voice dips and soars like never before. With the same band that had cut *Elvis Is Back!* on hand, the musicianship is stellar. Yet there seems to be a certain daring missing. In contrast to his previous demeanor, Elvis comes off as conformist and conservative on this album. He was going more for technical vocal perfection and paying less attention to the music's ambitions. There were a few welcome exceptions, but the malaise that had been diminishing his soundtracks over the past year was beginning to carry over. The difference here is that Elvis was the one in charge, and so he must take more of the acclaim and/or blame for the results.

Nineteen sixty-one was when things basically leveled off, quality-wise, in terms of the soundtracks vs. regular sessions. The results for the films stayed about the same, and the regular studio dates took a moderate dive. It was a strange state of affairs. The songs Elvis was singing weren't as good as before, but his singing was better than ever. Though there aren't as many of them as there should be, the few tracks that do show growth are outstanding.

Something for Everybody has some light touches of blues and country, but all the edges were getting polished off of Elvis. Encouraged by Parker and producers like Hal Wallis, he began to have the misguided idea that you couldn't come off as rebellious and make serious music. It was the one flaw in his creative makeup that got worse over time. Elvis enjoyed rock and roll, but the pre-rock influences of his youth were always going to make him a bit stodgier in taste than most of his audience.

"It's a Sin" is a case in point. Covering the most placid form of country music, Elvis makes the song less captivating by handling it genteelly. "Judy" has a classic pop structure, but his tone is too sugary and high-pitched on the refrain. There's no sense of danger. "In Your Arms" lacks the needed testosterone as well. There's a thin feeling to the sound, and the lyrics veer from clichéd to clumsy.

Thankfully, the rest of the LP isn't as slight, partially due to the presence of a new songwriter. Don Robertson had begun writing for Elvis in 1956, but after his initial luck placing a song, he hadn't scored again until this LP. Don had a talent for composing love ballads, and came along at a time when Elvis' focus was heading in that direction. Some of his songs lacked body, but each of them spurred Elvis on to give a good effort.

Furthering Presley's maturing persona, "There's Always Me" was one of Don Robertson's finest pieces. From the luxurious piano intro to the closing vocal crescendo, every second of "There's Always Me" exudes class. Elvis connected very personally to the romantic sentiments of the lyric, and rose ably to the considerable challenge the voicing presented.

After that, Robertson's "Starting Today" seems to be an afterthought. Not melodious and calming, but ultimately it's all icing without cake. There's no edge or bite to Elvis' singing—it's so careful and clinical. Not bad, just unexciting.

"Gently" is held back by being too gentle. The right elements are in place—the acoustic guitar playing has a warm tone, and Elvis' harmonies with the Jordanaires are positively sumptuous—but there's a certain spark missing.

"Sentimental Me" also can be put in the category of agreeable but not especially gripping. The catchy beat unfolds at a slow gallop, yet the merest hint of attitude would have made it exponentially more stirring. Elvis is wispy on the high notes, balancing it with a throatier resonance as he goes into the refrain.

"Give Me the Right" has a raw sensuality that's missing from most of the album. There's a great Millie Kirkham wail over the intro, and a pulsating rhythm steeped in blues and gospel. More polite than he would have been the year before, Elvis' every word is still laced with suggestion and yearning. By holding back, he sounds more alluring.

"I Want You with Me" also has a decidedly wild edge. Elvis had heard Bobby Darin's recording, and he followed it fairly closely. Unusually for this LP, he imparts a comparatively more defiant attitude. The music is festive, and the Jordanaires' Ray Walker has a grand time with the bass notes. Sounding much like he had in the fifties, Elvis finally sets aside perfectionism in favor of soul.

"Put the Blame on Me" has a pulse because Elvis' delivery is decidedly mischievous. Floyd Cramer's organ playing has a hedonistic effect, conjuring up a snake charmer. Though it lacks the kind of commercial hook required for single release, it reminds the listener that Elvis was no choirboy.

The Charlie Rich rocker "I'm Comin' Home" is one of the few Elvis songs of the period to originate from Memphis. It's interesting to hear Floyd playing the kind of fast triplets that bear Rich's stamp. Elvis doesn't fail to bring his own personality to the mix, but some of the smoother passages reveal how much he admired Charlie. Giving the album a needed touch of imperfection, Elvis gets slightly overpowered in the last verse.

"I Slipped, I Stumbled, I Fell" has a different background than the other songs as it stems from the autumn 1960 sessions for *Wild in the Country*. As noted, the gap between Elvis' regular sessions and soundtracks was rather small in 1961. As a result, it doesn't stand out like a sore thumb. With heavy use of slang, it's more gimmicky a song than Elvis might have chosen otherwise. Regardless, his performance is lively and the music beaty.

"(Marie's the Name) His Latest Flame"/"Little Sister" (Released August 8, 1961)

Elvis' best rock-and-roll 45 of the early sixties, each side of this pairing hit the Top 5 with ease. Truthfully, either could have sat comfortably on top the charts, had they not been competing with one another. Both were written by Doc Pomus and Mort Shuman, who in terms of creative ingenuity can be seen as successors to Jerry Leiber and Mike Stoller. "His Latest Flame" has an irresistible Bo Diddley beat and a more thoughtful storyline than most pop records of the day. The initial verses are handled in such a way that you don't guess the truth about his friend's new girl until they later spell it out. Elvis sings with utter buoyancy, displaying a peerless skill for handling the conflicting emotions called for. Floyd

Cramer's piano playing must again be singled out—he made the keys take flight. When it sounds that easy, you know it isn't!

"Little Sister" is a fiery blues-rocker with the bad-boy qualities of Elvis' best fifties work. His passion for the songs subject smolders, and the dirty licks of Hank Garland make the proceedings sound that much more carnal. One play dispels the notion that Elvis lost his ability to rock by the early sixties. When Elvis died, President Jimmy Carter took the then-uncommon step of a world leader making an official statement on the death of an entertainer. Among the things he said was that Elvis represented the vitality, good humor, and rebelliousness of America. If one record can be said to contain all those qualities in one tight package, "Little Sister" fits the bill.

Blue Hawaii (Released October 1, 1961)

Blue Hawaii has always been among the most popular Elvis LPs. With the islands having recently been made a state, interest in them was at a peak when the movie came out. In fact, it made such a big impression that, along with Memphis and Las Vegas, Hawaii is a place that still brings in considerable tourism due to Presley's association with it. Elvis never grew tired of visiting Hawaii, and it would be a frequent destination for both work and play as late as five months before he passed away.

Blue Hawaii isn't Elvis at his most adventurous, but the best songs do have a relaxed beauty that recall the location with vivid color. There are even authentic Hawaiian sounds, some markedly traditional. Despite the inspiration provided by the subject matter, however, there is an alarming amount of filler. At fourteen songs, the album could have used pruning, but even at this length there's a lack of good rock and roll. Elvis tried on several occasions to inject attitude into the cuts, but the session tapes make it clear that he was being steered in a staid direction.

The writers couldn't seem to put rock and Hawaii together without thinking along the lines of silly novelties. In a musical, one or two of these numbers wouldn't be out of place, but the album has a full five songs brimming over with corny humor. Granted, the ballads adapted well to the tropical setting, and it is these the LP thrives on, but this was a sign of things to come.

"Ito Eats," a typical calypso song of the day, is probably the weirdest song on the record. One is tempted to laugh at Elvis, not with him. Coming off as a parody of Elvis movie music, "Slicin' Sand" brings about more unintentional giggles. Aside from a dopey lyric, it sounds like rock and roll with a stiff shirt on.

"Almost Always True" has a fairly cool intro, but the words are so pat and jokey that it heads straight down as soon as Elvis begins to sing. In the movie, Elvis does it as a duet with co-star Joan Blackman; her absence from the LP meant that the jokes fell flat. Better than just scrapping her would've been to throw out the song altogether. To a lesser degree, "Beach Boy Blues" also suffers from its tie to the plot. If the words spell things out enough to pick up on what is happening, the material remains clichéd. It comes from a scene where Elvis' character is thrown in jail for fighting, but "Jailhouse Rock" this ain't!

"Rock-A-Hula Baby" suffices as a goofy bit of Hollywood madness. It's an oddball that provides a kind of entertainment, but with some credible rock and roll to be found in the music. The problem lies in what accompanies it. One unusual novelty song is fun; five severely diminishes the credibility of the album and the artist. Why this one stands out is because it has a knowing sense of the absurd.

Elvis' most frequent writer (particularly when it came to the sixties movies) was Ben Weisman. He wrote some great stuff but also penned many of Elvis' most insane numbers. Here he teams up with frequent partner Fred Wise and newcomer Dee Fuller. Fuller was the former collaborator and muse of the man who made the most eccentrically bad films of all time, Ed Wood. Used to working with unusual forms of creativity, she was attuned to Weisman's off-the-wall ideas. Sometimes this made for awful results, but "Rock-A-Hula Baby" demonstrates the amusingly weird underbelly of the Presley movie formula.

The rest of the material takes itself more seriously, with decent results. One exception is "Island of Love (Kauai)." Though pretty enough, it matches the other ballads too closely to have an identity of its own. On the other end of the spectrum is "Can't Help Falling in Love." Based melodically on the French love song "Plasir d'Amour," it benefits from a timeless quality that made it one of the most popular tracks in the Presley catalogue. Elvis' singing is wonderfully pristine in its beauty, and you can tell how hard he worked to get it perfect. Emphasizing the romanticism of the melody, the arrangement does the song justice by keeping things simple. Elvis used it to close almost every show he gave from 1969 to 1977, and it's been a standard at weddings ever since.

A ballad used in local or theme ceremonies, "Hawaiian Wedding Song" is also a classic. Passages from the native tongue are interwoven proficiently throughout, and Elvis' tender croon is immaculate. On one of Presley's most romantic albums, this stands out for having an especially warm quality.

"Moonlight Swim" had the potential to be a catchy, Hawaiian-flavored ditty, but the arrangement spoils it. With a simple production focused on Elvis' lead and the ukulele, this would have been endearing. Ultimately, it is too busy musically, and the duet with the female backing singers feels gimmicky and fey. "Hawaiian Sunset" is more on point, having a lovely melody and lyric. There's a relaxed, late-night feel that is charming, and a somnolent effect reinforced by the "sleep Hawaii sleep" hook. It captures a mood, painting a picture of the islands in sound. If it was safer stylistically than much of Elvis' work, that takes nothing away from the effort put forth.

"No More" is a melodic ballad written by Don Robertson and Hal Blair. They based the melody on "La Paloma," a popular Spanish folk song. Robertson's highly attuned sense of the romantic served him well, and Elvis gets to vocalize with the Latin affectation he was so fond of at the time.

"Blue Hawaii" was once popularized by Bing Crosby, and it made a fitting title song. With steel guitars and ukulele high in the blend, a mellow Elvis imparts a lucid vision of the place often called "paradise on Earth." It borders on dreary, but achieves its goal of enticement for both the film and the islands.

The writer of the traditional Hawaiian number "Aloha Oe" was Lili'uokalani. Besides being a song and fiction writer, she was also the last reigning Hawaiian monarch. The intro has a Hawaiian chant, over which Boots Randolph makes his sax sound Polynesian. Over a bed of languid native-styled instrumentation, Elvis sings straightforwardly in a mix of English and Hawaiian.

"Ku-u-i-po" was one of the most memorable numbers in the score. It has an absolutely gorgeous melody, and Elvis sings in his sweetest register. A fine combination of the standard Elvis ballad style with Hawaiian sounds, it has validity as a representation of tropical music. Meditative and flowing, "Ku-u-i-po" shows Elvis mastering yet another facet of the American music tradition.

"Good Luck Charm"/"Anything That's Part of You" (Released February 27, 1962)

"Good Luck Charm" is a melodious update of the "All Shook Up" formula. It doesn't have the same guts or attitude, but it's perfect as a laid-back companion. The beat is steady, Elvis playfully throws in a bunch of different grunts and groans, and the harmonies with the Jordanaires are pristine. Elvis' last single to top the charts until 1969, "Good Luck Charm" was more of a great record than a great song. With its inspired use of instruments blending with a merry vocal, it was the overall sound that appealed.

"Anything That's Part of You" didn't have the same instant familiarity, but this Don Robertson ballad was artistically fulfilling. Musically, Floyd Cramer's outstanding piano playing takes center stage. Robertson had taught Cramer what was known as the "slip note" technique, where a wrong note leads into a good one. This had the effect of making the piano sound more complex, and added some solid counter-rhythms.

As a composition, "Anything That's Part of You" was finely articulated, allowing Elvis to dig deep into himself and come up with a result that was refined and personal. The most interesting thing about his vocal is the way he used volume to express different emotions. He's soft on the verses, giving off a feeling of sadness. For the chorus, he gets quite loud, spilling over with feelings he can't seem to control. Suddenly composed, he quietly leads back into the verse.

Pot Luck with Elvis (Released June 5, 1962)

Pot Luck could almost be called *Something for Everybody Volume 2*. It follows the same formula in trying to showcase Elvis as an artist with range. His voice is again in fine shape, and he handles all the material with care. Yet there is an additional reserve—a toning down of style. The music is good, some of the songs represent the continuing evolution in Elvis' abilities, but there is no gutsy rock, blues, or country to be found.

Ironically, one of the songs closest to traditional rock and roll is the *Blue Hawaii* out-take "Steppin' out of Line." Toned down markedly from the early takes, it typifies how his music suffered from his having to work with movie producers who didn't understand what he was best at. Regardless, there's a likable rollicking attitude not found on many of the other selections.

Three songs originated from the brief Nashville June 1961 date. "Kiss Me Quick" is a disposable cha-cha, one of the many in the long line of Elvis' Latin-flavored indulgences. There's a bubbly tone to his voice, but the song is too fundamentally square to be redeemed.

"That's Someone You Never Forget" was one of only two genuine co-writes by Elvis, and like the second to come, Red West served as his partner. Elvis' contribution seems not to have extended much beyond the title, but as one of his best friends, West was able to impart some of Presley's personal sentiments. Though Red has said Elvis was initially thinking of a girlfriend, it was a somewhat ambiguous ballad about losing a loved one. With Elvis still grieving for his mother, it can be construed as a musical tribute. Though Elvis' singing is tender, as a record it's middling. As an insight into the man, not much else is as revealing.

"I'm Yours" is a lackluster ballad where Elvis sings a duet with himself using the magic of overdubbing. The organ, played by Floyd Cramer, dominates, sounding like something from an Italian roller rink. Released three years later as a 45 from *Tickle Me*, the thinness of the song is even more apparent, as the remix removed one of Elvis' vocal tracks and a spoken section. Still, the tinkering proved to be a good choice commercially, as it hovered just outside the Top 10—at a time when hits no longer came easily.

"Night Rider" dates from another quick Nashville session in October 1961. Elvis tried to remake it during the main March 1962 album sessions, but there was minimal difference. It's more or less Pomus and Shuman ripping themselves off with a milder "His Latest Flame" on the middle eight, and the "new" verses aren't particularly fascinating. Decidedly more common than offensive, it's not a bad piece of sax-driven pop.

Not enthralled with everything cut in October, and still needing over half an LP, Elvis went back to Nashville in March 1962 to finish the album. The finest cut was "Suspicion," a phenomenal mid-tempo ballad. Perplexingly, it wasn't picked to be a single for two years, and even then only to cash in on the hit by Terry Stafford. Eventually, it did go Top 10 in the U.K. in 1976, but Elvis' superior recording is the more obscure. A short and sweet Pomus and Shuman cut with an air of tension, the performance and production were flawless.

"(Such an) Easy Question" is attractive light pop. Giving it a bit of bite, Elvis handles his lead with an air of playful seduction. The Jordanaires are prominent, and the music is breezy. It too would be included in *Tickle Me* and released as a single in 1965. Attaining a valued #11 spot on the charts, this and "I'm Yours" are rarely included on hit compilations, though they rank among Elvis' forty biggest.

"Something Blue" is a brilliant ballad handled from an adult perspective far removed from the adolescent days gone by. Elvis' singing is full of nuance; listen closely to the last thirty seconds to hear some of his most proficient vocal phrasing. Though otherwise a bravura reading, the first take had a clever "Here Comes the Bride" intro that is missed here.

Not everything is done from such a lofty position of expertise. "Just for Old Time Sake" is a copy of the melody of "Old Shep" with a new lyric. Elvis sounds staid, if not aloof. "Fountain of Love" is another third-rate European-styled ballad, sticking out only because of how weak it is. "I Feel Like I've Known You Forever" has an agreeable melody, and Elvis takes his balladry seriously. Sadly, it is let down by a juvenile rhyming scheme, which in one case matches "your touch" with "too much." This (exact) rhyme worked with a flip rocker like "Too Much," but it sounds hackneyed on such a quiet ballad.

Rounding off the album is the driving "Gonna Get Back Home Somehow." Dramatic in tone, it is respectable filler that oddly seems to be a precursor to the tone of early James Bond movie themes. Elvis gets into the mood of the piece, giving it a needed element of integrity. Though the results were somewhat mixed, much the same can be said about the entire album.

"She's Not You"/"Just Tell Her Jim Said Hello" (Released July 17, 1962)

"She's Not You" is a good mid-tempo ballad, but is one of Elvis' less meaty offerings. His vocal is charming, sounding especially sweet on the chorus. The bass is mixed high to the point of distortion, but this is otherwise attractive (if frothy) pop. That it got to #5 speaks more to Elvis' popularity at the time than the song being exceptional. It would have made for a solid track on *Pot Luck*, but it had less going for it than "Suspicion."

"Just Tell Her Jim Said Hello" has many of the same pluses and minuses. Elvis' vocal is pristine, the melody is admirably catchy, and it's light as a feather. Having Elvis be "Jim" within the framework of the song is novel, and it also benefits from having something of a story. The beat kept on a triangle gets old, but "Just Tell Her Jim Said Hello" works because Elvis put in a high level of effort.

Girls! Girls! Girls! (Released November 9, 1962)

The first Elvis album to have more bad songs than good, *Girls! Girls! Girls!* is a major disappointment. It takes the mistakes of *G.I. Blues* and *Blue Hawaii* and multiplies them. There were still exceptions that gave Elvis something to work with, but some songs insult the intelligence of even a juvenile buyer. The worst tracks are the novelties. Embarrassing onscreen, they have even less reason to exist without the visuals. The only thing that remained intact was Elvis' voice. He was still enthusiastic enough to give whatever he could, and the energy on display made a difference on a number of occasions. The production is still clear and crisp, but *Girls! Girls! Girls!* was a big step down from previous standards.

As far as what went wrong, Elvis was given an odd assortment of styles that often didn't suit him. "Earth Boy" was the worst offender in this department. Bizarrely sung with children onscreen, this is a faux Asian–styled ballad. That it's politically incorrect is fine, considering the context of the time—the issue is that nobody then or now would want Elvis to sing it. Poorly written to the point of being asinine, "Earth Boy" makes Elvis seem like a fool.

"Song of the Shrimp" is a "Banana Boat Song" knock-off best left to the Harry Belafontes of the world. Here, Elvis actually has to sing from the shrimp's viewpoint! It might be harmless fun in isolation, but the album is full of such songs.

"The Walls Have Ears" is an ill-advised tango, acceptable onscreen but not on record. "We'll Be Together" was the most offensively audacious attempt to turn Elvis into Mario Lanza to date. His singing is great, but there's no creative thinking going on. One could falsely surmise that the writers had never even heard an Elvis Presley record, let alone written for him before.

"A Boy Like Me, a Girl Like You" heads into gushing teen-idol territory à la Fabian or Bobby Rydell. Totally unsuited to what an Elvis Presley record should be, it was written by Dudley Brooks and frequent Elvis choreographer Charles O'Curran. Logically, both should have been more attuned to his strengths.

"Because of Love" is another frivolous cut. It has a vaguely attractive melody, but there's no body, nothing to give it a little more bounce. U.K. singer Billy Fury had a minor hit single with it in England. Sad to say, his version outclasses Presley's because there was an effort at substance. Hollywood had already forgotten that it was Elvis' rebellion and good recordings that made him a star. It's understandable to a point why there was an attempt to clean up his image, but they took it to where his characters rang false and the music suffered.

"I Don't Want To" and "Where Do You Come From" are a step up, but they don't hold a candle to the best ballads Elvis was recording. The tonal quality is brilliant, but these should have been the worst songs he attempted. He was the biggest star in the world in 1962, yet the people he had vetting songs were unqualified and incompetent.

"Thanks to the Rolling Sea" and "We're Coming In Loaded" are both tied to Elvis' character's job on a fishing boat. Against all odds, they were catchy, ending up being two of the better songs included. "Thanks to the Rolling Sea" has minimal instrumentation, with Elvis above a thick wall of harmonies. The Jordanaires were present for this session, as were the Amigos, and it's likely they all sang together here. It may be a sea shanty, but it's a reasonable one.

"We're Coming In Loaded" has a hint of real rock and roll to it. Elvis sounds like he's enjoying himself, even scatting along to the music at the fade. The lyrics nearly ground it by being about having a boatload of fish, but the jovial ambience just about salvages things.

It was only with the three rock-and-roll songs (along with the out-take "Plantation Rock") that Elvis was able to make some classic music. "I Don't Want to Be Tied" has a lot of pep in its step. It's not gutsy, but Elvis imparts it with the joie de vivre of good early-sixties pop. It's akin to him being momentarily let off a leash.

Despite Parker pushing them away, Elvis was still a fan of Leiber and Stoller. "Girls! Girls! Girls!" was an upbeat novelty cut they had penned for the Coasters, and it turned out to be a good fit for the film's title. Though the Coasters were better suited to being outwardly funny, Elvis sounds happy to be singing authentic rock and roll. Boots Randolph gets to play an extended saxophone solo that is reminiscent of his signature tune, "Yakety Sax," which most listeners will know as the theme from *The Benny Hill Show*.

"Return to Sender" is the song the album was sold on, and is by leaps and bounds its best cut. There is a quality to the lyric missing elsewhere. Granted, the plot wasn't any heavier than getting love letters sent back, but it was a clever idea. Not missing a chance to growl or hum, Elvis sings the song with a great use of inflection. It holds up as impeccable 1962 pop, and it nearly topped the charts.

It Happened at the World's Fair (Released April 10, 1963)

From *G.I. Blues* on, each of Elvis' soundtrack LPs got progressively worse. With this album, even the facade of quality vanished. There were a scant ten songs, lasting just over twenty minutes in total, and the most memorable moments had already been released on the "One Broken Heart for Sale"/"They Remind Me Too Much of You" 45. Parker originally wanted to put it in a gatefold cover and charge more, but even he realized he would be pushing his luck.

By now, even Elvis' most forgiving fans noticed the steep drop in quality. Though some original followers couldn't come to grips with him expanding his style, most thoughtful listeners understood that he couldn't be the "Hillbilly Cat" forever. It was only when the material had deteriorated beyond reason that the average listener paused to wonder what had happened.

Through 1960, Elvis' records stood proudly among the finest music in any field. Now, a scant three years later, he was issuing some of the worst material ever recorded by a major talent. One of the most shocking falls in music history, Elvis' decline in the seventies pales against it artistically, if not personally. Here, Elvis was in the prime of his life, but the songs he was being made to sing are condescending to himself and his listeners.

Over and over, the LP comes off as an insipid imitation of what went before. "Beyond the Bend" tried to be a happy, cheerful song in the tradition of other Elvis movie openers. This time it didn't work. The melody is trite, the chorus ungainly, and it reeks of artificiality. "Relax" is an attempt at seduction in the same vein as "Fever," but the lyrics are too obvious to be sultry. For the first time, Elvis is feigning his natural sex appeal, and the supper-club trappings of the music don't help.

"How Would You Like to Be" is overlong and painful to hear. Another feeble children's song, onscreen the music was played on toys. There was no attempt to make it sound like real music for the record, and Elvis is reduced to singing a chorus of "Ho ho ha ha tra la la la la la." There's twenty seconds of a rock fill shoehorned in to remind listeners that this is not a reject from kiddie performer Danny Kaye. "Cotton Candy Land" is yet another song for the tykes, but the ersatz lullaby comes off as creepy. The lyric is fluffy, but there's an unsettling tone to Elvis' delivery.

"Take Me to the Fair" is formulaic, and plainly written to order. It has no life outside of the scene it was composed for, and it imparts the impression of being tossed off. Even though it is not burdened directly by the plot, "A World of Our Own" is equally flimsy pop. The sound is so soggy that the writers seem not to have a grip on the basic tenets of composing. "Happy Ending" is marginally better, with a glimmer of a gospel influence in the chorus. Still, it feels too polite, the musicians not inspired to take flight.

"I'm Falling in Love Tonight" is an agreeable Don Robertson ballad, but it sounds secondhand next to his best work. Elvis jumps at the chance to do something with heart, and the sound is lovely. Beyond that, there is an air of artifice—kind of a blurred replication of what a real Elvis ballad would sound like. Thankfully, Robertson came up with the goods on "They Remind Me Too Much of You." This utterly dazzling love song is only marred slightly by overloaded bass notes. The lovely piano playing (by Don himself) provides the perfect accompaniment to Elvis' reflective vocal. No doubt the singer rises to the occasion, infusing every intonation with dedication and care.

"One Broken Heart for Sale" contains a lot of the best qualities of Elvis' early-sixties persona. It's got teasing yet knowing vocal growls, the arrangement is bright, and the mid-paced rock tempo is sprightly. Why, then, was it the first major Elvis single to miss the Top 10 since 1956? The main reason was that an entire verse was dropped, leaving a master of little over ninety seconds. Why the verse was axed for the record remains a mystery, as the movie featured a somewhat tamer full-length version. This fine Otis Blackwell–Winfield Scott pop-rocker deserved better, and the lack of care in making it as good a record as possible is the only explanation for its relative failure. Certainly, reaching #11 was nothing to sneeze at for most artists, but Elvis had been so hot before this that there was a definite feeling of disappointment.

"(You're the) Devil in Disguise"/"Please Don't Drag That String Around" (Released June 18, 1963)

The last classic early-sixties single, "(You're the) Devil in Disguise" is an inspired rocker with a stop-start rhythm. The verses are smooth, the chorus sharp. Even on the wilder sections, Elvis has a sense of hurt in his voice, a tense restraint only finding release as he shouts out the title. It's a fantastic recording with a sense of happy abandon.

A nonchalant rocker with a pounding beat, "Please Don't Drag That String Around" is breezy and enjoyable. There's a confidence to Elvis' singing that would be missing in the next few years to come. The best part is how it is in constant motion—there are no breaks or pauses. A fine pairing in all ways, it almost got Elvis back to the top of the charts.

"Bossa Nova Baby"/"Witchcraft" (Released October 1, 1963)

The rollicking "Bossa Nova Baby" would prove to be the sole highlight from *Fun in Acapulco,* and its flip continued the party atmosphere. A belting slice of rhythm and blues, "Witchcraft" came from the 1963 "lost" album sessions. Had promoting the movie not been given such importance, it's likely the sides would have been reversed. Still gliding easily into the Top 40, "Witchcraft" was a great dance number with a restrained verse leading into an all-out chorus. Unusually for an Elvis record, the singing takes second place to the overall sound. The vocal is nicely measured, but the centerpiece of the track is Boots Randolph's extended saxophone solo. Though evidence of it was becoming rare on his albums, "Witchcraft" served to prove that Elvis could still rock.

Fun in Acapulco (Released November 15, 1963)

Fun in Acapulco is an odd album to assess. On one level, it is well sung, finely produced, and arranged with some thought. On another level, it was Elvis once again being forced to sing songs that made sense (barely) in the context of the film. Ultimately, this LP proves that most of the films were too stifling to do much with anymore. Making good music had long taken a backseat to what was required for the movies, and the songs reached new levels of lunacy with each project. Elvis' reputation was in deep trouble.

Maybe the biggest problem here is the misuse of the Mexican locale throughout. Nothing is hostile, but there's a smugness throughout the album. Though the album itself was flawed, the best *Blue Hawaii* music was illuminating. Here, "amigos" are thrown in cavalierly, and the Mexican rhythms are used in an inane context. That Parker wouldn't let Elvis go to Mexico to film undoubtedly cost the movie a lot of authentic local flavor, but of the songs themselves only a bellowing rendition of "Guadalajara" comes close to the real music or people.

Elvis' movie songs had been misguided before; now they were getting down-right strange. "The Bullfighter Was a Lady" is a ballad about a bull that falls in love with a lady matador. "El Toro" had Elvis letting loose the operatic qualities of his voice, but how many songs about bullfighting did there need to be? The insipid "(There's) No Room to Rhumba in a Sports Car" contains every bad cliché the title suggests. Don Robertson's "Marguerita" had decent stanzas, but the overblown arrangement lacked the subtlety that allowed his previous songs to shine. Elvis does the best he can to emote, but the setting is brutal.

Three songs are aimed at the aspiring tourist, but none conjure up the exotic imagery that would entice one to visit. "Fun in Acapulco" is harmless enough in isolation, but shares in the shortcomings of the whole album. Throw in some Mexican slang, insert a little extra percussion, and you have yourself a faux anthem with little feel for the subject.

"Mexico" is more phony, forced excitement, only this time there are a few pitiable attempts at humor. Though some awkward pauses are revealed by his absence, the duet film version with young Larry Domasin is unbearable. Even if the basic requirement of professionalism had been addressed, the composition is a patronizing chore to get through. "You Can't Say No in Acapulco" is the best of these because it comes across as a no-frills Elvis ballad. Sorely lacking by most standards, it's only worthy when compared with the overall standard of the LP.

More fun to watch than to hear, "Vino, Dinero Y Amor" at least has a faint spark. Good-natured fluff, "I Think I'm Gonna Like It Here" is also more suited for the screen than the studio. Even there, Elvis seems acutely embarrassed by lines like "Your troubles like bubbles will soon disappear in the air."

The wild "Bossa Nova Baby" is a fun piece of cheese from the period. There's a good beat and a funky little organ lick played by Dudley Brooks, and it provided the participants with a chance to let loose and enjoy themselves. Never mind that bossa nova is of Brazilian origin and has nothing to do with Mexico. Originally penned for the Clovers, it showed that Leiber and Stoller were still coming up with durable movie songs, even when no longer directly working with Elvis.

After the negative feedback for *It Happened at the World's Fair*, Parker decided to include "bonus songs" to fill out the movie albums. The first of these came from Elvis' May 1963 studio session, basically ruining any chance the intended album had for release. "Love Me Tonight" was an emblematic Don Robertson ballad. Romantic sentiment never failed to appeal to Elvis, often bringing out the best in his voice. If it lacked the distinction of Robertson's most rewarding pieces, a quick comparison with "Marguerita" speaks volumes on how much better the music was with Elvis taking the reins.

A fuzzy guitar line played by Jerry Kennedy put a bit of meat on the plate of the light rocker "Slowly but Surely." A gallop through familiar territory, it showed Elvis could remain playful under the right circumstances. Despite being one of the less remarkable cuts done for the unreleased album, like most "bonus songs" to come it largely laid waste to the soundtrack it accompanied.

"Kissin' Cousins"/"It Hurts Me" (Released February 10, 1964)

With the quality dropping rapidly, the decision to keep using movie songs as the top sides of singles was disastrous. If "Witchcraft" had been slightly better than "Bossa Nova Baby," "It Hurts Me" is on a different planet than "Kissin' Cousins." A gorgeous ballad written mainly by future country star Charlie Daniels, "It Hurts Me" had it all. The melody was striking, the lyrics intelligent, and the arrangement considered and classy. Elvis' vocal is among the most potent he ever pulled off. There's more depth than before, more open emotion. It's the first time Elvis sounds like his pain is personal.

He is maturing, in possession of an ever-increasing vocal dexterity, and this art is being relegated to backing up junk. Tellingly, after the January 1964 session that included "It Hurts Me," it would be well over two years before Elvis cut anything outside of movie fodder. That nobody in charge could grasp the fact that quality mattered is one of the tragedies of Elvis' career. Elvis could deliver the goods, but his real music was being brusquely shoved aside.

Kissin' Cousins (Released April 2, 1964)

Another new low, this was the first Presley record of any sort not to have at least momentary transcendence. Several of the songs are good, but none show signs of progression. A small buzz can be heard on some selections, as the actual technical quality of the sessions began to suffer. Elvis didn't bring his top game to the studio. Some tracks rouse him to try harder, but otherwise the material is excruciating.

"Smokey Mountain Boy" is on the level of a Cub Scout camping song. Something the kids on a *Peanuts* TV special might sing while hiking in the woods. Set to a milquetoast version of R&B, "Once Is Enough" finds Elvis in the iffy role of a twenty-nine-year-old senior citizen. Every single line on this mockery of a song is a worn-out cliché.

"Barefoot Ballad" is an offensive Southern stereotype of a song that Elvis' country character warbled onscreen. Disregarding the jug blowing for a second, that Elvis was told to sing in an exaggerated, cornpone manner is humiliating in itself. "Country Elvis" made a second appearance in "Kissin' Cousins," but because he is duetting with "City Elvis" without the visuals to differentiate them, on record it comes across as though he can't stay on pitch. A second tepid R&B attempt, "Kissin' Cousins" is ludicrous to the point of being stupid. The indefensible decision to put it out as a single put a serious damper in Elvis' hit-making ability.

"One Boy, Two Little Girls" is close to blatantly pilfering "A Boy Like Me, a Girl Like You," only it's become even worse in the interim. "There's Gold in the Mountains" is pop pap of the dullest sort. "Kissin' Cousins (Number 2)" exists because pre-set titles were passed out to Hill & Range writers competing to fill spots in the movies that called for songs. In this case, two different "Kissin' Cousins" were approved, and both ended up on the album. "Kissin' Cousins (Number 2)" opened the LP and movie, and has a quieter feel. It's not much better than the "Kissin' Cousins" chosen for the single, but it isn't as outrageously inept. Elvis comes across as dispirited, almost going into a monotone. When presented with multiple songs about kissing your cousin, one develops the tendency to lose hope.

Though obscured by what they are surrounded with, there were a number of palatable moments. "Anyone (Could Fall in Love with You)" at least sounded vaguely like real Elvis music. The Hawaiian tone on the lead guitar has a nice resonance, and Elvis does his best on lead. It was cut from the film over a half-dozen lesser numbers—further proof that the people making Elvis' movies were becoming evermore tone deaf. "Catching On Fast" bore a resemblance to rock and roll, but the horn parts had a clichéd air, and Elvis just isn't invested in it. The sudden ending was about the most creative aspect.

"Tender Feeling" was a sweet ballad that made nice use of the melody "Shenandoah." The lyrics are refreshingly straightforward, and Elvis puts them across gently and sincerely. As good as this is, it doesn't completely escape the trappings of the sessions. For instance, the mono mix is far better than the stereo version, as a hiss (which is much more distracting on CD) seems to have been eliminated. The taut, stringed intro and outro provide a welcome moment of musical experimentation on a record that is otherwise predictable.

Two songs from the May 1963 Nashville session round out the collection. With an annoyingly repetitive riff running throughout, the ballad "Echoes of Love" wasn't any better than the soundtrack recordings. It was recorded with more care, but that's all it has going for it. "It's a Long Lonely Highway" holds more interest. Light touches of R&B and an attractive, measured beat accompany a peculiarly heartening tale of abandonment and loss. Outwardly addressing a failed relationship, the integral message was to keep going in the face of obstacles. It was a life lesson Elvis felt acutely at the time.

"What'd I Say"/"Viva Las Vegas" (Released April 28, 1964)

Containing two of the most effervescent cuts from *Viva Las Vegas*, this was one of several Elvis singles this year that had their chart placement diluted by divided airplay. "What'd I Say" is the less well-known of these two performances today, but at the time it charted eight places higher, almost in the Top 20. Among the dozens of versions of this Ray Charles R&B standard, Elvis' recording is in the shadow only of Ray's epic original and Jerry Lee Lewis' hot cover. Restrained, compared with how he would handle it live in 1969, this low-key approach had a supple sensuality that worked on film. Elvis acts as the calm at the center of the storm of the frenzied background. Acclaimed session saxophonist Steve Douglas wails away maniacally, and the combined efforts of the Jubilee Four and the Carole Lombard Quartet lend the song a celebratory air.

"Viva Las Vegas" has undeniably gained stature over time. It wasn't on the fourth volume of the *Gold Records* series, and Elvis never even rehearsed it for his live show. But after first depicting the town (and the 1969 comeback) in the 1981 docudrama *This Is Elvis*, it has since been used in countless television shows and movies addressing Elvis or Las Vegas. It wouldn't be an exaggeration to call it the informal Vegas anthem, and for valid reason. The fast samba rhythm is laid under lyrics that encapsulate the luxurious, tawdry duality that defines the city. Having to fast-talk the lyric and hold long notes on the chorus, Elvis' larynx gets quite a workout. Amazing as ever under the right circumstances, his elocution is faultless.

"Ask Me"/"Ain't That Loving You Baby" (Released September 22, 1964)

The lovely ballad "Ask Me" hailed from the short January 1964 session. It had been attempted in May 1963, but Elvis thought he could better it. The 1964 version is smoother, Elvis has more assurance in his voice, and the instrumentation has an improved flow. There's a hint of the Latin sound in the music, but Elvis made the decision to sing with no trace of affectation.

"Ain't That Loving You Baby" had been recorded all the way back in 1958 but remained unreleased because Elvis hadn't felt like he achieved a proper master. On later takes, Elvis tried it faster (check out the 1985 *Reconsider Baby* LP for an edit of various fast takes that rocks unmercifully hard), but the one used here is mid-tempo. A vivacious piece of rock, the drums sound right out of a fifties striptease act. Less dated than the recording date would suggest, it was close enough to current tastes to not come off as an anomaly. Both songs lodged comfortably in the Top 20 but rose no higher because of the split radio play.

Roustabout (Released October 20, 1964)

This album was an unaccountably popular soundtrack, going all the way to the top of the charts. There's some decent pop and rock, but it isn't what you could remotely call a classic. To say it is one of the better movie albums of the mid-sixties isn't a ringing endorsement. Half the songs are silly, and all of it was archaic, considering the rapid advancements then happening in rock and roll. Not a painful listen, it wasn't a rousing one either.

"Little Egypt" was one of Elvis' few credible rock-and-roll songs of the era. Like "Girls! Girls! Girls!," this is a humorous Leiber and Stoller cut originally recorded by the Coasters. One really has to lament the fact that Jerry and Mike were driven away by Parker. Their penchant for writing quirky novelty songs with real musicality and wit could have fulfilled the needs of the soundtracks without dumbing down Elvis' music. A perfect balance of playful sexuality and wit, "Little Egypt" gives a tantalizing glimpse of what might have been.

"Poison Ivy League" attempts to be another funny number. The music is peppy, and Elvis puts forth a reasonable effort. It's unimportant that it isn't as self-knowing as "Little Egypt." It achieves its modest goal of being sound LP and screen material. "Hard Knocks" rocks along pretty well. Elvis makes an effort to sound tougher than usual, and the guitar work is pretty sharp. With Elvis lavishing some care, "One Track Heart" is respectable pop with a catchy hook.

The mild "Big Love, Big Heartache" ends weakly, though Elvis' attractive performance is more than passable. "There's a Brand New Day on the Horizon" is more typical of the decline in fortunes. The sound picture is muddled, the transitions from verse to verse come across as forced, and Elvis seems slightly lost.

The rest of the score is tied to the setting of the film, and is distinctly inferior to the less topical material. "Roustabout" is geeky, with abysmal lyrics and a generic backing. It was recorded at the last minute to replace a respectable rocker of the same name. "Carny Town" was short, and had Elvis acting like a barker. The music and vocal arrangements are all right, but the words fundamentally ruin it. As it doesn't have any quality to speak of, "It's Carnival Time" is twice as bad. It poorly incorporates the familiar "Entry of the Gladiators" associated closely with numerous fairs and circuses.

"Wheels on My Heels" should be better than it is. Elvis loved motorcycles; car and cycle songs were huge at the time; and along with Marlon Brando and James Dean, he nearly invented the fifties greaser. Bearing no trace of cool or rebellion, the lyrics are hokey, and Elvis sounds ill at ease. The worst song included was "It's a Wonderful World." The words are sappy as all get out, and there was nowhere to go with such a trite melody.

Girl Happy (Released March 1, 1965)

For those hoping that the follow-up to *Roustabout* would maintain the same modest standards, *Girl Happy* was a considerable letdown. As a film, it was more humorous and well cast than usual. On record, it was another dip in Elvis' fortunes. It attempts to present Elvis with rock-and-roll material, but it fails miserably.

Other than how out-of-date it sounded, the worst thing about the album is the technical amateurism. Suffocating the music, Elvis' voice is poorly balanced, and is even sped up on the title track. Songs cut out too quickly, or start hastily. Instruments sound hollow and off pitch. Bad songs are one thing; this was indicative of all-around disinterest in the final product. There was no way *Girl Happy* could have been a good LP, but it could have at very least had a proficient mix.

Elvis made an effort to some extent, but was disgusted by the flimsiness of the material. Eventually, this led to him walking out halfway through the sessions. He dutifully showed up to overdub the rest of his leads but came off more apathetic than ever before. The Beatles' success on an artistic and commercial level had to have fueled Elvis' realization of just how far off-track he now was. Presley was also starting a spiritual journey that put into sharp focus how insignificant his career had become.

"Girl Happy" works as a piece of camp, but Elvis sounded ridiculous with his voice sped up. That it remained one of the best tracks says a lot about how bad most of the soundtrack was. "Do the Clam" was an atrocious idea for a dance song, and the stereo mix is severe and disorienting. Using an overblown arrangement to try to pump it up, it too has a perverse kind of entertainment to it. If several notches better, "The Meanest Girl in Town" still only reaches the level of adequate. Not marred by bad playing or a poor mix, Elvis leaves the impression of being more awake.

"I've Got to Find My Baby" rocks enough to the point where it would have been given a decent reading a few years before. Here, however, the contrived excitement leaves Elvis sounding dispirited and unmotivated. "Startin' Tonight" is another weak rocker that doesn't move Elvis to put any expression into his voice. The intro is a roll call of colleges that doesn't mean anything on record, and the end just peters out. "Fort Lauderdale Chamber of Commerce" has an off-key piano, and is a sleazy tune that Elvis' character repeatedly sings to pick up girls. It too stumbles to a close with haste.

"Spring Fever" was one of those lame formula songs Elvis duets on with the co-stars in the film. Shelley Fabares could sing better than most of the actors who warbled with Elvis, but she was still edited out of the record on Parker's orders. "Wolf Call" is dated pap, with some of the worst lyrics Elvis ever had to muddle through. Not able to hide his feelings anymore, he sounds plainly ashamed to be singing it.

Being as it was the number that caused Elvis to walk, it should come as no shock that "Do Not Disturb" is plodding and artificial. It strives to be titillating, but there isn't a hint of heat. Elvis worked at it, take after take, eventually bubbling over with frustration. "Cross My Heart and Hope to Die" is equally pedestrian, though it at least has a sense of melodic flow.

"Puppet on a String" has a pleasant melody, but Elvis seems only slightly attentive. The off-key piano renders any argument of real quality null. Issued on 45 when nothing on *Harum Scarum* proved to be suitable for radio, it outperformed "Do the Clam" in denting the Top 20.

The only value came with the bonus song. An out-take from March 1962, "You'll Be Gone" is the second and final song Elvis helped compose. In early 1961, he came up with the idea of writing a new lyric to Cole Porter's "Begin the Beguine." Red West handled most of the task, but Porter refused to let them change his song. It sat on the shelf a while, and then Charlie Hodge came up with the idea for a fresh two-chord pattern. One of the countless Mediterranean ballads of the period, "You'll Be Gone" stands out for having a beguiling melody and Elvis' complete attention. His voice soars with longing, and the lyric, which concerns sexual desire, is direct. It's a shame Elvis never came up with any composition ideas in the future, considering the way his participation inspired him to give a little extra.

Harum Scarum (Released November 3, 1965)

Harum Scarum is where things get rough. The songs are badly mixed, with Elvis' voice overpowering to the point that the rest is muddy. This was done on Parker's instructions—Elvis hated drowning out his singers and musicians. It would be nice to say the songs make up for it, but they don't. There is an attempt to put a few Eastern sounds into the music, but it comes off as a joke compared to what bands like the Beatles and the Rolling Stones would soon do with these exotic textures.

A few songs are OK, though the mix hampers them greatly. "Shake That Tambourine" has abysmal lyrics but a good beat. It was at least competent, if not in any way exciting. Sporting a cool piano lick from Floyd Cramer, "Hey Little Girl" is faintly decent rock and roll, yet this is ruined for any poor soul who sees the film. Onscreen, Elvis looks like a pervert and a fool as he sings this fairly sensual lyric to a very young child. The look on his face is one of humiliation.

"So Close, Yet So Far (from Paradise)" is the only song with legs. With his voice more resonant than before, it's a big dramatic ballad of the kind Elvis would return to often in the seventies. Though the mix is as bad as on the rest of the record, there is something moving about "So Close." At the low point of his career, Elvis conveys a level of melancholy both tragic and inspiring.

The rest is best forgotten. The film out-take "Animal Instinct" has fleeting moments of interest, but none long enough to lift the track out of mediocrity. The others don't get that far. "Kismet," "Golden Coins," and "Mirage" are limp ballads with generic Eastern references. Elvis' voice doesn't fail him, even if he does sound bored to the point of being numb.

"Harem Holiday," "Go East Young Man," and "My Desert Serenade" are insipid efforts that try to convey the glamour of the Middle East locale. They are as cardboard as the sets. The tempos may vary, but all are poorly conceived and recorded. The bathetic "Wisdom of the Ages" was another film out-take, this one ineptly tackling the meaning of life. A bunch of gobbledygook about "the sands of time," in Elvis' catalogue it rivals only the 1970 misfire "Life" for airheaded "poetry."

"Tell Me Why"/"Blue River" (Released December 3, 1965)

Taken from the first set of sessions at Radio Recorders from January 1957, "Tell Me Why" is a fairly bland ballad. If the performance was somewhat overwrought, the commitment Elvis used to give even his lesser songs now stood in sharp contrast to his current work. Very much in the mold of side two of the *Loving You*

LP, "Tell Me Why" was well performed but ill considered. By the end of 1965, it sounded antiquated—which can't be said about Presley's best fifties output—and was only a minor success. "Blue River" is from the canceled 1963 LP, and was later issued on the *Double Trouble* album.

Frankie and Johnny (Released March 1, 1966)

That this is a minuscule improvement on the albums it followed and preceded isn't anything to be proud of. *Frankie and Johnny* gets away with a bit more than usual due to it being an early-twentieth-century period film. That doesn't excuse the ineptitude—it only means that the outdated sound is marginally acceptable. Suffering from the same atrocious vocal mixes that marred all of his 1965 masters, the sound is so bad that it strains all credibility that it was recorded at the same Radio Recorders studio that delivered many of Elvis' sharpest recordings.

"Frankie and Johnny" is a pretty decent version of the period standard. The arrangement seems thought-out, the touches of jazz rare on an Elvis record. Wanting good material desperately, he squeezed everything he could out of it. "Down by the Riverside"/"When the Saints Go Marching In" was a satisfactory medley of these gospel standards. The stultifying sessions left Elvis unable to emote, not loosening up even on songs he enjoyed singing in private.

There were a couple of ballads pretty enough to rise above the prevailing mood of languor. "What Every Woman Lives For" is a bit sexist, but it did inadvertently reflect the prevailing mood at the start of the 1900s. Lyric aside, Elvis' smooth vocals are worthy of a listen. It's admittedly bland, but "Please Don't Stop Loving Me" is the LP's one moment of honest emotion. It has a lovely melody, the lyrics are proficient, plus Elvis comes off as if he's feeling what he's singing.

With Elvis in the midst of the worst creative period of his career, memorable cuts are exceedingly scarce. "Chesay" is a mock-gypsy melody over a lyric concerning good luck spells. Sort of fun once or twice, but not anything to play regularly, "Everybody Come Aboard," "Shout It Out," and "Come Along" have old-time Dixie horns and are ornamented with ukulele and banjo. These songs sound happy enough, I suppose, but Elvis had so much more in him than doing second-rate vaudeville.

"Hard Luck" has good intentions. It's a blues that musically isn't half bad, but the lyrics are nothing like real blues. Elvis was undoubtedly the best white blues singer that ever was, but this time he sounds fake. "Beginner's Luck" is the worst ballad here. It has no personality, and is a mere clone of a dozen other movie songs.

"Look Out, Broadway" had a ridiculous rationale in the film, and without the visual it comes off as cornball. "Petunia, the Gardener's Daughter" is sad as it has no more wit or ability than your local grade-school play, with moronic jokes about "two lips" vs. "tulips." The situation was bad.

Paradise, Hawaiian Style (Released June 10, 1966)

The weakest LP to bear Elvis' name during his lifetime, there are only faint hints of his immense talent here. Elvis seemed to realize it was a joke, and his continual laughter during the sessions makes the out-takes a lot more palatable than the real album. The one quality track was cut from the film, and the recording quality is muddy. Snipped or not, "Sand Castles" towers over the other songs. The melody and vocals are beauties, and the lyric has some decent imagery. The acoustic guitar work is also striking in that it sounds informed by the folk-rock of the day. It hints at what Elvis could have been doing during this period, had the quality of his movies and their soundtracks not taken a downturn.

"Paradise, Hawaiian Style" is tepid, but is fairly well known for being included in the opening sequence of *Aloha from Hawaii*. In that it was written to be background music for Hawaiian scenery, its shallow artistic ambitions are fulfilled. "This Is My Heaven" has identical meager aspirations, and is (just) passable.

Distinguished only by being the worst of this sorry bunch, "Datin'" is yet another movie song written for children. Elvis couldn't stop laughing at the trite lyrics, so to get a complete performance it had to be spliced together from different takes. "A Dog's Life" found Elvis nine years removed from Steve Allen, singing a song to a dog—only this time, the song is actually about a dog. Even splicing couldn't hide the fact that Elvis could barely conceal his giggles. Elvis' session asides are funny, but an element of sadness lurked underneath the mirth.

The "one little slip" couplet in "House of Sand" has a pleasant structure, but the remainder of the song is horrible enough to cancel it out completely. "Queenie Wahine's Papaya" is merely an exercise to sing a tongue twister progressively faster. Trying to be sexy and clever, "Scratch My Back (Then I'll Scratch Yours)" doesn't cut the mustard in either department. The only thing that can be said about the last two songs is that the cast members' pitiful duets aren't reproduced on record. Elvis seems to be flirting with himself on "Scratch My Back," but that's a small price to pay.

Of interest only for how elaborately it was staged, "Drums of the Islands" is a wan attempt to incorporate real Hawaiian music. Seemingly written so the film can include gimmicky stop-motion effects, "Stop Where You Are" is appalling. Call it artificial, insipid, or simply wanting—it fits all these descriptions.

Audibly lacking passion for what he was being given, Elvis was inert for virtually the entire album. He was also visibly overweight, so RCA elected to use photo from *Fun in Acapulco* for the cover. He had been completely demoralized, but after hitting bottom he began an overdue fight back to the top. There were plenty of bad movie songs to come, but a corner had been turned.

Spinout (Released October 31, 1966)

Spinout was the first Elvis album in many years that hinted at artistic growth. Most of this is down to the three excellent bonus songs, but even the soundtrack is fairly enjoyable. A lot of the songs are formulaic, but the performances and arrangements are a step up from what Elvis had recorded for his movies since *Viva Las Vegas.*

These are generally better songs than he had recently been given, but it's Presley's improved attitude toward his work that makes a true difference. The musicians also step up their game, with Floyd Cramer on organ sounding especially contemporary. While not on the level of what leading groups were doing, it's still enjoyable. Mixed with more care than anything since *Roustabout,* that there isn't any garbage on the record makes for a welcome change.

"Stop, Look and Listen" is a frantic rocker with organ to the fore. If clumsy in places, there's an element of daring in Elvis' voice not often heard of late. If "Spinout" wasn't good single material, it does work as part of the album. Elvis' singing is well nuanced, and another hot keyboard line nearly makes up for the racing terms sprinkled throughout. With its snake-charmer motifs, "Adam and Evil" should be crummy, yet there's a zest to it that renders it inoffensively cheesy fun. It's as if Elvis decided that instead of despairing over the situation, he would make the best of it by having a good time.

"I'll Be Back" is a self-conscious finale to the movie, but onscreen and on record it benefited from Elvis' positive attitude. Much the same can be said about "Beach Shack." Out-takes show Elvis unable to contain himself over the "dum de dum" line. If lacking as a song, the bright mood means it goes down smoothly. "Never Say Yes" is a sprightly rocker with a Bo Diddley–influenced beat. While the lyrics are puerile, the prevailing high spirits once again push a mediocre track to a reasonable level.

Yet another rock-oriented song, "Smorgasbord" is the best of the cuts to come from the actual soundtrack. Elvis gets into the freewheeling vibe, the saxophone keeps things moving along steadily, and the lyrics can even be termed as clever, though the conceit of comparing ladies to buffet dishes wouldn't fly today.

With a reasonable facsimile of rock being the focus, there were only two ballads included in the flick. "All That I Am" is ambitious in form, yet pretty dull to listen to. A string section was something new for an Elvis record, but the song was too insipid to make an impression. "Am I Ready" is far more engaging because there's heart in it. Letting each line breathe, Elvis handles his vocal carefully. The resulting recording is undeservedly obscure.

If the film songs are fairly entertaining, it is the three bonus songs that make *Spinout* something special. Hearing these three brilliant songs makes you realize how good Elvis could have been throughout the entire decade, had his circumstances been different.

"Down in the Alley" was Elvis' best blues since "Reconsider Baby." Stemming from his May 1966 Nashville sessions, it was a pleasant shock that he could still even sing the blues. Here, on one of his most refreshingly raunchy recordings, Elvis sounds born anew.

Elvis' artistic rejuvenation was confirmed in spades on his cover of Bob Dylan's "Tomorrow Is a Long Time," another May 1966 cut. Elvis had been listening to a lot of folk, and had heard this song on Odetta's *Sings Dylan* album. Her elongated bluesy arrangement was perfect for Elvis, but he took the lyric to a different place. Where she comes across as soulful and resilient, Elvis is quiet and wistful. When he sings, "I can't remember the sound of my own name," you can hear the insecurity he was feeling. He also simplified the instrumentation, giving it a country tinge all his own.

By doing this kind of challenging material, Elvis was fighting valiantly against the morass of dead ends his career had become. Because of its sheer quality, "Tomorrow Is a Long Time" is one of the key performances in Presley's career. There's an intimacy that's very special, a lifting of the public mask. By doing a long track removed from the sounds that made him famous, Elvis gained greater freedom to experiment in the future. He was still aware of what was going on in music, and more than that, he still cared. Of all the countless cover versions of his songs, this is the one Bob Dylan loves most.

Finally, we have "I'll Remember You," a crystalline ballad from the June 1966 Nashville date. The promise of new maturity cultivated by "It Hurts Me" finally reaches fruition. Elvis' voice took on more weight as it deepened. Using shade and nuance, he expresses a heartbreakingly beautiful sense of longing. The musicians also excel, with the guitars having more complexity than in the past—a sort of delicate touch that meshes perfectly with the romantic air. After several years where Elvis seemed to be heading into creative oblivion, tracks like "I'll Remember You" were heartening. Though the cycle of bad films and songs hadn't yet come to a conclusion, the incipient signs of his return can be traced back to here.

Double Trouble (Released June 1, 1967)

After *Spinout* and *How Great Thou Art*, *Double Trouble* was a massive setback. The sound was muffled, the songs were terrible, and it came out at the worst possible time. Released the same day as the Beatles' *Sgt. Pepper*, it was worlds removed from what was happening in rock and roll. Three 1963 bonus cuts taken from the abandoned studio album were nice, but the *Double Trouble* soundtrack songs were so execrable that the album is one of Elvis' worst.

"Double Trouble" was an adequate title song in terms of tempo, but the lyrics are clumsy, and the sound picture unfocused. "Long Legged Girl (with the Short Dress On)" is tolerable faux hard rock. The guitar is dirty, but the lick is humdrum, and Elvis sounds detached. It wasn't a good single choice, but it has a pulpy cheese thing going. "City by Night" is the closest Elvis ever got to non-blues-based jazz. Had he tried harder, or been properly miked up, it may have risen beyond the level of a curio.

"I Love Only One Girl" is a strange amalgamation of traditional European sounds. Set to a series of sight gags, it's one of numerous movie cuts tailored to the screen at the expense of playability on record. "Old MacDonald" is outrageously insulting to the artist and audience—one of the all-time ghastliest ideas in Elvis' entire cinematic oeuvre. Putting on a brave face before the cameras, Elvis left the recording session in exasperation and embarrassment.

"Baby, If You'll Give Me All of Your Love" and "There Is So Much World to See" try to be hip, à la Tom Jones, but are hammy embarrassments. Elvis' vocals sound thick and syrupy, the arrangements are square, and the lyrics are self-conscious and lumbering. "It Won't Be Long" is no more than a mediocre rocker, cut from the film's final edit.

Finally, we have the hissy "Could I Fall in Love." In the movie, Elvis' character sings along with his own record, creating a self-duet. Why this was deemed a good idea for the LP is a mystery. That this soundtrack was partially recorded on the woefully cavernous MGM soundstage meant that you had a major loss of sound quality when Elvis did a simple overdub of a second vocal.

The three songs from Nashville 1963 aren't enough to save the album, but they do keep it from being the lowest of the low. "Blue River" is a swift, middling rocker. It's charming next to the soundtrack material, but feels like it could have been fleshed out. That it had to be extended by edits reveals it was filler from inception. Its use as the flip of a 1965 single was an act of desperation. "Never Ending" has also been a flip side, but this pretty ballad was worthy of the position. If the chorus is ordinary, the opening couplet is a lovely bit of poetry. Elvis' voice was sugary sweet, and the melody well considered.

The best of these songs was a country ditty entitled "What Now, What Next, Where To." Lyrically, it recalls the days of "I'm Left, You're Right, She Gone," while the music is pure 1963 Nashville. Floyd Cramer's piano lines are sophisticated, and Elvis' vocalizing is letter-perfect. Despite recording in Nashville often, Elvis didn't cut much country in the mid-sixties. This rare treat offers another hint at what he could have achieved, had the soundtracks not been such a draining diversion.

Clambake (Released October 10, 1967)

A schizoid record if ever there was one, *Clambake* has some of Elvis' best and worst recordings sitting awkwardly side by side. Combining most of Elvis' strong September 1967 session with the generally wretched *Clambake* score is the main cause of the split. To add to that, the soundtrack had some songs that were shockingly good next to others that hit a new low. What you hear is a desperate Elvis fighting off the shackles of a system that failed him years ago. Not yet completely free, he was winning the battle simply by making music with guts.

Outside of the stunning "Guitar Man," the first side is among the most lacking on any Presley album. "Clambake" is a take on "Shortnin' Bread" that begs ridicule. Was Parker completely clueless about how bad it would sound alongside real Elvis music?

"Who Needs Money?" was a plot-driven duet with Jordanaire Ray Walker that was slightly comical when lip-synched by co-star Will Hutchins. As a record, the only word for it is terrible. "A House That Has Everything" is a tedious ballad with no flavor, and with Elvis bored to the point of numb. Endeavoring to get across Elvis' character's message of love meaning more than money, it has a sanctimonious air hardly conducive to romance.

"Confidence" is the song "High Hopes," with adults trying to sing like children in the background. If that wasn't awful enough, it was performed on a playground to little kids, making Elvis look like a big oaf. It had nothing to do with the rest of the film, and Elvis looks almost ill at having to do it. The faux rocker "Hey, Hey, Hey" demonstrated that songs involved with the storyline fared no better. The lack of visuals concerning the "girls" he addresses at the end—or of any background to the convoluted lyric—renders it superfluous to the audio medium.

After that, "How Can You Lose What You Never Had" sounds like a masterpiece. It isn't extraordinary, but the soulful, country-tinged music is solid. Played either by Jordanaire Hoyt Hawkins or Floyd Cramer, the organ is slick, and Elvis makes an effort to overcome the clumsy words. Reflecting the unfathomable tastes of those who made these decisions, it was snipped from the film. "The Girl I Never Loved" is similar in that it is remarkably good for a mid-sixties soundtrack recording. There are a few nice changes where Elvis has to hold his notes over the appealing melody.

The remainder of the LP was cut at the September session, the best of which represents some of the finest material Elvis ever tackled. "You Don't Know Me" was first cut at the proper *Clambake* sessions in a respectable version used in the film. The soundtrack cut reflects Ray Charles' version, but for vinyl, Elvis slowed it down and simplified the arrangement. It gains a lot in intimacy, and there's almost a lachrymose quality to his voice that is affecting. "Singing Tree" is a slow ballad as well. The song has the peculiar conceit of being sung to a tree, but Elvis' voice is especially strong in the parts where he double-tracks himself in a technologically enabled duet.

Over the past five years, country music had been all but eradicated from Elvis' repertoire. With Elvis taking control again, the rest of his career would see it return to a place of prominence. "Just Call Me Lonesome" was first popularized by Eddy Arnold in 1955. Elvis' version is hard country in a fashion he hadn't attempted since the fifties. His deepening voice doesn't affect an accent—he just sings beautifully, with the accompaniment of Pete Drake's steel guitar high in the mix. There's a feeling of despondency infused into the cut. Whether it was the loss of his twin brother at birth, the death of his mother, or perhaps the feeling that he didn't know if he was loved strictly as a person, Elvis enigmatically remained something of a loner, despite having constant companionship.

"Big Boss Man" was a fantastic blues popularized by Jimmy Reed some years before. It's a very tough, gritty song—one that Elvis throws himself into. Jerry Reed's grumbling guitar starts things off, and an uninhibited Elvis gives it a masterful reading. Wailing and vivacious, Charlie McCoy's harmonica playing puts it over even more. Elvis never used an onstage harmonica player, and preferred to use Charlie Rich's rockabilly pop arrangement when he performed "Big Boss Man" in concert. It was only the lowly state of Presley's career that kept this from scoring high chart positions and sales.

"Guitar Man" is one of Elvis' most defining records. The tale of a guitar player trying to make it as a professional obviously resonated with him. Relishing the chance to put across his own experiences fictionally, he would never sound more sincere or true. Jerry Reed's sizzling acoustic guitar playing on his own composition is superlative, but even he never sang it with this kind of passion. Performing with attitude, it takes Elvis three short minutes to wipe out the schlock of the last half-decade. Running on sheer bravado, he careens through this fast-talking blues without a care in the world. The unedited master (found on the six-LP/five-CD boxed set *From Nashville to Memphis*) gets even crazier, with Reed strumming wildly, and Elvis swinging into "What'd I Say." The song suffered as a result of Elvis' lowered professional standing. One of his most timeless recordings, it isn't all that well known.

Speedway (Released June 25, 1968)

Speedway wasn't close to being the worst Elvis album, but at #82 it was his lowest chart position yet. The times had changed, and there was no longer a market for Elvis movies or soundtracks. That Elvis was concurrently shooting his NBC TV special when this record came out shows how much he himself had moved past them.

As usual, most of the best selections were "bonus songs." "Western Union" went way back to 1963 and the "lost" album. A blatant retread of "Return to Sender," it was probably considered too derivative to issue before. Be that as it may, "Western Union" is a sprightly pop tune that actually rocks harder than "Return to Sender." Fresher due to not being overexposed, the witty lyrics and fine vocal make this an agreeable enough indulgence. After all, answer songs or follow-ups to proven hits were a common practice in the fifties and early sixties.

"Mine" is a solid (if somewhat ordinary) ballad cut at the September 1967 Nashville session. Elvis' maturing voice is in fine fettle, melodically it's pretty, but it lacks a memorable hook to put it over as more than quality album-filler. "Goin' Home" was cut in January 1968 for *Stay Away, Joe*, and the improvement over the *Speedway* cuts is distinct, if subtle. Stylistically closer to where Elvis' own instincts would have led, the production is comparatively natural and warm. The lyrics try too hard to be poetic, but Elvis was committed again to making his music the best it could be.

"Suppose" and "Five Sleepy Heads" were cut at the *Speedway* sessions but removed from the finished film. "Five Sleepy Heads" is simply the old lullaby done straight. It's OK for a kids' record, but yet another song that shouldn't have been considered for an artist of the caliber of Elvis Presley.

"Suppose" is far more worthwhile. A slow, piano-based ballad Elvis had recorded semi-professionally at home, it was a song close to his heart. Benefiting from Elvis' full attention, the master was as good as his regular contemporary songs. Featuring an unusually vulnerable-sounding performer, it has dark lyrics that obliquely mention suicide. A sensitive love song of the type Elvis admired, it's frustrating that it was not used as this album's single.

The songs used in the movie were mostly outdated trifles. Nancy Sinatra was used as a selling point, even getting her own solo number. "Your Groovy Self" isn't her best cut, but it did sound more like what was on the charts than anything outside of "Suppose." It's sobering to remember that she was more popular than Elvis at the time. Their duet, "There Ain't Nothing Like a Song," is awful. Neither of the performers seems inspired, which is reasonable enough, considering how poor the song was from conception to mastering.

"Speedway" bore a slight resemblance to real car songs, but they had been out of fashion for four years. The piano playing was better than normal for a soundtrack, and musician Larry Muhoberac would go on to be a part of Elvis' 1969 live band. "Who Are You? (Who Am I?)" has the distinction of being one of Elvis' least convincing ballads. Pretentious, plastic, and boring is all that needs to be said.

"He's Your Uncle, Not Your Dad" is a lame novelty number about paying taxes. The mind-boggling dance sequence that accompanied it in the film had Elvis, co-star Bill Bixby, and a bunch of extras dancing and singing in the middle of an I.R.S. office. The scene ranks among the ten most ill-advised moments of Elvis' screen oeuvre—it has to be seen to be believed.

Not quite as traumatic were the songs chosen for the "Your Time Hasn't Come Yet, Baby"/"Let Yourself Go" single. "Your Time Hasn't Come Yet, Baby" was sung to a little girl in the film, but at least it was age-appropriate this time. Decent light pop, it loses a lot in the arid mix. The other thing holding it back was a disjointed vocal intro that takes a few seconds to get on pitch.

"Let Yourself Go" is a curate's egg. The 1968 remake for the *Singer Presents Elvis* special proves there's a decent song inside, trying to get out. By contrast, the 1967 master sounds terribly dated, which is no surprise as it had originally been submitted in early 1965 for *Harum Scarum*. The echoed, clapped intro is clever, and Larry's piano work is exemplary, but the backing vocals are infantile.

Speedway would mercifully be the last soundtrack LP. Not every Elvis album to follow was satisfying, but only the 1974 "comedy" LP *Having Fun with Elvis on Stage* would be an out-and-out disaster. Despite the limitations Elvis' personal decline would place on some of his performances in the mid-seventies, creatively he would never fall into such a deep hole again.

18

Hard Luck

1965

Nineteen sixty-five was the low point. Even some of the more agonizing 1976–77 live shows have more going for them than the stuff Elvis cut during what was otherwise one of the best years in rock-and-roll history. As he mentioned in a 1969 interview with Ray Connolly, all Elvis focused on at this point was riding the film contracts out until he could get back onstage.

Everything he did in 1965 was a soundtrack, and even the few decent songs were hampered by bad mixes. Elvis was still respected enough that his records sold moderately well, but his status would be swiftly eroded.

Studio Work

Elvis recorded the soundtracks for three movies this year. The results were appalling. Even the songwriters themselves weren't happy about having to write songs with titles like "Queenie Wahine's Papaya" or "Shake That Tambourine." Elvis didn't want to do them, but he had signed on the dotted line. Growing up poor, as he had, it just wasn't in his character to break his professional commitments. Up until this point, Elvis had tried his best with even the worst of songs, but now he just couldn't motivate himself. Though he attempted to get better songs and scripts, the people with the power to do anything about it only saw the cash coming in.

On Celluloid

Elvis was now being given roles his music and persona were completely unsuitable for. He resembled Valentino slightly, but even Colonel Parker realized that *Harum Scarum* was a bomb. Not that he helped the situation. Parker was so out of touch that he thought a talking camel could be filmed telling the story as it unfolded. Considering how pathetic the movie was, it would have fit right in. The only progression at all was that Elvis' voice was maturing nicely.

The next film was an improvement—how could it not be? *Frankie and Johnny* was a period piece set roughly at the beginning of the twentieth century. The songs were accordingly archaic, but most of them were very bad. "Frankie and Johnny" was a popular song of the era the film took place in, and was staged nicely as a casino performance featuring the cast. The notion of having Elvis

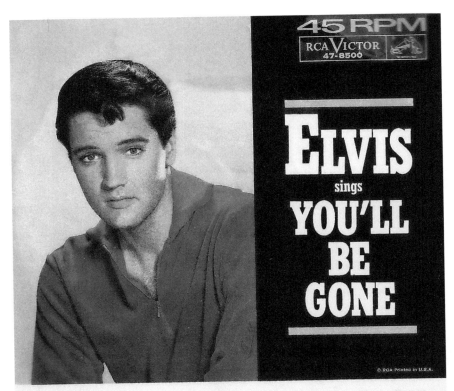

Elvis' career hit a new low with the release of "Do the Clam" in 1965. Too bad this pretty flip side he co-authored was ignored.

and leading lady Donna Douglas play the "real" Frankie and Johnny was a good one, but the only thing truly different about this movie was the setting. The plot ended up being yet another to center on Elvis' romantic escapades, wasting the opportunity to make a real movie.

Paradise, Hawaiian Style was the nadir of Elvis' career. "Sand Castles" was the only salvageable song, and it was cut from the film. The music would have been laughable if it hadn't been plain sad. Though the movie was set and filmed in Hawaii, a paunchy Elvis spent most of the beach scenes fully dressed. A pitiful attempt to cash in on the commercial success of Elvis' previous Hawaiian pictures, this half-assed movie made *Blue Hawaii* look like *Citizen Kane*.

Popularity and Impact

Based far more on his track record than on his current work, Elvis' music still charted highly. *Girl Happy* and *Harum Scarum* both hit the Top 10, as did a

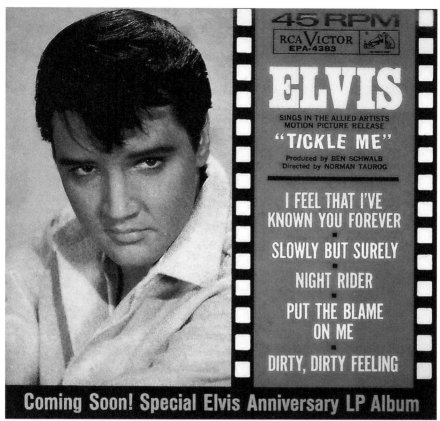

Tickle Me had one of Elvis' best post–*Viva Las Vegas* soundtracks by default, as all of the songs were sixties album cuts. With the EP being a shrinking format, this 1965 record didn't match the success of the two *Tickle Me* 45s.

comp of mostly unreleased material called *Elvis for Everyone*, released to mark the occasion of Elvis' first decade with RCA. Half of the tracks were excellent. Fans getting to hear such recordings as "When It Rains, It Really Pours" and "Memphis, Tennessee" forgave the fact that there was also a lot of filler. With no notes on the origin or date of the recordings, it would be a good ten years before there was any idea where many of the songs came from.

The *Tickle Me* songs were clearly better than Presley's current offerings, and the singles "(Such an) Easy Question" and "I'm Yours" nearly broke the Top 10. "Do the Clam" and "Puppet on a String" from *Girl Happy* were both moderately successful, with the latter's better quality resulting in an improved chart placing.

Elvis' big hit for 1965 was "Crying in the Chapel." Though he originally thought this out-take from *His Hand in Mine* was sub-par, it would be his only gospel smash. While it's unknown whether Elvis' consent was even sought prior to releasing the song, if he did change his mind, it was for the better. A beautifully nuanced recording, the only flaw was that its five-year vintage didn't allow for Elvis' current image to get a needed overhaul. "Blue Christmas" charted high on the holiday charts again, this time with the more appropriate "Santa Claus Is Back in Town" backing it. The success was welcome, but by now it was an oldie twice over.

By this time, there was no pretending that Elvis was a contemporary artist. His impact compared with Bob Dylan, the Beatles, the Beach Boys, and the Rolling Stones was next to nil. He still appealed to the more loyal (or less discerning) of his old fans, but he wasn't making many new ones. "Crying in the Chapel" reminded people that Elvis was still around, but his recent work was so poor, any goodwill generated was short-lived. Incoming cash was keeping Parker and RCA from insisting on—or even allowing for—a change. The needed turnaround would have to come from Elvis himself, but his fans were logically thinking this might never occur.

19

Sweet Song of a Choir

Elvis' Gospel Recordings

ospel music was a core influence on every major star from Sun Records' mid-to-late-fifties rockabilly period. Because of this, gospel was as equal a part of the genesis of rock and roll as blues or country. Perhaps the major difference in the American rock artists of the fifties and the "British Invasion" bands of the sixties is the fact that gospel wasn't a part of the latter's formative influences.

Elvis had a sincere love of gospel. He never received a Grammy for any of his secular work, but won three for his gospel records. If one thing ties his entire career together, it's the continued influence gospel music had on him.

The reason there isn't any gospel from Elvis' first two years as a recording artist is that Sam Phillips was strict about the types of songs he released. Elvis laid down a version of Martha Carson's "Satisfied" while he was with Sam, but it is the one master (that's one hundred percent certain) of Elvis' that was never remade, and is now lost. It lasted little over a minute long, and as such Steve Sholes probably didn't have a clue how to market it. By the time Presley's first gospel record appeared, his sound had completely changed. Around 1959, long before the historical ramifications of Elvis' Sun Records days became clear, Sholes either discarded or lost the tape.

What follows is a look at Elvis' original, non-compilation gospel releases. Elvis often included gospel on his later albums, and also incorporated it into his movies and television specials. All of this work is covered elsewhere.

Peace in the Valley (Released April 11, 1957)

Elvis' initial gospel outing was an EP recorded in January 1957, at Radio Recorders. He had recently sung the title track on *The Ed Sullivan Show,* and it had gone over well. What inspired Elvis to perform gospel at this point can likely be traced to the recent "Million Dollar Quartet" jam session. "Peace in the Valley" went to #25 on the singles charts, but Elvis admitted that the song wasn't quite the kind of gospel he grew up with. Nonetheless, it was a quality performance, with an appealing country-styled arrangement.

The rest of the EP was stiff, if heartfelt. Elvis' ballad voice was beginning to develop, but it wasn't where it would be even by the May *Jailhouse Rock* sessions. Ending with a nice crescendo, "I Believe" was decent in execution, but otherwise

(There'll Be) PEACE IN THE VALLEY (For Me) • IT IS NO SECRET (What God Can Do)   **EPA-4054**
I BELIEVE • TAKE MY HAND, PRECIOUS LORD

PEACE IN THE VALLEY

RCA VICTOR

A "NEW ORTHOPHONIC" HIGH FIDELITY RECORDING

ELVIS PRESLEY

© RCA Printed in U.S.A.

Though only hinting at what Elvis would eventually achieve in the gospel field, this 1957 EP reached a completely new demographic.   *Courtesy of Robert Rodriguez*

adds nothing to the standard. "It Is No Secret (What God Can Do)" is pretty, yet similarly indistinct. Considered by many to be the father of traditional black gospel, Thomas A. Dorsey penned the title track, and was also the composer of the wistful "Take My Hand, Precious Lord." It brings home the deficiencies in *Peace in the Valley*, in that the songs are all of the same mood and tempo. Taken alone, it's perfectly enjoyable, but as the final song in the lineup, it blends into the others without making an impression.

Peace in the Valley was hardly a mistake, but only the title track had staying power. This wasn't the kind of Southern gospel music Elvis heard in church, but rather four selections that it was thought would be appealing to the masses. Many have heard these songs since, as the EP was included in full on *Elvis' Christmas Album*, and later on the one of the ubiquitous Camden albums, *You'll Never Walk Alone*. Elvis hadn't as of yet found his individual voice in the gospel medium, but at least *Peace in the Valley* established it as part of his public repertoire.

His Hand in Mine (Released November 10, 1960)

His Hand in Mine was an important album displaying tremendous creative growth in the three years since Elvis' last gospel outing. Consolidating his diversity in a year where he was determined to master as many styles of music as he could, it was also a personal triumph for Elvis to finally record the less commercialized kind of sacred music he had heard in church. *His Hand in Mine* not only paid tribute to his childhood influences but also exposed many outside of the South to hardcore gospel. Listeners not brought up in the Pentecostal or Baptist traditions were in for a surprise as far as how much of Elvis' work could be traced back to Christian music.

One of Elvis' favorite gospel singers was Jake Hess. In the fifties, Hess was with a group called the Statesmen, who specialized in harmonizing over a reflective kind of gospel. Their records and shows acted as a bridge between Northern and Southern church music. "His Hand in Mine" sets the tone for the LP by having Elvis sing sweetly on top of the Jordanaires' backing. "His Hand in Mine" wasn't the best cut on the album, but it summed up what Elvis was reaching for. "He Knows Just What I Need" and "Known Only to Him" were two more Statesmen ballads that were delicately performed and arranged, as was the effervescent "I Believe in the Man in the Sky." The latter song sticks out because Elvis gave the Jordanaires part of the lead.

Along with the short and beautiful "If We Never Meet Again," Elvis included two more ballads: "Mansion over the Hilltop" and "In My Father's House," both thematically similar songs popularized by the Blackwood Brothers. Elvis tried out for their junior group the Songfellows shortly before he began at Sun, but he was rejected. As soon as Elvis got a local hit, they reconsidered, but upon advice from his father, Elvis realized that he should stay solo. All the same, the Blackwood Brothers were one of Elvis' parents' favorite groups, and also one he and his fiancée Dixie went to see live many times shortly before he found fame.

J. D. Sumner was a member of the group from 1954 to 1965, and this alone led Elvis to recall their music fondly over the years. Elvis even had the Blackwood Brothers sing at his mother's funeral. These ballads don't stand out as much as the title track or other faster selections, but they are carefully arranged and beautifully executed.

As with almost every backing group Elvis used, the Jordanaires had a distinguished career in gospel. Their music was often upbeat, which reflected the infectious, jubilee sound in both black and white forms of the genre. Unlike Elvis' musicians, the Jordanaires always received label credit—and no doubt they deserved it with this album. They brought in two fast songs that made the link between rock and gospel crystal clear. Elvis put his stylistic stamp on "Working on the Building," building up the tempo and excitement as the chorus is frequently repeated. It ended the LP on a hopeful and happy note, in sharp contrast to the thoughtful mood it began on.

The Jordanaires' other jubilee offering was "I'm Gonna Walk Dem Golden Stairs." Elvis sank his teeth into it, injecting passion without altering his clean delivery. This wasn't music of condemnation, or hellfire and brimstone; "I'm Gonna Walk Dem Golden Stairs" offers a message of faith in life after death. To those who fear death, or have recently lost a loved one, the pure joy found in Elvis' and the Jordanaires' singing offered comfort.

The Golden Gate Quartet were a black spiritual group that Elvis had loved for years. He was reacquainted with their music when Charlie Hodge bought him a copy of one of their LPs (likely *Golden Chariot*) while they were stationed in Germany. Elvis subsequently went to see them live while on leave in Paris, and there even was a tape made (sadly since lost) of him joining them onstage during the show. Elvis was eager to record their music upon his return to the States, and their secular hit "I Will Be Home Again" was fittingly included on *Elvis Is Back!* Naturally, Elvis also wanted to cut a few of their songs for *His Hand in Mine*, picking two that fit the jubilee sound he had so much fun singing publicly and privately.

"Joshua Fit the Battle" was based on the Old Testament, and was sung in both synagogues and churches. Jordanaire Gordon Stoker noted Elvis often memorized lyrics after hearing them only one time. He noted with a mixture of bemusement and respect that this was true even with a song as wordy as "Joshua Fit the Battle." Not only did Elvis master the song quickly—he had no doubt heard it, if not performed it, before—he made it swing.

Even better was "Swing Down Sweet Chariot," which other than the title (and the Golden Gate Quartet including a snippet to start their version) had nothing to do with the somber "Swing Low Sweet Chariot." With the Jordanaires harmonizing closely behind him, Elvis unabashedly rocked up the tale of Ezekiel. If the liner notes on Elvis' second album stretched things a touch in declaring his sound to be a modern version of folk music, four years later, "Swing Down Sweet Chariot" found him telling a biblical tale in the best folk-music tradition. He included the song in his few early-sixties concerts and cut an even more energized take in 1968 for his movie *The Trouble with Girls*.

How Great Thou Art (Released March 8, 1967)

After six years of albums that didn't match Elvis' early work, *How Great Thou Art* marked a clear return to form. *Spinout* had showed signs of creative recovery, yet it still was a soundtrack, with many of the attendant trappings. *How Great Thou Art* was the first big step in what would be a hard-fought comeback. If *His Hand in Mine* was a fine representation of the gospel Elvis had grown up on, *How Great Thou Art* brought the genre firmly into the sixties. Singing with more power than ever, Elvis finally updated his sound as well.

Producer Felton Jarvis did his first work with Elvis on these sessions, and as a big fan he brought much enthusiasm to the proceedings. It would be more accurate to term Felton a co-producer or cheerleader, as Elvis still made all the final decisions on his music, but Jarvis' presence did help Elvis realize his vision. For the first time since he left Sun, Elvis had someone other than himself at the mixing board who fully understood his music.

Along with his regular studio musicians and singers, Elvis brought in the Imperials Quartet to fill out the harmony. Jake Hess was the group's leader, and that alone got them the job. *His Hand in Mine* had paid tribute to Hess' sound in many instances, and now, to Elvis' delight, Hess was to be a part of the creative process.

How Great Thou Art was carefully programmed to put most of the slower tracks on side one, and the up-tempo material on side two. Friend Larry Geller remembers Elvis being uncharacteristically involved with the final sequencing and presentation. With Jake Hess present, Elvis took the opportunity to cut three Statesmen songs. "How Great Thou Art" had been done by many people, but Elvis based his version on the Statesmen's recording. It was to become something of a signature track, being the gospel song Elvis sang most often onstage in the seventies. There, it gradually gained intensity, but this original understated version has a delicate beauty.

Just how flexible Elvis' range had become was demonstrated on "Where No One Stands Alone." Elvis worked hard to hit the loudest notes with grace, and with a good deal of effort he made it happen. The song is haunting; starting out bare, it grows into a tour de force of harmony and sound. To call Elvis' performance inspired isn't strong enough—transcendent was more like it.

"If the Lord Wasn't Walking by My Side" showed off the lighter side of the Statesmen, and Elvis turned it into something close to a duet with Hess. Jake thought it was outrageous that Elvis wanted him so high in the blend, but Presley has rarely sounded more comfortable. One notable feature was how modern the organ part played by Harry Slaughter sounded. It's not exactly the Sir Douglas Quintet, but it sounds far more steeped in modern music than what was the norm in gospel at the time.

"Run On" was a fast-paced stomper that worked itself into a lather. Making something new from tradition, this Golden Gate Quartet number finds Elvis, the Imperials, and the Jordanaires blending their talents brilliantly. The arrangement has strong elements of contemporary rock, with only the words setting it apart. The interplay between Elvis and his vocalists sounds natural—a product of sustained hard work.

Elvis pushed the envelope even further with the strident "By and By." Though it wasn't different, vocally, from the fast gospel Elvis had cut before, the guitars (played by Scotty Moore and Chip Young) are distorted and steamy. Feedback wasn't heard much outside of hard-blues circles until Marty Robbins used it in 1961 on "Don't Worry." Some of Elvis' Nashville cuts like "Slowly but Surely" previously had a little feedback applied, but here it sounded almost angry. "By and By" has Elvis' full attention lavished upon it and points ahead a few years to when rock and gospel merged as something mainstream.

"In the Garden," "Without Him," and "Stand by Me" are solemn and worshipful in tone. Considering the solace Elvis took in his faith, they were truly revealing. "Stand by Me" is a particularly heartfelt performance that eerily looks ahead to Elvis' last few years in its description of desolation. All exhibit a maturity not previously displayed in public.

One of Elvis' few disappointments with *How Great Thou Art* was that he couldn't get one of his favorite bass singers, Jimmy Jones, on the sessions. As part of the Harmonizing Four, Jones had been one of the most influential voices in sacred music over the previous decade. Reflecting Elvis' taste in black gospel perfectly, Jones likely would have taken the job, had anyone been able to locate him in time. Elvis still went ahead and included four Harmonizing Four songs in his absence.

"Farther Along" was arranged similarly to the other ballads on the album. Elvis sings gently, with an exquisite tonal quality in his voice. The song has an interesting structure; there are brief periods where all the music and other voices stop to give us a word or two of Elvis singing a cappella. The song has also been recorded with slightly different lyrics as "Father Alone," Ike Turner's spare 1974 rendition of which was nominated for a Grammy award.

"Somebody Bigger Than You and I" stands out as a composition. The words are humbling and reassuring to the point where the phrase "He walks beside you" was altered to *He Walks Beside Me* for the title of a 1978 gospel compilation. With Jones absent, Elvis willed himself to sing in a lower tone than he had ever attempted before on record. This gave him a new style to build on, and it ranked alongside the two Statesmen ballads as a performance that exposed a new depth. As so often happened when Elvis felt a song down to his bones, not a single syllable is wasted.

"Where Could I Go but to the Lord" is something altogether different. It has the deep commitment Elvis gave the weighty tracks, but there's also a real sense of soul. That's a quality that cannot be learned, coming only to the most natural of talents. Listen to the syncopation of the finger snaps, the way Presley hits every word with just the right inflection; he literally exudes cool. "Where Could I Go but to the Lord" was skillfully revived in 1968 to open the gospel medley in the *Singer Presents Elvis* special. More than any other selection, this shows the line between rock, blues, and gospel to be almost invisible.

"So High" was another of the great jubilee songs that brought out the convivial side of Elvis' musical personality. With playful vocal interplay, a rousing melody, and lyrical wit, "So High" typifies that love he held for the genre—a love rooted in his enthusiasm for all things religious or spiritual.

"Crying in the Chapel" was Elvis' biggest hit from late 1963 to the spring of 1969. He saturated this religious ballad with an abundance of subtle nuances, each breathtaking in its perfection. The Jordanaires are mixed up nice and high, and their harmonies give it an extra dimension. "Crying in the Chapel" reminded people of Elvis' talent at a time when he seemed not to be using it. It was a nice idea to include as an extra thirteenth bonus track for the album, and despite its vintage, it closed the LP flawlessly.

"You'll Never Walk Alone"/"We Call on Him" (Released March 26, 1968)

Elvis cut this single for Easter release during his 1967 Nashville sessions. "We Call on Him" is a sedate gospel ballad lamenting the fact that people only pray during hard times. The arrangement and vocal are pretty, but the lyrics are overly precious. "You'll Never Walk Alone" is more inspirational than gospel, but Elvis' version is one of the definitive readings of this standard. Playing piano himself, Elvis kept the arrangement simple. He felt the song intently, and it was one of his strongest vocals—one he seemingly didn't want to end, since out-takes feature him singing the chorus several times over. An arresting recording.

He Touched Me (Released April 5, 1972)

Those who only look at Elvis' later work in terms of his slow decline in the seventies miss a lot. Elvis wasn't unhealthy to any great extent in 1971–72, but some have trouble admitting that some fine work was done in this period. *He Touched Me* was Elvis' best-conceived LP from *Love Letters* on, and it was the last one that was a clear musical influence on any particular genre. Recorded over the late winter and spring of 1971, Elvis is in fine voice throughout and shows a clear commitment to the material, which stood in marked contrast to the Christmas album he was talked into recording concurrently with this one.

Having backed Elvis onstage for the last two years, a newer lineup of the Imperials (minus Jake Hess) worked closely with him on this release. It had a different feel than any of Elvis' previous gospel outings. *His Hand in Mine* reflected the past of gospel; *How Great Thou Art* was gospel in its then-current form. *He Touched Me* looked toward the future of the genre, even having elements of what would later be known as contemporary Christian music. The fast songs have an unabashed rock feel blended with jubilee and traditional hymn-styled vocals.

Elvis is seen singing three selections from the album in his 1972 documentary *Elvis on Tour.* Judging by the film and their rare fun-filled outings onstage, "I, John" and "Bosom of Abraham" were the two songs Elvis enjoyed running through the most. Relying almost completely on the harmonies of Presley and the Imperials, both have minimal instrumentation and a charming homespun feel. Performed in the jubilee tradition, these were the types of things Elvis sang most with his friends and family to relax.

"Bosom of Abraham" was particularly loose and carefree, and though it didn't chart, it's easy to see why it was the 45. It can be learned fast, and it encourages the listener to sing along, no matter what their belief system is. "I, John" was wordier, and has more dogma attached, but is not any less of a recording for it. It basically shares the same rhythm as "Bosom," yet it doesn't wear out

The 1972 classic *He Touched Me* was the most contemporary of Elvis' gospel albums. It was arguably the last of his albums to break new ground. The nicely chosen photograph hailed from Elvis' summer 1971 Las Vegas booking.

its welcome. In their own way, these are two of Presley's best recordings, as fundamentally crucial to the understanding of the gospel medium as his fifties recordings are to rock and roll.

"He Is My Everything" and "There Is No God but God" are the only weak spots. The former is a remake of "There Goes My Everything" with gospel lyrics. It's not that the performance was bad, it's that remaking a hit to fill up a gospel album was a shoddy idea. Elvis thankfully only did this once. "There Is No God but God" is lightweight, receiving the kind of cutesy arrangement bogging down the sister release, *The Wonderful World of Christmas*.

Andraé Crouch's "I've Got Confidence" and Red West's "Seeing Is Believing" are far more significant. Andraé Crouch and his band the Disciples were at the cutting edge of black gospel, and Elvis was naturally drawn to their work.

"I've Got Confidence" is a song that reflects faith being tested in both biblical times and modern life. Elvis performs with all the energy of his best rock music, assuring the listener that "God is going to see me through." Christian rock was a new concept, this track being one the most credible fusions of the two forms.

"Seeing Is Believing" (which West co-wrote with Glen Spreen) moves along in the same style, this time addressing continued belief in a jaded world. Elvis defends his faith by pointing out the scenic marvels of the land. When discussing the stars in the sky, his clever retort is, "Only God can reach that high." Behind the lyrical ingenuity, Elvis was letting loose and getting into the message. Female session singers Mary and Ginger Holladay, plus Millie Kirkham, worked with him often; this is arguably the best they were ever integrated into his music.

"Amazing Grace" was one of the most frequently recorded songs of the era, and Elvis gives it a nice bluesy feel that was more pronounced on early takes. This has bona fide soul to it, accurately recreating the feel of a Southern church on Sunday morning. Elvis' version may not be the best known, but it does benefit greatly from his remarkable dedication and arrangement.

Ralph Carmichael was well known for working with Nat King Cole, among others, but by the mid-sixties was mostly concentrating on gospel music. His "Reach Out to Jesus" provoked Elvis to sing himself into a near catharsis at the climax. The slow tempo allowed him to give every word his rapt attention, and there is no doubt of his sincerity. What remains striking about "Reach Out to Jesus"—and almost all of *He Touched Me*—is how modern this music still sounds. By embracing the current teachings of people of all faiths, Elvis was able to put across biblical theology in a way that brought it up to date.

The slow and thoughtful "Lead Me, Guide Me" is a perfect example of how Elvis blended past with present. The lyrics make use of old English, but Presley made them relevant in an entirely new way. He reinvented the 1953 composition by Doris Akers almost completely by using only currently relevant lyrics and giving it a flow missing from the traditional choral voicing heard in Akers' rendition. The melody was completely fresh and is likely something Elvis worked out with the Imperials and other musicians. Considering how dark his final years were to become, the message of seeking out a higher power provides some sort of comfort to the many who care about Elvis through his music. That Elvis continued to turn to faith in his times of trouble speaks far louder than any sordid details of the era.

In contrast, "An Evening Prayer" sticks very closely to Mahalia Jackson's seminal recording. Elvis didn't possess quite the same technical purity, but he threw himself unabashedly into the moment while maintaining grace and composure. Because he tried so hard, he did manage to replicate a great deal of her passion.

Jerry Reed wrote "A Thing Called Love" in 1968. Elvis made good use of the Imperials' talents, having them sing some warm, clear wordless notes to begin the track and link the verses. Presley took the opportunity to sing bass, sounding uncannily like Johnny Cash. Before Elvis' recording was released, Cash in fact recorded the song himself and ended up with a sizable hit.

"He Touched Me" reflected new trends in gospel without losing the best of what went before it. The Imperials popularized this hymn in 1969, and Elvis' vocal arrangement was similar. He kept the close harmonies intact, while adding his own lead part on top. Presley also got rid of the strings, giving the song a whole new intensity by keeping it uncomplicated.

"He Touched Me" reflects being made whole spiritually in a way that's much more personal than what you would have found in previous eras. By the late sixties, music was becoming more confessional, and this extended itself to gospel. It's hard not to hear something of the born-again movement that was gaining popularity, but this had always been an element of Baptist or Pentecostal faith. Elvis put every fiber of his being into the song, and the final stanza is as intimate and powerful as anything he ever cut. Elvis was putting himself out there, letting the world know once more that he fully believed in God and Christ. In the face of his own growing personal tribulations, he was relying on his faith more than ever, and because of that, *He Touched Me* stands as one of his most powerful statements.

20

I Can't Remember the Sound of My Own Name

1966

Elvis had hit bottom artistically. He was well aware that music was going through a revolution as big as the one he had headed ten years earlier, and he made the painful realization that he played no part in it. He had three movies to make that didn't seem promising, and touring and television didn't seem to be options, yet he was inspired by the developments in popular, folk, and gospel music.

Having taken the time to develop his spirituality further, Elvis felt that a gospel album could get his career on track. It was agreed he would go to back to Studio B in Nashville that May to work with producer Felton Jarvis. Felton was near Elvis' age, had been a longtime fan, and realized Elvis needed quality material. With Hill & Range not seeming to have much on offer, he let Elvis decide where things would go. The outcome was, with a few minor exceptions, a categorical success, and from that point on Felton took part in every regular studio session.

Elvis had taken the first step in the right direction, but he was still bogged down in poor films. It would take some time before he had the chance to do another quality project, but now he had the focus to make them happen, if offered. The gospel record was scheduled for release at Easter 1967. In the meantime, his career continued to go downhill.

Studio Work

The session to record the *Spinout* soundtrack was held at Radio Recorders in February. The score was considerably better than the general 1962–67 standard. For the first time since *Roustabout*, the mixes sounded professional, and there was at least a vague resemblance to rock and roll. Though merely adequate, *Spinout* was a relief. The spate of sixteen soundtracks from *Girls! Girls! Girls!* in 1962 to *Speedway* in 1968 was topped only by *Viva Las Vegas* and the old songs in *Tickle Me*.

The May Nashville sessions (and the one-day follow-up in June) came at the right time, giving Elvis a needed boost. Felton provided so much positive energy that Elvis attempted to experiment in ways he had been discouraged to for years. The resulting *How Great Thou Art* stands as one of his best albums, a truly innovative work in the gospel field. Though it couldn't undo all the damage, it bought Elvis valuable time to finish up his film commitments. The secular music wasn't uniformly good, but an exquisite cover of Bob Dylan's "Tomorrow Is a Long Time" proved that Elvis hadn't lost the ability to create magic, when given sympathetic people to work with.

The next two film soundtracks almost hit the depths of 1965. *Double Trouble* and *Easy Come, Easy Go* were appalling films, and the music was even worse. A couple of the songs were serviceable, but it sickened Elvis to have to do numbers like "Old MacDonald" and "Yoga Is as Yoga Does." With Elvis' monkey Scatter apparently behind the boards, every nuance was lost in the muffled mixes.

This nearly LP-sized portrait came with the surprisingly decent *Spinout* soundtrack.

On Celluloid

As the soundtrack attests, *Spinout* rose above the pitfall standards of the movies made the year before and after. That's not an endorsement, but Shelley Fabares was back, and most of the songs took place on a stage setting. No risks were taken, with Elvis again cast as a race-car-driving singer going through a series of romantic entanglements. It wouldn't have been terrible for a light musical comedy of 1962, but unfortunately it was now 1966, and the music and cinematic worlds were vastly changing. Seen today, *Spinout* is harmless fluff; seen through the filter of 1966, it can only have appeared to be gauche.

Elvis' next film would try to cash in on the "Swinging London" craze by being set partially in England. However, Parker's refusal to let Elvis work outside of North America meant that *Double Trouble*, which was based around a series of adventures Elvis' character has on a European tour, had to be shot in Hollywood. The songs were almost all lame, the plot was contrived, and the humor fell flat. As far as humiliation goes, few things could have been worse than the sequence in which Elvis had to sing "Old MacDonald." Considering his unfulfilled desire to perform in Europe, the film can be seen as a cruel joke.

Easy Come, Easy Go was Elvis' last film for Hal Wallis, and the only praise it can be given is that it bettered their most recent project, *Paradise, Hawaiian Style*. Elvis looked significantly leaner, but his role called for him to do nothing more than alternate between bemusement and anger at the events surrounding him. In an abysmal attempt to bring Elvis up to date, he is seen with hippies and doing yoga. The songs are putrid, with the exception of the relatively decent "You Gotta Stop." Elsa Lanchester, a star from Hollywood's golden age, sang a duet with Elvis on "Yoga Is as Yoga Does." The scene was staged so appallingly that Elvis rightly considered it an insult.

Popularity and Impact

Nineteen sixty-six was the first year Elvis didn't have a Top 10 pop LP or 45 since 1955. "If Every Day Was Like Christmas" almost topped the special Christmas charts, but with the exception of the easy-listening listings, Elvis' chart placements were in rapid decline.

The two gospel singles taken from *His Hand in Mine* were catalogue items that weren't issued with hit-making in mind. Elvis' soundtrack singles never bothered the Top 20 after 1965. "Frankie and Johnny" reached #25; "Spinout" only made it #40. Neither was a bad result, considering the standards the soundtracks had dropped to, but they had nothing to do with what was happening in music. The beautiful "Love Letters" was a welcome return to new studio cuts, but Elvis' popularity had declined to where it struggled to reach #19.

Elvis issued three soundtrack LPs in 1966, and considering the contents (*Spinout* aside), they did well to reach the Top 20. They did set a new low, however, in that every previous secular Presley LP—and all but three compilations—

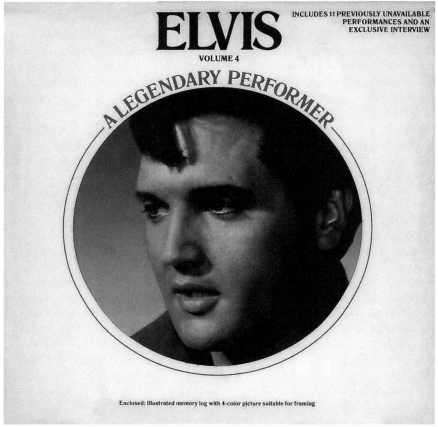

The *Legendary Performer* series featured attractive die-cut covers. This shot was taken during the filming of *Double Trouble*.

had placed in the Top 10. *His Hand in Mine* also bettered these LPs in getting to #13. *Frankie and Johnny* and *Paradise, Hawaiian Style* were two of most pitiful albums ever issued by an important performer, but on the strength of the "bonus songs," *Spinout* was above average.

Other than the "Love Letters"/"Come What May" single and the three studio cuts on *Spinout*, Elvis' new commitment to his recording career had yet to surface. *How Great Thou Art* was in the can, but it wasn't geared toward bringing people back to theaters, or getting Elvis in the Top 10. Except for the fluke hit "Crying in the Chapel," Elvis hadn't made any real impact since *Viva Las Vegas*. As 1966 came to a close, it wouldn't have been outrageous to suggest that he was only to become a relic of the past.

21

Just Pretend

Borrowed Songs and Other Oddities

Elvis Appropriated

With a catalogue as extensive and influential as Elvis Presley's, you are going to find people trying to jump on the bandwagon. Some attempted to look or sound like Elvis, but some outright "borrowed" his songs. Today's mass media would ensure that this wouldn't pass without comment, but in the fifties, it was a quietly accepted practice. The most blatant and unusual knock-offs are fascinating in their boldness, and contain merit as performances.

Elvis' Sun sessions have influenced people for over fifty-five years, but at times they were purely copied. In a 1988 interview for a Beatles recording-sessions book, Paul McCartney admitted that the only song he and George Harrison wrote together, "In Spite of All the Danger," was copied from an Elvis number. He would not say which song it was taken from at the time but revealed that the song was recorded at the debut amateur recording session by the Quarrymen (the Beatles' first name).

"In Spite of All the Danger" was recorded in the spring or summer of 1958, and was finally released on the Beatles' *Anthology 1* three-LP/two-CD set in 1995. It turned out to be "Trying to Get to You" with new lyrics. It's pretty assured, considering their age, and since it only was for private use, "In Spite of All the Danger" is a harmless homage.

Conway Twitty sounded a lot like Elvis on his early recordings, and it is well established that Ben Weisman and Fred Wise slightly rewrote their Elvis out-take "Danny" for him as "Lonely Blue Boy." However, Twitty did occasionally rewrite songs with slight changes and record them—usually as B-sides or LP cuts—which was ignored in those less litigious times. "Mystery Train" was transformed into "Long Black Train" and issued on the 1961 *Touch* LP. It's a fantastic recording, with a danger all its own.

Roy Hamilton ranks among Elvis' top vocal influences. They met in January 1969, when both were recording at American Sound, and the meeting went so well that Elvis gave Hamilton a fantastic song he was planning to cut called "Angelica." The flip of Roy's ensuing single was a melodious ballad entitled "Hang-Ups." Over the coda, Reggie Young plays his signature riff from "Suspicious Minds."

This popular 1956 pin changed back and forth between two different photos. It's a neat novelty even today.

Jimmy "Orion" Ellis may have been a soundalike, but he rarely recorded Elvis material during his Sun Records tenure. The 1981 LP *Fresh*, being entirely new compositions, was arguably his best, though one selection wasn't as "fresh" as it seemed. Singer/songwriter Buddy Harris recorded an LP for Shelby Singleton's Plantation in the late seventies, later penning the *Fresh* ballad "If I Can't Have You." Recorded and arranged with flair, it's a great performance of an almost note-for-note remake of Elvis' "Don't Leave Me Now," with perhaps a dash of "Don't Ask Me Why" or "Give Me the Right" blended in. It's another case of songs being obscure enough for reviewers not to comment on.

Elvis Recording Trivia

Let's look at the unexpected origins of a few songs, and information about selections Elvis considered but ultimately didn't record. The criterion for inclusion is that the information has previously gone unpublished, or that it's too intriguing not to chronicle.

During the course of the recording sessions for Elvis' second film, *Loving You*, Jean Aberbach from his song publishers Hill & Range made an odd suggestion. For no reason that seems conceivable, other than owning the publishing, he suggested that Elvis might want to record the children's song "Peter Cottontail"! Elvis quickly dismissed this as something of joke, but Aberbach was probably responsible for a Paramount musician's instrumental rendition playing during the film.

Several of Elvis' movie songs were obscure recent recordings by other acts established in the fifties. Bill Haley cut a 45 of "Yeah, She's Evil!" in 1964, and the following year Elvis and the musicians doubled the tempo on the retitled "The Meanest Girl in Town" for *Girl Happy*.

Rick Nelson released an LP in 1965 titled *Spotlight on Rick*. With comparable frenzy, Elvis cut Rick's rocker "Stop, Look and Listen" for *Spinout*. Inadvertently, the album also contained a Red West co-write with Joey Cooper, "I'm a Fool." It became a hit almost concurrently for the trio of Dino, Desi, and Billy.

One might notice that the rendition of "I Got a Woman" played during Elvis' 1969–77 concerts had a different arrangement than the one used before. It was largely based around Rick Nelson's 1963 cover, recorded while James Burton was Nelson's lead guitarist. Upon joining Elvis' group, Burton simply used the arrangement he was most familiar with.

When Elvis recorded "Only Believe" in 1970, he was going back to a favorite from his army days. Among the records he had in Germany was the Harmonizing Four's version of the song under its more common title, "All Things Are Possible." After first considering it for *His Hand in Mine*, Elvis eventually recorded it ten years later for an Easter 1971 single.

Elvis' arrangement of "Bridge over Troubled Water" was not based on Simon and Garfunkel's hit but rather on B. J. Thomas' take on the song. Included on Thomas' *Everybody's out of Town* LP, it was released two months before Elvis laid his version down in Nashville.

Never afraid to experiment with the production of his records, Elvis made use of several unusual instruments. A good example is found on the Christmas ballad "It Won't Seem Like Christmas Without You." To add more flavor, Elvis made the suggestion of using a toy piano. This uncommon adjunct is most notable on the intro.

A fan of Mac Davis, Elvis frequently recorded his compositions in the late sixties. He planned to record a track from Davis' 1970 LP *Song Painter* entitled "Home," written about the soldiers serving in Vietnam. Elvis' desire to appeal to audiences on both sides of social issues may have led to him discarding it.

At Presley's March 1972 recording session, as well as providing "Burning Love," Dennis Linde submitted an ornate ballad called "Don't Leave Me Here All Alone." While Elvis may have felt closer to the lyric, the synthesizer-heavy version found on Linde's 1972 self-titled LP seems an incongruous choice. It was later released as a UK (and possibly a domestic) 45, appropriately enough as the flip to Linde's own cut of "Burning Love."

RCA considered recording an "Elvis Live at the Sahara" album in May 1973, after Isaac Hayes and several other artists cut live albums there. The probable reason RCA did not do so was that, as of May 1973, Elvis' last two LPs had been live, and a third would have been redundant without a complete change in set-list and format.

As the composer of "Mystery Train," Junior Parker was the first person to record it. (Sam Phillips would claim co-credit on Elvis' version.) Parker's version had some train-whistle effects played by saxophone. Elvis never did forget the original, and at times during the seventies he had his orchestra play the horn riff. The most common version that contains this modification comes from a Dallas concert from June 6, 1975. The show was partially included on the 1980 eight-LP boxed set *Elvis Aron Presley*.

Elvis would go to great lengths to make a recording have the right feel. To get in the right mood, he would do things like install a Christmas tree, sing in different positions, or adjust the lighting. The most elaborate measures occurred during his "Jungle Room" sessions. Every couple of songs, he would have the room's light bulbs changed to the color he felt best suited the lyrics or tempo.

22

Suppose

By this point, Elvis' career was in deep trouble. Generating only a fraction of the money it had before, his movie music no longer bore resemblance to anything current. And though Elvis was starting to make strides in the studio, his now-tarnished reputation meant that even his good records were dismissed by most disc jockeys. Elvis was depressed by these developments to the point where he almost had to be forced to show up on the set of *Clambake*. When he did consent to start filming, he had put on a good deal of weight, which showed clearly.

While some of his friends have said he never wanted to settle down, Elvis' marriage to longtime girlfriend Priscilla Beaulieu on May 1st did seem to shake him out of his torpor. He lost weight, cut back on his pill use, and—after getting the pedestrian film *Speedway* out of the way— began a three-year period of artistic and personal renewal. If *How Great Thou Art* could be seen as a fluke good album in a sea of mediocrity, and if Elvis' best new secular songs were still being buried on soundtrack albums, changes were taking place that would soon make themselves clear.

Studio Work

Elvis recorded his soundtrack for *Clambake* in Nashville in the middle of February. No doubt the music he had to record for this picture played a part in why he was so reluctant to make the film. On the first night, some surprisingly strong material was cut, but the rest was as bad as ever. A reworking of the song "High Hopes," "Confidence" was one of Elvis' worst recordings.

The *Speedway* sessions were recorded in June on the MGM soundstage. Elvis again consented to this arrangement only because he figured it wouldn't make a difference. Indeed, many of the tracks were stupid, but Elvis salvaged a few of them. "Suppose" was a song he liked so much that he had tried to make a master of it at home. There was an overdub session for that version that turned out pretty, but he decided to record it again for the movie.

Going back to Nashville in September, Elvis held an excellent session that found him recording a few single and album cuts. He wanted to record a number by up-and-coming songwriter and performer Jerry Reed. When they couldn't get Reed's signature guitar sound down, they had Reed himself join in. The results were fantastic, but Hill & Range reps tried to bully Reed into signing away some of his copyrights. He refused, and Elvis insisted the "Guitar Man" record be released anyway. The rest of the sessions weren't as jovial as a result, but Elvis still laid down some fine music.

Elvis returned the next month to record songs for his film *Stay Away, Joe.* The music and film finally broke away from the stifling formula that had been in place since 1962, but there was still a song called "Dominic" that was so ridiculous that Elvis put his foot down and refused to allow it to be released on a record.

EPA-4387

Paramount Pictures
Presents

ELVIS PRESLEY

in

HAL WALLIS'

Production

EASY COME, EASY GO

Co-starring

| DODIE MARSHALL | PAT PRIEST | PAT HARRINGTON | SKIP WARD | FRANK McHUGH |

and

ELSA LANCHESTER as Madame Neherina

TECHNICOLOR®

Directed by

JOHN RICH

Written by

ALLAN WEISS and ANTHONY LAWRENCE

SIDE 1	SIDE 2
EASY COME, EASY GO (ASCAP) 2:08	**YOU GOTTA STOP** (BMI) 2:16
THE LOVE MACHINE (BMI) 2:47	**SING YOU CHILDREN** (BMI) 2:05
YOGA IS AS YOGA DOES (BMI) 2:07	**I'LL TAKE LOVE** (BMI) 2:10

© RCA, New York, N.Y. • Printed in U.S.A.

ASK FOR ELVIS' 1967 COMPLETE FULL COLOR CATALOG

Easy Come, Easy Go has the ignoble title of being the worst-selling Elvis record ever issued. The reasons were twofold: the EP format was obsolete in the domestic market, and the music was mostly awful.

On Celluloid

Clambake had a few redeeming points. Co-stars Shelley Fabares (back for her third Elvis picture) and Bill Bixby enjoyed a good chemistry with Elvis, the comedy elements coming off quite well with their support. Still, this was a silly, antiquated film with mostly silly and antiquated music.

Speedway was slightly better, but in truth it was a pale imitation of *Viva Las Vegas*. The basic outline was identical: Elvis was a race-car driver who fell in love with a girl who resisted his advances at first. Bixby returned to play Elvis' business manager, and Nancy Sinatra was cast as Elvis' love interest. There were some OK comedy bits, but it was lightweight fluff that seemed surreal by the time of its summer 1968 release.

Stay Away, Joe wasn't going to win plaudits, but it brought an end to the *Blue Hawaii* prototype. Elvis got to play a wild adult who drank, had sex, and had a good time doing it. His acting was better than it had been for ages. If *Stay Away, Joe* lacked distinction, it was awfully fun. The cast was likeable, with key roles given to Burgess Meredith and Katy Jurado. The growth found in this and subsequent Elvis movies showed that he was trying to turn things around. Appearing trim and tan, and having finally grown back his fifties sideburns (they weren't pork chop until 1968), he even began to look like his old self again.

Popularity and Impact

If *How Great Thou Art* hadn't returned Elvis to the Top 20, this year would have to be written off. Fortunately, the album was well promoted on radio by a special Easter broadcast that was one of Parker's very few inspired ideas of the time. It ended up winning a Grammy for Gospel Album of the Year, and was a bright spot that came at a time when one was sorely needed.

The *Double Trouble* and *Clambake* soundtracks only made it into the Top 50, and the EP for *Easy Come, Easy Go* didn't even chart. The few that picked up *Clambake* had to have been shocked at how good the bonus songs were, but by now Elvis soundtracks had worn out their welcome.

The two new non-soundtrack singles, "Indescribably Blue" and "Big Boss Man," dented the Top 40. The latter was an excellent bluesy rock-and-roll single, but Elvis' string of bad releases had made buyers and radio wary of him.

The noisy but limp "Long Legged Girl" from *Double Trouble* tanked, as did a reissue of the 1961 cut "There's Always Me." Why RCA and Parker thought that a soundtrack recording or a previously released song would reverse their fortunes is a head-scratcher. Parker didn't seem to have a clue what to do anymore except try what worked before. As 1967 ended, Elvis' career was on life support. Elvis would soon be back on top, but that was in spite of Parker, not because of him.

23

Don't Count Your Chickens

The Strange Saga of Jimmy "Orion" Ellis

More than any other performer who made the attempt, Jimmy Ellis was able to capture the sound of Elvis Presley's voice. Except Ellis wasn't faking it—the singer who would become best known as "Orion" naturally sounded very close to Elvis Presley. He had more vibrato, but his best recordings can fool casual listeners. Jimmy never got out from Elvis' shadow, but he made some first-rate recordings that won him a dedicated following.

Beginnings

Born Jimmy Bell in Pascagoula, Mississippi, on February 26, 1945, Jimmy grew up in Alabama, where he was adopted at age two by Robert and Mary Faye Ellis. He was an Elvis fan from a young age, and later in life questioned whether his birth father could have been Elvis' father Vernon, as that first name is all that is listed for his father on his birth certificate. While this seems all but impossible, his vocal similarity—as well as a physical resemblance to the Presley side of Elvis' family—did cause Jimmy to wonder. Nonetheless, he was a real fan, and Elvis led him into a lifetime love affair with music.

Fresh out of high school, Jimmy had an offer to join the Milwaukee Braves, but he chose college instead. With the help of his campus friend Jimmy Youmans, Ellis cut and wrote his first record in 1964. "Don't Count Your Chickens"/"Love Is but a Love" was a fun pairing released on the small Georgia record label Dradco. It didn't get anywhere, but Ellis had won some local contests, and now began to perform in small clubs. His voice sounds higher here, but fairly close to Elvis'.

Sunrise

After several years breeding horses, Jimmy began to seriously consider a career in music. He recorded some cuts that were brought to the attention of record mogul/producer Shelby Singleton, who had bought the Sun Records label from

Sam Phillips and from 1969 to 1983 put out a series of reissues and new titles on the revamped Sun International label. Not sure what to do with a singer so close in timbre to Elvis, Singleton came up with a plan. He requested that Jimmy do both sides of Elvis' first Sun single and try to get as close to it as possible.

Jimmy's debut Sun single was thus "That's All Right"/"Blue Moon of Kentucky," and Singleton released it with no name on the label. While it was obvious that it wasn't recorded in the fifties, Shelby wanted people to wonder if Elvis out-takes were being used over new music tracks. The ruse worked to a certain extent, and apparently RCA only backed off legally when a voiceprint proved it wasn't Elvis. Singleton reissued it under Jimmy's name, but this would set the pattern for the rest of Ellis' career.

Shelby issued a second single by Ellis in 1973, "Changing"/"I Use Her to Remind Me of You." Both were fine ballads that presented Jimmy in a more contemporary light, but they garnered little action. Perhaps Ellis' biggest chance came when he signed a one-single deal with MCA Records later that year. "There Ya Go"/"Here Comes That Feeling Again" was another quality set of love songs that showed Jimmy in fine voice, but although "There Ya Go" was featured in an episode of the popular *McCloud* series, it too failed to find an audience.

In the mid-seventies, Jimmy lived in California, but his sole accomplishment was to win an episode of *The Gong Show*. Around 1976, Elvis was made aware of Jimmy after he was given a few of his records by an acquaintance, Steve Kelly. Kelly would later work with Ellis, and told him that Elvis liked his music, particularly "I Use Her to Remind Me of You." Elvis told Steve that it had tricked Vernon when he heard it.

Moving back to Georgia, Ellis was signed to Bobby Smith's Boblo Records. From 1976 to 1978, Ellis released five singles, one LP, and one 8-Track. These sessions resulted in some of Jimmy's very best work, but the LP of Presley covers, *Ellis Sings Elvis*, was something the singer had mixed feelings about. The singles were originals, and released near the time of the 1978 album was "I'm Not Trying to Be Like Elvis"/"Games You Been Playing." Though the more cynical could charge that using Elvis' name in the song title was a cheap tactic, Jimmy's self-penned song was a sincere attempt to explain himself as an artist while paying his idol some respect. In it, Ellis decries the Elvis impersonators, little knowing that this was his ultimate fate.

Other notable Boblo singles include the lively "Tupelo Woman"/"Just Out of Reach" pairing, which came close to Elvis' better mid-seventies work. The best record Jimmy ever made was "Movin' On"/"My Baby's Out of Sight," featuring a pair of up-tempo ballads that capture him at the height of his creative and vocal powers. "Movin' On" was written by Walter Earl Brown, who back in 1968 had penned "If I Can Dream." Had Parker not been so brusque with Brown, it is likely that Elvis would have gotten a shot at the track himself. Elvis' loss was Ellis' gain, but only from an artistic standpoint, since Boblo didn't have the resources to push their products properly.

Reborn

By late 1978, Ellis' career seemed at a standstill. He was to star in a Broadway musical called (ironically) *Elvis Lives*, but it fell through at the last moment when Colonel Parker used his muscle to have it stopped. Wanting to help Ellis out, Bobby Smith convinced Shelby Singleton to re-sign him to Sun. Singleton still felt Jimmy needed special promotion, and first used him on a Jerry Lee Lewis LP, *Duets*. Ellis was told to overdub his voice over old Jerry Lee masters, and Shelby released the record with the artist listed as "Jerry Lee Lewis and Friends." Two selections were duets the Killer cut with Charlie Rich in 1959, but the others hailed from the new sessions with Ellis.

"Save the Last Dance for Me" proved to be a fairly big success, reaching #26 on the country charts. Many speculated that it was a lost duet between Elvis and Jerry Lee, which is what Singleton was pinning his hopes on. Syndicated columnist James Bacon even claimed Elvis told him about the record before he died, but any fan of Lewis' could hear it was a doctored version of Jerry's 1961 original.

Duets and its follow-up, *Trio +*, which had Ellis overdub his voice onto Charlie Rich and Carl Perkins songs (as well as a few more by Lewis), saw him tampering with Sun classics that needed no augmentation. However, if heard dispassionately, they are entertaining. If Ellis had mixed feelings about doing them, where Singleton steered him next wouldn't do anything to alleviate his concerns.

Orion was a book penned by Georgia journalist Gail Brewer-Giorgio in 1977. She had approached Jimmy about doing a movie based on it, and the book ended up with Singleton, who had his wildest idea yet. The book is basically the Elvis Presley story, except for the twist ending where Orion Darnell fakes his death to get away from his self-destructive lifestyle and stifling fame. Singleton told Jimmy he should become the living, breathing Orion and keep his identity private. In order to complete the ruse, Jimmy would wear ornate masks whenever he was in public. It certainly was novel, but it was obviously meant to capitalize on the rumor that Elvis may have faked his death.

Glory

From the start of Ellis' tenure as Orion on Sun in 1979 until it ended three years later, he built a fairly big following in the South. Sure, many were there because they were curious, or thought it may be Elvis, but Ellis proved himself a fine performer, winning some real fans who didn't care who Orion was. Others who called themselves fans were slightly delusional. It was claimed by this fringe that Ellis was covering for a second Orion, who was Elvis; one even tried to pull off his mask!

The entire Sun Orion catalogue was well recorded and thought-out, and the Orion singles often made their way to the lower regions of the *Billboard* and *Cashbox* country charts. Ellis was never particularly happy with the ruse, but he had tried so long to find success that he acquiesced. The first Orion LP, *Reborn*, was excellent, but the tasteless cover had a drawing of Orion rising from his coffin. It was replaced with a nice photo of Jimmy in the mask, but the LP, which featured an excerpt of the book on the back, had the stigma of Elvis' death hanging over it, as three cuts were covers of "death discs" popular in the early sixties. Many more were cut, but thankfully the LP changed direction. Rockers like Ellis' "Washing Machine" and "You Can Have Her" are filled with high sprits, and even the moribund "Honey" sounds good, coming from Ellis.

The late 1979 follow-up, *Sunrise*, was even better. A cover of Kenny Rogers and the First Edition's "Stranger in My Place" brought out a fine vocal from Ellis, and he was able to impart new things even on old warhorses like "Turn Around, Look at Me." "I Heard You Knocking" and "You Can't Judge a Book" are superb interpretations, informed by Smiley Lewis' and Bo Diddley's originals. Ellis' "It Ain't No Mystery" has a dark atmosphere, and leaves one wishing he had written more.

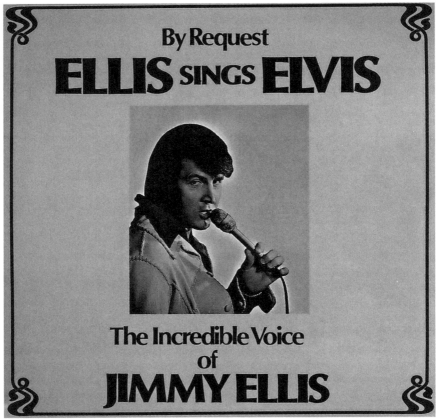

Jimmy Ellis' debut album hardly helped the singer to establish his own identity. Ironically, it would be the only LP to actually bear his name.

In 1980, Orion released three themed LPs: *Country*, *Rockabilly*, and the gospel record *Glory*. The first two albums demonstrate Shelby's goal of recording Jimmy with simplicity, and in the spirit of the original Sun label. *Country* was highlighted by story-songs like "Texas Tea" and the moody "Long Black Veil." The latter tied into the whole Orion mystery, as it's sung from the perspective of a ghost. The ballad "Am I That Easy to Forget" closed the album with a fifties feel.

Rockabilly is notable for being a prime example of the eighties rockabilly movement. Oldies like "I'm Gonna Be a Wheel Someday" and "Rockin' Little Angel" are energetic romps, but it's the relatively new songs that come closest to being cutting edge. "Crazy Little Thing Called Love" is one of the most acclaimed Orion records, being that it gives an idea of what Elvis may have done, had he lived. Queen themselves told Ellis that they liked his version of the song best.

Glory is an OK album, but Ellis wasn't happy with how it turned out. He intended the songs to be simple and stark, and was dismayed to find that they had been overdubbed with extra voices and instrumentation. Tracks like the fast-paced "I Surrender All" suffer the most, as it tries to be too commercial. "Just a Closer Walk with Thee" hits home as it's got a sense of style and is slightly bluesy.

Glory went against Shelby's practice of minimizing the Elvis songs by having five selections done by Presley, bringing comparisons that aren't favorable to Ellis. While his voice is strong, the passion Elvis brought to his gospel recordings is missing. Ellis doesn't try to dodge the notes, but Elvis was able to push them out with a zeal nobody's duplicated.

Fresh, from 1981, was far better. Ellis wrote the up-tempo opener "Some You Win, Some You Lose," and Singleton staff writer Buddy Harris handled most of the rest. It's his best album. The mood is jubilant; even the ballads have a fun air. "Look Me Up (and Lay It on Me)," is a fantastic rock-and-roll record with a rough-and-ready vocal. "Baby Please Say Yes" is cut from the same mold—sprightly, upbeat, and rockin'. If Ellis at times seemed drawn to mediocre adult contemporary mush, there is no hint of it here.

"Born" is a tasteful, straight-ahead love song, beautiful and direct. "If I Can't Have You" copies Elvis' "Don't Ask Me Why"—and in a more original way, "Ain't No Good" also drew influence from the *King Creole* album. A blues-flavored gem, Ellis growls the lyrics over an imaginative, Dixieland-styled backing. It should have been Ellis' crossover to the Hot 100, but it was buried on a flip side.

A TV-advertised LP called *20 All Time Favorites* was ill conceived. The record suffered sonically for packing too many songs on each side. "Orion" hadn't had enough chart action for such an LP, so it was filled out with well-known standards of the seventies, and a solo version of "Save the Last Dance for Me." The Orion singles weren't completely ignored, but some were left out in favor of numbers more familiar to the general TV watcher. It doesn't seem as if the ad was aired much, and it didn't make the rounds nearly as much as Suffolk's Slim Whitman or Boxcar Willie albums. That Ellis was being marketed in the same way seemed to negate his talent, and did nothing to back Sun's claim that he was "The Superstar of the Eighties."

Minus "Save the Last Dance for Me," the new material was issued around the same time on Sun as the *Feelings* LP, which contained a mere eight songs and was easily the most dispensable record of Ellis' pre-nineties period. Many of these weren't necessarily identified with Elvis, but were part of his catalogue. Even without using Elvis' arrangements, Ellis suffers by comparison. Tracks that were non-Presley, like "Somewhere My Love" and a surprisingly good "Feelings," went too far into lounge-lizard territory, while covers of "He'll Have to Go" and "I Can't Stop Loving You" have panache but only half the creativity Elvis brought to them. *Feelings* as (very) light listening served its purpose, but it was the polar opposite of *Fresh*.

Sadly, *Feelings* marked the end of an era. Ellis would record a few more singles for the label, but his LP *Surprise* was canceled after Jimmy rebelled against the mask. Once he pulled it off, during a 1982 appearance, Shelby felt that he couldn't effectively promote Ellis and ended his association with the singer. The first single from *Surprise* had already made it out by then. "Honky Tonk Heaven" was an excellent rocker that almost matched a recent version by Jerry Lee Lewis, while "Morning, Noon and Night" was a melodic ballad with a top-notch lead.

There Ya Go

The rest of Ellis' career had flashes of brilliance but was rather sad. He never got on a major, and though everyone now knew who he was, he rarely had the chance to perform under his own name. In 1988, Gail Brewer-Giorgio's *Is Elvis Alive?* made the masses aware of the performer Jimmy Ellis, but his story was couched in her conspiracy theory, and thus brought little of the kind of attention Jimmy wanted. Some new fans did discover him through the book, but overall it only muddied the waters.

Jimmy continued to perform live, but by the late eighties he mostly did Elvis songs. In that he did his own styled show, he never quite became an impersonator, but as he aged, his voice thinned to an extent, and his gigs domestically got smaller. The only way it seemed he could sell tickets was trading on Presley, and it was depressing to a somewhat bitter Ellis that it had to come to this.

New Beginnings from 1989 was his last vinyl LP, a comp of his better mid-eighties recordings acting as a new album. He did record some tracks for the project but was upset when a joke song not intended for release called "The Way My Dog Loves Me" took the place of hard rockabilly tracks like "Old Pipeliner" and a scorching cover of Carl Perkins' "Restless." Most of the ballads were too safe, and the high notes came harder. Rockers like "Back on the Street" and especially "Old Time Rock" recalled the Sun days with style, but perhaps the most interesting song was taken from a 1987 single he did under the name Steven Silver.

"Down in Mississippi" had been released on the tiny Vulcan label and was subsequently mentioned in Brewer-Giorgio's book. It was a song written from the perspective of a still-living Elvis, yet it was an impressive performance that rose above the novelty factor. Initially, Ellis was dead set against doing the song, only acquiescing when he was offered $5,000 cash. He even did a one-time-only performance as Steven Silver in the same month he did Orion and Jimmy Ellis shows!

In the nineties, Ellis periodically cut some good music, but much of it was tame and cheaply produced with heavy synths. He tried to get away from being Orion by performing and recording under the name Ellis James, but his audience was mostly the diehards by then, and it seemed pointless. His gospel CD *Because He Lives* was decent, and occasional numbers like the fine country-rocker "Plastic Saddle" or the "Separate Ways" knock-off "Looking for a Way" rose above the dross. (He put all three of these on his 1990 album *Genuine*.) By the time of his last two CDs in 1997—skimpy holiday offerings that would have fit on one vinyl disc—even the technical competence of his recordings was in question. Both recordings contained a faint buzz throughout.

A 1996 CD called *Steady as She Goes*, recorded with the legendary country producer Larry Butler, was probably his last real chance, but Ellis' tiny label couldn't afford to capitalize on the prestige, and it flopped. It was no better than any of his other recent work, yet one wonders why Butler couldn't get it issued on a bigger independent. It was released three times—credited to Orion, Ellis James, and simply "Ellis"—but that didn't help either.

Jimmy found some measure of success outside music as a bail bondsman and running a convenience store, but the latter brought about his early demise when Ellis and his ex-wife Elaine were viciously killed in an armed robbery on December 12, 1998. Though the culprits were caught, it was a sad end to a life that had never quite been his own. Jimmy Ellis never achieved sustained fame or fortune, but—as often happens—he has posthumously developed a strong following. Official and unofficial releases of his music are put out with regularity, and there is supposed to be an all-encompassing documentary in the works. Because of the Elvis and Sun Records connection, Orion will never be forgotten, but with a little luck, maybe Jimmy Ellis won't be either.

24

Goin' Home

T he birth of Elvis and Priscilla's daughter, Lisa Marie, on February 1st was one of the happiest moments of Elvis' life. Though their marriage began to falter soon after, the boost came at a crucial time. Elvis had his usual three movies lined up for the year, and they had caught up with the times. Still, none of them were good enough to stop Elvis' Hollywood career from imploding, and he wasn't sorry about it.

The game was over—the movies had to stop, and it was time for Elvis to take a major risk. Parker thought getting Elvis on TV again might be beneficial. He envisioned an NBC special with Elvis singing one hour's worth of Christmas music. Elvis didn't like the idea, but he went to meet the potential director, Steve Binder.

Binder, known for his work on the rock-and-roll program *Shindig*, thought that the idea as Parker described it would kill Elvis' career. He envisioned a special where Elvis could get back onstage and sing to his fans. He also felt that, through the use of various production numbers, Elvis could say something about himself. Elvis loved the idea and told Steve that he would take care of Parker. The Colonel didn't like being bucked, but Elvis stood up to him, and the special went on the way he and Binder wanted it. Singer Sewing Machines signed on to be the sponsor, and filming took place over the last two weeks of June.

Elvis had been working the past two years to get himself out of the doldrums, but the formally titled *Singer Presents Elvis* was the key factor in his comeback. That the music produced is some of Elvis' most vital work renders it an important event in the history of rock and roll. The special is discussed in detail in the next chapter, but it cannot be overemphasized how important a role it played in Elvis' career.

Studio Work

Elvis held a January date in Nashville that ended up being the last time he worked with Scotty Moore and D. J. Fontana in a studio setting. In fact, except for the informal section of the upcoming TV special, it would be the last time he worked with them at all. Though they would overdub certain things in the future, the Jordanaires were also out of the picture after this outing. Elvis hadn't made a conscious decision to get rid of anyone, but that's how it played out.

It was an odd session, set up for a single and two more selections for *Stay Away, Joe*. While the gap lessened, the movie songs still suffered by comparison to Elvis' regular material. Jerry Reed was there to play guitar, and Elvis eventually decided on recording his composition "U.S. Male." Strangely, though the music cut was good, Elvis was not in a working mood. He managed to get down only one song on each of the first and third nights, and on the second he clowned his way through the movie songs.

Though the mood in the studio seems to be fun, Elvis couldn't get his mind on the task. He performed well when he buckled down, but he had never acted so strangely while working before. Maybe it was the nerves he had as an expectant father; maybe he was fed up with not having anything suitable from Hill & Range. Some have suggested he was high, but no matter the cause, what normally would have taken one night took three.

In March, Elvis went to Western Studios in Los Angeles to record the *Live a Little, Love a Little* score with the core of musicians that had become known as the Wrecking Crew. Led informally by drummer Hal Blaine, they had gained fame playing on a multitude of hits coming out of mid-sixties L.A. The songs Elvis recorded were a mixed assortment—some pretty hip, some sounding like lounge music. This was the most modern-sounding soundtrack Elvis had done to date, yet the music was more influenced by producer Billy Strange than anything Elvis would have come up with. It was the first time Elvis worked with orchestration, and he enjoyed the experience enough to incorporate it into most of his sessions thereafter.

Elvis went back to Western in June to record the TV special soundtrack. He was performing certain segments of the show live, so this session consisted solely of the various production numbers to be used in the special. At times, Elvis would sing live to a backing track during filming, and at times he mimed to what he cut here. For the LP, it was decided that the more formal studio takes would be used, and they were universally wonderful. Several of the cuts are over-arranged, but Elvis sang with so much zeal that he made you focus only on him.

Elvis held two more soundtrack sessions in October. The first was for *Charro!* at Goldwyn, the second for *The Trouble with Girls* at United. The *Charro!* recordings were last-minute additions to the movie, and you could tell. Elvis performed well enough, but of the two tracks, "Let's Forget About the Stars" was as bad as any movie song, and "Charro" was a faux–spaghetti western piece by Mac Davis.

The Trouble with Girls had a better collection of songs. It wasn't right for the period the movie took place in, but "Clean Up Your Own Back Yard" was the toughest slice of rock Elvis had done for a movie since "King of the Whole Wide World" in 1961. He also took the opportunity to better his 1960 recording of "Swing Down, Sweet Chariot," and even the novelty numbers came off as reasonable.

Live Performance

Elvis' informal and formal live TV studio appearances were astounding. After years of keeping his desire to perform bottled up inside him, Elvis unleashed seven years of raw energy onto the enthralled crowds. The two informal "sit down" shows alone would have brought Elvis back from the brink of obscurity. Elvis poured every bit of himself into his performances, both of which rank as the most invigorating moments of his career. This is a man finding his true essence again against incredible odds, and there is little in the recorded history of music that is so deeply felt.

The two "stand up" shows weren't as defining—after all, how could a faceless band and orchestra match the dynamic Elvis still had with Scotty and D. J.? Nevertheless, notwithstanding that some of these big arrangements were shaky, Elvis' kinetic movements and the palpable excitement in his voice make these shows almost as fascinating.

On Celluloid

Attempts continued this year to update Elvis' onscreen image, but they ultimately proved futile. Elvis' film career had become such a joke that it would have taken another film the caliber of *King Creole* to make things right. None were near that, but they are enjoyable today in that Elvis looks good and tries harder.

Live a Little, Love a Little plays like a daring late-sixties sitcom. The presence of the future second Darrin of *Bewitched*, Dick Sargent, certainly adds to that impression, but the film is charming in its somewhat distant take on modern love affairs. Elvis' co-star Michele Carey was sexy and fairly funny in a few scenes, and depicting her having more than one lover certainly made for a change in pace. As tame as it is by the standards of the last forty years, that people were now going to bed with each other in Presley films itself marked a big departure.

Elvis gets the chance to be surly, playing against his character's two employers with a degree of cunning not seen since the days of Vince Everett. Also worthy of mention is the freaky scene where Elvis is drugged and dreams about singing "Edge of Reality." He plays this against the cast and a bizarrely clad man playing a talking version of Carey's character's pet dog.

Charro! is fairly predictable by comparison. It was supposed to be a hard-hitting western with violence and nudity, but it ended up being bowdlerized before it hit theatres. According to Charlie Hodge, Elvis liked the character he was given to play, but he came to be resigned to the fact that the powers that be wouldn't allow him to take the role where it had the potential to go. Elvis didn't sing anything except the title song (off-camera), his acting is good, and the characters have more depth than one had come to expect from a Presley film. However, this is an unexciting film, the lack of action moving the plot along sluggishly. *Charro!* was a missed chance, but the story would have had to have been revamped considerably to have changed Elvis' screen rep.

Having less lofty ambitions, *The Trouble with Girls (and How to Get into It)* works swimmingly as a lighthearted ensemble piece. It takes place in the late twenties, covering the end of the Chautauqua. It was a traveling education program, with entertainment offered as well. Elvis plays the manager of the outfit, looking resplendent in his white suit and hat. In addition to a young Dabney Coleman playing a crucial role, the film included cameos by Vincent Price and Joyce Van Patten.

The music and production style is unapologetically 1968 during the staging of "Clean Up Your Own Back Yard." Other than that, there is a certain degree of period detail, beyond the fact that plastic football helmets did not exist at

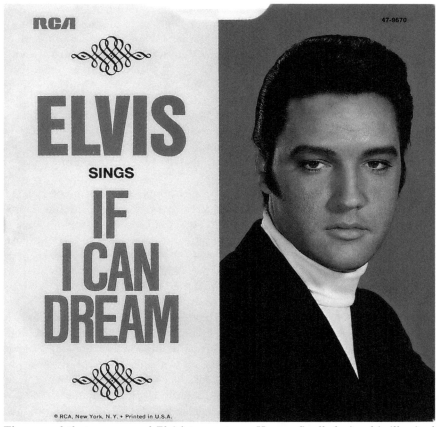

The record that announced Elvis' true return. He was finally losing his ill-suited Hollywood look. *Courtesy of Robert Rodriguez*

the time. Three of the songs Elvis sings do recall twenties-era ditties, and the Chautauqua was enough of an obscurity by the time *The Trouble with Girls* was lensed that there was a degree of historical interest.

Elvis' acting technique had improved, and from *Stay Away, Joe* on you see more of his actual sense of humor and personality. The scene where Elvis is laughing at Marlyn Mason's histrionics feels genuine, and you even get to see him singing the jubilee classic "Swing Down, Sweet Chariot." To sum it up, *The Trouble with Girls* is a fun film that would have been properly acknowledged, had Elvis still been a box-office draw.

Popularity and Impact

As far as Elvis' movies went, they no longer had any popularity or impact. Only Elvis' most stalwart fans went to see them, and thus, *Stay Away, Joe, Speedway*, and, *Live a Little, Love a Little* were ignored until they began to play on television.

Elvis' standing wasn't too high as the year began, but critics started to notice all the rock and roll he was cutting. "Guitar Man" was one of Elvis' most marvelous 45s but sat just outside the Top 40. "U.S. Male" continued the same rootsy sound and got Elvis inside the Top 30. "You'll Never Walk Alone" has a lot going for it but was one of Elvis' worst showings ever. The soundtrack singles "Your Time Hasn't Come Yet, Baby" and "A Little Less Conversation" didn't do anything either, despite the latter being another premium performance. It took the TV special and the complete turnaround offered by "If I Can Dream" to get things back into shape. If its #12 placing would have been disappointing six years before, now it was an out-and-out blessing.

With people out of the habit of buying Elvis, the fourth volume of the *Gold Records* series topped out at #33. Considering that only one of the hits it contained broke the Top 10, it was lucky to get that far. Elvis had had more Top 10 hits since the third volume appeared, but the series no longer held the pretense of being a comprehensive look at Elvis' sales success. Instead, it was set up as an anthology of 45s going back to 1960 that hadn't been on an album before. The music was mostly good, but the plot seemed to have been lost. The series wouldn't resume until long after Elvis' death.

If any evidence was needed, *Speedway* made it clear that the Elvis soundtrack record had become a dead duck. Climbing only to #82, the album's high volume of bonus cuts meant it was better than many of the soundtracks that had reached the Top 10 in years gone by. Times had moved on, and few wanted Elvis the actor. Even fewer wanted to hear the formulaic music found in the *Speedway* score. That it was Elvis' last truly hackneyed movie and soundtrack didn't matter—it was too late in the day to do anything but ride out the remaining film commitments.

The TV special finally brought around the drastic reversal Elvis needed. Soaring to #8, the resulting LP was an excellent blend of Elvis classics old and new. With TV once again serving to sell his music, all it had taken was for Elvis to be true to himself again. It wasn't easy. It had taken a lot of work to override Parker, not to mention the stress of singing publicly again. Yet Elvis had triumphed above everyone's expectations, and upon getting quality product, the public forgave him overnight. Not only were people back on his side, he deserved every bit of the acclaim. For the first time since 1960, Elvis' future seemed limitless.

25

Saved

The Comeback Special

T he history and significance of the *Singer Presents Elvis* special has been mentioned throughout this book, so what follows is a discussion of the music and format of the original seventy-six-minute cut that Elvis watched with director Steve Binder. Information on the fifty-one-minute 1968 broadcast version is also included to give the reader insight into what the public was exposed to at the time.

Oddly, neither of these cuts was included on the DVD releases. The stand-alone disc should be avoided. It's a new edit that's ineffective at displaying what was accomplished. The triple-disc version has all of the footage described, the essential unedited concert performances, plus almost every take of the production numbers. In substituting something that is a cross between them, however, the drawback is that it doesn't have either 1968 edit. As the DVD sets are now out of print, one hopes the box version is reissued with both of the 1968 cuts, plus the takes left off the original 2004 edition.

Introduction—"Trouble"/"Guitar Man"

The first few frames that open the special (a quick, silent *Singer Presents Elvis* title card has been cut from all official releases) make it clear that the old Elvis is back. Looking every bit the rocker he once was, he begins the seminal "Trouble," his face in tight close-up. He sings the first verse, and the camera pulls back to reveal a quasi-tribute to the 1957 "Jailhouse Rock" sequence. Behind Elvis is a wall of people in silhouette made up to look like him. He launches straight into a scorching "Guitar Man" that left no doubt that *Singer Presents Elvis* was going to bear no resemblance to the plastic products Elvis had been making in Hollywood. Playing a scratchy guitar and wailing his heart out, the outstanding standard of the performances is quickly established.

The First "Sit Down" Segment

Binder had observed the magnetic energy of Elvis jamming in his dressing room with friends, and he felt that it should be translated to the stage portion of the show. Scotty and D. J. were called in, and the results were frenzied. First heard completely on the classic *Burbank Sessions Volume 1* double-LP bootleg, these performances at Burbank Studios are Elvis at his apex. Wearing his iconic black leather outfit, a slim Elvis looked better than ever.

Fragments of the informal concerts were broken up and placed into different parts of the special. This first live section included "Lawdy, Miss Clawdy" and "Baby What You Want Me to Do," with Elvis joking about his curled lip and discussing how the police once filmed his show because they thought he was obscene. Like everything he attempted that night, "Lawdy, Miss Clawdy" is pure adrenalin and guts. "Baby What You Want Me to Do" was a Jimmy Reed blues song Elvis enjoyed jamming to. Worried about how he would be able to improvise for an hour, Binder told him to use "Baby What You Want Me to Do" as a safety net anytime he was stuck. Not only did that give the show structure, Elvis took it as a challenge to keep bettering his performance. Not used in the special was a version from the stand-up show that Elvis played his heart out on. It didn't better the small group renditions, but it does provide a cool alternative.

The "Stand Up" Segment

Held on June 29th, these two shows were the ones that had originally been scripted, before the concept of the "sit down" performances took hold. Featuring Elvis accompanied by an offscreen band, the decision to supplement them with an orchestra yielded mixed results. The strings and horns worked well on the ballads but made the fast numbers sound kitschy. It didn't really matter. Slinking around the stage like a jungle cat, Elvis sang and played everything terrifically.

All the oldies used here are given Elvis' full attention in a way that may be shocking to those who have only heard them performed after early 1970. The horns and flutes do get to you after a while, but Elvis rocks the hell out of "Heartbreak Hotel" and "Hound Dog." Prowling across the stage, diving to his knees, Elvis plainly owns the small crowd. For "Hound Dog," he even threw in some of the original "Big Mama Thornton" lyrics. Outside of a horribly lush introduction, "Can't Help Falling in Love" sounds fine with more adornment. It's again instructive to hear this fully dedicated version next to the ones he would perform later.

"Jailhouse Rock" comes off as the least produced of all the rockers, and Elvis tears into it full throttle. It's a song he never did justice again, so it's wonderful to have this energized version preserved. At one point, Elvis is on the floor with his leg stretched out in front of him, totally lost in the moment.

"Don't Be Cruel" is the sole letdown. The problem Elvis had with it onstage from this performance on is that it was taken too fast. The original record and early live performances come off as classy, because there's a subtle cool to them. Not helping here is the flute being high in the blend. Binder was smart to cut this out of the broadcast edit.

"Love Me Tender" suffers less from being over-arranged because there's a flow missing from the original record. No longer halting and unsure, Elvis only grew comfortable with this ballad as he matured. As it turned out, it would rarely come off this well again. Upon his return in Las Vegas, "Love Me Tender" quickly devolved into the song where Elvis kissed ladies in the audience.

One song that didn't make either cut was a sloppy but dynamic version of "Blue Suede Shoes." Likely left out because the band missed its cue at the early show, and Elvis stumbled on a line at the second, both performances were kinetic displays of Elvis rocking his heart out. Note the way he ends the first version—growling, pushing the band to keep going on, playing to the crowd. It's a short moment, but one that's revealing in how Elvis still considered the audience, even though he likely knew it wasn't going to air.

"Sit Down" Show Interlude

We return to the "sit down" portion of the show with a humorous version of "Are You Lonesome Tonight?" Even at his 1961 Hawaiian show, this was a number Elvis often had fun with. Skipping the narration that usually cracked him up, you can still sense that he's having fun. Likely because of Elvis' tomfoolery, only a few lines were used in the 1968 broadcast. The director's cut has it complete. Both edits lead to Elvis doing a half-scripted, half-ad-libbed commentary about the changes in music since the late fifties that cuts to the next sequence.

Gospel Medley

With Elvis having made some advancements in gospel music, it was natural that this genre be represented. Elvis' religious search had continued to be of high importance to him, and this was a way to express his faith without proselytizing directly. It was arranged in a sequence of four songs, with Elvis backed by the Blossoms.

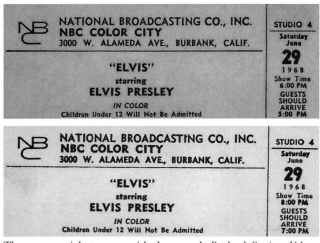

These repro tickets came with the superb *Burbank Sessions Volume 2* bootleg LP.

Elvis doesn't feature in the first number, where ballet-type movements by a male dancer accompany Phil Spector's ingénue Blossoms singer Darlene Love's vocal solo, "Sometimes I Feel Like a Motherless Child." Looking the picture of perfection in a red suit and scarf, Elvis saunters out singing "Where Could I Go but to the Lord." Singing straight from his soul, his level of supremacy is remarkable. This melds into a faster ditty called "Up Above My

Head." There's a dance section that could have been condensed, but Elvis is invested enough in what he is doing to where the positives snuff out the negatives.

Keeping the incremental tempo increase going over all four numbers, the feverish "Saved" was a smoking way to conclude the set. Leiber and Stoller had written it in 1961 for LaVern Baker, for whom it was a Top 40 pop hit. Burning up the set with vitality, Elvis grits his teeth and sings the most dangerous-sounding vocal of his life. Belting out the lead with zeal, he sounds completely truthful in the lyric about seeing the pits of hell and finding himself sermonizing the path to salvation. Whatever else Elvis ever was, right then and there that's who he truly believed he was. On film, the conclusion gets a little overrun with dancers toward the end, and a truly marvelous moment where the Blossoms sing solo lines regrettably got cut off the soundtrack LP.

The Third "Sit Down" Segment

A nice long fragment dominated by Sun Records launches with Elvis introducing Scotty Moore and D. J. Fontana. They promptly go into an icy-cool version of "That's All Right." That it wasn't included in the broadcast cut may come down to the network pushing for recognizable hits.

Elvis is next seen doing the earliest surviving performance of his version of "Tiger Man." The song was a wild howler recorded by Rufus Thomas for Sun in 1953, though from this point on Elvis mysteriously referred to it as being a part of his own Sun Records period. He roars through it like a genuine jungle cat, pressing himself—and his larynx—to the limit. Trading his acoustic for Scotty's lead guitar, Elvis played the instrument with which he is most synonymous more brilliantly than ever before or again. Despite this being a moment of conquest-based transcendence, it was not included on the original 1968 broadcast, and had to wait until a 1969 rerun. On record, it had already been issued on the makeshift tie-in *Singer Presents Elvis* LP.

"Trying to Get to You" continues the focus on the early days with a superlative performance that saw Elvis reveal fresh emotions within it. With Elvis having since metaphorically lived out the trials and tribulations described in the lyric, it was plain that his interpretation of the song had expanded to something that delved much deeper. Most stunning about the way Elvis is singing is the level he is willing to go within himself. You hear that it's not been easy, but you sense how good it feels to be back. "Trying to Get to You" captures the moment Elvis realized his dreams were again within reach. For all that, this defining performance curiously didn't make it past Binder's personal edit.

Having not yet shown one frame of anything past the gospel medley, the 1968 broadcast version joins back in with another stab at "Baby What You Want Me to Do." It's better structured than the previous rendition, and the fun Elvis had made it a worthwhile performance each time. Not only is it exuberant, "Baby What You Want Me to Do" is steely rock and roll.

"Blue Christmas" is the one moment in the 1968 broadcast version that isn't in the longer edit. Put in at Parker's insistence that there be at least one Christmas song, Presley vocalizes adroitly throughout. Elvis' heavy electric playing gives the cut a harder feel than the 1957 master.

"One Night" reaches a whole other realm of performance. Hollering beautifully, Elvis wrings every last bit out of himself, attacking every lyric, unable to sit still. This almost matches "Trying to Get to You" in the catharsis department. The way Elvis uses his voice is fascinating. He's singing so hard and passionately, there is this rasp that may come off as harsh in other vocalists. Throwing off the shackles of all self-protection or pretense, Elvis exhibits nothing but soul. Fortification of the spirit that rocks insanely to boot—that's what *Singer Presents Elvis* is all about.

"Memories" is a touching (if faintly cloying) Mac Davis ballad Elvis used to end both his "sit down" sets. A fittingly sentimental close to the shows, Elvis was enamored of it in 1968–69. He had released it as a single and, against the advice of Sam Phillips, would also include it in his 1969 sets. The girls he is seen singing it to seem in total awe.

"Guitar Man" Medley

Binder wanted to make some kind of statement on the way fame had led Elvis off course, and how Presley was now finding himself back at his roots. By weaving "Guitar Man" in and out, this medley was a way to tell a fictionalized capsule version of the Elvis saga. Butchered on the broadcast version, and incomplete on the DVD, the director's cut is the only way to properly view the segment. It is so cool to see Elvis act in something conceptual, rather than linear, but his sublime performance is interrupted by bloated dance numbers and other unnecessary bits of business.

It starts off with Elvis on a trippy electric road, emoting silently over the short blues song "Nothingville." Written to order by Mac Davis, it's a brief, effective mood piece. Going on to an ersatz busy main street, Elvis sings a verse of "Guitar Man" and gets pulled into a brothel. The only segment the network refused to air at the time, it was daring for the period. "Let Yourself Go" is the featured song, but Elvis had to sing it with the actresses. Elvis and blonde co-star Susan Henning had an erotic spark that is readily felt, but their innate sensuality aside, the self-indulgence of this "too hot for television" portion—complete with a bizarre, twenties-styled dance interlude—comes off tacky and corny.

Having run from the cops, Elvis comes back out on the colorful road to sing another fragment of "Guitar Man." After that he promptly goes back to the main street, where there is a carnival. A solid version of "Big Boss Man" is sung to what looks like the boss of the setup and a pretty girl he's been mistreating. Kept lean and to the point, this is the best thing shot for the medley so far. The broadcast version skipped straight from "Nothingville" to here.

With the "big boss" having broken Elvis' guitar, Presley sings a crystalline "It Hurts Me" to the girl. Fighting attackers with karate, his physical skills at the time were impressive. If the silly setup is tolerable when Elvis is on the screen, a *West Side Story*–inspired dance sequence is out of place. Peculiarly, this abrasively off-track moment was the only part kept in the broadcast version, while "It Hurts Me" and Elvis got trimmed out completely. It should have been the other way around; as it was broadcast, even the little sense the dance made was lost.

Back out on the crowded color street, Elvis sings a little more "Guitar Man" before we cut to a club where a belly dancer is onstage. In a nod to his old gold-lamé outfit, Elvis is seen wearing a gold vest as he sings an abbreviated "Little Egypt" behind her. "Trouble" follows, and we see a sequence where Elvis gradually works two stages that are incrementally nicer, with more elegant clothes at each venue. We then cut back to the "stand up" show, where Elvis finishes "Trouble" and sings a newly written concluding verse to "Guitar Man." Over

The incredible energy and passion of Elvis during the *Singer Presents Elvis* special is perfectly encapsulated on the cover and contents of this 1976 bootleg.

applause, Elvis picks up his guitar and walks off the stage onto the colored road. This was nicely executed, and holds up because the focus is on Elvis.

"If I Can Dream"

For the finale, something special was put together. Binder knew that Elvis believed in basic equality for all men, and he wanted the show to end with something that conveyed this. He asked Earl Brown to compose a song along those lines, and what resulted was "If I Can Dream," a powerfully written ballad about brotherhood. Elvis loved the message and took it to heart. Coming during Vietnam, and in the wake of the assassinations of Bobby Kennedy and Martin Luther King, "If I Can Dream" was a bold step for Elvis. Singing from the heart with everything he could summon up, Elvis made this moment into something all can relate to.

Dressed in white against huge red letters making up his name, Elvis sings with all the relief and inspiration one acquires when they have put their life on the right path. Moving his arm back and forth, building to a climax, Elvis lays his soul on the line. Raw footage shows the crew applauding after each take—a particularly unusual happenstance on a set. A triumphant climax, this firmly clinched Elvis' turnaround. As the special aired, he was back in the charts with an important new single, and it had to have felt good.

Credits

As Elvis plays along, an instrumental of "Let Yourself Go" is shown over the credits, providing a neat way to get a little more music into the show.

26

Change of Habit

1969

This year was almost perfect. It's like 1956 again, with only the movie lacking to some extent. *Change of Habit* and most of its soundtrack were too self-consciously modern, but Elvis gave a natural performance. It's a shame that the promise he had shown as an actor never got fully developed.

The American sessions were the first Elvis had held in Memphis since 1955, and some argue they were the best since then as well. The lesser cuts reveal some of the problems that would pop up in the seventies, as far as being middle-of-the-road or overproduced, but a good number of Elvis' most accomplished performances stem from these dates. Indeed, the topical "In the Ghetto," the elaborate "Suspicious Minds," and the sensitive "Don't Cry Daddy" were strong enough to give Elvis another run of Top 10 hits. Along with *Elvis Is Back!*, *From Elvis in Memphis* has often been called Elvis' finest LP. Not every song was of equal quality, but Elvis' commitment and vocal intensity remain unmatched anywhere else in his catalogue.

Elvis' comeback shows in Las Vegas were astounding. Now possessing sharp and graceful movements honed from hours of karate practice, the concerts were his best visually. With Elvis finally having the material to back up his broad creative vision, it was also a musical triumph. Elvis no longer limited himself to one genre, and now appealed to a huge cross-section of people. He had become America's preeminent entertainer.

Studio Work

Most of the details on the two Memphis sessions can be found in the reviews of the records that resulted. What's important to remember is the risk Elvis took in undertaking them. Though he had artistically redeemed himself with the NBC special and his 1966–68 non-soundtrack sessions, Elvis still had a way to go in erasing his Hollywood image.

Elvis' friend Marty Lacker had been working with producer Chips Moman as a production assistant. Knowing that Chips' American Studios was now the hottest spot to record in Memphis, he suggested to Elvis that he cancel a planned Nashville session to try something new. Chips and his house band put out the kind of soulful records Elvis loved, and Presley quickly agreed to the session.

Needing to finish up before he flew to Hollywood to shoot *Change of Habit* in March, Elvis held two lengthy sessions in January and February. He and the

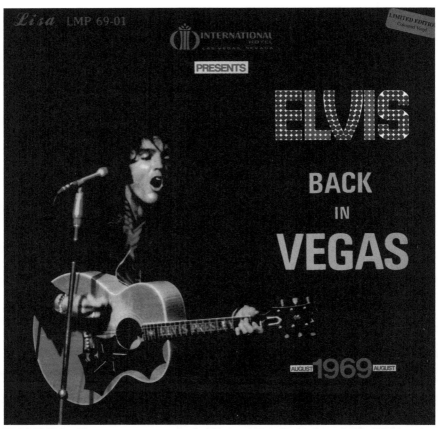

Elvis' 1969 Las Vegas concerts may be familiar now, but it wasn't until this 1986 bootleg that a full show was released. This clear audience recording hails from August 14th and reflects the tremendous quality of the 1969 performances.

American crew quickly proved their worth to each other, developing the kind of rapport Elvis hadn't enjoyed since Hank Garland had been forced to leave the business. If Elvis having to prove anything to anybody sounds unusual, one must remember that his standing in the industry had taken a big hit.

Chips Moman was an exacting producer, working Elvis hard. In the prime of his life, and in a good frame of mind after the success of the special, Elvis delivered with a breathtaking intensity. Presented with a set of new material of variety and quality unmatched since 1960, Elvis immediately carved out a new, more mature image. Not only was his voice stronger and more powerful in its maturity, he could still rock like he had a decade earlier.

Elvis had established he could handle any type of music he put his mind to. What was proved in Memphis was that he could handle it as well as anyone else at the time. By doing so, he won over a generation who had previously been unable to relate to his current work. Maybe he was never again a trendsetter, but that Elvis didn't have to become a strict oldies act lies largely in what he accomplished at American.

The Colonel didn't like it that Chips, like Steve Binder before him, wasn't willing to play ball. Elvis would never work with either man again—in fact, they were barred from seeing him at all. Tragic as that was, Chips got Elvis back on the right track. If Elvis' own issues meant that his instincts lessened with time, at least he never again took his hands off the reins. He would occasionally do songs he didn't like as favors to his song-publisher friends, but the overall direction of Elvis' career to come was—for better or worse—his own.

Live Performance

After the success of the *Singer Presents Elvis* special, Elvis insisted on making his overdue return to the concert stage. Once a deal to play the new International Hotel in Las Vegas was established, Presley held a series of auditions to form the nucleus of what would retrospectively become known as the T.C.B. band. Along with Elvis on vocals and rhythm guitar, the lineup consisted of James Burton (lead guitar), John Wilkinson (rhythm guitar), Charlie Hodge (rhythm guitar and background vocals), Larry Muhoberac (piano), Jerry Scheff (bass guitar), and Ronnie Tutt (drums). He also utilized two of the best contemporary vocal groups, the soul-based Sweet Inspirations and the Imperials Quartet. Topping everything off were the twenty-seven musicians who made up the Bobby Morris Orchestra.

On July 31st, Elvis began his triumphant monthlong engagement. At his peak in many ways, he was never slimmer, his energy was amazing, and his voice blended rock-and-roll grit with a newly developed range and maturity. With the exception of some dates recorded for a live album, a pre-arranged set-list was more closely adhered to here than at anytime later. This doesn't detract from the shows, as they were ideally structured. The blend of classic Presley hits, contemporary covers, blues, and new material gave audiences ninety minutes with an artist who had developed an unerring mastery of modern music.

Some have argued that, as a rock star, Elvis sold out by playing Vegas. That's not correct, because Elvis no longer strived for strictly the same audience as his younger competitors. Besides, some great bands played Vegas during this time, and Elvis being there turned the town around. From 1969 on, Las Vegas was no longer the sole province of middle-aged high rollers. Instead, "Sin City" became a destination that people of all ages and most income brackets could enjoy.

On Celluloid

Change of Habit fulfilled the last of Elvis' movie obligations and was a somewhat curious end to his cinematic career. He looks slender and vibrant, and as a ghetto doctor he even got to stretch. The movie itself wasn't so hot. Talented as she was, Mary Tyler Moore didn't have much chemistry with Elvis, but that wasn't even a problem next to the script.

By trying to force too many movie-of-the-week dramatic situations into one film, *Change of Habit* floundered under its own ambition. Issues like rape, race, and autism have to be handled with care, and at times the film seems close to exploiting these topics rather than exploring them. Crossing Elvis with Jesus as Mary has to make a choice between being a nun or being with Elvis' Dr. John Carpenter character, the ambiguous ending came across as heavy-handed. In the shadow of Elvis' comeback, it quietly faded to black, along with his acting career. It gets points for presenting Elvis in a different way, but on the other hand it's more dated than anything he ever did.

Popularity and Impact

Elvis won back most of his old fans in 1969, and made a large number of new ones besides. Rock and roll—at least as defined by Elvis—was no longer considered a social menace. Unless they wanted to risk credibility, even harsh critics of the past couldn't ignore the sheer quality of Elvis' best music. This also went for the public—people of all ages were open fans of his now. Playing Las Vegas may have caused hipsters to sneer, but by doing so, Elvis showed a lot of people in and out of the business how important he and his art actually were.

On the record front, it was almost like the good old days. *From Elvis in Memphis* and *From Memphis to Vegas* were both strong titles that engendered goodwill. Both narrowly missed the Top 10, but their impact on Elvis' career belied chart positions. By tying into events that generated a lot of new public interest in who Elvis was today, the LPs were marketed with a flair that became rare as Parker's addiction to gambling took hold.

Despite there still being too many irrelevant Presley singles issued, the three 1969 Memphis titles—"In the Ghetto," "Suspicious Minds," and "Don't Cry Daddy"—were not only the biggest Presley hits in years, they were also among his finest. Two years ago, having one Top 10 hit would have been an insurmountable challenge; now, Elvis had three. "His Hand in Mine" was a catalogue item; topping off at #35, "Memories" fared better as part of the TV album than alone.

The 45 that should have hit as hard as the Memphis singles was "Clean Up Your Own Back Yard." If anything, this sampler from *The Trouble with Girls* served as a direct precursor to what Elvis would do in Memphis several months later. The only reason it too only got to #35 was because of the stigma the movies carried with them. The message was finally brought home, and nothing recorded specifically for *Change of Habit* reached 45. The song it pilfered from the Memphis sessions, "Rubberneckin'," was put out on 7-inch, but only as the flip to "Don't Cry Daddy."

27

Standing Room Only

Elvis Live on Vinyl 1969–77

D uring the last eight years of his career, Elvis' focus was on live performances. It would be wrong to say that he lost interest in record-making completely, but during that period his studio visits gradually became more of a chore. The live albums were an easier alternative, containing proven hits with a longer shelf life than the concurrent studio albums.

After the first three, these albums are not exactly creative highlights in Elvis' career, but they did make sense from a commercial standpoint. Usually built around events, the concert albums seemed to sell themselves. That together they get repetitive does not detract from the impact each release made individually. What follows is a review of the pluses and minuses of each live album and stand-alone single released from 1969 to 1977. Live recordings popping up on LPs of mostly studio recordings are covered in the studio LP reviews. Taken together, these albums give a fair (if incomplete) overview of Elvis' peak and slow descent as a concert performer.

Elvis certainly held better concerts than some released on RCA during his lifetime, but these albums remain the most historically important, and contain the concerts the general public was most exposed to. These LPs shaped the general view on Elvis as a performer in the seventies, and it is only because of the interest they sparked that this era eventually underwent detailed examination.

From Memphis to Vegas (Released October 14, 1969)

Covering the 1969 Las Vegas season where Elvis returned to live performances after an eight-year absence, the live half of the double-LP set *From Memphis to Vegas* was a stunning recording. What makes this record stand out from later issues of 1969 material is that the mix is so much more punchy. Later released on its own as *Elvis in Person*, the only problem with it is that the double-album should have contained a complete 1969 concert.

In 1969, Elvis sang every song with feeling and commitment. From an uninhibited "Blue Suede Shoes" to the beautiful "Can't Help Falling in Love," each track is a winner. Highlights include an impassioned cover of Willie Dixon's "My Babe" that Elvis was very physical with onstage. The little exclamation of "Oh God" he gives after the first verse makes the track even more exciting. A hard rock "Johnny B. Goode" is one of the few covers of this standard worth investigating. Elvis related to the story of the track as much the author Chuck Berry did, and he brings to it a reality many others can't convey.

A rip-roaring reinterpretation of "I Can't Stop Loving You" makes one forget that it had previously been a country ballad, and the medley of "Mystery Train" and "Tiger Man" is explosive. Even the Bee Gees' "Words" comes out masculine and powerful. Best of all was an almost eight-minute tour-de-force version of his upcoming "Suspicious Minds" single. With Elvis literally somersaulting across the stage, it was one of the most electrifying performances in the history of rock and roll. Reaching #12 on the *Billboard* charts, the success of this album meant that a follow-up was a foregone conclusion.

On Stage, February 1970 (Released June 23, 1970)

Except for two cuts slipped in from his August 1969 shows—a good if not particularly distinct "Yesterday" and a fine version of Del Shannon's "Runaway"—*On Stage* was indeed recorded in February 1970, during Elvis' second gig at the International Hotel. Entirely made up of songs he had never recorded, *On Stage* displayed the more contemporary bent of Elvis' 1970 shows. The cover photos feature Elvis looking his very best, and the record has him sounding his very best.

Elvis' early-1970 shows were tremendous, and again it would have been nice to have a complete performance. Still, an argument can be made that an entire concert recording might not have had the same contemporary impact as an album of Elvis doing fresh songs. Besides, the placement of "See See Rider" as the opening cut is likely what led Elvis to use it as his main intro from 1972 on. It would never again smoke as strongly as it does here, however.

Elvis did not throw away one moment, each song having a creative arrangement and powerful vocals. Subsequently covered to death, "Sweet Caroline" sounds revitalized as something other than an audience singalong. "Walk a Mile in My Shoes" comes across as a personal anthem, and an electrifying one to boot. "Proud Mary" has a clean crispness missing from other renditions, and, stripped of all MOR leanings, even "Release Me" sounds like vital country-rock.

Besides being one of the first ballads to feature Elvis' voice in full bloom, "The Wonder of You" became a Top 10 hit all around the globe. Elvis' new command of his voice and the warmth he coveys keep it becoming too schmaltzy. A case in point is the arrangement of "Let It Be Me," which would sound gooey and glitzy if not for the passion in Elvis' delivery.

As one of Elvis' finest ever rockers, the highlight of *On Stage* was a cover of Tony Joe White's "Polk Salad Annie." Even divorced of the stunning visuals that Elvis gave to it in his physical prime, his stinging vocals and the steamy lead guitar of James Burton will leave your sound system sizzling. Elvis loved the pure Southern vibe of this song, and seemed still to enjoy it even in the depths of his 1976–77 decline.

This is an obscure Japanese quadrophonic version of the *On Stage* LP. As with all quad mixes, differences can be heard from the stereo releases.

"An American Trilogy"/"The First Time Ever I Saw Your Face" (Released April 4, 1972)

The highlight of Elvis' show in 1972 was "An American Trilogy," and on vinyl it was no less of a stunner. Since Elvis *was* America for so many around the world, this song comes across today as a true statement of purpose. It was a medley of three nineteenth-century songs: "Dixie," which was associated with the Confederacy; "All My Trials," a black hymn; and "The Battle Hymn of the Republic," which had been an anthem for the Union. Conceived by Mickey Newbury, its intent was an effort toward harmony. This measured rendition from Las Vegas in February 1972 is Presley's definitive recording. Though Newbury had the hit in the U.S., "An American Trilogy" has become one of Elvis' many signature numbers. The flip is reviewed in chapter 29.

Elvis as Recorded at Madison Square Garden (Released June 18, 1972)

With Elvis' debut Madison Square Garden shows being a major media event, it was only natural that an LP containing the gig would be issued. What *was* rather surprising was that it was issued a mere eight days after being recorded. Elvis hadn't even finished his tour yet, so other than preparing the set-list, he had no input into how the album was mixed or packaged. Thankfully, he was still performing almost as well as ever in 1972, with his June tour being the highlight. The King sparkles throughout, and as he had recently revamped the lineup, many of the songs had not been issued live before. Giving the listener at home an idea of how well Elvis paced his shows, it was his first LP to contain an entire concert. Two sets on June 10th were taped, and the tighter evening show was the one RCA selected.

By 1972, Elvis had slowed down a little—some of the oldies felt perfunctory by then—but the funk-infused rearrangement of "Hound Dog" was punctuated by brilliant James Burton riffs. Jerry Scheff's newly instituted bass solo on "Polk Salad Annie" kicked butt, and Three Dog Night's "Never Been to Spain" appeared in a fantastic, horn-infused rendition, showcasing Elvis at his most soulful.

The show offered plenty of variety. One of Elvis' favorite records at the time was Ray Price's "For the Good Times," and he delivers a delicate yet commanding performance of it here. "The Impossible Dream" was already an old warhorse, but Presley's sincerity pushed it into the autobiographical realm. He felt so close to it that he even considered making it a single in early 1971.

A huge seller, *Elvis as Recorded at Madison Square Garden* reinforced Elvis' reputation as a top concert performer. A #11 hit, it has sold five million copies in the U.S., with Canadian sales alone adding another two. Eddie Murphy has gone on record as saying that listening to this album when he was growing up inspired him to enter show business. It's not as scorching as previous live albums, but it's a solid piece of entertainment, as well as a great representation of seventies Elvis before the decline.

Aloha from Hawaii Via Satellite (Released February 4, 1973)

Documenting Elvis' recent TV spectacular, the *Aloha* recordings became his very next album. Releasing two live albums in a row would normally have been a risk, but a high-volume publicity campaign—and subsequent massive ratings—saw to it that Elvis had his first #1 album in nine years. The special itself, and the story behind it, are discussed in chapter 33, so let's delve into the actual album. Released as a gatefold with a die-cut cover, the double-LP was released domestically in Quadraphonic sound only (excepting the stereo record-club issue) through the early eighties. The mix isn't especially dynamic, but it did have a live ambience. Having dieted and cut down his pill intake, Elvis looked great, but *Aloha from Hawaii* was a commercial, not artistic, landmark.

Elvis Recorded Live on Stage in Memphis (Released July 7, 1974)

After *Aloha*, Elvis' casino gigs seemed to lose much of their excitement, but he was still performing well on tour. Elvis hadn't played Memphis since 1961 when he scheduled five shows there during his March 1974 jaunt. They were well received, and Elvis himself wanted to record a new LP at the final show on March 20th.

He told reporter James Kingsley, "Man, I'm ready and prepared for this recording session." He said he'd been nervous for his first hometown show the previous Saturday, but he got a warm reception. "They were great and I appreciate it." Recording at the Astrodome was discussed, he added, but "I wanted to record a live session in my hometown in Memphis. After all, this is where it all started out for me." Clearly an album he put some thought into, even the cover art was nicer than usual. Both the front and back featured photos of Graceland.

The shortcoming of the release was the decision to edit the set-list, leaving out superb performances of "Polk Salad Annie" and "Steamroller Blues." It's conceivable that RCA and/or Elvis wanted to avoid repetition with previous live albums, but the decision dimmed the show's more contemporary fire.

There remained a degree of spirit. Olivia Newton-John's "Let Me Be There" was limp country-pop that Elvis toughened up to reasonable country-rock. "Trying to Get to You" and "My Baby Left Me" were the best blues and rockabilly interpretations Elvis did onstage during the mid-seventies, and also welcome was an unexpected, off-the-cuff version of "Blueberry Hill."

With gospel now a bigger part of his show, two selections from that genre were included. The power-packed "How Great Thou Art" is terrific, and deserved the Grammy it won, but "Why Me Lord" was a rough-going J. D. Sumner spotlight. Sumner was a fantastic bass singer, but the lyric seemed bizarre when sung so low. Arguably better for J. D. was his dive-bomber act during the "I Got a Woman"/"Amen" medley. "Amen" was based on Otis Redding's recording, and Elvis did this pairing at countless seventies dates. It may get boring when heard repeatedly, but the edited version here is reasonable.

Selections like the rock medley were crassly uninspired, but this show was a huge improvement over *Aloha*. Neither are done any kind of justice, but the rock medley was the only place at the time to hear Elvis do Joe Turner's follow-up clone to "Shake, Rattle and Roll," "Flip Flop and Fly," along with Loggins and Messina's "Your Mama Don't Dance." Following the pattern of many of Elvis' post-1968 releases, *Live on Stage in Memphis* charted at #33 pop while reaching #2 country.

Having Fun with Elvis on Stage (Released August 19, 1974)

This infamous album featured Elvis' between-song stage patter. *Why* this album exists is hard to explain. Elvis had a witty sense of humor, but his jokes don't make sense when taken out of context. Pressed on Colonel Parker's Boxcar label as an item to sell during Elvis' summer 1974 Las Vegas Hilton shows, the proceeds allegedly went to charity. Funny that, two months later, it came out as a full-blown RCA release. This was a boon to collectors, but it made Elvis look bad.

Critics harped that Elvis didn't care about what he put his name to as long as it made money. Getting to #130 on the pop charts, it was Elvis' lowest showing for a full-priced new album, but some sort of unnatural event made it #9 on the country listings. What his detractors couldn't have known is that Elvis was furious that the album came out. Other than its odd conceit, probably the most offensive aspect of the release was the fact that at first glance it seemed to be a

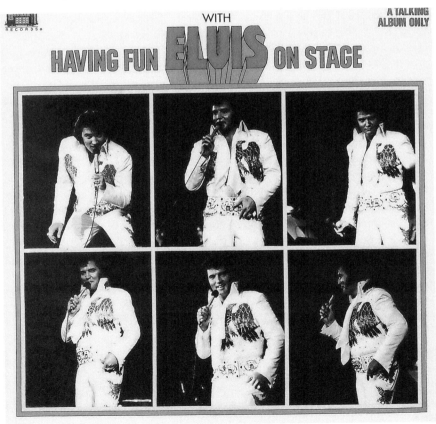

This bizarre set of between-song patter on the Colonel's Boxcar label was to garner poor press upon its release as a full-price RCA LP. Though given a production credit, Elvis didn't even know about it until it was pressed.   *Courtesy of Robert Rodriguez*

true live album. Sure, it was billed as "A Talking Album Only," but it also lacked notes to explain what it was.

The only thing that comes close to being valuable was a somewhat bowdlerized 1969 monologue. A loose overview of his career to that point, it was a decent example of Elvis' off-the-wall, self-deprecating humor. Too bad more moments like this were omitted in favor of water requests. The sound itself is taken largely from low-fidelity mono soundboards, several of which have been put out officially or unofficially since Elvis' death.

It's more entertaining than Elvis' worst soundtracks, but *Having Fun with Elvis on Stage* remains the most disposable Presley release. Unexpectedly enough, a *Having Fun with Elvis on Stage* series of bootleg CDs and 10-inch LPs came out around 2000. There was a reissue of the original album alongside new collections compiled in the same spirit. If nothing else, they confirmed that there is a market for anything Elvis.

Elvis in Concert (Released October 3, 1977)

This posthumous double-album may not belong here in the strictest sense, but it likely would have been Elvis' next release, had he lived. Some speculate that the *Elvis in Concert* TV special would have been canceled if not for his death, but no evidence suggests that. Recorded on June 19 and 21, 1977, the show chronicled what became Elvis' last tour.

The first LP presented material used in the final cut of the special, while the second contained—with one exception added at the last minute—tracks that ended up on the cutting-room floor. Elvis was not in good shape, and this is his most painful album. He tries valiantly to deliver, and the effort he makes (feeble as it is at times) is heartwarming and heartbreaking.

Though the first show featured him generally at his worst, a moment of grandeur came with an inspirational rendition of "How Great Thou Art." The purity of his intonation as the notes are stretched out at the climax constitutes some of the most moving vocalizing Elvis ever did. The second night was better, featuring several highlights. "See See Rider" and "That's All Right" show an Elvis who could still rock a little and enjoy himself onstage.

Elvis' humor came through clearly on "Are You Lonesome Tonight?," and though they were pale shadows of his youth, he even had fun with old standbys like "Hound Dog" and "Jailhouse Rock." Uncommon songs like "Hawaiian Wedding Song," "And I Love You So," and "Fairytale" disprove the theory that Elvis' set was overrun with oldies. "You Gave Me a Mountain," "My Way," and "Trying to Get to You" were bravura vocal efforts, and it is surprising that the latter didn't make the final cut of the special.

"Love Me," "Teddy Bear"/"Don't Be Cruel," and "Johnny B. Goode" are weak performances by an audibly sick man who hadn't cared for these numbers for years. When he does an aching "I Really Don't Want to Know," you can hear that

Elvis' talent is still there. It was more that he gradually had lost the stamina and inspiration to put it across for an entire show.

The LP ended up reaching #5, with "My Way" becoming a fair-sized hit. A revelatory version of "Unchained Melody" should have been included, but was held back for issue as a posthumous single. You can't compare these recordings to any concert he did from 1954 to 1972, or many held from 1973 to 1975, but the Rapid City show was good for its era. The *Elvis in Concert* album and the subsequent "Unchained Melody" single were heavily overdubbed, and ended up sounding over-produced. While the un-dubbed shows reveal how bad a shape Elvis was in, he received some undue criticism for arrangements he had nothing to do with.

"My Way"/"America" (Released October 3, 1977)

The flip to the "My Way" single came from a soundboard cassette recording made in Las Vegas in December 1975. Elvis sang "America the Beautiful" (called just "America" on the sleeve) from the end of 1975 to the end of 1976 to celebrate the bicentennial. Though he was in mediocre-to-poor shape during most of his 1976 concerts, this was one number that seemed to rouse him. Being that he was in better vocal condition, the initial December 1975 Vegas outings are the best. Being that this comes from cassette and not multi-track, the audio quality is lacking.

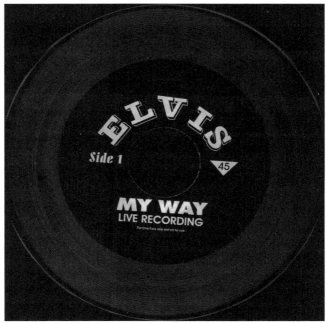

Colored vinyl failed to obscure the fact that this boot version of "My Way" came straight from the *Aloha* LP.

28

Got My Mojo Working

1970

Most would agree that Elvis was at his mature peak in 1970. The Nashville sessions held in June show a further ripening of his voice, and in some ways he never sounded better. Presley's voice had smoothed out into an opulent baritone capable of handling music of every style. Elvis found his place in modern music without losing the fundamental strengths of what he built his name on.

As far as concerts go, the 1970 shows set new standards in success and presentation. The film footage shot that summer for the documentary *That's the Way It Is* shows Elvis knocking out those attending his third engagement at the International Hotel. The documentary is seen today as the ultimate record of Elvis in his Las Vegas prime, but the shows he performed in February were even more high-spirited. Elvis also played an outstanding engagement at the Houston Astrodome, which spurred on a return to touring. His two tours in the fall were rapturously received.

Studio Work

Elvis' June and September sessions in Nashville showcased an artist still revitalized by his comeback. Some songs were over produced, but a lush element had been intermittently present the year before in Memphis. Thirty-four masters were cut in June. Everything was sung well, and only a few cuts were downright poor. Several demonstrated sustained creative development, and progressive singles like "I've Lost You" found Elvis getting more personal with his music. Oddly, Elvis wasn't in the best of moods during the short September booking, organized to finish a country album and record a new single, but the end results were nonetheless satisfying.

Containing only four live recordings, the *That's the Way It Is* LP was not a soundtrack. With Elvis unlikely to connect with the same market that bought albums by Led Zeppelin and Black Sabbath, it was mostly aimed at a more mature audience. A nice release with superb vocals, the only hitch was not having enough rockers to balance it out.

Elvis Country has no such problem, being the most carefully programmed LP Elvis ever released. It contains a great blend of songs that cover the many different aspects of the genre—who else but Elvis could convincingly reinvent a warhorse like "Whole Lotta Shakin' Goin' On"? It was one of the most satisfying projects of his career.

Live Performance

On January 26th, Elvis returned to the International Hotel to perform a series of shows with a contemporary slant. With a set that featured the live debuts of "See See Rider," "Polk Salad Annie," "Proud Mary," "Walk a Mile in My Shoes," "Don't Cry Daddy," "Kentucky Rain," and "The Wonder of You," this was Elvis' best engagement—the high-water mark in his performance career.

Two key changes had been made in the lineup, with Bob Lanning now handling the drums, and Glen D. Hardin taking over the piano bench. A less ornate form of the trademark Elvis jumpsuits replaced the two-piece karate outfits from the year before. Not only were these more distinctive, they also gave Elvis the ability to move without fear of ripping his pants.

Perhaps the finest new element was how fluid the lineup had become. Not only did this keep Elvis and the band on their toes, it also gave extra value to the many fans returning for multiple performances. Eighty percent of the *On Stage* LP was recorded at this time, and it was to be the only Elvis concert album with all new songs. It is an LP that noted critic Dave Marsh once heralded as a fundamental example of "swamp rock." While too varied to put into one specific bag, it does have solid examples of the genre.

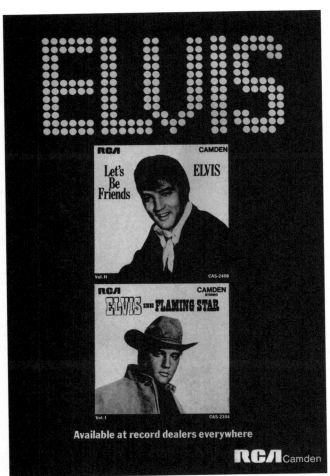

A 1970 ad for Camden's *Let's Be Friends* and *Flaming Star* LPs. The Camden releases were cheap and had nice covers, but they lacked aesthetic value.

In late February, Elvis played a short stint at the Houston Astrodome—his first non-charity tour shows since 1957. Poor acoustics and a small stage meant that the venue could not accommodate an orchestra. Backed by the core group, Elvis played to an average of 80,000 spectators a day. Though he was displeased with the sound, the ecstatic reception proved that a return to full-time touring would mean a whole new level of personal and professional achievement. On a more delicate note, it was strongly suggested to Elvis that he not bring the Sweet Inspirations with him. Balking at this blatant bigotry, he said he would only come if his group came with him. As he had since the fifties, Presley admirably stood up for racial equality and tolerance.

After a deal fell through on a live closed-circuit telecast that Elvis had invited Ringo Starr to be a part of, Presley and Parker decided to do a documentary focused around Elvis' upcoming return to the International, which was scheduled to commence on August 10th. With Tutt back in the fold, and Joe Guercio taking over from Bobby Morris, filming took place at an adventurous time. Later in the engagement, Elvis added Kathy Westmoreland, a classically trained vocalist whose beautiful soprano voice immediately made an impact. She would remain with the show until the end.

The concerts were for the most part extraordinary, but Elvis was showing signs of boredom by the end of the run. He had dropped many of his new songs, and he wasn't taking some of his more common oldies like "Hound Dog" or "All Shook Up" as seriously anymore. They still had energy, but they were notably faster and shorter than before. Elvis was nearly as artistically committed as he had been the past year—he just didn't want to be playing the same room so often.

To add to the boredom, events that transpired during this gig meant that Elvis was mostly stuck in his room. A false paternity suit and a serious death threat curtailed his previously generous time with fans, and he no longer felt completely safe in public. Though both these incidents didn't result in anything but temporary personal turmoil, Elvis was never a carefree individual again. They were part of the catalyst for the decline that slowly followed.

Two short tours held in September and November featured sets that were slightly less creative than those for Elvis' Astrodome gig, but in every other respect they were victories. Rapturously received by fans old and new, Elvis presented a short show by later standards, but one that was more physically dynamic. The Hugh Jarrett singers filled in for the Imperials on the September dates, reuniting Elvis with the former Jordanaire,

This pin shows Elvis riding his horse at Graceland in 1970. It was one of his favorite hobbies during the period.

who led the ensemble. When the Imperials came back in November, Elvis took the opportunity to fulfill his longtime ambition of performing a gospel number onstage. Closer to the record here than it would be subsequently, "How Great Thou Art" was a powerful display of Elvis' deep spirituality.

On November 14th, Elvis played two shows at the Inglewood Forum in Los Angeles. Perhaps the most celebrated of his early-seventies dates, they presented a star at the very top of his game. Though they got frequently tangled up, the long fringes on the new suit Elvis wore at the evening show accentuated his frenetic movements in a dazzling fashion. Still, there were signs of trouble ahead. Elvis continued to be plagued by the paternity accusation, and there were more death threats on the road. Outside of one show where some fans claimed (in retrospect) that he was stoned in Las Vegas that summer, the evening performance at the Forum gave the first hint that Elvis' private life was no longer as satisfying as his career. He had been visited between shows by a process server concerning the paternity suit, and was legitimately shaken. The show that night was superb, but Elvis' onstage dialogue featured out-of-character bragging, almost like he was justifying himself. Though he had been on top of the world only months before, there was, as his friend Jerry Schilling put it, "a change in the air."

On Celluloid

Elvis' early Las Vegas engagements not only led to his return as a live artist. One of them also revived his film career. In early 1970, Elvis and his manager Colonel Tom Parker decided to make a documentary. Elvis wanted to convey where he was at currently, and it was also a way to entertain those who could not come to see him in Vegas. He called the resulting film, *Elvis: That's the Way It Is*, his best in a decade.

The first half of *Elvis: That's the Way It Is* chronicles how Elvis, his fans, his entourage, and the staff of the International got ready for his summer engagement of 1970. While the Colonel is conspicuous by his absence, this section gave the audience a chance to see what went into staging a Las Vegas show. Shot in the month leading up to his opening night on August 10th, we get a fairly candid look at Elvis during his various stage rehearsals. He comes across as a guy who likes to have fun but is also a perfectionist. He comes across as even-headed, too, with a healthy respect for those who work with him. The high regard his musicians obviously held him in seems well deserved. While there is no doubt who is in charge, Presley listens to suggestions with an open mind and is never afraid to admit his own mistakes.

In the last twenty-odd years, audio and video bootlegs—along with a handful of official releases—have given the Elvis fan a chance to see and hear much of the unused rehearsal material. On the days when the camera was present, the rehearsals weren't conducted exactly the same way as normal. As the movie had an accompanying studio album, Elvis was encouraged to do more new material. Indeed, once his shows were no longer being filmed, he reverted to a more conservative set. This is partly explained by most of his new music not coming out until the end of the year. Unfortunately, it also points to the fact that Elvis often gave up on challenging material if it didn't get an immediate response.

The second half of the movie is footage of Elvis onstage during the first week of his monthlong engagement. This concert footage shows Elvis near his physical peak, having lost quite a few pounds during the rehearsals. Finally achieving the sheer volume and power he had always strived for, Elvis authoritatively sailed through his excellent selections, performing a diverse mix of country, rock, and ballads. Highlights include "I've Lost You," "Suspicious Minds," and the showstopping "Polk Salad Annie."

Visually, one of the highlights is the strobe effect during "Tiger Man." After being named one of the Jaycees' Outstanding Young Men of America the following year, Elvis admitted in his acceptance speech that as a child he often dreamed he was the hero of a comic book. By perfectly syncopating his movements, Elvis takes on nothing less than the dimensions of a superhero. The effect was so out of the ordinary that "Tiger Man" was not only used to open the movie—a second performance also featured during the concert segment.

Elvis enjoyed watching *That's the Way It Is*, proud that he had brought who he really was to the screen. The fan interviews are kind of bizarre, seeming to concentrate mainly on the fringe diehards, but while a 2000 re-edit had more footage of Elvis, it lost the flavor of the period. Especially galling was the decision to replace several of Presley's then-current songs with oldies he had started to get sick of.

Popularity and Impact

As 1970 began, Elvis was doing better, creatively and personally, than he had in a decade. If his singles didn't chart as well as the previous year's releases, some were as good. "Kentucky Rain" has become a classic, even though it missed the Top 10. "The Wonder of You" had been a hit for Ray Peterson, but Elvis' live rendition was the first of his larger-than-life ballads, and it went Top 10 without a problem. "I've Lost You" was more creative, but unexpectedly didn't make it past #32.

Elvis played it safer with a fine cover of Dusty Springfield's "You Don't Have to Say You Love Me," getting results with a #11 placement. The next single was "I Really Don't Want to Know," which reached #21. The flip was "There Goes My Everything," which at #9 gave Elvis his highest position on the country charts since the fifties.

Though each 45 was solid, it's sad that Elvis' more challenging work didn't sell as well as his more conventional ballads. Elvis continued to experiment a lot in the upcoming year, but the public has a rather shallow image of this period. Elvis is often portrayed as having abandoned his sense of aesthetics, but nothing could be further from the truth.

This button features a great candid shot taken in Las Vegas on August 22, 1970.

Though Elvis didn't get back into the Top 10 LP charts, *On Stage* did very well at #13. When *That's the Way It Is* only hit #21, it started to become clear that it was the handling of Elvis' catalogue that was slipping, rather than the quality of his records. Two Camden albums crowded the market when released at roughly the same time. Further diluting the sales of Elvis' new title, *From Memphis to Vegas* was simultaneously issued as two separate albums.

Camden's *Let's Be Friends* arrived early in the year. Though it ran too short, it had unreleased songs of a mostly recent vintage. Half the tracks were pretty good, the Memphis cuts unadorned and charming. Still, some of these tracks were terrible, and the album wasn't promoted as having archive recordings.

Almost in Love and a reconfigured *Elvis' Christmas Album* came out in November. They were musically sound, but all the tracks were previously released, except for an out-take of "Stay Away, Joe," which was accidently used in place of "Stay Away." *Almost in Love* used what was likely the only bad photo of Elvis in 1970, and *Elvis' Christmas Album* used an obviously retouched picture from *Speedway*. Pickwick would make the jackets even worse when they reissued them in 1975, but all Camden titles moved a lot of copies, with the holiday title becoming one of Elvis' top sellers. They were fairly harmless, but liner notes or a smidge of perspective would have helped.

RCA did one thing right that year in issuing a fantastic boxed set called *Elvis 50 Gold Award Hits, Volume 1*. It didn't have notes, but it did list the original release date and go in the proper order. On top of that, these were the original mono cuts of the single mixes. To this day, *Gold Award Hits* and its follow-up are the only "best of" albums (except for the mono *Golden Records* series) to use the versions that were the mono sixties hits. The four-record set also had excerpts from the discontinued *Elvis Sails* EP, and included Elvis' current concert program. Some vintage photos would have been nice, but it was one of the best Elvis packages ever released.

29

The Next Step

A Guide to the Comeback

hough Elvis' 1968 *Singer Presents Elvis* television special has rightly been seen as a major turning point, it was not the first step in what has come to be known as his "comeback." If you go strictly by his non-soundtrack studio recordings, the entire period of 1966–72 represents Elvis as a mature artist trying to create a new sound for himself. The first several years of this period have some of the trappings of the soundtrack recordings, and Elvis was never quite as inspired in the studio after his 1969 Memphis sessions, but his dedication during this era is obvious.

The soundtrack recordings that will be reported on here are the ones released on full-price LPs or 45s from *Stay Away, Joe* on. There often remained a great disparity between these and the regular records, yet several attempts were made to break out of the mold.

The 1966–72 recordings didn't change popular culture like his early work, but they do make up some of Elvis' most interesting and creative music. From the mid-sixties on, Elvis did far better on the country, easy listening, and overseas charts than on the *Billboard* pop single or LP listings. This wasn't down to lack of quality, having more to do with the fickleness of American rock-record buyers and disc jockeys of the day.

For those who don't follow fifties rock and roll, these records are the best introduction to Elvis Presley. Hearing Elvis in a somewhat more modern setting may help those who like "classic rock" (but are predisposed against "oldies") discover his genius. In the best-case scenario, those who listen to this work for the first time will go on to discover that Elvis' early records—and pre-Beatles rock in general—had more to it than they thought. Conversely, those who think Elvis never equaled his early work, or lost his artistry, are bound to reconsider notions of what Presley achieved as a vocalist and stylist through his entire career.

"Love Letters"/"Come What May" (Released June 8, 1966)

Best known in a 1962 version by Ketty Lester, the ballad "Love Letters" was the first step in Elvis' career rehabilitation. Recorded in May 1966 at Elvis' first regular studio session in over two years, "Love Letters" presented a more mature singer than heard before. With a deeper voice, and an updated sound, it didn't deserve to only scrape the Top 20. The diminishing of Elvis' reputation—and

Lester's record being a hit only four years before—were the main factors as to why this nuanced elegant reading didn't become a smash.

"Come What May" was lacking by comparison, but was an adequate enough rocker for a flip. The honking sax and jerky lead guitar were too close to what Elvis was laying down for his soundtracks. The only thing that stands out is the fun Elvis seemed to be having scatting the fade. "Come What May" is also notable in being the last Elvis single to make it onto a regular domestic RCA LP

Elvis' early-1970 Las Vegas appearance was the high-water mark of his later career. This soulful shot from the engagement featured on the front cover of his 1971 concert program.

or CD. Alternates were used in the nineties, and the briefly lost master was only included on the FTD label and the *Complete Elvis Presley Masters* boxed sets from Franklin Mint and Sony.

"If Every Day Was Like Christmas"/"How Would You Like to Be" (Released November 15, 1966)

Red West both wrote and cut the initial vocal for the holiday offering "If Every Day Was Like Christmas." Elvis was ill the day of the June 1966 Nashville session, and he came in a few nights later to overdub his lead. Attractive melodically, with a nicely nuanced vocal, the song shot to #2 on the Christmas charts. Having more depth than Elvis' previous holiday fare, Red's lyrics are well thought-out and contemplative. The only thing wrong with the single was the horrid and inappropriate flip side.

"Indescribably Blue"/"Fools Fall in Love" (Released January 10, 1967)

Taken from the June 1966 Nashville session, "Indescribably Blue" has a good enough vocal, but it's over-produced. The backing vocal from Millie Kirkham is shrill, and the big sound feels like much ado about nothing. Barely gracing the Top 40, it wasn't strong single material. "Fools Fall in Love" came from the May outing, and is comparable to "Come What May" in quality. It's close to the feel of the soundtracks, but Elvis sounds more engaged.

"Guitar Man"/"High Heeled Sneakers" (Released January 3, 1968)

Though it didn't break Elvis out of his current rut on the charts, this was his best single since "(You're the) Devil in Disguise" five years earlier. "Guitar Man" was already included on the *Clambake* LP, and the bluesy "High Heeled Sneakers" was the perfect complement. Sounding as tough as anything Elvis cut in the fifties, "High Heeled Sneakers" gets a premium performance that captures Presley growling out the lyrics. The arrangement is tight, but it also has the rollicking atmosphere of a jam, with superlative harmonica played by Charlie McCoy.

"U.S. Male"/"Stay Away" (Released February 28, 1968)

With Elvis' third rock-and-roll single in a row, people finally started to notice the positive changes occurring. Another fast-talking Jerry Reed song, with Reed himself playing guitar, "U.S. Male" was a great illustration of Jerry's lyrical wit, a takeoff on the macho attitudes found in country and rock music of the day. Elvis spits out the words with perfect comedic timing. Musically, the song is tough, with the rhythmic stops and starts of the bass and guitar solo being particularly funky. It was Elvis' first Top 30 hit since 1966, and the last single to feature Scotty Moore and the Jordanaires.

"Stay Away," like its parent film *Stay Away, Joe*, showed Elvis taking more care in cinematic side of his work. It wasn't as good as what was being cut outside of the soundtracks, but it was a marked improvement on recent film songs. Using a sped-up country-styled version of the melody from the folk classic "Greensleeves," "Stay Away" is an interesting experiment.

"A Little Less Conversation"/"Almost in Love" (Released September 3, 1968)

Taken from the movie *Live a Little, Love a Little*, this single further closed the quality gap between soundtrack and studio work. With Elvis now working with more orchestration than before, the session was led by Billy Strange at Western Recorders Studios. "A Little Less Conversation" wasn't a well-known song until an out-take from the *Singer Presents Elvis* special received a questionable remix in 2002. The original is far superior, with Chuck Berghofer playing a sizzling bass line, and Hal Blaine pounding out the drums. Elvis' zippy delivery, well suited to this straight-ahead bedroom rocker penned by Mac Davis, has a blend of buoyancy and arrogance. The version used on the 1970 Camden LP *Almost in Love* is a tamer alternate.

"Almost in Love" is about the closest Elvis got to being a lounge singer. As with everything he cut in the late sixties, his vocals are powerful, but the song is a soulless drag.

"If I Can Dream"/"Edge of Reality" (Released November 5, 1968)

Included on the NBC soundtrack LP and special, "If I Can Dream" was Elvis' first Top 15 hit since 1965. "Edge of Reality" stems from *Live a Little, Love a Little*, and is a most audacious cut. Backed by foreboding horns and strings, Elvis sings this vaguely trippy ballad using the full power of his voice. It doesn't measure up to his best music, but there is something to be said for trying something different.

Elvis (Released November 22, 1968)

Though formal studio takes were often used in place of those Elvis sang live to backing tracks, this is nearly the complete soundtrack to the *Singer Presents Elvis* special. The LP patterns itself exactly after the fifty-one-minute broadcast cut, the only important omission being the second version of "Baby What You Want Me to Do." The LP also edited sections that didn't involve Elvis' participation, and a one-line snippet of "Are You Lonesome Tonight?"

Knowing how many sublime performances were left out originally doesn't hurt the LP the same way it did the trimmed special. Elvis is fantastic all the way though. The visuals obviously added another element, but in the days before home video, it was important that this be a good album. With the special getting rave reviews, this LP got Elvis back into the Top 10 at #8. It holds up very well purely as music.

"Memories"/"Charro" (Released February 25, 1969)

Both sides of this record were written by Billy Strange and Mac Davis. The top side is taken from the NBC LP, and "Charro" is the title track to the film. Like the movie, "Charro" is a diluted copy of what was being done for spaghetti westerns of the period. Heavily orchestrated, it worked fine over the credits, but is little more than a piddling novelty as a record.

From Elvis in Memphis (Released June 17, 1969)

This is a milestone LP. With the guidance of producer Chips Moman, the American Sound Studio sessions gave Elvis' career a new lease on life. These recordings were the last to provide Elvis with a stream of Top 10 hits, and the first to overhaul his old image(s). Helping bring out the best in Elvis were the American Studio musicians, later known collectively as the Memphis Boys. They featured Bobby Emmons on organ, Bobby Wood on piano, Reggie Young and Dan Penn on guitar, Ed Kollis on harmonica, and Gene Chrisman on drums, with bass guitar duty split between Tommy Cogbill and Mike Leech. Together, the bulk of these guys played on well over 100 hits during the late sixties and early seventies. With that kind of track record, it would have been shocking if they hadn't been able to make Elvis sound commercial.

Of course, the songs had to be there too, and what makes *From Elvis in Memphis* stand out is that every cut feels fresh and vital. The role Chips and the musicians played in this is important, but the key factor was the power Elvis Presley had when he was feeling good about himself and his music. Even standards like Hank Snow's "I'm Movin' On" sounded born anew. The source was old-fashioned country and western, but the music was modern soul at its hottest. Topped off with Elvis' animated vocals, the results were entirely contemporary.

"Wearin' That Loved On Look" opened the LP and made its intentions clear. Elvis sounds tough, uncompromising, and alive. There's a new level of sexuality present in his performance—an ability to express that side of himself without worrying about having to answer to a backlash. Times had changed, and now Elvis was taking the chance to change with them. There's real excitement, gospel-like backing vocals, heavy-duty percussion, and a sense of uninhibited syncopation. The studio players being a real band gives the music an extra snap, and Elvis responds to the challenge of leading them. Not only was he working hard for himself and his fans, he also wanted to regain the respect of his peers.

"After Loving You" was a solid beat ballad with a good lyric; Elvis turns it into a declaration of his new freedom. Not wanting to lose the power of the moment, he pushes everyone to new heights. Each repetition of the chorus is incrementally more intense, but he doesn't sound winded. Elvis had enjoyed jamming to this Eddy Arnold hit for some time, but any hint of Arnold's reserve or manner is obliterated by the raw passion Presley offers.

"I'll Hold You in My Heart (Till I Can Hold You in My Arms)" is much the same. Elvis finds a mood, and by repetition builds his voice into ever-greater displays of passion. The feel is loose and affable, and the false start left in the intro works to set up the rough-and-ready tone. Elvis plays the piano quite well; arguably, he was as skilled at it as he was guitar. He wasn't a formal musician by any standard, but there's a lot to be said for feeling over formality.

There isn't a banjo anywhere close to Glen Campbell's signature tune "Gentle on My Mind." Elvis treats the song seriously, fashioning the cryptic lyric into a story of strength and survival. The music and arrangement are tastefully propulsive; listen for the little breaks of harmony and bass fills throughout. Elvis felt what he was hearing, and performs here as much as he would to a crowd. It doesn't matter that the public isn't watching; he wants everyone present to be with him.

Jerry Butler's hit "Only the Strong Survive" is powerfully soulful and has a message of inner fortitude. Elvis' love for his mother may have drawn him to the lyric, which is dressed in the guise of motherly advice. Even if it doesn't vary much from the original, it's pretty amazing that Elvis matched Butler in intensity. It also gains meaning by virtue of being recorded at a time when Elvis was tapping into his inner strength to regain his artistry.

"Power of My Love" is sexy rock and roll, gaining an erotic charge from the overall atmosphere. Elvis' sneering lead makes it clear what's on his mind, and the band (particularly the female singers) seem to tune into that. He's pervasively ardent, but there's a hint of satire that tells you he's not taking himself too seriously. "Power of My Love" excels simply by being unencumbered rock of the kind Elvis once made his name with.

Not every track is a statement, but good albums need to alternate intensity with a sense of calm. "True Love Travels on a Gravel Road," for instance, is a positively minded country love song that Elvis sings with heartfelt sensitivity. "It Keeps Right On A-Hurtin'" is likewise an agreeable mid-paced country ballad that Elvis performs attentively.

"Any Day Now" is faster paced, and one of the more deeply felt selections. At American, Elvis gave everything a sense of courage and hope, even when singing a sad lyric. The song retains its R&B roots, but has something more human to it. Elvis had gone through so many things by age thirty-four, and in his late-sixties music you can tell he felt every bump in the road intently. The middle eight is sung with delicacy, but there are raw nerves on display as well. When he says he's holding on for dear life, you can feel that clearly. "Any Day Now" is basically a song about a relationship, but Elvis turned it into a personal declaration. It provided an intelligent 45 (and LP) companion for "In the Ghetto."

"In the Ghetto" was a record that meant quite a bit to 1969. Not only was it Elvis' biggest hit in four years, it was also special for his taking a public stance that not everybody agreed with. Even if it wasn't without precedent, that a Southern figurehead like Elvis Presley was willing to address race was a significant step forward.

With acoustic guitar to the fore, the record was essentially a folk song with the sound picture expanded to include strings, horns, and backing vocals. The lyric is phrased in such a way that it condemns not only society's treatment of poor blacks but also how the poor of any race or creed are often not given an equal shot. Elvis had lived in poverty all his early life, and to this day is sometimes looked upon badly for growing up poor and Southern. Going against an unjust stereotype of his own, he had always been a racially sensitive, intelligent person.

That "In the Ghetto" took a stance against racism and social class was not lost on Presley. He put a lot of thought into whether he should do the song, and he thought even harder about its issue as a single. "If I Can Dream" had been about universal brotherhood, but "In the Ghetto" was riskier for being specific. In interviews, Elvis made it clear that these two songs didn't mean he saw himself as a "message singer," but he also made it clear they were too important to pass up. That "In the Ghetto" was the song that reintroduced Elvis to the general public was not insignificant. It woke a lot of people up.

"Long Black Limousine" is an allegory for Elvis in a way that had yet to be lived out in 1969. It deals with a small-town girl who wanted nothing more than fame. The singer plays the boy she left behind, describing the way she got her wish—only to be killed while being driven in her dream car. She is finally brought home for her funeral, again riding in a "long black limousine." Of course, Elvis didn't die in this manner, but he did want success badly in his youth. Having seen the dark side of what celebrity can bring, he sings this with wisdom that seems far greater than his thirty-four years.

There is a sense of indignation about what fame entails. At his most passionate, and in the prime of health, Elvis still carried a sense of foreboding about him. "Long Black Limousine" opened the sessions in Memphis and acted as a sort of catharsis for him. Intent on regaining the crown that would soon sit uncomfortably on his head, Elvis seemed to know that going back to his music full-time might cost him dearly. Performing was what he was put here to do, but perhaps Presley had an inkling about the way things would eventually go. This hint of foresight is what makes "Long Black Limousine" so chilling today.

"Clean Up Your Own Back Yard"/"The Fair Is Moving On" (Released June 17, 1969)

Released the same day as *From Elvis in Memphis*, and coming in the midst of the American Sound singles (with a flip taken from those sessions), "Clean Up Your Own Back Yard" marked the point where the soundtrack songs again reached the level of Elvis' normal work. Though too modern for *The Trouble with Girls*,

"Clean Up Your Own Back Yard" was contemporary Southern rock at its apex. Another Davis-Strange collaboration, the guitars are tough, the rhythms pulsating, and the backing singers appropriate and soulful.

It had been a good ten years since Elvis got a movie song with attitude, and he seems to relish being a philosophical storyteller. Coming in the midst of three Top 10s, the only logical reason "Clean Up Your Own Back Yard" stalled at #35 was its being from a soundtrack. Record buyers were long trained to avoid movie songs, but this time they were unwise to leave it on the shelf.

"Suspicious Minds"/"You'll Think of Me" (Released August 26, 1969)

When it comes to a record like this, not much needs to be said. All readers have heard it, and most treasure it. With a hypnotizing guitar riff and excellent all-round musicianship, "Suspicious Minds" was a sublime Mark James composition that Elvis transformed into pure gold. Elvis had sounded vulnerable in the past, but here there's a hurt in his voice that's beyond emoting. Anybody can vocalize lyrics, but it takes a special performer to immerse himself so completely in a song.

When "Suspicious Minds" returned Elvis to the top of the charts, it solidified his legend. There were many great performances and records to follow, but this was the peak of the mountaintop.

From Memphis to Vegas (Released October 14, 1969)

The studio LP of this two-record set was later sold separately as *Back in Memphis*, and contains the second and final LP from American Sound. Elvis' performances are all good, but that's not the case regarding the songs. Being the second pick, it seems logical that this LP would not be as masterful as *From Elvis in Memphis*. However, the album also suffers because some fantastic songs were being held back for singles. "Suspicious Minds" additionally wasn't considered, as it was the centerpiece of the live album. A third strike is that, despite having a charm not present in some of the tracks here, a few of the less-produced songs from these sessions were thrown onto RCA's Camden titles instead.

With those caveats in mind, this is still a fairly sound record. "You'll Think of Me" is a brilliantly produced ballad, having been previously used as the flip side of "Suspicious Minds." Being a song of a broken relationship, one might expect Elvis to sound deflated. Instead, he sings with an assurance that makes one think the subject of the song has accepted that the romance has ended. This is in sharp contrast to how Elvis handled most of his "love gone wrong" ballads in years to come, mostly coming off shattered on the later cuts. That was partly a creative decision dependent on what he felt best suited any given song, but Elvis' buoyant mood and health in 1969 also made a difference.

Another fine ballad is "Do You Know Who I Am?" The song has an eerie atmosphere hinting at the influence of Phil Spector, and Elvis sings with deliberation. The part where he harmonizes with himself (through the magic of overdubbing) is particularly beautiful in its warmth. Carl Wilson of the Beach Boys once described Elvis' voice as a "miracle," and "Do You Know Who I Am?" proves him right. It is unquestionably one of Presley's most haunting recordings.

"Without Love (There Is Nothing)" is pretty special as well. It's drawn out in spots, and a tighter arrangement would have been more effective, but Elvis sings like his life depends on getting this down perfectly. The slight rasp he had from June 1968 to March 1970 gave his songs an earthy quality only found elsewhere in 1954–60 recordings. Elvis' soaring last stanza is brilliantly affecting to all but the most stoic.

None of the other ballads on this half of the album are top-shelf, and this happened to be the first Presley release where slower tempos dominate. Elvis' dedication keeps them from being a chore, but they only rise a bit above average. Neil Diamond was not an artist Elvis covered too often. If Presley was able to rock up "Sweet Caroline" onstage, "And the Grass Won't Pay No Mind" is one of the rare occasions where he sounds derivative. Oddly enough, though "A Little Bit of Green" has nothing to do with Neil, it too was performed in his style. These songs aren't as poor as the soundtracks, yet they are anomalous in how little Elvis imparts of his persona, and are a rare moment of misdirection from the American team on what would suit him best as a current artist. Not coincidentally, Diamond had recorded at American himself.

"Inherit the Wind" is considerably more interesting due to Elvis following his own instincts, but it's pretty tame compared with much of his current music. The overdubbed strings are heavy-handed and invasive. "This Is the Story" is also too serious for its own good. There's nothing objectionable about what Elvis, or what the core band came up with, but the horns and voices suck the life out of the final master.

"The Fair's Moving On" and "From a Jack to a King" also suffer from being overdone. The latter is OK in that it was an old favorite of Elvis and Priscilla's, and has a sense of fun. What it lacks is a decent arrangement. The "la las" by the female backing singers are silly, and the song should have flowed instead of being choppy.

Being that the lyrics make gauche use of carnival terms, "The Fair's Moving On" isn't much of a song. This time it is Elvis that lays it on too thick. The song isn't worth emoting so heavily on, and it's likely an acoustic arrangement would have been better.

The album's masterpiece comes with its sole rocker, "Stranger in My Own Home Town." Being that Elvis hadn't recorded in Memphis for fourteen years, and had felt so alienated during the mid-sixties, this gutsy Percy Mayfield gem about a prisoner coming home from jail reflects his mood. For Elvis, the Memphis sessions were comparable, creatively, to being released from prison.

Elvis had been given a good degree of leeway for his TV special, and for previous Felton Jarvis–led sessions, but he had long been encouraged to tone down his music for the sake of his films. With Chips Moman pointing Elvis in a decidedly contemporary direction, he was able to take his recent progress even further. If nothing else, "Stranger in My Own Home Town" decisively proved Elvis once again had his finger on the pulse of modern rhythm and blues.

Elvis leads the band into a wonderfully tight, uninhibited take on a song previously reflecting the stylings of Mayfield's friend Ray Charles. Dripping with attitude, and a clear sense of purpose, Elvis turns it into a full-on strut. The American musicians crank up the heat, with Reggie Young's electric sitar sounding downright funky. "Stranger" perfectly demonstrates where Elvis took music, and also where music took him. Utterly stupendous.

"Don't Cry Daddy"/"Rubberneckin'" (Released November 11, 1969)

The third single from American Sound kept up the standards set by its predecessors. "Don't Cry Daddy" is the type of song that, in the wrong hands, could turn into sentimental mush. In the midst of his second prime, Elvis interpreted the song as a sober tale of loss. It describes a widower encouraged by his young children to start life over. No doubt this brought Elvis back to 1958, when he had to comfort Vernon over Gladys.

Beautifully sung, and double-tracked in certain passages to mimic the sound of a duet, "Don't Cry Daddy" confirmed the new sophistication Elvis was striving for. Chips Moman's production was equally as tasteful, especially in how the strings add a sense of both darkness and calm. The public responded in their droves, giving Elvis yet another Top 10 hit.

Being good-time rock and roll, "Rubberneckin'" was a whole different animal. Though part of the Memphis sessions, it was selected to be used in a scene from Elvis' last theatrical picture, *Change of Habit*. Showing a modernized, self-assured Elvis off to the world, it's a shame that the footage wasn't edited to be a real music video.

With a tight syncopated groove running through it, "Rubberneckin'" is one of the funkiest Elvis records. It is also one the most sensual numbers in the Presley canon, particularly the way the female backing singers moan in seeming ecstasy. No doubt about it, the "real" Elvis was back!

"Kentucky Rain"/"My Little Friend" (Released January 29, 1970)

"Kentucky Rain" is the fourth and final single from the Memphis sessions. Though it sold the fewest copies of the four, it's easily as good as what came before. With true inspiration, songwriters Eddie Rabbitt and Dick Heard paint a vivid portrayal of a protagonist searching for his wayward true love. Elvis sings with the kind of passion that only comes with time and experience. The arrangement is excellent, full of dramatic fluctuations in tempo and an exquisitely executed chorus. It shouldn't have languished in the lower end of the Top 20.

"My Little Friend" is little more than cute. It's not awful, but the lyric is a tad awkward. The bouncy country melody is decent enough, and Elvis sounds relaxed, but there's no substance. Perhaps what killed it the most were the overdubs. The strings overwhelm the fragile melody, and the interludes are intrusive, bearing little relation to the basic track.

"The Wonder of You"/"Mama Liked the Roses" (Released April 20, 1970)

Getting Elvis back into the Top 10, "The Wonder of You" was his first and most successful live single. "Mama Liked the Roses" stems from the Memphis sessions, and pales in comparison. Though the ballad is heartfelt, it was overproduced in the overdub department. The end result is syrupy, and the recitation hits you over the head with sentiment. Elvis' voice is truly lovely, and it's a unique record, but subtlety should have been key.

"I've Lost You"/"The Next Step Is Love" (Released July 14, 1970)

The release of "I've Lost You" proved two things. The first was that Elvis was staying contemporary, and the second was that this was not necessarily how the masses wanted him. Those who stuck with him through the movie years seemed glad that Elvis had matured with the times. Casual fans seemed more interested in who Elvis had been than who he was now. That Elvis was trying to sound like a man of his age in 1970—and not a fifties revivalist—didn't go down well with rock-and-roll purists.

A dark ballad about the ending of a relationship, "I've Lost You" was one of the best tracks from Elvis' June 1970 Nashville session. With Elvis wanting to prove himself most on songs where he could hold notes for dramatic effect, "I've Lost You" was ideal for his fully matured voice. Arranged with taste and moderation, it set a template for the rest of his career. This was the first of a number of songs he cut with an increasing focus on love lost and loneliness. As "I've Lost You" comes earlier than most, it has a freshness missing from those in its wake. For some, these songs are a drag to get through, but they are the most personally insightful of Elvis' career. Though it's doubtful he always had any one individual in mind, he had growing trouble figuring out who loved him for being ELVIS—or if anyone loved him for himself.

"You Don't Have to Say You Love Me"/"Patch It Up" (Released October 6, 1970)

The solid "You Don't Have to Say You Love Me" landed just outside the Top 10 and was included on Elvis' next LP, *That's the Way It Is*. "Patch It Up" would be included, too, but live versions of it and "I've Lost You" were used in place of the studio master. "Patch It Up" was recorded during the June 1970 Nashville sessions, and was one of Elvis' hardest rockers of the early seventies. Propelled by a driving rhythm, with Norman Putnam front and center, the song has a groove to it that makes up for its minimal lyrics. Elvis' energy level is astoundingly high when one considers that this was the last of over thirty songs he had finished in a mere five days. Sinking his teeth into his vocal, Elvis' scat singing on some of the out-takes show him to be enjoying himself immensely. "Patch It Up" may not have a lot under the surface, but its blend of rock and soul was a diversion from Elvis' current focus on ballads.

That's the Way It Is (Released November 11, 1970)

This is a fine LP in one way, and a slightly disappointing one in another. Though marketed as the soundtrack to the 1970 documentary of the same name, most of the LP stemmed from the June 1970 Nashville sessions. The documentary was on Elvis' third International Hotel engagement including footage from the July–August rehearsals and the first three days of his August run. It's not that the music on the *That's the Way It Is* LP was bad—it just wasn't close to what was heard in the movie.

Perhaps the other problem with the LP was there was only one rocker on it. As *Back in Memphis* had demonstrated, showcasing only one facet of Elvis' talent made for a somewhat tepid listen. The songs here are generally better, but there is nothing close to "Stranger in My Own Home Town" to break the contemplative mood. Though people who generally favor Elvis' wild side should steer clear, *That's the Way It Is* does capture him at a time when he was still at the peak of his powers. Being that his voice had never sounded deeper or fuller, he makes even the most ordinary songs sound vibrant.

The live performances do come from when the movie was being shot. "You've Lost That Lovin' Feelin'" was a mainstay of Elvis' set over the next few years. Using lights and movement to dazzling effect, it was theatrical in presentation. On record, it's good, though it isn't that daring a remake. Elvis sings the heck out of it, but other than being a little earthier, there isn't a huge difference, musically, from the Righteous Brothers' hit.

Though Elvis adds sensuality, "I Just Can't Help Believin'" is also only slightly altered from B. J. Thomas' hit record. This was partly done out of deference to the audiences in Las Vegas, where a certain familiarity is expected. Elvis does an excellent job with the song vocally, and the movie footage shows him working

This 2012 FTD release captured the alternate takes from the original *That's the Way It Is* LP. The cover photo was similar, but far more flattering than the original. Though he took neither of the shots, Parker's photographer Ed Bonja remembered that personal jealousy on the Colonel's part meant that the best photos weren't always chosen.

hard at getting it right for the show. As Thomas' record hadn't taken off in Britain, U.K. fans made it a huge hit for Elvis in late 1971.

"Patch It Up" and "I've Lost You" are both nicely done, but the decision to use these live recordings was a mistake. Opening side one with "I Just Can't Help Believin'" and side two with "You've Lost That Lovin' Feelin'" was fine, as it didn't spoil the flow of the studio work. But as far as "Patch It Up" and "I've Lost You," the superior Nashville masters fit better with the other songs. On the other hand, as neither lasted in Elvis' set beyond the summer of 1970, their only downside is being out of place.

The rest of the LP (bar a tampered-with "Bridge over Troubled Water") features quality studio recordings. "Bridge over Troubled Water" was a focal point of Elvis' early-seventies set. It was a song he placed importance on, and in

June he had recorded a fine master of it. Adding some tension to the end, Elvis turned it into another vehicle for his long notes. With all the voices and orchestration, he also made it into something more ornate. Unfortunately, whoever did the final mix of this album all but ruined what Elvis had cut.

In the only time an Elvis studio cut attempted to disguise itself as a live recording, the ending was abruptly chopped off with overdubbed applause. Even worse was the lowering of the natural levels on the intro and first verse. On vinyl, this almost invites surface noise to intrude, and on tape and CD it often hissed. The five-LP/three-CD *That's the Way It Is* boxed set from 2000 corrected this. The un-doctored master has been issued several times on comps, but that doesn't help this album.

"Stranger in the Crowd" isn't memorable, but it does pick up the pace. Not approximating anything near rock, it's adult-contemporary pop. It is thoughtfully sung and arranged with a contemporaneous lilt, but should have had more meat on its bones.

Though gushing romantic lyrical sentiment meant it too could have sounded lightweight, "Mary in the Morning" goes to another level. It was done with delicacy, and musically there is a mix of folk and pop, with a harmonica adding country seasoning. Elvis' singing is quiet, making for a contemplative mood. If "Mary in the Morning" wasn't stunning, it ought to have proved to Felton and Elvis that sometimes less is more.

"Twenty Days and Twenty Nights" is a strong story-oriented ballad, not overly embellished. The harmonic parts featuring a double-tracked Elvis are precise, and the imaginative idea of repetition in the coda has a mesmerizing effect on the ear.

"How the Web Was Woven" was a single for Jackie Lomax, issued on the Beatles' Apple label. Elvis heard the song due to the British songwriting presence in Hill & Range's catalogue. Here, rather than matching Jackie's bouncy reggae direction, it received the full Presley ballad treatment. Highlighted by David Briggs' excellent piano out front, Elvis finds nuances in the lyric that make it considerably more meaningful. In 1970, Elvis was knocking out great vocals left and right, yet "How the Web Was Woven" stands effortlessly among the best. Elvis sings with a sad, bluesy tone that keeps one riveted. It's a great example of the command Elvis had over the human voice.

"Just Pretend" is a standout love song with sumptuous gospel-tinged organ by Charlie McCoy, flawless vocals, and even a warm nod to "Love Letters" in the fade. Elvis' enthusiasm for the chorus is infectious. Each time he sings it, he lets himself get further drawn in. Fervent and strong, he doesn't want the moment to end.

"The Next Step Is Love" is one of the most appealing and creative inclusions. It's mid-paced, with horn parts influenced by Beatles producer George Martin and lyrics that reflect a thoroughly modern outlook. Elvis appears to have been keeping up with the British scene more than rumor would have it. It's not psychedelic in any way, just baroque, à la "Penny Lane." It has a steady groove in that the beat rarely pauses, and Elvis demonstrates his vocal dexterity by staying with the music.

"You Don't Have to Say You Love Me," which went up to #11, is the LP's biggest hit. Its lavish production helped set Elvis' Las Vegas image in stone. Elvis turns on his biggest voice to sing this Dusty Springfield hit, changing what was originally a sigh of despair into a roar of determination. When he says, "believe me," he's pleading with his soul. Indisputably showy, this record has electricity surging through it. Elvis never had sung with this much masculine authority before. He still sounds like he's on top.

Elvis Country (I'm 10,000 Years Old) **(Released January 2, 1971)**

Elvis' albums tended to be grab bags of different styles. This worked because he was one of the few artists who could shift from genre to genre with ease. Still, some longed for Elvis to do an album focused on one particular area of his talent, but he had only done so with his gospel releases. *Elvis Country* changed all that, and it is easily his most conceptual album. That it was top-shelf made it even better.

Though Elvis hadn't gone into the studio with a country LP in mind, as the proceedings evolved he and his producer Felton Jarvis decided that the country tracks together would make an excellent album. Once the concept was firmed up, Elvis took care of details he usually ignored. First of all, he gave the album the subtitle *I'm 10,000 Years Old*, and he put excerpts of "I Was Born About Ten Thousand Years Ago" between each track to unify the songs further. Elvis was drawn to the phrase because he felt he had lived thousands of years during his short lifetime. He also provided the first photograph ever taken of him, at age two with his parents. The country attire they are shown wearing snugly fit the theme.

The recordings were taken from the June and September 1970 sessions. Elvis was confident, hardworking, in excellent shape, and arguably never sang better. With his country audience growing rapidly, and rock audiences now embracing rock-and-roll "roots" music, this album was well timed. At #12, it was the highest charting studio LP Elvis had on the pop charts, post-1965. It also shot up to #6 country. There are no weak spots whatsoever.

With acoustic guitar and harmonies to the fore, "Little Cabin on the Hill" was a Bill Monroe/Lester Flatt bluegrass number that Elvis loved to sing. It had even turned up as one of the songs he ran through during the Million Dollar Quartet jam in 1956. It's charming, with all of the participants giving it a nice homey atmosphere. Charlie McCoy's harmonica playing is excellent throughout these sessions, and the overdubbed banjo and fiddle add a lot to the mood.

In concert, Elvis threw "Whole Lot-ta Shakin' Goin' On" (as it is spelled on the cover) away as part of a medley, but this version is almost epic as Jerry Lee's. The bass and drums set up a driving rhythm unheard on any other version. Kicked into high gear by what he was hearing behind him, Elvis gets more animated with every verse. The speed quickens, his voice gets fierce, and he sounds almost crazed by the end. The un-faded out-take shows Elvis continuing another few minutes by scat singing, almost veering out of control with excitement. Hearing music take Elvis to another realm is exhilarating.

Nothing else is that ferocious, but "I Washed My Hands in Muddy Water" comes close. Elvis was a fan of Charlie Rich's mid-sixties material, and Rich's was the rendition this is based on. A blend of country, rock, and blues, it was a perfect fit for both former Sam Phillips protégés. The difference in Elvis' version is that he gives the melody a sense of urgency. He sings the tale of delinquency and jailbreak as proudly as a peacock. Rebellious as any Elvis cut, this was also jammed on after the fade.

"The Fool" was a rockabilly hit for Sanford Clark in 1956, and was one of the songs Elvis casually recorded while in the army. It's got an upbeat blues tempo, giving Elvis a chance to show off his bass voice. What's unique is how male-centered it is. Elvis often sang songs that appealed to a female viewpoint, but this is a "good old boys" classic about pouring out your heart about an ex at the saloon. As wealthy as Elvis got, he never lost the ability to relate to people of all types.

"It's Your Baby, You Rock It," an easygoing, mid-paced ballad, is the lone new song. Elvis enjoyed the lyrics and even began using the term in conversation. At a different session, this may have ended up schmaltzy, but the country setting gave it a solid foundation.

"Faded Love" is an old Bob Wills swing number that Elvis brought a completely new feel to. A bit of blues is blended in with the country sentiments, and the arrangement is rock. A new rhythm line is utilized, too, providing a chance for the musicians to show off a bit. Elvis rides on top of it like a bucking bronco, never losing his perfect sense of timing. It's yet another song that kept on going past the fade. Elvis liked making this album.

"Make the World Go Away" and "There Goes My Everything" are the kind of big-voiced ballads Elvis made a staple of his seventies repertoire. Both originally date from the mid-sixties, and they give Elvis something to really emote to. "Make the World Go Away" is a little heavy on the strings, but James Burton plays a gutsy, twanging lead guitar.

"There Goes My Everything" became a Top 10 country hit as the flip of "I Really Don't Want to Know." The breath control Elvis displays is utterly stunning. He knew exactly how long to hold or stop a note. More than that, his performance is as emotionally involving as it is technically brilliant.

"Funny How Time Slips Away" is a Willie Nelson standard done so many times that even in 1970 it was hard to add something to it, yet Elvis does this by slowing the tempo to a yearning country-blues. Lyrically, the song is exceptional, addressing a guy running into his old love, acting both emotional and distant. Elvis alternates between being proud and sorrowful, making it clear that the latter is what he is feeling deep down. He performed this live from 1969 until his death, usually placing it near the end of a show as a type of farewell.

When Ernest Tubb made "Tomorrow Never Comes" popular, he did it as a traditional western toe-tapper. There was nothing wrong with that, but Elvis heard a darkness in the song that he brings to the fore. Almost operatic in the notes Elvis reaches, it starts off gently, with basic backing. Slowly, Elvis' voice gets more passionate, the music and strings build up, and by the last verse, Elvis is spitting out the words with venom. "Tomorrow Never Comes" is a great piece of theater that came from Elvis' way of reworking a song until it felt right. Elvis never ended up singing it onstage, as the vocal gymnastics were quite hard to reproduce. Even for the record, they had to splice on the astoundingly powerfully held note at the end.

Recorded in September 1970, "Snowbird" was a recent hit for Anne Murray, and was Elvis' nod to current trends in the country field. The arrangement is countrified pop that flows effortlessly from verse to chorus. Some have chided Elvis for doing such a light number, but the tone he gives the words lends it depth. Wistfulness and regret were written into the lyric, but Elvis expresses this in such a mature way that you get swept up in his performance.

"Rags to Riches"/"Where Did They Go, Lord" (Released February 23, 1971)

Elvis recorded these two cuts at a quick September 1970 Nashville session to finish up the *Elvis Country* LP and cut a new single. The better songs were on the album; the single was his first misfire after two years of classic 45s. Elvis was in good voice, but the material wasn't adventurous enough. "Rags to Riches" was too adult-contemporary for most rock-oriented DJs, and too pop for the country market. It managed to get to #33, but it made Elvis seem dated again.

"Where Did They Go, Lord" is not too bad, but it didn't provide much contrast in being another breast-beating ballad. Being that Elvis' voice was in remarkable form in 1970, his performance itself can't be faulted. The wah-wah pedal effects are a nice touch, but it otherwise feels very safe stylistically.

Love Letters from Elvis (Released June 16, 1971)

After six excellent albums in a row, *Love Letters* was the first in a long time that didn't fully satisfy. It's thought that Elvis having to cancel his March 1971 session early brought about this LP, but since he hadn't vetoed the songs it probably would have come out anyhow. Though he looks great on the cover, the live shots were becoming predictable, and the back looked ten years out of date. As all the songs come from the June 1970 sessions, the vocals are impeccable. Being third choice, however, most of the tracks are slight.

One of the things Elvis can be commended for is never recording an album of studio remakes, but he did redo songs on rare occasions. With David Briggs feeling he could play piano better on "Love Letters," Elvis agreed to try it again. The only real difference in the end was that Elvis' deepened voice sounds more certain. Naming the album after the song sponged off of the 45's success, but it is an awfully good song, and is different enough for an LP cut. It was the best ballad by a long shot.

Little of the new material is sound, and Elvis comes across best on rockers like "Cindy, Cindy" and "Got My Mojo Working." "Cindy, Cindy" was hastily arranged, the horns are intrusive, and the band is sluggish. Only a snarling Elvis is dynamic. On the other hand, "Got My Mojo Working" is a classic—a superbly tough and speedy take on the old blues—and Elvis rocks his socks off. A lot of Elvis' best seventies work came out of studio jams, and his bemused laugh at the end says it all.

After that, everything else is rote. "When I'm Over You" is an OK mid-tempo track sung with diligence. Aside from the violins being too upfront, it isn't bad. Elvis always sang gospel with some inspiration, so "Only Believe" is also one of the better tracks. It's not a stunner, but Presley obviously has a feel for the song. The arrangement is overdone, and the Imperials could have been brought forward a tad more, but it's adequate.

"I'll Never Know" sounds sincere but syrupy. There's a decent melody, but the lyrics are hackneyed and the arrangement soporific. Quiet and unassuming, "It Ain't No Big Thing (but It's Growing)" and "If I Were You" are pleasant country ambles that fail to make an impression. Much worse is "Heart of Rome." Harking back to Elvis' Latin fixation of the early sixties, this is ridiculously over the top, with Charlie Hodge providing some awful harmonies.

"This Is Our Dance" is a waltz, of all things. Sounding out-of-date despite the vocal being decent, it's the kind of white-bread frilly ballad Elvis once made obsolete. "Life" is strange. It tries for some sort of statement on the cosmos and meaning of life, but ends up with nothing but a plethora of clichés and other-worldly sound effects. One doesn't have to wonder why this didn't break the Top 50! The only thing *Love Letters* has over the records to follow was the shape of Elvis' voice at the time, yet even on peak form, Presley couldn't do anything when the material wasn't there.

"I'm Leavin'"/"Heart of Rome" (Released June 22, 1971)

"I'm Leavin'" may not be Elvis' most influential single, but it is one of his finest recordings. His most fully realized folk-influenced master, it best represents the new directions he was going in during 1971. The song has a vague, dreamlike atmosphere that Elvis contributes to by singing very gently during the verses. Quickening the pace, the chorus is more forceful but still very clean. With acoustic guitar to the fore, the playing is also hazy, with the complexity of the arrangement never overwhelming the intimate feel.

With slightly esoteric lyrics expressing self-doubt, "I'm Leavin'" was a huge departure for Elvis—perhaps too big of one. Radio airplay was minimal, and it only hit a semi-adequate #36. Those that heard this record treasured it, and Elvis was pleased with the results. Performed on and off until the end of 1975, it was a song played during Presley's most creative sets. If any one record in the Elvis catalogue is a lost masterpiece, "I'm Leavin'" fits the bill.

"It's Only Love"/"The Sound of Your Cry" (Released September 21, 1971)

The very modern approach of this 45 split Elvis fans into two camps. One side felt that Elvis had gone too pop with these selections, and the other side didn't mind Presley going into that area. Not everything Elvis tackled had to be rooted in the traditions of years past, and today it is intriguing to hear Presley records so firmly contemporary to the seventies. The top side originates from Elvis' May 1971 Nashville session, and the flip was cut at the same venue the previous June.

"It's Only Love" is a very produced record. Strings and backing vocals take a conspicuous role, but the mono mix also gave the rhythm section prominence.

Japan has long been known for having rich, quiet vinyl. The Japanese 45 sleeve of "It's Only Love" shares the same artwork, if not language, with the 1971 American release.

Elvis concentrated hard on his vocal, and it shows in his effort to reach the more challenging notes. Giving Elvis a chance to inject drama, "It's Only Love" sounds fresh today in that there's little to compare it with in his other work.

The problem lies in the marketing. There was next to no publicity for "It's Only Love." Elvis was making records that sounded a part of 1971 radio, but he didn't have the proper push an established artist needs to sell records. "It's Only Love" sat just outside the Top 50. It's hard to fathom that his musical experimentation wasn't being promoted as such.

"The Sound of Your Cry" is an unabashed big ballad that fans either love or despise. The young Elvis wanted to be a lush ballad singer, loving the genre as much as gospel. He couldn't hold or push out notes at the beginning—it was something that he aspired to, and had to train his voice to do, over time. Elvis was drawn to these types of songs in that they presented him with more of a challenge than the rock or blues that came to him naturally.

That's not to say that "The Sound of Your Cry" is a particularly innovative record, but it is excellent pop. Something so slick may not win over the rock-and-roll traditionalist, but others—and most importantly Elvis himself—didn't care about that. Elvis simply saw it as a song he could throw himself into. That the ending was edited down lessened the initial impact. Available on the bizarre 1981 LP *Greatest Hits Volume One*, the long edit finds Elvis getting intense while repeating the chorus over and over. Even if it doesn't suit all tastes, that it's an involved performance by Elvis at the top of his vocal game renders it worthy.

Elvis Sings the Wonderful World of Christmas (Released October 10, 1971)

This album may be one of Elvis' most heard of the seventies, but it's one of his worst non-soundtrack outings. Elvis did not want to do this album, but he did so because it was expected of him. It did extremely well in the holiday market, but the project left a bad taste in his mouth. The production and arrangements are tame on the whole. Other than the fact that Elvis is singing them, selections like "The First Noel," "Silver Bells," and "On a Snowy Christmas Night" have nothing to offer. "Winter Wonderland" is also pretty pedestrian, with only a tacked-on rock-and-roll ending being notable. Sure, an Elvis fan is going to like these recordings over most other versions, but Presley was bored, and he brings nothing to the table.

"The Wonderful World of Christmas" and "It Won't Seem Like Christmas (Without You)" have Elvis going through the motions, but they sound slightly contemporary. "If I Get Home on Christmas Day" was a ballad Elvis tried a bit harder on, but it's still melodically dreary.

Making one wish the EP format was still viable at the time, there are four tracks worthy of Elvis. One is a fine ballad by Glen Spreen and Red West called "Holly Leaves and Christmas Trees." The melody has a bit more substance to it than most of the other songs here, and Elvis responds to the moodiness of the piece.

"I'll Be Home on Christmas Day" is a song Elvis toiled hard on, recording several different versions of it before he was finally satisfied with one of his earlier attempts. It's very bluesy, and one can tell why he wanted to do it justice. There's a lot of feeling, and it creates atmosphere on what had so far been one of Elvis' most trite projects.

The two songs chosen for the single were quite solid, with "Merry Christmas Baby" being particularly rewarding. Doing it as a slow blues jam, Elvis pulls out all the stops by reaffirming himself as the best white blues singer there ever was. These types of songs came so easily to Elvis that he never seemed to realize how many singers would kill for his mastery of the idiom. "Merry Christmas Baby" has been recorded by many great artists, such as Chuck Berry and Ike and Tina Turner. As good as their records were, nobody put their stamp on it like Elvis. Even on a project he had no passion for, Elvis couldn't help but be great when he really dug a song.

It seems less likely that Elvis would excel on "O Come, All Ye Faithful," but with a country-styled basic track over a tasteful choral backing, excel he does. Though some traditional feeling is retained, there is a modern beat behind it, which keeps proceedings from getting dull. Elvis is credited on the LP with the arrangement. This may have been a ploy for Hill & Range to claim publishing, though it's likely Elvis did have input, considering the work he put into his vocals. Doing his own harmonies over his main lead, his voicing is intricate, and the resulting thickness is pleasing to the ear. If the LP is far too patchy, at least the single showcased Elvis at his best.

Elvis Now (Released February 20, 1972)

This album has taken a lot of flak over the years, but most of it is musically above average, if not always excellent. The problem is in its execution. As a 1969 cut and two 1970 tracks were included, it wasn't entirely Elvis "Now." It's not all that unusual to use an old master on an LP, but in this case it went dead against the title. Elvis fans were kept in the dark about track origins before recording-session books began to appear in the mid-seventies, but anyone who owned *Elvis Country* would recognize that "I Was Born About Ten Thousand Years Ago" wasn't a new recording.

The LP lacked any sort of common theme or feel. There were gospel songs, pop offerings, some country, a bit of folk, and even Rick Nelson's hit arrangement of the standard "Fools Rush In." *Elvis Now* didn't lack for variety, which on one hand was good. However, when the 1971 masters are looked over in their entirety, one can see how a more cohesive LP could have been readily produced. It was disappointing that Elvis was not taking the time to carefully put together his new releases so soon after his comeback, but the music reveals that only his post-session sense of follow-through was an issue.

"Hey Jude" is among the most disliked of Elvis' non-soundtrack masters, but it's hard to hear why. Even if it was more of a tryout than an attempt at a definitive take, the soulful elements that make Presley's 1969 recordings unique are present. Elvis sings it in a higher register than was normal, yet he still sounds persuasive in his approach.

"I Was Born About Ten Thousand Years Ago" is obviously given a better showcase when heard in its entirety and revealed to be a gospel-tinged hard Southern rocker. Elvis has his usual blend of humor and machismo, and if the Nashville musicians were a little less soul-oriented than the ones in Memphis, they were equally as masterful in modernizing Elvis' sound.

Also from 1970 was the ballad "Sylvia." The arrangement is too slick by half. Elvis tries his best to give his vocal some feeling, but comes across as shouty. There are some interesting counterpoints in the melody, and one wishes that a subtle arrangement had been attempted, with Elvis sounding relaxed.

The rest of the LP hails from the three 1971 Nashville sessions, and much of it is stronger. Elvis' folk-inspired songs are his most forward-thinking masters. What makes these so nice is that none them are over-sung, sped-through, or drawn-out.

"Early Morning Rain" was among the unquestionable highlights, and an example of the pleasant tone Elvis gave his folk-oriented work. Like Johnny Cash before him, Elvis took folk material into country territory. "Early Morning Rain" conveys a sense of desolation without sounding weak or desperate. Elvis' deep tones sound properly world-weary and experienced. Heard under sedate conditions, it works magic.

As the opener, "Help Me Make It Through the Night" set the tone that *Now* was a departure. Elvis enjoyed Kris Kristofferson's compositions, but he was discouraged from recording them because Kris wouldn't give Hill & Range part of his publishing. Though RCA even went to the trouble of shutting off their tape machines during "Help Me Make It Through the Night" when they recorded parts of Elvis' February 1972 Las Vegas shows, nobody could dissuade Elvis from putting it out. There's a charming twang that comes through in Elvis' voice when he lifts it higher during the verse. Unlike "Sylvia," Elvis keeps the mood dignified when going for extended notes by never losing the pleading tone he began with.

"Until It's Time for You to Go" was a major hit in the U.K. and a minor one in the U.S. At the time, critics said that Elvis' delivery was too masculine, but he hardly could have copied Buffy Sainte-Marie and come off serious. Actually, Elvis sounds quite gentle, and he doesn't overpower the music. A beautiful recording, "Until It's Time for You to Go" is a classic love song because it's realistic.

The flip of "Until It's Time for You to Go" was a contemporary track called "We Can Make the Morning." If lyrically it over-reaches in its attempt at poetry, Elvis sings with dedication. Though it has been put down for not being rooted in his background, Presley was smart to stretch out with modern pop from time to time. It was legitimate creatively as it continued Elvis' lifelong determination

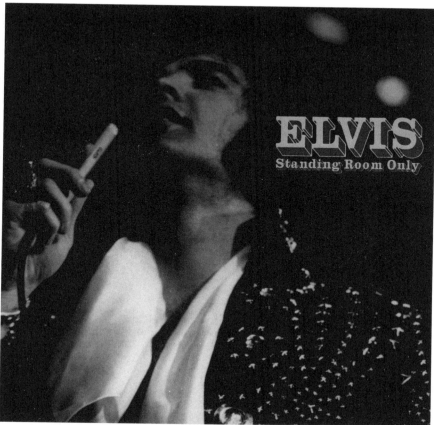

Elvis' intended 1972 album *Standing Room Only* went unreleased until 2009. When it was replaced by the Camden *Burning Love* LP, his credibility took an unfair hit.

to tackle anything that took his fancy. With some pleasing harmonizing with the Imperials, and some insanely long held notes at the fade, "We Can Make the Morning" is ostentatious, but in the best possible sense.

"Fools Rush In" was a pop standard of the forties, as recorded by the likes of Glenn Miller and Frank Sinatra. A 1966 home recording has Elvis singing along to an easy-listening arrangement by Nelson Riddle, but when it came time to record it in the studio, Elvis had another source in mind. Elvis had long been a fan of Rick Nelson, which was a factor in why he hired James Burton in the first place. Now that he had James in the studio, it was natural that Elvis would eventually try out a Nelson song. The results were charming, with Elvis paying homage by copying the record as close as possible. The arrangement (especially Burton's parts) is nearly identical, and Elvis attempts to sound younger than usual. It wasn't original, but it was a hell of a compliment to Nelson.

"Miracle of the Rosary" was an unusual choice for Elvis, being that the sentiments are of the Catholic faith and incorporate the "Hail Mary" prayer. The
incongruity is explained because Elvis recorded it as a favor to songwriter Lee
Denson, who had been his neighbor in the Lauderdale Courts housing projects.
Elvis sings it well, but it's too sugary for its own good.

Conversely, Elvis rocks up "Put Your Hand in the Hand" to a degree not even
hinted at in recent hit versions by Anne Murray and Ocean. The Imperials had
recorded it the year before, and Elvis got most of his good-time feel from them.
It has the very commercial, modern gospel-rock sound that Elvis was exploring
at the time, and could have likely been a Top 5 hit had Ocean not got to it first.
Like "Miracle," it was conceived as a part of Elvis' 1972 religious LP, *He Touched
Me*. They picked the right ones to extract, as "Miracle of the Rosary" was simply
too greatly at odds with real gospel, while "Put Your Hand in the Hand" was
already proven in the secular market. The only difference is that the former was
the worst moment on *Now*, and the latter was a highlight.

"An American Trilogy"/"The First Time Ever I Saw Your Face" (Released April 4, 1972)

"The First Time Ever I Saw Your Face" was one of Elvis' 1971 folk excursions.
He had originally considered it as a duet with either Temple Riser or Ginger
Holladay. Choosing in the end to record it solo, he put forth a dedicated vocal
with a gentle undertone. It's a choice example of Elvis' early-seventies ballad
sound.

"Burning Love"/"It's a Matter of Time" (Released August 1, 1972)

Both this and Elvis' next single were recorded during his lone 1972 recording
session at RCA Studios in Hollywood. Just one place short of topping the charts,
"Burning Love" was Elvis' biggest hit of the seventies. Though he was in the
mood to cut ballads, "Burning Love" eventually got him rocking hard. With
stinging guitar licks by James Burton, a second overdubbed guitar line by the
song's author, Dennis Linde, great vocal backing from J. D. Sumner and the
Stamps, and a tight arrangement, Elvis sounds full of life, and more sensual than
ever. Though the FM rock-radio format tended to ignore Elvis, "Burning Love"
was simply too outstanding to pass over.

"It's a Matter of Time" has lived in the shadow of "Burning Love" to some
extent, but it's also a premium performance. Perhaps the best thing about it is
how Southern Elvis' voice sounds. Stridently country in tone, the production is
controlled, in complement to Elvis' relaxed delivery. "It's a Matter of Time" was
a brilliant coupling for "Burning Love," simply by being so different. It helped
that it was virtually as artistically rewarding.

"Separate Ways"/"Always on My Mind" (Released October 31, 1972)

With Elvis' divorce looming, this single acted as a succinct commentary on the situation. "Separate Ways" was co-written by Elvis' friend Red West, and is likely the song that best reflects Presley's feelings at the time. Lyrically, it expresses a gradual acceptance of the breakup, and the hope that his daughter will one day understand it. Musically, it's an appealing ballad and an intelligent blend of country and folk. Though not a common subject for the Hot 100, "Separate Ways" defied the norms and made it to #20.

Having one of the best lyrics Elvis ever tackled, "Always on My Mind" is a wonderful composition. Elvis was very focused during his 1972 session, and he expresses every word with feeling. Footage of him recording it at a "mock" session for the *Elvis on Tour* documentary shows how much this song of romantic regret meant to him then. Shaking his head back and forth, Elvis maintains his composure and delivers a powerful performance. The record version is equally effective, with the fluid beauty of the melody being a perfect complement to Elvis' emotional lead. Though Elvis would record many more songs of this type in years to come, none matched "Always on My Mind" for raw emotion. Ronnie Tutt's drums have an edge to them not unlike those heard on hard-rock ballads of the era.

Elvis (Released July 16, 1973)

Popularly known as the "Fool" LP in order to differentiate it from Elvis' second album, this is another cobbled-together release that didn't do justice to the music. For the most part, the material is good, but the album suffers from a lack of identity. The cover is a fine shot from the *Aloha* special, but with no notes and just a few LP ads on the back, it looked no different than the Camden budget issues.

Actually, had it come out the way producer Joan Deary originally conceived it, the album would have been far more slipshod. She wanted to combine the after-show selections from the *Aloha* taping with a mishmash of other live and studio cuts. She didn't even know the title of "Reconsider Baby," and intended to use the June 10, 1972, Madison Square Garden matinee performance of it under the title "A Blues Jam."

Horrified by what he heard, Felton Jarvis stepped in. If his results were only one step up from Deary's, at least it was no longer jarring. Jarvis chose some 1971 and 1972 studio masters that had not yet been issued, as well as a 1972 live performance from the called-off *Standing Room Only* LP.

Of the skimpy ten selections (which had sadly become industry standard for all but modern rock albums) only the overblown Latin arrangement on "Padre" is a real misfire. It had been a favorite of Elvis' since he heard Toni Arden's 1958 hit, but it is one of the few songs that lives up to the glitzy stereotype unduly put

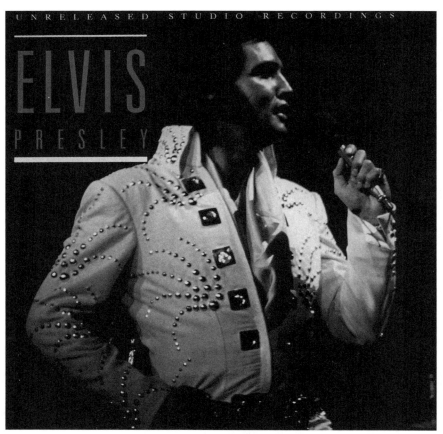

This boot issued some of the rehearsals filmed for *Elvis on Tour* in professional sound quality. The front cover photo dates from the 1972 tour in June instead of the April one featured in the movie.

upon all of Elvis' seventies recordings. It's obviously unfinished: Elvis blows the note at the end.

Also sounding strained was "Love Me, Love the Life I Lead." Elvis never felt he got his lead vocal down properly, but either he wasn't consulted about what would go on the album, or he was talked into letting it be issued. It too is extravagant, but it had a more contemporary sound and personal relevance to Elvis.

Other 1971 selections included three songs Elvis sang alone at the piano. All are heartfelt, and thankfully only one had any kind of overdub. "I Will Be True" and "It's Still Here" are Ivory Joe Hunter ballads that capture Elvis at his most natural. While various fans feel Elvis' 1971 masters show him in vocal decline, that only applies to the tracks that bored him. Heard here in a warm and unadorned setting, one can hear that his voice was as expressive and beautiful as ever—when he was inspired.

"I'll Take You Home Again, Kathleen" was also a longtime favorite of Elvis', which, along with "I Will Be True," can be found as a 1959 home recording made in Germany. There are some strings on top that don't need to be there, but Elvis infuses it with the same kind of care and delicacy he gave the Hunter tracks. Despite the aesthetic drawbacks, these three songs alone make *Elvis* a record worth picking up.

In the same league as the piano recordings was Elvis' brand of folk-rock. It's a shame that all the songs of this type from 1971 weren't put on the same album. "That's What You Get for Lovin' Me" is a Gordon Lightfoot number Elvis had heard sung by Peter, Paul, and Mary. Elvis did have the female backing and the acoustic guitar put up front, but the country-rock undertones and wry delivery are all his own.

"Don't Think Twice, It's All Right" is the most widely acclaimed track on here, and for good reason. Excerpted from a long jam, Elvis' take on this Dylan classic is flowing and energetic. It has a jaunty pace, with James Burton's country-styled acoustic guitar to the fore. Elvis remembers few of the lyrics, but he chews up every word by adding a sense of humor (and ego) to what was a mournful ballad. The unedited long versions have a charm of their own, but this choice passage is very effective. Those who criticize "Don't Think Twice" for the lacking the original verses miss the point. What matters is the mood it conveys.

Not nearly as substantive is a February 1972 live take of "It's Impossible." Not too many people would cover both Bob Dylan and Perry Como on one album, but Elvis' musical makeup was uniquely his own. Elvis performs well, but it's the kind of safe choice often used against him by critics. What lazy journalists who portray Elvis as artistically selling out overlook is that crooner-styled pop was only a small part of his repertoire. Furthermore, Elvis didn't see the need to categorize what he did to make purists happy. He had enjoyed cutting this kind of bland pop music even at Sun.

Two studio cuts from the 1972 Hollywood sessions round out the album. Mixing a quiet verse with a strident chorus, "Where Do I Go from Here" is similar to "Love Me, Love the Life I Lead," except for a decidedly country flavor. With Ronnie Tutt's drumming getting wild toward the end, "Where Do I Go from Here" is also far better realized. The lyric is one of the few of the time that don't deal with a specific relationship, but is more about yearning for the past in general. Elvis was increasingly reflective as years went by, and he never stopped trying to figure out why he was who he was. Needing a creative outlet to express things he had trouble dealing with, Elvis began to openly expose himself through his music.

Elvis has been given a hard time for recording so many songs of lost love in the seventies, but with his marriage crumbling, these were songs he related to. Most weren't aimed specifically at Priscilla but reflected the doubt that plagued him throughout his life. "Fool" is good example of the self-recrimination Elvis was feeling by this time. It's not that Elvis was always depressed and brooding, but these ballads seem to be something he needed to help him work through his darker moments. With some pleasant shifts of tempo in the middle eight, "Fool" is well sung. Though some prefer the lighter touch he gave his early-sixties ballads, the deep resigned tones of Elvis' mature voice give the song far more credibility than he could have before.

30

Love the Life I Lead

1971

O
ften ignored, 1971 remains the most underrated year in Elvis' career. He wasn't as consistent as he was during 1969–70, but that doesn't mean that his later work isn't worthy. Elvis was becoming less raw as a vocalist, but he still had a lot of range and power. While he was not yet disinterested in his work, he did have certain career goals that weren't being encouraged by his management.

After fifteen years at the top, he still wasn't getting the opportunity to tour overseas. Elvis was still in good enough shape to go, and it may have inspired him to go further with his live show. Parker has been made scapegoat for certain things he shouldn't be, but this was a major mistake.

Another glitch was Elvis' continuing to be instructed not to do songs outside of his publishing catalogue. This was fine in the fifties and early sixties, when writers were willing to give up a percentage in order to get an Elvis record, but the industry had changed. As Elvis noted at his 1972 Madison Square Garden press conference, many of the writers were now recording their best material themselves. Elvis had begun what was shaping up to be an excellent modern folk album, but he was forced to cut his March session short due to flare-up of glaucoma. When he returned to the studio two months later, it was dictated that he would do a Christmas album. True, he was allowed to cut more folk and gospel, but by 1971, Elvis should not have been told what he could or couldn't do.

By the end of the year, Elvis' lean, panther-like physique had vanished. While the weight gain was still too minor to dampen his physical intensity onstage, Elvis was losing his self-discipline, partly due to the end of his marriage. The psychological effects of his separation and divorce were to have a distinct effect on his music, but Elvis enjoyed his share of highs along with the lows. A Jaycees award and a lifetime award Grammy saw him finally get some long-overdue recognition for his civic and artistic contributions.

Studio Work

Though hampered by the Christmas album, Elvis was interested in new directions. Distinguished by his focus on contemporary folk and gospel, the three sessions he held in Nashville have moments that show him continuing to flourish creatively. A good amount of the material stood too far away from a rock or blues base for most critics to appreciate it, but a number of Elvis' most experimental tracks date from these sessions.

Despite the wrongheaded direction of some of the decisions made, much of what Elvis recorded in 1971 had quality. Some of the Christmas material features a bored artist, but with the exception of outright missteps like "Padre," most of his other work holds up. Several songs would have been better without Felton Jarvis' ornate vocal and string overdubs, but there were a notable amount of good arrangements mixed in.

Elvis didn't have the raw power of 1969 or the clarity of 1970, but though some fans/historians are openly hostile toward them, his 1971 vocals often carried a deep resonance. Some may be aghast at the fact that he went more pop on some selections, but even purists have to admit that tracks like "Bosom of Abraham," "Merry Christmas Baby," and "Early Mornin' Rain" show Elvis

The best vinyl release of 1971 concert performances is this 2010 boxed set. Stemming from Elvis' vastly underrated fourth International stint, it was the last time his voice carried the edge of his initial comeback.

going in some remarkable areas. "I'm Leavin'" has often been justifiably cited as an excellent performance, but other singles like "It's Only Love" and "Until It's Time for You to Go" also deserve attention for their sophistication, and the expressiveness of Elvis' voice. Even "O Come, All Ye Faithful" had a mature approach.

While they weren't compiled with aesthetics in mind, LPs like *Elvis Now* and *Fool* are much better than their reputations would have them and contain some of Elvis' most rewarding 1971 work. Forget the critical harping and hear them on a purely musical level. There are many rewards.

Elvis' gospel work was particularly good this year, and the LP *He Touched Me* won him another Grammy. The most contemporary of Elvis' gospel records, it provided insight into where this genre of music was going in the early seventies.

Live Performance

Of all Elvis' concerts, the winter 1971 International Hotel engagement is the most undervalued. Elvis was still slim and retained much of the fire that had characterized his recent work. He seems to talk a bit less, but he had yet to lose the passion in his voice when performing his classic hits. There was some interesting changes to the show, namely at the beginning and end. The buildup to Elvis' entrance onstage had always been exciting, but now, with "Also Sprach Zarathustra" (the theme from *2001: A Space Odyssey*), the effect was astounding. He also temporarily dropped his perennial set-closer, "Can't Help Falling in Love," in favor of a grandiose rendition of "The Impossible Dream."

There aren't many circulating photos or recordings from Elvis' July debut at the Sahara Hotel in Lake Tahoe, but the little that does exist makes it seem quite exciting. While some of the fifties material was now given token status, Elvis was audibly thrilled to be onstage after a five-month hiatus. The jumpsuits were more ornate than they had been previously, most notably a dazzling series of "Cisco Kid"–styled outfits. The gig lasted two weeks, but was regrettably scheduled right before another monthlong residency in Las Vegas.

The audience at the newly renamed Hilton saw basically the same show, but a lack of rest drained Elvis' vitality. Performing nearly 300 times on the same stage in a little over two years naturally brought with it a degree of boredom. The 1971 Elvis wasn't capable of doing anything that could be called tragic, but this was the first clear sign that his comeback was leading to its own dull patterns. Success alone was never enough, and Elvis needed a constant change of pace to feel satisfied. Thankfully, touring had not yet become routine.

Elvis rose to the occasion in November, launching a full-scale tour that (with the exception of Houston) brought him to cities he hadn't played for fifteen years—if ever. A still-athletic Elvis may have gained a few pounds, but his further incorporation of martial arts gave his movements extra grace and drama. Presenting a longer, more eclectic set, the addition of his longtime idol J. D. Sumner had an invigorating effect.

This summer 1971 Las Vegas shot served as the cover of Elvis' 1972 concert folio. The "Cisco Kid" suit had flash but also a tasteful quality that wasn't to be maintained.

With the Imperials leaving over a contract dispute, J. D. offered up the services of a new gospel quartet he had formed called the Stamps. Elvis agreed to use them on the condition that J. D. would appear with them. With the arrival of J. D. and the Stamps, Elvis' best known seventies lineup was in place. Elvis had fun with Sumner and his impossibly low voice, but he was honored to be sharing the spotlight with him.

Popularity and Impact

Seeing Elvis live hadn't yet lost its novelty in 1971. His Nevada and tour shows drew plenty of press, and most of the notices were deservedly positive. On record, it was to be more of a rocky year. In *Elvis Country*, Presley had his most confident and consistent record of the seventies. The critics liked it, it was well received in the charts, and most importantly it connected with the public. *Love Letters* was such a poor follow-up that Elvis undid much of the goodwill of the last three years. It made #33 pop, a number that was not matched on that chart by many studio Elvis LPs to come. (*Moody Blue* was to give Elvis one last respectable pop showing, but only in the wake of his death.)

Love Letters was conspicuously the first new LP that Elvis hadn't taken an interest in compiling since *Speedway*. His drug and depression issues weren't yet out of control, but he was losing focus. Monotony seems to have been the number-one factor. It wouldn't be fair to say Elvis let his gun-and-badge collecting, martial arts, and now fairly open string of girlfriends completely overtake the music. What did happen is that Elvis let his non-musical interests take away from time he needed to spend on planning long-term creative goals.

Elvis did have a little more say on his *The Wonderful World of Christmas* album, but it was still a disappointment in that he didn't want to do it in the first place. The 45 of "Merry Christmas Baby"/"O Come, All Ye Faithful" presented a better alternative from a creative standpoint, but it failed to sell. The album itself topped the Christmas charts, but it scarcely improved Elvis' standing.

"Rags to Riches" and "Life" were both wrong for the 45 market. "Rags" made Elvis look square, and "Life" was terrible. "I'm Leavin'" and "It's Only Love" were both solid. The former had more depth, but the latter sounded just as contemporary. With Elvis having seemingly tarnished his name with his last two singles, these didn't do well either. "I'm Leavin'" should have topped the charts, but Elvis' lack of discretion in what he recorded was biting back. As the year ended, Elvis was a top concert attraction, but his days as a hit-maker seemed numbered.

His status as a recording artist was not helped by the release of three Camden albums. *You'll Never Walk Alone* benefited from the gospel theme and the inclusion of a few previously unreleased songs. With material ranging from 1957 to 1969, it didn't flow, and even a budget album feels like a rip-off when it contains only nine tracks. *C'mon Everybody* and *I Got Lucky* reissued the *Follow That Dream*, *Kid Galahad*, *Viva Las Vegas*, and *Easy Come, Easy Go* EP cuts that hadn't appeared on LP before. Good music sat next to bad, and of course there were no notes, historical photos, or care taken with the track order.

Even *The Other Sides—Elvis Worldwide Gold Award Hits Vol. 2* was a disappointment. This time out, the songs weren't placed in chronological order, nor could any other theme or reason be deduced from how they randomly appeared. The format was stretched to include EP cuts, which would have been fine had they collected all the songs that had crossed over onto the Top 40 singles listings. No dice there, either. Real 45 mono mixes were used throughout, but with some essential non-LP and even hit singles not presented, *The Other Sides* failed to live up to its predecessor. Even the release dates were missing on what could well have been the definitive Elvis hit series.

31

Where Do I Go from Here?

1972

The last year you could call him reasonably healthy, 1972 presented the best chance to see the full-blown seventies-era Elvis in all his glory. While some don't like the flash, his voice was strong, his shows were focused, and his material was well chosen. The band was tight, and the sets had little horseplay and a lot of music. Informed critics and fans would hesitate to say Elvis was up to the level he had been onstage from 1954 to 1970, but the casual observer would plausibly have enjoyed these more formal affairs the best.

Using his full seventies live band in the studio for the first time (minus bass player Jerry Scheff), the songs emanating from Elvis' short 1972 recording session were by and large solid. If only a few of these cuts reached the heights of 1969–70, track by track, this 1972 endeavor was his most consistent outing of the seventies. Not only was it creatively fulfilling, but Elvis also managed to get himself a #2 Hot 100 hit with the rocker "Burning Love." However, its success oddly meant that Elvis' artistic intentions were pushed to one side. Instead of turning the session into a well thought-out album, RCA flippantly included "Burning Love" as the title track to the poorest of its budget titles to date. Elvis didn't lose money, as the LP hit #22 on the charts (an amazing feat for a cut-price item), but artistically he lost face in a big way.

Thankfully, Elvis' return to film that year did reveal him as he was currently. If the stage moves were less scorching than those found in *That's the Way It Is*, *Elvis on Tour* was made with more care and respect. Elvis even took the time to do his first extended interview in ten years, talking candidly to his producers/directors Bob Abel and Pierre Adidge. In the interview, he admits the mistakes of his Hollywood years, and one also gets a sense of how much he enjoyed performing live. With this film, Elvis finally achieved his goal of being in an award-winning movie. *Elvis on Tour* deservedly won the Golden Globe for best documentary of 1972, capping off a year of success that was stunning even for Elvis.

Studio Work

Elvis' sole 1972 recording session from March 27th to the 29th was brief but of excellent quality. It was the first since 1960 that Elvis had held in RCA's

This shot was taken during Elvis' first 1972 Las Vegas stint. This album was a 2012 LP boot of his penultimate performance, on February 23rd.

Hollywood studios, a place he had avoided after the bad experience at the early sessions for *G.I. Blues*. This time, everything seemed to be in place, and the sound was certainly up to standard.

Separated from Priscilla, Elvis was in the mood to record ballads about lost relationships. Tellingly, one of the titles was "Where Do I Go from Here." No matter how you feel about his latter-day focus on ballads, Elvis' creative coming to terms with his fractured personal life makes for fascinating listening. The myth about Elvis hating "Burning Love" is not supported by recorded evidence. The hard-rocker may not have been his main focus, but the out-take first released on the *Platinum* boxed set in 1997 reveals his delight in playing the scream off of Stamps member Donnie Sumner at the end.

These songs, plus a batch of February 1972 Las Vegas live cuts of new titles, were to make up the LP *Standing Room Only*. On the back of "Burning Love," what could have been Elvis' biggest seventies LP of new material was abandoned.

Not only would it would have showcased Elvis' artistic growth of the period—in concert and in the studio—it would have also gone a long way in keeping his image current. In the end, the live songs were duplicated on Elvis' Madison Square Garden and *Aloha* albums, and the studio cuts came out piecemeal.

Live Performance

When Elvis opened back at the Vegas Hilton on January 26th, he brought with him a revamped show. "See See Rider" was now in place as the opener, and selections such as "Never Been to Spain," You Gave Me a Mountain," and "American Trilogy" revealed him to have more vocal power than ever before. Elvis' singing had developed in volume, and he now had the ability to really stretch out his notes. The change of lineup invigorated him. Even "Hound Dog" received a respectful treatment that harked back to its blues roots. If a few of the Vegas shows displayed a continued sense of ennui, they were much better than the ones from the previous summer.

Elvis hit the road in April with a film crew in tow. *Elvis on Tour* traced his whole career, significantly treating him as an important contemporary artist. The shows weren't dissimilar to the ones Elvis gave in Las Vegas, though it was clear he preferred the variety offered by different venues.

The June tour received a lot of media attention when Elvis performed a three-day engagement at Madison Square Garden. Elvis had never played New York City, and it was known for being tough from both public and media quarters. A trimmed-down Elvis knocked them dead, and the LP, *Elvis as Recorded at Madison Square Garden*, finally gave buyers a complete concert. It was Elvis' biggest album in three years. Sparkling throughout the tour, he sometimes added rarely preformed gems like "My Babe" or a killer medley of his own "Little Sister" with the Beatles' "Get Back."

The next Vegas booking began on August 4th, with sixty-four concerts held over the next month. It was a punishing schedule, considering the physical nature of his stage act, but Elvis was (for now) up to the challenge. Looking regal, he once again gave a show that was musically and visually a treat. Younger fans may have been dismayed that rock and blues only made up a part of his repertoire, but Elvis performed songs such as "My Way" with an authority few others managed to muster.

At the end of the engagement, Elvis announced a new TV special. Devised as the first live multi-country satellite concert, it would take place in Hawaii as a charity benefit for the Kui Lee Cancer Fund. With the Madison Square Garden LP and his new "Burning Love" 45 reestablishing him as a top record-seller, a documentary destined to win a Golden Globe, and now the immense goodwill and publicity generated by the satellite show, Elvis had reached a level of notoriety that went beyond ordinary fame.

A tour in November concluded with three dates in Hawaii, the last of which was originally scheduled for the transmission day of the special. Since this would have overlapped with the newly released *Elvis on Tour*, the date was pushed back to January. This actually worked out to Elvis' benefit, as he could get used to the venue and take the time to work up a new set. Elvis gave solid performances during this eleven-day jaunt, highlighted by a rousing rendition of "Burning Love." Though the weight he had gained since closing at the Hilton slowed his movements down, he was determined to get back into fighting shape for the upcoming broadcast.

On Celluloid

Elvis and the Colonel were pleased at how well received *That's the Way It Is* had been, and it was decided to make a quasi-sequel. Centered on the April gigs, it documented the extensive effort involved in producing a first-class tour. *Elvis on Tour* also had sequences (supervised by the up-and-coming Martin Scorsese) of archive footage that gave a proper perspective on Elvis' musical and cultural achievements. Providing the film's narration by way of an off-camera interview with the film's producers/directors, Elvis was finally able to articulate his views about his past and present.

Filming began in March of 1972, at the RCA recording studios in Hollywood. Elvis had just completed his recording session the day before, and understandably didn't want to worry about the camera until his new material was finished. In order to show how he made records, it was decided to make part of his filmed rehearsal into a mock session.

By 1972, Elvis had altered the presentation he gave physically. Although he moved less than before, his movements had become sharper. While *On Tour* has plenty of stage action, Elvis did not get as intense as usual. He explained to producers/directors Bob Abel and Pierre Adidge that he feared that the severe look on his face while performing his karate routines would make him look bad on film.

Despite this, Elvis' visual impact had not diminished. His increasingly lavish jumpsuits gave the King a distinctly royal air. Mostly, Elvis was seen in his "Blue Nail" suit, as Abel and Adidge deemed the April 9th evening show in Hampton Roads, Virginia, to be the best they shot.

In the early seventies, a lot of young rock fans didn't have any reverence for the performers who were prominent before the Beatles. *On Tour* helped change this, as it landed Elvis several major features in highly revered rock periodicals of the day. Not only did the coverage lead younger readers to discover who Elvis had been in the fifties, it also made them curious as to what he was doing now. Awarded the Golden Globe for best documentary of 1972, Elvis was so excited by the news that he ran from the bathroom where he was watching the ceremony before he had time to fully pull up his pants!

This dynamic shot from the spring 1972 tour came as a bonus with the Camden *Separate Ways* LP. The "Burning Love" suit remains iconic.

Popularity and Impact

Elvis was deservedly riding high. He was still big news as a concert attraction, and his record sales perked up in the last six months of the year. While some criticized him for no longer being strictly a rock performer, Elvis had long made it clear that he was going to sing whatever he felt he could do something interesting with.

Elvis' new singles and albums of 1972 were all quality outings. *Now* wasn't compiled well, but it did present him as someone with a firm grip on current gospel and folk trends. The more carefully compiled gospel album, *He Touched Me*, landed Elvis his second Grammy award.

Though it hardly sold upon release in the U.S., by sheer force of will "An American Trilogy" later become an Elvis Presley standard. Mickey Newbury, who had conceived of this patriotic medley, had had a minor hit with it the year before, and while that normally wouldn't have stopped Elvis' record from hitting, his last eight singles hadn't made the pop Top 20. It took "Burning Love" to reinvigorate him as a rock-radio and chart presence.

The Madison Square Garden LP and "Burning Love" 45 should have proved that promotion and aesthetics played key roles in sales, but RCA seemed more interested in making quick money. Again, it was the Camden releases that made Elvis look like he no longer cared. *Elvis Sings Hits from His Movies Volume 1* wasn't a horrible way to put out choice cuts from deleted soundtrack albums, but the selections were random, and hardly what you can call "hits."

The *Burning Love* LP, billed as the second volume of the "Hits from His Movies" series, was far worse. Never mind how the included single blew everything else away—there were even deeper problems. The songs were mostly still in print, and Camden oddly chose several mired in the plots of their respective travelogue. This had the effect of giving the LP a peculiarly international feel. Despite the critical drubbing, money talked, and "Separate Ways" was also put out on a poor self-titled Camden LP. The cover was awful; the songs (though of better quality) went all the way back to 1956, with no reason or rhyme. *Standing Room Only* was indeed a big loss.

Elvis was still making great strides as an artist, but the impending divorce, TV special, and a packed live schedule meant that he didn't take care of details regarding the marketing and packaging of his music. It's not that he didn't care, but he didn't come to the realization that an artist was now expected to present his or her work with sophistication—a quality Colonel Parker sorely lacked.

32

Find Out What's Happening

T he year 1973 marked a turning point. It started off with great commercial success, but in retrospect it was when Elvis' mental and physical
health went out of control. He didn't spend every day in misery, and
nor was he yet what you would call extremely overweight, but the events of 1973
nearly killed him, and he would never quite recover. It's not that Elvis didn't
work hard: he did two full months in Vegas, two fairly extensive tours, and a few
weeks in Lake Tahoe, performing a staggering total of 158 shows. He also managed to record three albums, largely at the legendary Stax studios in Memphis.

The quality of the work varied wildly, mainly because Elvis' life was a mess.
For the first time, he couldn't do all of his scheduled performances. He canceled
seven shows in Vegas and a further eight in Tahoe. This means Elvis had been set
to do a whopping 173 shows that year—a figure that would tax even the healthi-
est performer. Yet Elvis wasn't feeling good at all. He had always been prone to
over-taking even over-the-counter medicine; now, misuse of prescriptions actually
put his life in jeopardy.

Studio Work

Besides two minor and three fair-size hits, the Stax sessions are generally obscure.
They did get a kind reception from the country-music community, but the fairly
snobby rock critics of the day saw Elvis only in terms of his past. It's true that few
recordings got near to what Elvis did in his prime, but these sessions were the
last time he worked extensively in a formal studio.

The tracks cut at his first Stax session in July 1973 have been unfairly
maligned ever since the musicians involved spoke of Elvis looking physically ill
and acting depressed to biographer Jerry Hopkins in the late seventies. Not all
of the songs were top-shelf, but he only seemed vocally off on the last day. The
deluxe reissue of the resulting *Raised on Rock* album includes studio chatter and
out-takes that show Elvis to be working harder, and in better spirits, than we were
led to believe.

Raised on Rock stands (if possibly to my ears alone) as one of Elvis' better
mid-seventies LPs. While he was in a better place at the follow-up sessions in

A June 23, 1973, matinee performance. Elvis' 1973 tours were considerably better than his Nevada engagements that year.   *Photo by Erik Lorentzen*

December, there was more filler recorded. True, two fantastic singles came out of it, with "If You Talk in Your Sleep" and "Promised Land," but the other Stax LPs, *Good Times* and *Promised Land,* lack musical unity. All three of these albums remain too obscure, and each deserves the kind of reappraisal one would give if the details of Elvis' private life weren't public. Taken on their own terms, they blend bona fide hidden gems with some of the worst non-movie dross of the Presley catalogue.

Live Performance

With the resulting double-LP going to #1, and television ratings going through the roof worldwide, there is no question that the *Aloha from Hawaii Via Satellite* project was one of Elvis' most successful. If not remarkable creatively, it was a conceptual and commercial triumph.

Elvis opened his eighth stint at the Las Vegas Hilton on January 26th. It was at this point that his health first became an issue. Elvis' voice was restrained and nasal on some nights, and for the first time shows had to be canceled. The setup of the monthlong engagements was grueling for a man half his age. Elvis was expected to play two shows every single night, without a day off. A slender Elvis looked fine, but this was where the final decline began.

Other than offering a few outings to the additions made to the set for *Aloha*, this was Elvis at his least inspired. He wasn't yet in a state where he wouldn't please a less-discerning crowd, but these shows were plain boring. The pressures of work had to be a part of it, but Elvis had previously maintained decent self-control. His looming divorce couldn't have helped. In February, Priscilla's boyfriend Mike Stone made the suggestion that Presley see less of his daughter. Infuriated, Elvis had what can only be called a nervous breakdown.

Attacked onstage on the 18th of the month by drunken spectators (one of whom had a hidden sword), Elvis took too much of something later that night and began to believe Mike Stone was behind the incident. He came to his senses after his binge ended, but for a few days he ranted on about putting a hit on Stone. Once the worst had passed, and Red West had (reluctantly) made it clear that it could be done, Elvis dropped the idea and never brought it up again. To put this oft-repeated event in perspective, that Mike Stone is still alive today proves that Elvis didn't, wouldn't, and couldn't have gone through with it.

An eight-day tour at the end of April brought about a complete turnaround. Thrilled to have a new challenge each night, Elvis was every bit as engaged as he had been during his last tour. An increased drug regimen had brought about a slightly swollen face, and now, as his colon began to malfunction, Elvis had to deal with a permanent distention of his stomach. He didn't look bad yet, but the change was commented on.

What's more important today is that Elvis' voice was back at full throttle. Now being featured in less intimidating circumstances, "Steamroller Blues" was one of many songs that spotlighted a performer much less inhibited than the one seen in *Aloha*. The only obstacle in the otherwise smooth operation came when personal problems forced Jerry Scheff to resign. Emory Gordy was brought in to replace Scheff on bass, having fit in terrifically on the studio session the previous year. Elvis did not like to change his lineup, but Gordy proved himself to be up to the task.

Probably booked well in advance, the May 4th opening at the Sahara should have been pushed back in light of the canceled shows in Vegas. With the previous tour ending on April 30th, Elvis barely had time to fly in and rehearse before embarking on thirty-four shows in two weeks. Elvis appeared to be progressively more tired as the days passed, and the strain in his voice returned. The concerts may have been better overall than his last stand in Vegas, but he wasn't near the level he had been on the road. Apart from his ever-growing intake of pills, the altitude in Tahoe aggravated recent breathing problems to such a great degree that he ended up leaving four days early.

Elvis was in dire need of rest, and the month off that followed seemed to do the trick. In fact, he had rarely sung better than on the tour held from June 20th to July 3rd. Trekking around both the North and South, Elvis played extended gigs in many of the cities he visited, so great was the demand. He gave five shows in Atlanta and three shows each in Uniondale and Pittsburgh.

Having previously performed a one-song set on the *Grand Ole Opry* in 1954, Elvis played his only full dates in Nashville on July 1st. The addition of country numbers like "Help Me Make It Through the Night" and "Faded Love" electrified the crowd, winning over an audience usually jaded by the constant influx of live music.

If one date stands out, it is the June 28th show in St. Louis. Noted Elvis photographer Sean Shaver, who saw him literally hundreds of times, has cited it as one of the high points of Presley's career. Shaver says the reason this show stood out was the quality of Elvis' singing. Elvis performed vocally demanding numbers such as "How Great Thou Art," "I'm Leavin'," and "An American Trilogy" on the tour, and to hear any of these shows in soundboard quality would be enlightening.

On August 6th, Elvis embarked on his annual "Summer Festival" at the Vegas Hilton. Regrettably, he again seemed disengaged. Opening night began with a samba-infused "2001," which was played only once. A medley of "Trouble" and "Raised on Rock" deftly demonstrated the continuing influence of rhythm and blues on Elvis' work. The set also sprinkled in rare performances of "Memphis" and "Help Me Make It Through the Night."

After the promising start, most of the rare songs were dropped. The next several weeks blurred together. Though most performances were passable, few stood out. An improvised snippet of Ray Charles' "Crying Time" was done on the 12th, and a request led to the one and only airing of "It's a Matter of Time" on the 25th, but most of the time Elvis didn't exert himself.

For the closing show on September 3rd, Elvis played with the set and had some somewhat self-indulgent fun. He rode out on his friend Lamar Fike's back at the start, rolled around on a bed for "What Now My Love," and made plenty of other sometimes humorous—but mostly uncharacteristically mean-spirited—asides. He made a particularly strong objection to the Hilton firing his favorite waiter, which suggests perhaps that the fate of his friend Mario was what set Elvis off. That he went public with his complaint reflected dissatisfaction with his life and addiction. A healthy, happy Elvis would have dealt with things like this offstage.

Though blind to his own role in the mess Elvis was now in, Colonel Parker understandably thought Presley was being unprofessional. Elvis became enraged when Parker confronted him on it and fired the Colonel for a few days. Though he had been mostly in the wrong, this would have been the perfect chance for Elvis to start afresh. Sadly, Parker scared the financially naive Presleys with a huge bill, and they soon dropped the whole thing.

Elvis took a breather from touring for the next four months. It was his longest break from the stage in over two years. His health and drug problems came to a head in October, just days after his divorce was finalized. Admitted to hospital in a critical condition, Elvis had to remain there for an extended period.

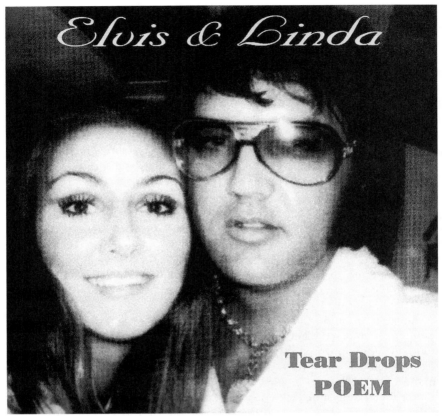

Elvis' girlfriend Linda Thompson would later find success as a songwriter. This boot 45 catches them having some decidedly dirty laughs at her brother Sam's house in 1973. The sleeve shows them during the summer of 1973 tour.

Seeing that his client could no longer be expected to do two shows a night for a solid month, Colonel Parker renegotiated Elvis' contract at the Hilton so that the engagements now lasted two weeks. This helped somewhat, but Elvis still had to perform twice nightly.

Popularity and Impact

With interest in Elvis' live appearances at a new high, *Aloha* got people listening as well as watching. It more or less formed public opinion on where Elvis was at the time, but that's unfortunate to some extent, as it was hardly his best concert of the period. The "Steamroller Blues" 45 concluded Elvis' run of three Top 20 singles in a row. On the still-potent AM radio dial, it got a lot of airplay.

Fool was one of many seventies Elvis albums that did better in country than rock. *Raised on Rock* didn't do particularly well on either chart (with country sales slowing due to the title), but though the lyrics got slammed for being inappropriate, the contemporary title track sounded right at home on the few stations that picked it up. Along with *Aloha*, Elvis was doing well with a cheaply packaged, poorly mixed, self-titled TV mail-order album. It sold more than most regular Elvis LPs, and was the direct result of Colonel Parker's biggest blunder.

With Elvis needing some quick cash for his divorce, he agreed to a deal with RCA whereby he sold them full rights to his back catalogue. He and Parker would no longer receive royalties from material recorded before 1973, nor could they tell the company how to package any of this work. Elvis was now sold on TV-only albums, in record clubs, and so on—all avenues Parker had rejected in order to keep Elvis from blending in with other artists. Though the $4-million-plus deal was unheard of then, and helped in the short term, Elvis and Parker were clearly in considerable financial and personal trouble to not realize how much was to be eventually lost.

Nobody could have predicted just how popular Elvis became when he died. However, it's hard to believe that Parker would have even considered such a deal before his gambling got out of control. On top of needing quick cash, Elvis went along out of insecurity over his longevity. Though he had to have seen how popular he was, he often told friends that he didn't know if his music would last. Being poor in his youth, naive in business, and a fan of instant gratification, Elvis frankly was taken advantage of. When Priscilla sued to get Parker's hands out of the till in the early eighties, the court basically found him and RCA guilty of collusion and fraud with regard to the 1973 buyout. It seems the Colonel arranged for side deals that meant he got a far bigger cut than his client.

33

It's Hard to Comprehend

The Satellite Special

There is no doubt that Elvis' *Aloha from Hawaii* TV special and LP project was one of his most out of the ordinary and commercially successful. Being the first live satellite entertainment broadcast carried by a single performer of Elvis' stature, it has a place in history above and beyond the content of the show itself. Since the actual content is often overlooked, I will review the concert song by song. I will also examine how the public reacted to the show and LP then, and in the years since.

The Facts or FAQ

Colonel Parker first got the idea for the special in February 1972 after watching President Nixon's historic trip to China. Noting how the footage of Nixon's visit was seen worldwide via satellite, Parker thought staging a worldwide satellite special would be a good idea for his client. Not only would it be a great way to strengthen Elvis' name in many different markets, it would also offset the demand for Elvis to tour abroad, which Parker refused to consider. He also failed to consider that a worldwide TV special would only make fans want to see Elvis more. But at least this would appease them, and Elvis, for the time being.

On the plus side, Parker intended from the beginning to make the show a fundraiser for a charity yet to be determined. On July 8th, he announced to the press the concept of *Elvis: Aloha from Hawaii Via Satellite*. Elvis was scheduled to end his November tour with three concerts on the islands, and it was planned that the television special would be a straight transmission of one of the shows.

Soon after the news was announced, Jim Aubrey from MGM got in touch with Parker and asked him if they could delay *Aloha*. MGM's *Elvis on Tour* documentary was set to open around the same time, and Jim feared seeing Elvis onstage for free at home would stop people from paying to watch him in the theaters. Parker acquiesced and scheduled two stand-alone concerts to take place at the Honolulu International Center arena on January 12 and January 14, 1973. The first would be a full dress rehearsal, filmed in case there were technical glitches during the live broadcast on the 14th. Elvis announced the new date at a press conference held between shows in Las Vegas on September 4,

Souvenir
Folio
Concert
Edition

Volume Seven

Aloha from Hawaii was a huge success commercially, but the performance was less vital than those that went before it. Taken at the *Aloha* rehearsal show, this shot of a slim Elvis was in marked contrast to the performer seen at the venues where this 1977 concert book was sold.

1972. Overall, a somewhat tired Elvis seemed amazed to being doing something on such a grand scale.

On November 20th, two days after he ended his tour, Elvis held a second press conference in Hawaii to announce that the concert would benefit the Kui Lee Cancer Fund (as suggested to Parker a month earlier by journalist

Eddie Sherman). Lee was a celebrated Hawaiian singer and composer who died at age thirty-four due to cancer of the lymph glands on December 3, 1966. Coincidentally, only the month before, Elvis had included Lee's song "I'll Remember You" as a bonus on his *Spinout* LP. Elvis further announced that the aim of the show was pure entertainment, without any kind of message attached.

After flying to Los Angeles, Elvis headed to Las Vegas on the 28th to meet the show's director, Marty Pasetta. Despite being taken aback by Marty's forthright manner, Elvis got along well with him. Pasetta, having seen at a November show in Long Beach that Elvis was reducing his movements, suggested an elaborate set with big colored lights and a huge sheet of foil to give off a mirrored effect. Though Parker shot the idea down, Elvis overruled his manager. He loved Pasetta's ideas and didn't even object when the director told him to lose some weight. Elvis set his mind to do so, and by the time he arrived in Hawaii on January 9th he was twenty-five pounds slimmer.

The dress rehearsal went well, and Elvis was asked to perform four more selections to bring the live broadcast up to a full hour. By the time he started his show late the next evening, everything was up and running from a technical standpoint. It was now up to Elvis as to how things turned out.

Song by Song

The focus is on the main performance from January 14th, but the songs are compared and contrasted with how he did them on the 12th. It is interesting to see the effect going out live had on Elvis. He is looser in the rehearsal, and more "on" at the beginning. He has a typical seventies Elvis haircut, and plays less to the camera. He cut his hair for the main show, and got going only as it went along.

Introduction: *Also Sprach Zarathustra*

Used at all but one show from 1971 to 1977, this dramatic piece (a.k.a. the *2001* theme) never failed to heighten audience expectation. In that this was going out globally, it likely packed quite a punch for those who saw America as being personified by Elvis Presley.

"See See Rider"

With the exception of a handful of shows, and the June 1972 tour, Elvis used this as his opener from January 1972 forward. With Elvis sounding and looking restrained, the version recorded for *Aloha* was a lesser rendition. His voice is clearer at the rehearsal, but it still doesn't hold a candle to his best performances of this iconic rocker.

"Burning Love"

Though this was Elvis' biggest hit of the seventies, he only made it a regular part of his show on his November 1972 tour, and during most of his concerts from 1975 through June 1976. The fallacy that he didn't enjoy performing it live stems from this lackadaisical run-through of what was usually an intense slice of rock and roll. While among the more stylistically appropriate selections, the key element of excitement is missing. Elvis even tones down the most sensual lyric, changing the daring "licking" to the benign "reaching my body."

One has to go to the rehearsal for passion, and even then there are lyrical foul-ups one wouldn't expect on an important occasion. At least Elvis used the sexy wording that time.

"Something"

While this ballad was seldom a regular in Elvis' act, it had been performed with more passion. There are moments of power, but Elvis sounds uncertain and subdued. There's a thickness to his voice during some of his 1973 shows, and the early segments of *Aloha* document it. At the main concert, Elvis was more focused, yet not engaged.

"You Gave Me a Mountain"

This was the first exceptional performance. Elvis sounds rejuvenated. Though he felt them personally, not every emotional ballad of loss was a good match for him. "You Gave Me a Mountain" is an exception, powerful without being overpowering. Upon viewing the less gimmicky, re-edited footage released on DVD, one can sense Elvis' tight interaction with his band. If his movements were sharper during the rehearsal show, he outdid himself vocally during the broadcast.

"Steamroller Blues"

The hit single, one of the most iconic performances from *Aloha*, vibrantly closed the first side. Elvis bites into the satirical lyric. Some less-than-observant critics have dismissed this performance as overblown, overlooking that Elvis couldn't help but make his blues shouting sound serious. He starts out a little reserved, but the mix on 45 (which focused less on the vexing horns and more on the band) shows just how credible this is as 1973 rock. The rehearsal version (best heard on *Elvis' Greatest Hits Volume 1*) is even more raw—proof that Elvis did still enjoy the rock medium.

"My Way"

One of Elvis' strengths was to take songs and make them his own. It would be nearly impossible for anyone else to encroach on Frank Sinatra's territory, but Elvis completely reinvents this ballad as a statement of purpose. This composition remained fresh to the end, the lyrics being among those Elvis afforded personal meaning to. The *Aloha* version was solid, and significantly better than his unissued 1971 studio attempt. While lyrical miscues slightly mar the rehearsal recording, it was one of the highlights of the main show.

"Love Me"

There were certain songs Elvis seemed to do out of obligation by 1973, and it is to his credit that he kept these to a bare minimum for *Aloha*. Despite it once

This single from *Aloha* featured artwork that differed from the live shots that had become routine. The 45 also had a raunchier mix.

being one of his favorite tracks, Elvis throws "Love Me" away. He did end it with power at the rehearsal, but he was, in both instances, more focused on the fans than the music. It is rather sad in retrospect that the crowd responds more strongly to the familiar material, even when hearing a halfhearted attempt. Only Elvis was to blame that this song got more perfunctory over the years, but blind acceptance for the hits couldn't have inspired him to raise his standards.

Oddly, he introduces "Love Me" as a medley of his songs, suggesting that there was going to be another oldie or two that were ultimately cut. One may have that impression, but Elvis does not perform additional tracks at the first show, and his medley comment was identical enough, both times, as to be scripted. Perchance it's an error that Elvis and the cue-card writer overlooked.

"Johnny B. Goode"

Added to the main show, this is not one of Elvis' most memorable renditions of this venerable rock-and-roll milestone. An inspired Elvis was a significant interpreter of Chuck Berry's work, yet he seemed to lose power on this over the years. James Burton's guitar work alone makes it worth a listen, but still the best that can be said is that it wasn't predictable.

"It's Over"

This is too middle-of-the-road for Presley, but it's a fair performance, once again covering a relationship gone bad. Elvis has a Southern feel vocally, in contrast with the grandiose arrangement. Despite some inherent flaws, Elvis nails the ending, especially at the rehearsal.

"Blue Suede Shoes"

Another of his classics that seemed to get less effective over time, Elvis' air of detachment differs from his band's enthusiasm. With Elvis only seeming to get into it on the very last verse, one can't help but think he included it only because he needed a few oldies in his set.

"I'm So Lonesome I Could Cry"

An exploration of pure country that strips things down to its bare essentials, again Elvis sings in an appealing Southern tone. He did put some thought into his *Aloha* set, this being a song he had never performed before in public. Regrettably, despite it being one of the sole (if infrequently performed) high-lights of his winter 1973 Vegas season, he would never include it in his set again.

"I Can't Stop Loving You"

Quickly added to the main show, this song had also lost some of the energy Elvis gave it upon his initial comeback. Fortunately, he never completely lost his passion for it. One of the more outwardly dynamic performances of the *Aloha* show, the ending is quite impressive, as were the vocal inflections on the chorus.

"Hound Dog"

All that goodwill goes out the door with this performance, the worst version of "Hound Dog" to date. Elvis had done the song with a degree of interest in 1969–70, and when it became stale in 1971 he revamped it with a sinister blues intro. For reasons unknown, he dropped the blues section here, rushing through the song in less than a minute. He gave the song zero respect, yet the crowd loved it at both shows. To add insult to injury, Elvis doesn't even do the halfhearted moves he attempted at the rehearsal.

"What Now My Love"

This is a fine performance of a song that was too conservative for Elvis. He had become attached to the lyric after hearing a recitation on Charles Boyer's *Where Does Love Go* album. He held back a little at the rehearsal rendition, but the last verse is sung so majestically that it saves the tepid performance. Elvis was much more intense at the main show, and again it's the climax that impresses. It would have been too esoteric for the new markets being reached with the special, but Elvis did occasionally recite "What Now My Love" in the melodramatic style of Boyer.

"Fever"

Perhaps keeping in mind the different cultures that would be watching, Elvis sings this with more restraint than normal. Still, this performance was played more for the audience in attendance than for the viewers at home. Elvis has a blast taunting the girls, repeatedly making them scream with the slightest of movements. At the rehearsal, he was more focused on singing, and his movements were sharper. This certainly makes for a better record, but it does lack the spontaneity of the main performance.

"Welcome to My World"

This was a song that Elvis never performed live either before or after the *Aloha* special. It was likely chosen because of the lyrical nod to the worldwide audience. To be honest, it doesn't work outside of that concept. The Jim Reeves recording was a classy example of the early-sixties Nashville sound, but this horn-heavy rendition loses the delicacy. Elvis doesn't seem inspired, appearing hardly to know the song at the rehearsal. He does do better at the main show, though not enough to salvage it.

"Suspicious Minds"

This was the most divisive part of the special. While there was a huge drop-off from what Elvis gave "Suspicious Minds" in 1969–70, it has a visual excitement missing from the rest of the show. No doubt Elvis was bored with the song, and at the rehearsal he almost ruined it by playing with the audience at the end. Looking lithe and tan, and augmented by a strobe effect that wasn't present on the 12th, Elvis pulled it together at the main taping.

Introductions

After introducing his band, Elvis takes the time to talk about the Kui Lee Cancer Fund and thank the audience for bringing in three times the money that was expected. Unfortunately, the little moment of warmth and humor in his introduction of Jack Lord and Charlie Hodge was cut out of both the album and the American version of the special. These edits had the effect of making Elvis seem less personable than he was that day.

"I'll Remember You"

In that Elvis had just mentioned the money raised for the Kui Lee Cancer Fund, it was only natural that he followed his announcement by performing Lee's "I'll Remember You." Moved by the occasion, Elvis reaches within himself to give the song a remarkable depth. With an absolutely stunning vocal, he was upping his game.

"Long Tall Sally"/"Whole Lotta Shakin' Goin' On"

The final last-minute addition to the set, this medley is tossed off without much thought. Sure, it's better than hearing him do a hackneyed "Teddy Bear"/"Don't Be Cruel," but for such an important show, one wonders why Elvis didn't choose to do something like his dynamic medley of "Little Sister"/"Get Back." Though the medley fails to bring out the best in Elvis, Ronnie Tutt and James Burton have a hell of a good time with the fifties classics.

"An American Trilogy"

To this day, this remains a song that exemplifies the excellence of Elvis live in the early seventies. If it is slightly less stoic than the 1972 live master, the versions delivered at both the rehearsal and main show were shining examples of a consummate artist. Elvis' vocal was powerful, and he used physicality to demonstrate how much the song meant to him. Although not explicitly religious, "An American Trilogy" has the solemn dedication usually reserved for his gospel recordings. J. D. Sumner and the Stamps also get a chance to shine, their solo allowing Elvis and his listeners a moment of quiet reflection.

"A Big Hunk o' Love"

This was a fifties rocker Elvis liked to perform. He doesn't move much but his vocal sizzles. It was easily the best rock and roll from *Aloha*, Glen Hardin taking advantage of the chance to pound his piano into submission. With Elvis egging his players on, even the orchestra managed to sound gutsy. While the fast numbers tended to be the weakest part of this show, "A Big Hunk o' Love" removed any doubts that he was still the king of rock and roll.

"Can't Help Falling in Love"

As good as it was, Elvis rarely took this song seriously live. The arrangement is nice, but it being the finale, Elvis often spent it kissing girls and handing out scarves. While that definitely pleased the front rows of the audience, it doesn't come across well on record or film. Still, at least at the main show, there was a celebratory air as it came to a close. Not wanting to leave without a grand gesture, Elvis unexpectedly throws off his beautiful cape as he hits a spectacular final note. The look of triumph he gives the camera (edited out of the American special, but seen on DVD and the extended *This Is Elvis*) was magnificent. Both proud and relieved, he had managed to pull off his satellite special with style.

NBC Bonus Session

After the show, Elvis came back to do insert tracks for the U.S. airing later that year. Four of the better *Blue Hawaii* songs are remade, along with "Early Morning Rain." First released on the *Mahalo from Elvis* budget album in 1978, the original edit was marred by inclusion of Hawaiian scenery. The *Aloha* deluxe DVD allows us to see this session in full.

It has been said that these should have been filmed on a separate day, and that Elvis resented having to do them. In retrospect, the session has a unique mellow feel that might not have been achieved had it been done under a different circumstance.

"Blue Hawaii"

Perfected in one take, the mood of this song is immediately apparent. These were stripped-down arrangements that reflect Elvis' own maturity. His voice may not be as pristine as it was in 1961, but the deepness of his tone gives these 1973 renditions their own appeal. It was a good choice for the special; Elvis' love of the island was evident.

"Ku-u-i-po"

Though it took three attempts to get it right, this song seems to benefit the most from the understated ambience. Singing with the gentle rhythm, Elvis gave the lyrics special attention. The 1961 recording was pretty, but only here can you hear how beautiful the melody is.

"No More"

This wasn't Hawaiian in lyrical content but rather in the arrangement. Improving on the original, Elvis hits high notes with a confidence only time can impart. Requiring a false start and two full takes, Elvis mastered it with seeming effortlessness. He hadn't performed most of these songs professionally in twelve years, but he doesn't give that away. While "No More" didn't make the final cut, it was no less successful than the other material.

"Hawaiian Wedding Song"

Funnily enough, it was a song Elvis had been performing over the last fourteen months that required the most takes. Take three was stronger than the final take four, because the closing duet between Elvis and Kathy Westmoreland is mixed better. That he revived it before the special, even singing it to Priscilla on their wedding day, strongly suggests that Elvis took more time because it was a favorite. Confirming that the atmosphere brought out something different, the strolling country feel was never duplicated.

"Early Morning Rain"

Though not quite as solid vocally, this comes very close to matching the 1971 master. Even without a tropical theme, its meditative mood fit musically with the rest of the set. With Elvis deeply focused, and polishing it off in one take, it was a fantastic conclusion to a very memorable evening.

Impact and Conclusion

If his initial motives were selfish, it cannot be argued that Tom Parker promoted *Aloha from Hawaii* with great skill. The original live broadcast went out to about ten countries, including Australia and most of non-communist Asia. Twenty-eight to thirty European countries (though oddly not England) saw it the next day, with America finally catching it on April 4th. It achieved high ratings everywhere it was shown, and was well received by the general public. The LP came out on

February 4th, and despite some carping about it being yet another live album, it went to #1. "Steamroller Blues" came out on 45 one month later, rising to #17. On LP, CD, VHS, and DVD, *Aloha from Hawaii* has remained a consistently strong seller.

As *Aloha* was such a big event, one has to question why Elvis didn't go all-out. One of the theories is that by now he was so addicted to drugs that he could no longer deliver. This is demonstrably untrue, however, as every credible source around Elvis says he did not misuse drugs in the month or two leading up to the special. Another theory is that he was too nervous to deliver. This has merit only up to a point. Though his voice wasn't at its best, it did open up considerably within the first twenty minutes.

Wishing to appeal to a worldwide audience, and not wanting to make a live album filled with the same songs as the one issued only six months before, Elvis dropped the more edgy material from his set. He also moved less, perhaps out of deference to the conservative factions that would see him. Some have theorized that this was something he did so he could stay on his mark, but that had never stopped Elvis before. Even the 1977 *Elvis in Concert* special, filmed when he was out of shape, had more action.

Elvis was going through a self-conscious phase where he wanted to be taken seriously purely as a singer. From his November 1972 tour through the rest of 1973, he did not move much. Unfortunately, this made for a less exciting visual experience, giving fodder to those who claimed Elvis had abandoned his roots.

These flaws do not mean *Aloha* lacks entertainment value. If not the best of Elvis in the seventies, it does aptly cover a variety of songs—at least one for all tastes. People have become almost too harsh in their assessment of *Aloha*, even complaining about his appearance at a time when he looked terrific. If *Aloha* was not Elvis' most rewarding musical endeavor, it had enough quality to sustain it. Elvis admirably achieved his goal of delivering pure entertainment, and *Aloha from Hawaii* will always remain iconic as one of the landmarks of his career.

34

Don't Mention My Name

Elvis focused exclusively on performing in 1974. He had no need to record as he already had two LPs in the can. The concerts were somewhat routine as the year began, but Elvis' joy of performing was coming through clearly as the spring and summer progressed. He even revamped his set for his summer Vegas Hilton engagement. Though he returned to his old format after the opening show, many new songs remained.

During the first week of the Vegas booking, Elvis seemed better than he'd been for two years. He had slimmed down, he looked healthy, and he seemed inspired to mix things up. The last week of the gig showed signs of trouble, but the music continued to be well performed.

While the subsequent tour and Tahoe gig largely followed the same set, they showcased an Elvis who was burned-out mentally, physically, and vocally. The division among Elvis historians and fans about why these events occurred is deep, but a close study of films, videos, and recordings helps untangle the truth from the glare of rumor and guesswork.

Live Performance

After being off the road for nearly five months, Elvis was back at the Hilton doing a more reasonable two-week gig. Opening on January 26th, Elvis was heavier than he had been before, but more focused than the previous August. This season did not present Elvis at his most dynamic, but he was genuinely excited about his new vocal group, Voice. Elvis got behind the ensemble, going as far as to let them perform "Killing Me Softly" during his set. J. D. Sumner also got to perform a solo, turning in a guttural (and frankly grating) "Why Me Lord" that Elvis sometimes mischievously interrupted. Emory Gordy had made the decision to return to studio work, so bass player Duke Bardwell became the latest addition to the band. With neither man thinking that the other was giving enough effort, it is often said he and Elvis didn't hit it off. There was some truth in that, but Duke's staying for over a year would suggest Elvis thought he was at least competent.

The set was fairly rigid, but there were some new additions. Although the arrangement was identical to the one he started using for "That's All Right," the occasional performance of "My Baby Left Me" brought out the best in Elvis and the band. Although rock-oriented fans took umbrage over songs like "Spanish Eyes," "My Baby Left Me" was proof positive that Elvis could credibly reproduce his original rockabilly sound.

In March, Elvis went on one of his longest tours. The twenty-day excursion wasn't too different, musically, from the last Vegas show, but Elvis' demeanor was livelier. The show wasn't as fiery as years past, but it was still evident that Elvis found touring more inspiring than his casino bookings. On March 3rd, Elvis made a successful two-show return to the Astrodome. The orchestra had to be left behind again, but with the exceptions of "2001" and "An American Trilogy," Elvis was able to present his normal program.

The highlight of the tour was a five-date return to Memphis. Elvis hadn't played in his hometown since 1961, and he wanted to preserve the moment for a new album. To avoid repetition with previous releases, a number of terrific songs were cut. Even on the edited LP, the warmth Elvis and his hometown fans shared is readily felt. Elvis won a well-deserved Grammy for his performance of "How Great Thou Art."

A short West Coast tour in May was well done, the highlight being an enthusiastic one-time-only performance of "You Can Have Her" in Los Angeles. With barely a pause, Elvis began his third stand in Lake Tahoe, and it went better this time. The High Sahara room had the smallest occupancy of any venue Elvis played in the seventies, and every seat had a good view.

An incident where Elvis' guards used strong-arm tactics against an obstinate drunk resulted in a drawn-out lawsuit. It was the first in a chain of events that would cost Elvis not only a fair amount of money, but also some of his closest friends. (See chapter 40.)

Elvis only took three weeks off before launching another tour that ran from June 15th to July 2nd. Though the schedule was three days shorter than in March, Elvis played the same number of shows. With tickets in exceedingly high demand, Elvis had no trouble selling out four gigs in Fort Worth and three in Omaha. Many were impressed with the vitality Elvis exhibited throughout the dates, the only downside being that he hadn't altered his set-list to any great extent since January.

The glad spirits of previous tours were evident, most notably during Elvis' bemused interaction with his more ardent admirers. Throughout the year, Elvis had been performing a greater amount of blues-based material. The upcoming Vegas season would bring this more to the forefront, but additions like a soul-infused "Big Boss Man" gave an early preview as to the direction Elvis was heading in.

Having a rare six weeks off, Elvis used the time to completely retool his show. When he opened for another two weeks in Las Vegas on August 19th, he did a set completely unlike any other. Dispensing with "2001," Elvis came onstage to

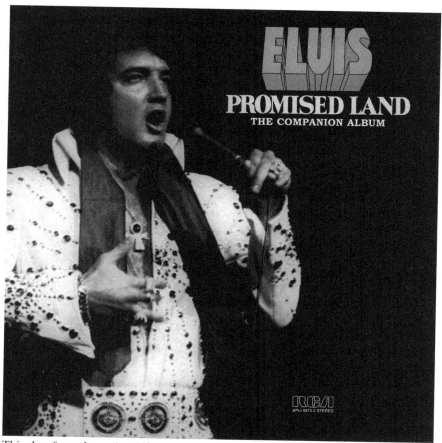

This shot from the spring 1974 tour was used on the FTD vinyl release *Promised Land: The Companion Album.* It was a big improvement over the unflattering original artwork.

the rocking beat of "Big Boss Man." The show was well-rounded in presenting all facets of Elvis' abilities, yet the one aspect that stuck out was how focused he was on the blues.

Going by the evidence of this season, and some of the material he cut at Stax Studios, contemporary soul and funk were styles Elvis took to readily. The show that evening saw Elvis taking a classic fifties blues record like "Down in the Alley" and graft a hard seventies edge onto it. Unfortunately, few of Elvis' real fans got to see him on his opening nights, as that was the day celebrities and the press would make up the preponderance of spectators. Seeing as they were less familiar with Elvis' catalogue than his true audiences, they didn't give him the reaction he was expecting.

Elvis reintroduced "2001" the next night and threw in a few more oldies. While he went back to a traditional structure from the second show on, most of the new selections remained in the show. During the concerts, Elvis often wore two-piece leather suits that showed off how lean he had become. There was still some colon distention, but he looked better than he had sixteen months before. Being in better shape, Elvis was again able to get physically into the music. The staging of "If You Talk in Your Sleep" had the most dynamic visual theatrics Elvis attempted after 1971. Donning his karate uniform, kicking and punching at invisible assailants, he left the audience breathless.

When Elvis felt good over the following three years, he did longer sets that included more spontaneity in general. However, he would never be as fit or dynamic again. None of his tours or gigs would match the sheer volume of rarities he unearthed over these two weeks. "Promised Land," "Never Been to Spain," "Good Time Charlie's Got the Blues," "I'm Leavin'," "Until It's Time for You to Go," "It's Midnight," "Softly as I Leave You"—it was an exciting panorama of modern music performed by a committed (if somewhat moody) Elvis.

For personal reasons, closing night was one of Elvis' most noteworthy shows. The most interesting musical inclusion was a three-song showcase for Voice, for which he backed them up. This in rough form was the start of Presley implementing a series of band solos that would evolve into a permanent part of the set. But the show is notorious for a speech Elvis made that showed his fury at an unnamed member of the hotel staff. Causing much controversy, the show (dubbed "Desert Storm" by bootleggers) has often overshadowed how good musically Elvis was that summer.

To understand how this went down, an alteration Elvis implemented in the show's structure must be discussed. On the last night, and over the last week of concerts, Elvis talked to the audience about the controversy that had been surrounding his life the last several years. These speeches began after Elvis had the flu and couldn't perform his shows on August 26th. The main things bothering Elvis were false rumors about heroin use and the stories printed in movie magazines about his divorce.

The long and personal monologues show Elvis sometimes angry and at other times boastful, but mainly they show him sharing his personal thoughts on his life and interests. What has been largely overlooked is that Elvis rehearsed these dissertations to be part of the show. This may seem somewhat odd, but that he planned these talks is obvious when one listens to every day of the last week. On closing night, you can even hear Charlie Hodge feeding Elvis lines.

Why did Elvis do this? Not having felt that his changes musically on opening night were wholly successful, he seemingly felt that talking part of the time he was onstage could be another way to give his performances a fresh dimension. The talking may not have pleased non-fans that came to see him casually, but until the "Desert Storm" show, Elvis hadn't been totally out of line. After all, the less-controversial subjects Elvis talked about, like karate and his jewelry, were interesting to fans and the curious. An onstage karate demonstration one night did see some people leave, but most stayed because Elvis was opening up in a way he hadn't before—and it was entertaining, in a fashion.

The talking during this gig has evoked mixed reactions from fans in the years since. It's the only time Elvis let his feelings out in public, but his behavior on the final night has to be deemed at least odd. Elvis actually got so angry discussing the heroin rumor he threatened to break the neck of the person he considered responsible. All of this has been attributed by armchair analysts to some sort of nervous breakdown, speed abuse, or even dabbling in cocaine. Yet despite the fact that Elvis was addicted to a growing pharmaceutical regimen by this point, that may be too simplistic an answer.

Bodyguard and friend Sonny West, who has always been vociferous about Elvis' drug abuse, said that the challenge of proving the heroin rumor wrong led Elvis to get straight over the rest of the engagement. Road manager Joe Esposito is usually diametrically opposed to everything Sonny says, but he has "Desert Storm" occurring during a "slim and sober" period. Slight exaggeration aside, that the same story comes from two different factions means there is some validity to their claim.

Even if it wasn't down to drugs, Elvis clearly got too comfortable with the public, and he forgot himself. Nevertheless, his charisma and musical performance were so strong that many in the crowd applauded his angry outburst. The show also got a rave review by upcoming Elvis author W. A. Harbinson in *Disc* magazine. Elvis did axe the majority of the planned talking from his set, but things were about to get worse.

The fourth tour of the year ran from September 27th to October 9th. A major *National Enquirer* article that followed, plus latter-day recollections, have given this run a very bad name. Fighting flu-like symptoms and serious intestinal problems, in little over three weeks Elvis had gone from fairly slender to noticeably overweight. He lost much of the weight over the first few nights, but in not feeling well, Elvis overmedicated, and he was clearly out of it onstage on a number of occasions.

Video and audiotapes from the tour don't completely bear out the sharp critiques these concerts have attracted. Certainly, Elvis was hoarse the first few nights, but he wasn't (as has been accused) holding half-hour shows, swearing profusely, or unable to move. He had slowed down physically, compared with Vegas, but nearly all the new songs remained. Contrary to the myth that refuses to die, audio evidence and reflections from audience members reveal that a few shows were actually good. Others, like his second show in College Park, Maryland, were his first to be downright bad.

Elvis' general condition hadn't gotten nearly as dreadful as it would become, and even the dire nights were decidedly better than the worst concerts from his final year. Despite some ill-tempered moments, he seems eager to vary his songs. This isn't a top-shelf tour, but the first College Park concert and others like Detroit weren't the disasters of legend. They were, however, a big fall from what he had done in Vegas just weeks before. Though full of speculation and half-truths, the *Enquirer* article did prove that someone in the troupe was gossiping about the now-troubled performer.

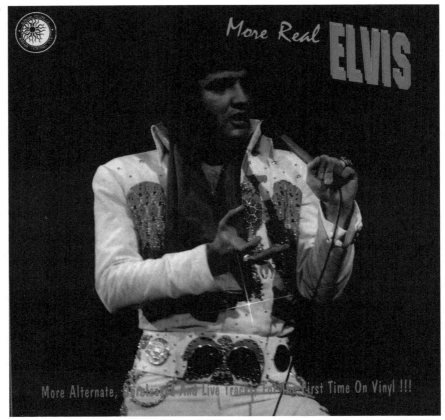

This entertaining 10-inch boot from 1998 was the second and final *Real Elvis* LP. The artwork uses a photo from the summer tour of 1974.

Immediately following the tour, Elvis held a four-day stint in Tahoe to make up the canceled 1973 dates. He was, as Duke Bardwell put it, running "out of gas." Other than premiering some new suits, and the continued refinement of (or reliance on) band solos, nothing memorable happened. After he closed, an exhausted Elvis didn't work for six months. Though he had planned to make a martial arts documentary, he gave it up as his health got worse and his weight soared.

Popularity and Impact

Though Elvis' LPs continued to reach mediocre positions on the pop charts, all of the 1974 releases did well on the country listings. Elvis had better luck on the Hot 100 when "If You Talk in Your Sleep" and "Promised Land" made considerable inroads into the Top 20. Concert-wise, there continued to be amazing success, but it was worrying that Elvis was getting more attention for his past than his present. Nostalgia runs in twenty-year cycles, so original fifties rock and roll was making a huge comeback. Following the buyout, the use of Elvis' catalogue was in RCA's hands. After she successfully masterminded the Madison Square Garden project, Joan Deary was put in charge.

Deary came up with a nicely packaged LP documentary called *Elvis: A Legendary Performer*. Though the *Worldwide Gold Award* sets and the *Golden Records* series were fine hits collections, only the original *Golden Records* release in 1958 provided annotation that gave Elvis' music a sense of history. By including recording dates, a lavish booklet of vintage articles and photos, and a focus (though later recordings were sometimes used) on Elvis' revolutionary 1954–61 era, *Elvis: A Legendary Performer* was the first LP to succinctly sum up why Presley was an important artist. It even drew raves from the die-hards, as it included previously unreleased material from the heights of Sun and the 1968 comeback. Woven together with period interviews, this record said more about Elvis than anything else—outside of Jerry Hopkins' book and radio projects—had before.

Perhaps, on the surface, it was unusual that Parker was unhappy about the album. He successfully had it delayed, so as not to interfere with the *Raised on Rock* release, but he couldn't stop it from coming out. What bothered Parker (other than his ego being bruised by not being consulted) was that Elvis had a past so illustrious that it was bound to make people forget new products.

As early as 1960, unfair comparisons were drawn between Elvis' new and old music. Yes, it was fantastic that Elvis' initial artistry was being recognized, but it was unfair to expect him to continue to shape his era. That Elvis remained a consummate artist in the seventies would largely be overlooked until the nineties, when nostalgia again took hold.

That Elvis gradually grew contemptuous and lackadaisical about performing can be understood in this context. Yes, a healthier Elvis would have done something like "Jailhouse Rock" better, but that's not what he was about anymore. In 1972, he had said it was hard to live up to an image, and day by day, what he saw in the mirror became harder to take. Elvis never really coped with growing older, and as he approached forty it seemed he now was "caught in a trap."

35

Fairytale

A Consumer's Guide to the Later Years

his chapter chronicles the studio LPs Elvis cut over the last four years of his career. Separating the music from the personal drama isn't unproblematic, but balance is sorely needed in summarizing the most hotly debated music in Elvis' catalogue.

The mid-seventies weren't the easiest time of his life, but Elvis managed to deliver interesting work almost to the end. There have been cogent arguments that Elvis wasn't attuned to the times, but he surely wasn't going to become a Sex Pistol. Comparing him to artists from a different era and place isn't really helpful. Looking at his fellow Sun label artists from 1973 to 1977, do any match the success Elvis was having?

Only Jerry Lee Lewis is more artistically solid in this era, but he was always a far more careful artist. Johnny Cash can be seen as more consistently engaged, but was just as up and down musically. Carl Perkins didn't challenge himself near as much as before, nor did Charlie Rich who, after the success of *Behind Closed Doors*, recorded a lot of material even Elvis would have found too middle-of-the-road. Many fifties artists didn't even have record deals by the mid-seventies.

As sad as it is that Elvis let himself go, he was doing better work in the studio than most performers of his era. After 1970, he wasn't at the forefront of what was current, but he never used the "golden goodies" format. For someone who only had to come out and do an easy set of obvious hits, or remake other hits of the fifties and early sixties, he excelled in the range of his shows and albums.

Raised on Rock/For Ol' Times Sake (Released October 1, 1973)

The first LP to come principally from Elvis' sessions at Stax studios, *Raised on Rock/For Ol' Times Sake* is one of the most unfairly maligned records in the entire Presley catalogue. I would go so far as to say that, as a whole entity, it was actually his best latter-day LP. Elvis wasn't in the best of spirits, or in the best of shape, but this has little bearing on the music. It's been claimed Elvis sounds bored on this album, but I can't hear it. Presley's delivery is less intense than it would have been three or four years previously, but his voice has a bluesy feel that's refreshingly laid back.

Elvis told U.K. fan Tony Prince in a rare backstage interview that he intended this to be a blues album. It didn't quite come out that way, but *Raised on Rock*

A June 23, 1973, matinee performance. Elvis' outfits were ornate on the front and back. One of the biggest requests he got from women while he was onstage was to turn around!

Photo by Erik Lorentzen

was Elvis' most blues- and rock-oriented LP of the seventies. Notably, it was not the blues and rock of 1956. The music has a contemporary feel that proves Elvis had indeed been following the output of Stax.

"Raised on Rock" was a fantastic performance of a Mark James composition. Both Elvis' voice and the arrangement have a menacing quality that is nicely dark. The lyrics have come under fire because Elvis helped create the rock movement, but he was as big a fan of rock and roll as any other kid growing up in the fifties. Even if Presley hadn't been relating something that applied to himself, it's a great song that still sounds invigorating.

"Find Out What's Happening" moves along nicely, with a cocky Elvis getting strongly in the groove. Burton's guitar solo could have been more forceful, but it does recall Elvis' rockabilly beginnings. The funk-infused "Just a Little Bit" and "If You Don't Come Back" sound like nothing else Elvis did. The former keeps a steady groove that Elvis vocalizes to, and the latter has great interplay with female backing vocalists Mary Holladay, Ginger Holladay, Kathy Westmoreland, and Jeanie Greene. It was written by Leiber and Stoller, who were also represented by the ridiculously contrived "Three Corn Patches," which is half-saved by a bemused Elvis and a kicking band.

The ballads are refreshingly sparse and humble. From the Stax sessions, we get the haunting Tony Joe White track "For Ol' Times Sake," which can be related to Elvis' continued feelings of uncertainty in the wake of his divorce. It's not that Priscilla was the only love of Elvis' life; it was more to do with the public way she left, and the idea that he held of marriage as a lifelong partnership. It's an utterly devastating performance, and one of Elvis' most open moments on record.

The initial Stax sessions were halted when Elvis' microphone was stolen and a quality replacement wasn't available. You can hear the problem on the meandering, country-styled "Girl of Mine." Elvis sounds distracted, and the tonal quality is muffled. It wasn't a good vehicle to begin with.

To finish the LP, a recording session was set up at Elvis' home in Palm Springs in September 1973. The idea was to overdub some music tracks with lead vocals, but Elvis only ended up doing the beautiful "Sweet Angeline." The words themselves aren't much, but there is a quiet dignity to everything cut that day.

Wanting to record with his new backing vocalists Voice, Elvis laid down two additional ballads. The delay in finishing the LP meant there was no time to overdub, so the music has a lovely sparse feel. A stark rendition of the standard "Are You Sincere" finds Presley reviving his blues-tinged delivery from Stax.

Also cut was Voice member Donnie Sumner's straightforward "I Miss You." Elvis rides the melody beautifully, and his relaxed approach turns what could have been a mediocre recording into something unique. Intriguingly, Elvis is said to have produced demos with Voice after he finished the album. As this seems to be the only time Elvis produced another group or artist, they could prove fascinating.

Good Times (Released March 20, 1974)

This album has a couple of tracks held for a single from the July Stax outing, but it was largely made up from the return visit in December. *Good Times* has moments that capture the better qualities of the previous album, but it also veers at times into the lounge-singer territory *Raised on Rock* actively eschewed.

"She Wears My Ring," "Take Good Care of Her," "Spanish Eyes," and "My Boy" were not the type of songs Elvis should have gone near—at least with the kind of arrangements he used. Though "My Boy" was a fairly big chart success, and "Take Good Care of Her" wasn't truly horrid, these songs reinforce the notion that Elvis had sold out. Even the gospel "If That Isn't Love" seems closer to easy listening than necessary.

The other five songs on the album have more musical variety and a less blasé Presley. Three were up-tempo, Dennis Linde's "I Got a Feelin' in My Body" being the funkiest gospel song I've had the pleasure to listen to. The organ solo by David Briggs puts the synthesized excesses of the era to shame, and Presley is positively electric. The part where he stops and sings, "I've gotta, I've gotta, I've gotta" with a layer of echo applied is most striking.

From July, Tony Joe White's "I've Got a Thing About You Baby" was a lighter version of soul unfolding in a melodic fashion. There's a sense of magic present that makes its relative failure as a single a true anomaly. That Elvis was able to shake off depression and make a record brimming with positivity is something pretty special.

"Talk About the Good Times" was another funky moment of jubilance. A Jerry Reed gospel-rocker, it gives Elvis plenty to chew on. This has an authentic gospel revival-meeting vibe, and sounds fresh upon repeated play. Even in 1973, Elvis still liked to record his lead live with his singers and band. This gave Felton some problems with sound balance, but the interplay that makes "Talk About the Good Times" so fun to hear couldn't have been obtained otherwise.

The remaining two ballads continue the run of songs Elvis saw as personal. "Lovin' Arms" stands in vivid contrast to mush like "Spanish Eyes" in that it has a great melody, well-written lyrics, a production that keeps things basic, and a vocal of nuance and feeling. Holding back in spots for dramatic effect, when he does reveal the pain, it stands out. Though "My Boy" did really well chart-wise, "Loving Arms" would have made for a much more palatable 45 that wouldn't have garnered any critical snipes.

"Good Time Charlie's Got the Blues" ends the album on a reflective note. Elvis sounds like he has lived out every implication of the lyric, although he notably cut a verse that references pills that perhaps cut too close to the bone for public consumption. The strings and voices were used intelligently, and don't water down what Elvis and the band were relaying.

In all, *Good Times* had the worst and best of the era side by side, but the good stuff makes it worth the half-hour one invests in playing it. It did very poorly on the rock charts, but was Top 5 country.

Promised Land (Released January 8, 1975)

Coming out on Elvis' fortieth birthday, *Promised Land* received an unduly harsh review from critic Robert Hilburn. Tearing the record apart, he suggested Elvis retire. Actually no better or worse than other recent albums, it's neither a classic nor an embarrassment. Taken from the December 1973 Stax sessions, the success of the featured singles led RCA to keep the album in print a decade longer than the other Stax offerings.

Of the songs not released on 45, Waylon Jennings' "You Asked Me To" was a standout. Elvis was two years ahead of the pack in noticing his work, since Waylon didn't break real big until the middle of 1975. The female voices are a little much, but there are some nice harmonies by the Stamps and Voice on the chorus.

"Your Love's Been a Long Time Coming" and "Mr. Songman" were everyday mid-paced pop. Elvis sounds fine; it's the arrangements that are ordinary. The same could be said about "Love Song of the Year." It's pleasant, but remarkable only in the way the concluding harmonies seem to faintly recall the Beatles' "All You Need Is Love." Only slightly better, "There's a Honky Tonk Angel (Who Will Take Me Back In)" did garner more dedication from the players and Elvis. The country ballad had potential, but it was weighed down by a sluggish tempo.

Red West and Johnny Christopher came up with the pulsating, R&B-flavored "If You Talk in Your Sleep." Elvis comes across as defiant in his menacing delivery. The horns are no-nonsense, adding a sense of drama that matches the lyrical theme of infidelity. An unexpected Top 20 hit, it proved listeners still liked Elvis to sound gutsy. Used as the flip, "Help Me" was a conventional ballad Elvis would often perform live.

"Promised Land" was an honest to goodness rock-and-roll classic that even garnered praise from fifties purists. A longtime fan of Chuck Berry, Elvis had recently seen him perform this witty composition at the prestigious Las Vegas Hilton lounge. Reinvented here as a full-force slice of pure rock and roll, James Burton's sizzling lead guitar is more than matched by a tuned-in Presley.

A second straight Top 20 hit, it succeeded on the strength of Elvis' own elation and drive. The one Presley track from this era to be continuously revived in movies and television, "Promised Land" was included on the 1981 *This Is Elvis* soundtrack. It was heard with a fascinating overdub of Elvis singing high harmonies over his lead.

"It's Midnight" was the flip of the Berry cover, and one would have to search hard to find more of a contrast. Downbeat and weighty, Elvis held his last note an incredibly long time. It wasn't his preeminent breakup ballad, but a wah-wah guitar pedal provided interesting melodic contrast.

Tim Baty from Voice came up with the quietly brilliant "Thinking About You." The only song with an overt folk influence included on the album, the attractive guitar riffs have an earthiness that make one wish Elvis hadn't strayed from that direction. Another song of love lost, this time there was no overt self-pity, no grand gestures, and no vocal gymnastics.

There's something unexpectedly heartening about Elvis' interpretation. He tries to put on a brave face, but there's a little crack in his voice that tells you he's heartbroken. The line "Life is fine, and I'm doing fine" is the giveaway. With it, the singer revealed himself to be not "doing fine" at all. Not wanting to end the entrancing atmosphere, the unedited master finds Elvis singing three repetitions of the chorus.

Elvis Today (Released May 7, 1975)

This album was of roughly the same quality as *Promised Land*. There are few bad moments, but only half of the album stands out. Elvis recorded it in March 1975, sounding rested after six months off the road. It was clearly conceived as an LP, and Elvis went out of his way to perform most of the songs live.

Today gave Elvis an executive producer credit, some nineteen years after becoming his own producer. The two 1974 live albums also list this credit, but while it was applicable for the Memphis show, Presley had nothing to do with compiling *Having Fun with Elvis on Stage!*

The exciting, Jerry Lee Lewis–influenced "T-R-O-U-B-L-E" was a hit years later in a neutered rendering by Travis Tritt. The original 1975 Elvis single was in every way superior, showing the stark contrast between a journeyman and a genius. The rapid delivery allowed Elvis to have fun it with live, and the piano playing of Glen Hardin reached a new apex. It doesn't have the focus of "Promised Land," but it proved Elvis didn't hesitate to record rock and roll that caught his interest.

"I Can Help" is a lively cover of Billy Swan's hit from 1974. It's not all that different musically, but Elvis' voice carried a command the comparatively frail-sounding Swan didn't come close to. To put an old rumor to rest, Elvis was never heckled with "You need help" while performing this song, as he never added it to his set.

"Fairytale" was an unusual country offering from the Pointer Sisters that can be disquieting to those who only know them by later hits. The blend of soul and country appealed to Elvis, and he didn't dilute the formula in his recording. It became a personal favorite live, but in introducing it as "the story of his life," Elvis was assumedly referring only to the title.

There are a couple other country tracks on *Elvis Today*, including an innocuous cover of "Green, Green Grass of Home." Elvis had once asked his disc jockey friend George Klein to play the Tom Jones version repeatedly on air while driving home from a movie shoot. Despite the song having meaning for Presley, the final recording was oddly tepid.

Much better was his run through the Statler Brothers' hit "Susan When She Tried." Burton plays like a true country picker, and Elvis loved attempting the bass harmonies. An altogether fascinating performance, it was regretfully one of the few on the album not tackled live.

The most soulful recording was Elvis' cover of the fifties R&B standard "Shake a Hand." Elvis makes an error in trying to evoke the era with his arrangement, but the attention lavished on the vocal is laudable. It's slightly longer than most Elvis cuts, but he seems into the moment enough to stop it from dragging.

The somnolent "Woman Without Love" was a clichéd ballad with outdated sexist sentiments. Less painful was "Bringing It Back," penned by Imperials member Greg Gordon. It was poor single material, but it worked well within the context of the LP. The lyrics were pretty, in a rudimentary poetic sense, spurring Elvis to put passion into his delivery. It was performed by Voice during their mini-set at the infamous "Desert Storm" show.

"And I Love You So" had been a recent hit for writer Don McLean. It was more romantic than what Elvis typically sang at the time, and in the studio he crooned it directly to girlfriend Sheila Ryan. Though pretty, the arrangement lacked ingenuity.

Lastly, we have "Pieces of My Life." This shouldn't work. It's very produced, and not dissimilar to a few dozen other songs from his later years. Yet "Pieces of My Life" somehow stands alone in that all traces of pretension or bombast were eradicated. Elvis based it on Charlie Rich's mournful version, but he gave it a new level of pathos. Increasingly puzzled by how his life had turned out, Elvis was feeling regret over some of his choices. More of this was to come on his next LP.

From Elvis Presley Boulevard, Memphis, Tennessee (Released April 20, 1976)

This album divides Elvis fans, then and now. In one way, it's the hardest Elvis album to sit through, the mood bleak and somewhat depressing. On the other hand, it feels like a statement of some sort, and very much a creative whole.

Unfortunately, typically shoddy Parker packaging was taken to a new extreme. Though *From Elvis Presley Boulevard* had an iconic concert shot taken, appropriately, at his June 10, 1975, Memphis gig, that it says "Recorded Live" on the front is misleading and untrue, precipitated by the fact that the live albums were selling far better at this point. The only upside to this tactic was that RCA had not doctored the tapes to make them appear to be a concert recording.

The album actually stems from the first of two 1976 sessions held in the "Jungle Room" at Graceland, though extensive overdubs meant this couldn't even be construed to be "live in the studio." Elvis' voice was far better than it would be on the road for most of the year, but it shows signs of his rapidly declining condition. Though Presley could hit all the notes, sustaining them was a frequent problem.

"Hurt" was a no-holds-barred cover of a Timi Yuro oldie that Elvis toweringly masters. The drama of the ballad would inspire Elvis, and it would quickly become one of the select highlights from his last fifteen months on stage. Even during his worst shows, he seldom failed to skillfully execute the challenging

Elvis with his backing singers during his final Las Vegas stint. Presley had become quite vocal about his distaste for the town.   *Photo by Erik Lorentzen*

extended coda. Arguably as over-the-top as some of the other songs on the album, the performance has more of a melodic quality. An air of fifties nostalgia permeates the music, but it's conveyed in an unobtrusive fashion.

"For the Heart" was a great country-rocker that would launch the career of the Judds in 1983. Elvis sounds cool and totally at ease, and the song likely would have made his live show had he been in better shape. The fun lay in the zooming bass played by Jerry Scheff, and the vocal interplay Elvis has with J. D. Sumner.

As far as the rest of the album is concerned, only Elvis' reinvention of "Blue Eyes Crying in the Rain" had any frivolity to it. It has a solid feel, with J. D. adding a few good background lines. For once the voices, band, and strings all feel as if they belong together.

The charmless "Solitaire" and "The Last Farewell" are the worst of these recordings. They seem to go on forever, and are practically ruined by Felton's overdubs. There's not much that could make these more appealing; Jarvis simply tried too hard. "I'll Never Fall in Love Again" was a better song, but Elvis can't sustain his upper range.

Elvis' voice is fragile on "Never Again," wavering off pitch on the second-to-last repetition of the title. Only his sincerity pulls him through. Besides, it was lost in the haze of voices used to cover up his mistake. "Love Coming Down" wasn't far from the lower rungs of the sessions but was partially saved by an unexpectedly well-conceived middle eight.

"Bitter They Are, Harder They Fall" is dark. Elvis sounds desolate, to the point where some have argued he was crying out for help. It wasn't a conscious thing, as Elvis was too proud to admit outright that he was in need of assistance. However, in recording songs like this, and then going out on the road so out of condition, he likely no longer cared about keeping up appearances.

"Danny Boy" was a song Elvis had loved from his youth, and one he had recorded at home while in Germany. Elvis decided to cut it for the album after Vernon told him it would be a good choice. He could have done it with more precision earlier in the decade, but this 1976 performance was extremely potent. He was still in possession of a remarkable voice, and playing armchair analyst is a tricky thing. Though this song may have come across differently before his death, he sounds as if he knows and accepts that he hasn't got long to go. A welcome respite from big production, it basically relied only on Elvis' voice and a piano accompaniment.

"Danny Boy" provided a hard challenge for Elvis at this point. Session out-takes show him having considerable problems finding the right key and pitch. You can sense the feeling of accomplishment when he successfully ends the track singing in falsetto.

Thirty years ago, there was a lavish LP-sized book by Roy Carr and Mick Farren called *Elvis: The Illustrated Record*. While it slavishly followed the traditional train of thought about Elvis' music, their take on *From Elvis Presley Boulevard* went against the mold. Summing up what Elvis was trying to convey, they likened it to a blues recording. They made a good point about how despair was what drove this LP and made it such a personal statement. I cannot improve on the way Carr and Farren summed the album up. Today, it indeed remains a unique piece of "required uneasy listening."

Moody Blue (Released July 19, 1977)

Unable to get Presley to finish a studio album, Felton Jarvis did put out one last Elvis LP. Even though it's a mish-mash of 1976 studio recordings and 1974 and 1977 live cuts, *Moody Blue* somehow manages to hang together. It had a refreshing variety, and was discernibly more upbeat than his last four studio outings. Although the origin of the songs was disparate, Elvis had indicated back in late 1975 that he wanted to do an album that was half live and half studio. Felton Jarvis also spoke of Elvis approving the lineup and mixes at Graceland earlier in the year, so this was something Presley was involved in putting together—at least to a small extent.

The studio work was considerably better than what was found on the last album. Two of the songs were taken from the same February 1976 sessions, but they had already proved themselves to be a success in late 1976 when the "Moody Blue"/"She Thinks I Still Care" 45 went to #1 in the country charts. "Moody Blue" had a disco backbeat and some swooping violins, but the Mark James composition was refreshingly free of artifice.

Though Elvis might have gone deeper into disco—with potentially disastrous results—had he lived few more years, "Moody Blue" itself was infectious. What keeps it grounded is that it stayed within the parameters of a normal pop single. Besides, it had been a long time since Elvis released a happy song about relationships. Here, the somewhat enigmatic lyrics address a free spirit.

"She Thinks I Still Care" was a country standard covered by numerous artists. It's a good interpretation, but comparatively paint-by-numbers next to a far superior blues arrangement that went unreleased.

The rest of the studio cuts were done in October 1976, back in the "Jungle Room." Elvis sounds like he had found a new lease on life, doing a set that had a lightness of touch missing since the Palm Springs foray from 1973. Part of this was due to an upswing in his health that unfortunately proved to be brief. Looking better than he had for several years, if nowhere near his prime, Elvis had recently lost a lot of weight. All of this came together to make these sessions a lot less laborious (if admittedly less productive) than the previous one.

In no way reflecting Elvis' personal life, his last single proved to be a welcome return to basic rock and roll. Like "For the Heart," "Way Down" builds on Scheff and Sumner's bass parts. It quickens the tempo and replaces the good-time feel with some genuine sensuality.

The flip is a thoroughly modern rendition of "Pledging My Love," the Johnny Ace classic from 1954. "Pledging My Love" also happened to be Ace's last record, too, after he bizarrely shot himself playing Russian roulette. Elvis based his arrangement on Delbert McClinton's recent cover, though Presley in contrast sounds looser yet curiously more forceful. It returns Elvis right back to where he started, with a song he could have easily recorded twenty years before—a sense of closure unforeseeable at the time it was recorded.

The last studio song Elvis ever recorded also seemed to bring him back to his roots. It's a blues-steeped cover of Jim Reeves' country ballad "He'll Have to Go." As he had been doing since 1954, Elvis took this country song and gave it an R&B infusion, a rolling, lazy feel akin to "Merry Christmas Baby." Though many of Elvis' looser moments were edited down for public consumption, "He'll Have to Go" runs to nearly five minutes. This length allowed Presley to dig into the lyrics, making them more gutsy with every pass. As much as he had changed over the years, Elvis never lost the sense of the immediate, nor the ability to blend various influences into something uniquely his own.

The only lovelorn ballad was an offering by respected musical writer Andrew Lloyd Webber. "It's Easy for You" was theatrical in its refrain, but otherwise it was a direct (if sorrowful) kiss-off to an ex. Coming as the last song on the album, it provides a coda to a body of work that is unparalleled. It may be another song that only seems to be haunting in light of Elvis' death, but there is an element of something coming to an end that makes its placement slightly chilling.

The new live cuts were recorded in April 1977, and thankfully two of them captured Elvis during one of the best nights he had all year. The Ann Arbor show of April 24th can't be compared to triumphs of years past, but Elvis was in a good mood and willing to give a little extra to make his album work.

"Little Darlin'" has been chastised for being silly, something Elvis should have never considered at this point. Hogwash! Elvis certainly had no need to fall back on novelty records from the fifties to generate a crowd, but the man was just having a bit of fun, and his audience seems to appreciate it. No, it wasn't daring, but it endowed *Moody Blue* with the kind of light contrast sorely needed in his recent work. If it's a moment of indulgence, it's done without aiming to be anything more than entertaining.

Creatively, the most significant addition to Elvis' show in many years was "Unchained Melody." It came from the same era as "Little Darlin'" but is worlds away in creative ambition. On his better nights from his New Year's 1976 tour on, Elvis would sit at the piano and have Charlie hold his vocal mic. He would then start to play the song without any accompaniment, before being joined minimally halfway through by his players and singers. Pouring every bit of himself into every word, his performance created its own magical aura. To make it fit for release, Felton filled out the song with overdubs in the second half. They come in far stronger than Elvis' band did in concert, but the final master had an unobtrusive polish and was approved by Elvis personally.

If the musical merits of Presley in his last years will never come to a general consensus, even his most dismissive and hardened critics can't credibly claim that Elvis was a completely spent force at the end in the face of "Unchained Melody." It is rare to find such naked emotion, and that Elvis could have done a more refined and controlled version in 1970 ceases to matter. Coming at this stage, exposing the vulnerability of the man beneath the legend, "Unchained Melody" was a coda that couldn't have been better if it was planned.

To Elvis, "Unchained Melody" was the centerpiece of the album, and on his last tour he said it would be the title track. Obviously, the commercial considerations of calling the record *Moody Blue* ended up outweighing the artist's wishes, but that too seems to make a final poignant comment on the contradictions of Elvis being a creative genius, but one who was often unable to stand up to those who marketed him.

The album was completed with a recording from two nights later in Kalamazoo, where Elvis performed the Olivia Newton-John song "If You Love Me (Let Me Know)." Yes, it's pure pop confection, and yes, Elvis should have chosen weightier songs at times, but he kept it in the show for three years because he plain enjoyed singing it. Obviously, he does give it a little more grit than the Australian balladeer could manage, but it goes by harmlessly. It also allowed Jarvis to finish the album by reusing the Memphis recording of "Let Me Be There" from 1974. Conspicuously the only time Elvis or Felton resorted to using a previously released cut, it did match the generally good spirits of the LP.

Moody Blue was never going to win any awards on aesthetic conception, yet it was more satisfying than many titles envisioned as a whole. Both the LP and its single probably would have done reasonably well had Elvis' death not made *Moody Blue* one of his best sellers. If not a definitive last masterpiece, *Moody Blue* was Elvis' strongest album in years, serving him well in the months to come and revealing little of the turmoil and problems he was going through in his final years. The original intent was, in all probability, an effort to counteract the gloom hanging over *From Elvis Presley Boulevard*. Instead, circumstances turned *Moody Blue* into a finale—a send-off that, considering the condition he was in, showed Elvis in the best possible light.

36

If You Got a Problem

1975

Elvis' physical decline and depression continued through early 1975, but he seemed far happier after a second visit to the hospital afforded him a chance to recuperate. Physically, Elvis was heavier than before, but this year was smoother than the two preceding it (and obviously the two following it). As to why 1975 was a solid year musically, it's hard to say. Elvis was in the hospital twice, and had to cancel nearly an entire Vegas engagement. In spite of this—or maybe because of it—he seemed to relish being onstage.

Along with those from August 1974, the concerts are categorically the most rock-oriented shows Elvis held in his later years. Going out of his way to perform fairly fresh hits like "The Wonder of You" and "Burning Love," he seemed to have rediscovered his recent catalogue. You aren't getting the groundbreaking live performer of 1954–70, nor are you getting the focused one of 1971–72, but you are hearing Elvis enjoying himself again, and sounding on top of things vocally. *Elvis Today* wasn't his all-time best album, but it was good enough for Elvis to use extensively in his set.

Studio Work

Pleased with what he laid down in 1972, Elvis returned to RCA studios in Hollywood for the March *Today* sessions. Of the ten masters, only "Woman Without Love" was off, and the best show a renewed playfulness. "Shake a Hand" and "Fairytale" really get him engaged, Elvis seeming to live every word of them. He once again proved he was the king of rock and roll with "T-R-O-U-B-L-E," a classic from the get-go. Even many of his harshest latter-day detractors admire this performance.

As trouble-free as the sessions were initially, Elvis had to fight to get the album to sound like he wanted it. After the tracks had been sent to New York for a remix, Elvis was unhappy with the results. He insisted that his songs be mixed in Memphis from now on, and he even threatened to leave RCA for the independent White Whale label.

Compared with Jerry Scheff, Elvis never quite felt his replacement Duke Bardwell fit in. Though Bardwell had played on the session, Elvis asked that the returning Scheff overdub bass on the entire LP, which he did, excepting the "T-R-O-U-B-L-E" 45 that was already being pressed.

Live Performance

After two years of highs and lows, Elvis' concerts of 1975 would prove even. Though his first hospital stay meant that he postponed his usual January Hilton opening until March, he was eager to get back to work. Continuing on the bluesy path of his previous gig, the engagement that opened on March 18th was a worthy run.

Along with a generous selection from the soon-to-be-released *Elvis Today*, he reintroduced more recent hits like "You Don't Have to Say You Love Me" and "Promised Land." A new series of two-piece suits failed to obscure Elvis' elevated weight, but despite his being heavier, his healthy complexion and ebullient disposition alleviated most concerns. The band stayed the same, but for the duration of the run, David Briggs was added on electric piano.

The tour that went from the last week of April to the first week of May was solid, if subdued. Jerry Scheff was back—something fans, the band, and Elvis himself all welcomed. The most important date was on May 5th, when Elvis played a show to aid tornado victims in Jackson, Mississippi, which raised a little over $100,000. The prospect of helping his home state had been the impetus for Elvis to schedule the tour to begin with.

By the time Elvis played his next dates, which ran from late May to the middle of June, he had lost enough weight to be able to wear jumpsuits. The inclusion of the physically demanding "Mystery Train"/"Tiger Man" medley was among the signs that Elvis felt far healthier. On "Mystery Train," Elvis had the orchestra mimic the train horn that had been a feature of Junior Parker's original 1953 recording. Like the previous tour, the concerts took place down South. Numbers like "How Great Thou Art" and "An American Trilogy" weaved a remarkable spell on the crowd. Bringing out the best in the whole troupe, the final show took place in Memphis. It was appropriate that the cover of Elvis' 1976 home-recorded LP *From Elvis Presley Boulevard* was shot during the performance.

Elvis went back out on July 8th, delivering shows that were fairly spectacular. He had gained back some weight, but it didn't seem to slow him down. Elvis' stage attire ranged from the attractive eagle designs to the dreadful Gypsy and Aztec suits. The two shows he held in Uniondale on the 19th were musically as impressive as the Madison Square Garden shows three years before. A big surprise at the matinee was an off-the-cuff gospel medley of "Bosom of Abraham" and "You Better Run." That evening, Elvis sat at the piano and performed a stunning version of his 1968 single "You'll Never Walk Alone."

The remainder of the tour was quite adventurous, with Elvis throwing in some never-recorded personal favorites like "Susie Q" and "Turn Around, Look at Me." The three closing shows in Asheville, North Carolina, saw Elvis dispensing with a formal set-list and singing whatever felt right at the moment instead. Over the three-night engagement, rarities like "Shake a Hand," "Pieces of My Life," "Memphis, Tennessee," "Something," "Wooden Heart," and "Return to

This 1983 film can–shaped boxed set of movie songs oddly used Ed Bonja's classic shot from June 10, 1975. Though indifferently compiled, it is a conceptually impressive package.

Sender" were all aired. "That's All Right" was used as the opener on the final night, an evening where Elvis went so far as to place a request box at the arena's entrance. By pushing himself outside his comfort zone, Elvis had held a tour that musically promised great things for his future.

On a personal level, Elvis' behavior was cause for concern. Before his July 20th evening show in Norfolk, Virginia, Elvis had been told that his risqué comments about Kathy Westmoreland during her intro were bothering her. Though he and Westmoreland hadn't dated in years, Elvis grew jealous when she began seeing one of the band members. In a foul mood already, Elvis insulted her onstage and extended his barbed remarks to the Sweet Inspirations. Kathy, Sylvia Shemwell, and Estelle Brown all walked offstage. Elvis retreated into pills, which made his demeanor even more odd. He gave Sylvia, Myrna Smith, and Estelle a tear-filled apology and some expensive gifts, but Kathy wasn't won over so easily, and she didn't go on the next night.

She came back on the 22nd after an encounter where, she claims, Elvis, with his gun drawn, offered her a gift or a bullet. She thought it was a joke but nervously took the jewelry to make sure. Later that night, Elvis had an argument with his physician, Dr. Nick, and recklessly waved his gun around. As he put his arm around his father, a bullet dislodged, zinged about the room, and finally ended up hitting the doctor in the chest. It was an accident, and the spent bullet didn't hurt Nichopoulos, but it still revealed how careless Elvis could be when under the influence. To be fair, Elvis never did get the chance to give his side of these kinds of stories, and he was giving terrific shows concurrent to this happening. Still, Presley wasn't making life easy for himself, or for those around him.

Enjoying the new excitement it had brought into his set, Elvis continued using the request box when he opened at the Hilton on August 18th. Losing his breath on the flight over, he almost didn't make it to Vegas. It may have been something he took or only a severe panic attack. Nevertheless, it shook everyone up. When he had to cancel the engagement six shows in, nobody around him was terribly surprised, yet the concerts he did perform were as unpredictable as they were engaging.

Film footage shows Elvis tiring quickly but putting a lot of physical effort into his act. As well as bringing back some karate moves, he dons funny glasses and plays with puppets. He was trying altogether too hard to please the crowd at the expense of his health. He went back into the hospital to rest and try to regulate his medicinal intake.

Elvis came back to finish his gig in December. Now giving a more sensible sixteen performances over the two weeks, the request-box format was abandoned in favor of a traditional set. Elvis had gained more weight during his time off, and his eyes over his last twenty months almost always looked tired. But his voice was in tight shape, resonating through the showroom. The increased dexterity of his low range meant demanding numbers like "Just Pretend" and "It's Midnight" were performed with solid poise. Voice had broken up during the time off, but Sherrill Nielsen (who was singing duets with Elvis on songs like "Softly as I Leave You" and "Spanish Eyes") remained. With the bicentennial coming up, Elvis decided he wanted a fresh patriotic song to replace "An American Trilogy." A thunderous "America the Beautiful" would be one of Elvis' focal points over the next year, seldom failing to draw a strong response.

Nineteen seventy-five ended with a stand-alone New Year's Eve show in Pontiac, Michigan, for which 60,000 people—his largest audience ever—withstood ice-cold conditions to see Elvis at the Silverdome stadium. Unfortunately, poor acoustics, a stage setup (with Elvis standing on a rider) that meant he couldn't interact with his band, and the embarrassment of ripping his pants early in the proceedings meant that this was one of his worst shows to date. It didn't help that he changed into the unflatteringly low-cut V-neck suit that revealed his distended and bloated abdomen. It was an unsettling omen of things to come.

Popularity and Impact

Elvis retained his drawing power throughout the year in Vegas, and on the road. Somewhat irrelevant comments about his weight now peppered nearly every review, but the improved quality of the shows was also frequently remarked upon. Elvis' record sales were decent, if unspectacular. His dominance over the country charts stood in sharp contrast to his mild pop success, but it was a reality that Elvis' past continued to outshine his present.

It's a sad reflection on both RCA, and the everyday consumer, that a poorly mastered mid-priced random collection of hits and well-known covers entitled *Pure Gold* (with fake stereo again used to ill effect) generated greater sales than his new albums. Had Elvis made an early music video, or done an occasional TV spot, it's conceivable that his music would have risen higher on the rock charts after 1969. As a country artist, he was scoring big time, but something

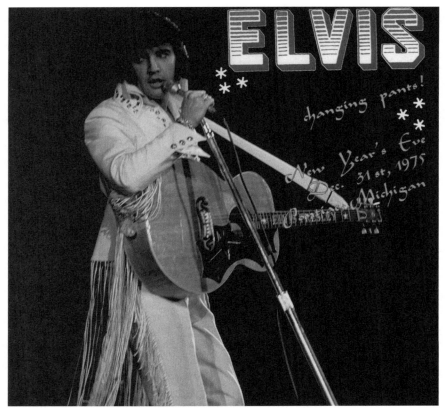

This two-LP bootleg features a stunning photo from November 14, 1970. Conversely, Elvis looked very ill by the time of the New Year's Eve 1975 show it contains. The final 1975 performance marked a new low that would sadly set the standard for most of 1976–77.

like "T-R-O-U-B-L-E" should have permanently put to rest the impression that Elvis had become a boring Vegas crooner.

Further obscuring Elvis' current achievements, Pickwick had bought out RCA Camden and reissued all of its Elvis titles along with a two-LP best-of culled from these albums called *Double Dynamite*. The low price of these items meant they were often carried in department and drug stores and bought by completists, fans on a budget, or those who took no notice of Elvis as a continuing creative force. Though *Double Dynamite* had a shamefully short playing time, it was by mere chance an interesting showcase for some of Elvis' most unfairly neglected singles and movie cuts.

Even though a few were decent, all the budget albums did was clog the market. Because Elvis' new releases were packaged so similarly, they began to fall between the cracks. Presley should have exerted more control on how he was promoted, but he was continually kept in the dark about these albums. After the 1973 buyout, Elvis had unwittingly given up any say on how his older music was presented, and even Parker's influence was now somewhat muted.

Many of the titles coming from RCA in England, Germany, Australia, and Japan were thoughtfully compiled. Not inadvertently, his new records did consistently better in these markets. No matter, in what should have been his biggest market, the American Presley catalogue was getting more confusing with every repackage. These records not only hurt his current image but also caused quality music to appear substandard.

37

Medicine Within Me

The Effects of Drugs on the Music

Undoubtedly, the specter of drugs hangs over Elvis' public image. This is not abnormal for a rock-and-roll star, but what is odd is how much the consensus on his music is now shaped by something that he managed to keep largely quiet until his final months.

That much of Elvis' personal decline comes down to drug use should not blind us to his continued worth as an artist. Since 1977, we have heard literally hundreds of conflicting stories about Elvis' use of, abuse of, and attitude toward drugs. The conflicts haven't been confined to just one person's word against another; many of Elvis' "friends" contradict themselves when trying to sell a new product. The debates and arguments have gone on too long. Few have written about Elvis' drug use without inserting a bias.

I don't profess to be anything more than a fan that has studied and researched Elvis' career closely. However, I have read around 400 books and countless articles on the man. I also have listened to, and watched, nearly every moment of his life that has been unearthed. This is no more than my two cents in an attempt to try to offer perspective and compassion on what I have read, heard, and seen.

I must disclose that it took me a long time to admit to myself that Elvis had a drug problem. As I got older, I realized it was nothing to be ashamed of or to condemn him for. Because it remains such an issue for so many, I decided to offer my views. I hope these are balanced, truthful, and understanding.

Except for what's in his medical records, we don't know exactly how much Elvis ever took. Everything else is opinion and/or hearsay, to some extent or another. That's not to say that some people around Elvis haven't offered honest views, but as a researcher I feel dates and facts are needed to back their stories up.

That's why the existing recordings, photos, and footage play a crucial role in untangling the web of drug stories. That said, there is no way to know exactly how many days he was straight, how many he was a little buzzed, or how many he was really out of it. One must also keep in mind that everything Elvis ever did wrong has been made public, in not always the most sensitive fashion. If that was to happen to any one of us, our lives could easily be sensationalized, or our character made to look bad.

The Fifties

It's doubtful Elvis took anything all that worrisome before the army. His girl-friend Anita Wood noticed that, as early as 1957, Elvis was fascinated by pills. He was well-read on the subject, but what he used didn't seem to be narcotic at the time. Maybe he tried this or that once or twice, or kept a supply of over-the-counter medication, but it certainly wasn't a hugely notable or destructive part of his life. Because of this, his music and performances were in no way affected during this time.

The stories of Dewey Phillips or actor friend Nick Adams getting Elvis hooked have not proved credible. Some have said they think Elvis was loaded on downers during a 1956 television interview with Hy Gardner. In truth, he was just tired, and trying to copy some of his idol James Dean's mannerisms. The pattern of blaming Elvis' various moods and demeanors on drugs starts early, and until his final years it seems pretty unfounded.

In the army, Elvis was first given amphetamine pills for a functional purpose. He mainly used them initially for the purpose of being up when he needed to be. I'm not saying he didn't like it, or that he shouldn't have shown restraint, but they probably seemed harmless at the time. One must remember that in 1958, we knew next to nothing, medically, compared with what is known now. It is also notable that Elvis started to have emotional issues after losing his mom. It's not abnormal to try to cloak the pain.

The Sixties

Although pills seem to have become a crutch by the mid-sixties, they were more a reflection of Elvis' frustration at the work he was doing, as opposed to anything found in the music itself. Yet his personal life was changing as early as 1960, when he made a group of friends he was traveling with turn back home when his pills weren't packed. He was a regular user of various uppers and downers for most of the period, and a serious fall on a hair-dryer cord in early 1967 was the first sign something bad might come of his use.

Some of his friends have said he would sometimes go weeks in the sixties without taking much. It also seems he cut back considerably from mid-1967 to mid-1970. His drug use wasn't healthy, but I don't think it was killing him. Elvis wasn't in a pattern of massive abuse, but he was developing the habit of using drugs when he was emotionally down.

For Elvis, I feel the occasional use of street drugs was not a problem at all. Except for his interest in spiritually, Elvis wasn't really of the sixties generation. He clearly had some sort of hang-up about extensively doing drugs of this sort because of the legality of it, and perhaps he didn't understand that the pills he was taking were far more toxic than soft drugs.

When discussing the trial of Elvis' personal physician Dr. George Nichopoulos, Memphis writer Stanley Booth summed the situation up in a

1982 article, "The King Is Dead: Hang the Doctor": "In spite of Dr. Nick's talk of rewards, the state's firm assumption seemed to be that Presley was, as Geraldo Rivera suggested on *20/20*, 'Just another victim of self-destructive over-indulgence who had followed the melancholy rock and roll tradition of Janis Joplin, Jimi Hendrix, and Jim Morrison.' The idea of Presley following in the tradition of Joplin, Hendrix and Morrison is one that defies chronology, sociology, musical history, and common sense."

Coming into the seventies, we have the greatest era of debate, so I will take a year-by-year look, attempting to piece together the impact drugs really had on Elvis' life and career.

1970

The summer of 1970 seems to be the point where Elvis was using more again, but he was in great shape most of the time. Perhaps the weight he briefly gained during the rehearsals for *That's the Way It Is* showed him not taking quite as good care of himself, but I don't think he was out of it. Maybe one or two shows, or the September session, were affected, but overall I think Jerry Hopkins got it right when he wrote that drugs only had the potential to be a problem in 1970. Elvis' chops were still intact.

This April 1972 photo gives no indication of the decline to follow. It was used as the concert book cover in 1973, by which time some distressing changes had become apparent.

1971

The drug use seems to have gotten worse in 1971, but he wasn't in bad health yet. He was going down the wrong road, but I don't think he was out of it most of the time. He was in pretty good shape, and still seemed somewhat together, but this was the point when the warning signs should have been seen. Maybe the few very close to him saw something wrong, but it was a couple more years before most realized what was happening to him. The shows and the sessions may have been patchier than before (though many were still amazing), but I don't really put it down to drugs yet as much as boredom about his emerging pattern.

1972

This is the point where most say Elvis began to abuse pills, as opposed to using them. Still, he wasn't stoned out of his mind 24/7. I can't see it in the rehearsal footage shot for *Elvis on Tour*, and I agree with the viewpoint that Elvis appeared out of it at the September *Aloha* announcement because he had not had time to rest after his first show. The November press conference does show an Elvis who may be under the influence, but what many base this assumption on should be examined closely. Much of the controversy around the surviving clip is based around Elvis stopping in the middle of a statement and pausing before he can get his thoughts out. Drugs could have played a role in this, but he did the same exact thing on a local Memphis TV show called *Dance Party* in 1956.

Few have said Elvis was at the point to where he needed baby-sitting yet. There were signs he was slowing down a touch, but he was getting older. Elvis' weight had gone up and down since 1961. Now there was a bloat in his face, a sign that something was going on internally. Still, this is his last good year.

1973

This is when most agree that Elvis was first really in danger. What a Las Vegas doctor gave Presley in the guise of "acupuncture" damaged his health for good. It seems the needles he used were dipped in concentrated doses of Demerol that almost killed Elvis in October. Presley's basic knowledge of pharmaceuticals has led to him being called an expert on the subject, but he had long disregarded suggested doses. Now fully in the grip of a major problem, this was only one of several close calls that year.

For the first time, drugs first played a major role in Elvis' creative life, and he was now canceling random shows in Tahoe and Vegas. A handful of performances found him in a very odd mood. It's not that Elvis was falling down disoriented in public, but he did display a lack of control several times. On autopilot during his casino engagements, he did manage to do two highly rated tours away from the stifling environment of Nevada.

The two sessions he held at Stax were the last time Elvis recorded much. It may have taken him longer, but he still seemed willing to work. Some of the problems at the sessions and onstage were medically induced, but he was down mentally for various reasons besides the pills.

At this point, Elvis' personal life still had more effect on what he chose to record than how he sounded. There were a few songs Elvis couldn't rouse

June 23, 1973. Elvis' declining health was beginning to lessen his endurance, but for the time being he still enjoyed the challenge of his tour shows.   *Photo by Erik Lorentzen*

himself to redeem, but the varying quality in the material has been too closely tied to his personal life. That's sad, as some people miss the greatness of the later Elvis simply because he was in a decline. Elvis at this point couldn't do what he did at the turn of the decade, but it's revelatory how good he actually still could be, when his work of this period is taken on its own terms.

1974

The first seven months of this year went by with Elvis seeming to be healthier and stronger. Owing to the fact that he took more time to work on his set than he had for several years, I don't think the controversial summer Vegas stint started off badly at all. Even during the second week, he was doing solid shows musically, looking pretty good, and a fraction of the talking was interesting. If Elvis looked and sounded good, however, he wasn't in a great frame of mind. The "Desert Storm" concert made it clear that Elvis was no longer able to conceal his emotional problems in public.

The fall tour that followed was indicative of a decline, but it wasn't as severe as some make it sound in retrospect. Still, there's no question Elvis had gained weight and seemed ill some nights. No doubt both fans and critics were now noticing something amiss. Drugs played their insidious role, but Elvis appeared burned-out on all fronts.

Elvis' problems went further than what he was taking. He was working too hard, and when he did get ill he wasn't given enough time to get himself together. Despite occasional temper tantrums, Elvis was gradually losing his confidence. He was without a doubt suffering some kind of depression.

It's said that Elvis used cocaine at this point, but he never made it a regular habit. None was found in his autopsy, and Elvis' complex discomfort with street drugs would have made it something he did with some measure of guilt. Yet street drugs were a way to fool himself into thinking that prescriptions were altogether different. He seems to have bought the powder only a handful of times, but he was also being given liquid cocaine. This isn't illegal for a doctor to use, but it sure wasn't meant to be handed out for people to use freely.

1975

One could argue Elvis' last seven years were a fairly consistent period of personal decline, but this doesn't hold fast for him creatively. Nineteen seventy-five wasn't a good year health-wise, but he did manage, for the most part, to get it together live. He made out-of-character comments at times, but most shows were respectable.

Sure, Elvis' weight was getting bad, and he was going in and out of the hospital, but he had rekindled his interest in live performance. It's hard to say what was going on, but maybe he was recuperating as an artist while going down the tubes physically.

1976

This was a terrible year. Some say they can hear a vocal decline as early as 1971, but Elvis' singing remained effective in most cases. Sadly, by 1976 something had audibly happened to Elvis. The initial studio sessions, held in Graceland's "Jungle Room," were bleak, mood-wise, but his singing wasn't bad. He couldn't summon up the power of years past, but the tonality was still acceptable. Worsening breath-control problems can be tied to his excessive weight and ill health, but these problems were highly exacerbated by drug use.

What becomes clear at this point is that Elvis suddenly couldn't cut it live. I'm not saying every show was appalling, but what he told Felton Jarvis and others at the time was true. Elvis Presley was sick of being "ELVIS PRESLEY." He looked bad, and he was unhappy to an extent to where sobriety would only have been the start of the total turnaround he needed.

There was a brief comeback late in the year. Elvis had lost a lot of bulk, and though the shows weren't great by earlier standards, they were a step in the right direction. A short December tour was one of Elvis' most entertaining, post-1972. In fact, one could be forgiven for briefly thinking that things were on the upswing.

1977

Things had gone off the rails, but it would be wrong to say Elvis became a bastard who didn't care about music or his fans. On evidence filmed that year for his CBS special, it seems he wanted to be a decent guy and give his fans a good show. Yes, he failed the latter to some extent, but one must consider that he was now very ill, had a bona fide addiction, and was unhappier than ever. I lean toward the theory of a heart attack being what actually felled him, but he obviously wasn't taking care of his health. Even if Elvis didn't overdose, his misuse of pills led to the state where his heart would stop.

I don't want to make excuses for Elvis, but it would be wrong to think he wanted to die. As in all cases like this, he simply got in over his head. Elvis was the one who ultimately hurt himself, but are the people that gave him drugs—from the army sergeant on down—blameless? Elvis trusted the wrong people initially, and by the time he did have a problem, he knew how to get what he wanted. He then declined because people were all too willing to help him continue to get it.

Though everyone around Elvis claimed later to have been *the* one to have tried to help him, I doubt there were many heroes around. The one thing that every book written by one of Elvis' friends has in common is that it wasn't "their" fault. To be blunt, the lure of getting associative fame and monetary gain blinded most that were supposed to be helping the man. Today, we can learn from Elvis' mistakes, but when possible they should be kept separate from the music.

38

I Can Roll, but I Just Can't Rock

1976

Nineteen seventy-six is often agreed to be the point where Elvis' decline really started to affect him. His weight shot to an all-time high, most of it stemming from an unhealthy bloat he attained as his body began to break down. He worked very hard, but the unevenness of the last three years had now reached a point where the bad moments weren't evenly matched by the good ones. With a total of ten tours, two casino engagements, and two sets of recording sessions this year, one couldn't complain that Elvis wasn't prolific. What did rankle was the quality of much of this work, especially onstage.

The year ended on a high note, with Elvis seeming to pull out of his continued funk, but it would prove to be a temporary respite. As far as development, Elvis continued to give longer shows, but they didn't differ much from his 1975 sets. This was rectified to some extent on his last tour of the year, but overall, the only thing that sets the 1976 concerts apart from the 1975 shows is that Elvis didn't perform them nearly as well. While Elvis' studio recordings didn't deteriorate as severely, they also revealed a lot about the state of his emotional and physical health.

Studio Work

During the mid-seventies, Elvis was becoming less inclined to go into the recording studio. After the upset over the *Today* LP, Elvis wanted more control over the sound of his recordings. It also can't be denied that he got lazier as his health continued to decline. So it was an unusual blend of ennui and perfectionism that dictated that all of Elvis' sessions this year were to be recorded at Graceland, using RCA's mobile recording studio.

The initial Graceland session from February was mostly downbeat, but Elvis was in much better voice than he would be for his upcoming live shows. *From Elvis Presley Boulevard* documents his inner search and sudden loss of the ability to handle the pressure cooker of superstardom. Still trying to understand why he was "Elvis Presley," he doesn't seem to come to any conclusions. One break from the gloom was the splendid "For the Heart." This is the closest Elvis got to rockabilly in his final years, and he obviously still had the touch.

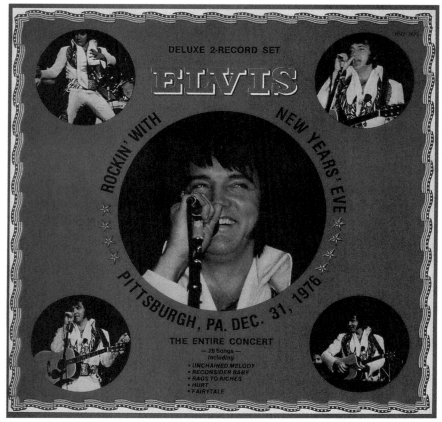

One of the best Elvis record covers of all time appeared on this 1977 boot. The photos and recordings featured Elvis on a brief upturn—destined to be his last.

The second session in October was much more upbeat, and Elvis sounded relaxed. Onstage, he was stagnating, but in the studio he was still cutting fresh, interesting material. All the songs he did here had quality, but "Way Down" was the standout. It's real rock and roll, but a modern take on it. This and the other three songs cut at what would prove to be his final recording date all helped make up the studio half of his 1977 release *Moody Blue*.

Live Performance

Elvis was pretty pedestrian for most of the year. The problem wasn't the music itself but his lack of stamina, and the sickly quality of his voice. It's kind of an unappealing nasal sound that's fairly shocking, coming from a singer who was in a league of his own for almost his entire career. Elvis was going out too often, playing short tours in generally small cities. Considering the toll such a heavy workload would take on any individual, it is perhaps surprising that the year ended far better than it began. Before getting a full month off, Elvis went on the road in March, April, May into June, June into July, July into August, and August into September, and between April 30th and May 9th he also managed to squeeze in a fifteen-show Sahara Tahoe engagement. Is it any wonder that the excitement of touring began to wear off, or that the tours now rarely differentiated from each other?

The March concerts were reasonable. Elvis had a solid three months off to recharge his batteries, and some fresh blood playing behind him. Shane Keister replaced Glen D. Hardin on piano, Larrie Londin took over from Ronnie Tutt on drums, and David Briggs (who had played the Pontiac show) was made a full-time band member. Two of the three new members didn't last, and in the case of Londin this was a particularly unfortunate loss. Tutt had agreed to return in April, and did an exemplary job, but Larrie was a genuine fan that seemed to give Elvis' spirits a much-needed boost. In April, Keister was replaced by former Voice member Tony Brown, who undeniably had an advantage due to his familiarity with the material.

Elvis seldom did a show that didn't have at least a few decent performances, but he had become chronically out of shape, and he was clearly worn out on several occasions. Settling on two nearly identical suits designed especially for the bicentennial, by the third tour of the year he had even stopped rotating outfits. Opposite to the situation back in 1973, the only time he seemed to work hard was in Tahoe. The shows were longer, had a higher quotient of scarce material, and were overall solid entertainment.

On average or decent nights, Elvis could still please the crowd on the strength of his charisma. More discerning fans mostly objected to his uncharacteristic reluctance to try out new material. "Hurt" was the exception to the rule, giving Elvis the chance to display an incredible operatic-styled bellow. The months passed somewhat uneventfully, with a standout show being his final appearance in Memphis on July 5th. In good spirits, Elvis even played a couple of songs on acoustic guitar.

More overweight than ever, there's no arguing that Elvis looked very ill. Perhaps it's the very unflattering bangs and chin-wide sideburns that made him look worse, but even in 1977, Elvis often looked better than he did during the bicentennial summer.

After his brief break, Elvis went back on tour in October. On the first show, held on the 14th in Chicago, he looked slimmer than he had for two years. The lack of bulk seemed to infuse him with his old fire. He literally worked himself sick, as his karate instructor/bodyguard Ed Parker was to find out all too well on the way back to the Arlington Heights Hilton, when Elvis vomited on him. The set and vocals were still an issue, but Elvis' improved effort and state of mind meant that his presentation became more impressive.

If anything, his short West Coast gig in late November was even better, and he maintained the pace when he started his last Vegas stint on December 2nd.

Sadly, his time at the Hilton was marred by some unfortunate circumstances. Firstly, Elvis badly twisted his ankle on the 5th, and when he refused to cancel the subsequent shows he required heavy painkillers to go on. He was doing solid shows again by the 10th, and his professionalism was astounding, considering that his father, Vernon, had had a mild heart attack earlier that day.

This was Elvis' last casino engagement. While the final Vegas gig may not have been as dull as those he held in 1973, after the first few days he wasn't on fire, either. He was notably better than he had been during the summer, but he seemed to have low energy, often standing stock-still. He now openly berated Las Vegas onstage, and was by all accounts sick to death of playing there. Still, it can't be said that he didn't try to do a good set when he was up for it. There was an acoustic part of the show, where he would laugh and joke around with Charlie Hodge on a politically incorrect version of "Are You Lonesome Tonight?" Sometimes he even played "That's All Right" or "Reconsider Baby." Along with the piano piece that Elvis implemented on his next tour, the guitar segment was the best part of his later shows. However, he only did these sections when he was inspired—and that wasn't often enough.

From October on, Elvis was able to resume his normal practice of wearing multiple jumpsuits during a tour. Due to his weight loss, he was even able to use a few that were designed all the way back in 1974. Though the last two months were encouraging at times, nothing could have prepared anyone for the impressive five-date tour at the end of December. With a wide range, admirable projection, booming volume, and good pitch, his voice sounded as good as it ever did in his last four to five years. The movements were still toned down, but the performances were visual, climaxing in a theatrical fall backward at the end of "Hurt." As was always the case when he was motivated, Elvis dusted off a number of rare songs, including "For the Good Times," "The First Time Ever I Saw Your Face," and "Such a Night."

The New Year's Eve show in Pittsburgh effortlessly stands up to any concert he did from 1973 on. He was in a terrific mood, belting out "Big Boss Man" with an intensity that blew away all the recent bad memories. Elongating his piano segment, he managed a one-time-only, vocally stellar airing of "Rags to Riches." The group didn't really know the song, but it was still engaging in its spontaneity.

The other song Elvis did at the piano was something a little bit special. Performed every night on this tour, and on some of the better shows the following year, "Unchained Melody" presented Elvis nakedly singing his heart out over his own basic accompaniment, with minimal input by the band. For the people who attended the shows on this tour, it must have been wonderful to see a consummate stage performer rediscovering his gift.

Counting down the New Year with the crowd, for a moment it seemed that the old Elvis was back. This did not prove to be true, but for one glorious evening, Elvis must have thought that 1977 would be a great year. Being the last show Elvis did without an attendant sense of foreboding, it was the end of an era. All too soon, the memories of those that had rung in the New Year with Elvis would become inexorably poignant.

Popularity and Impact

Despite the mediocre shows outnumbering the good, Elvis being a personification of America for so many meant that his run of success on the concert circuit continued. True, he now was playing a greater number of small towns, but this was partly dictated by where his audience now stemmed from.

If the country charts were the only place in the U.S. where Elvis continued to make an impression with his new material, his records were doing incredibly well in that market. Outside of *Raised on Rock* (which probably missed due to the title and comparative lack of country material), every album Elvis released after *Aloha* did markedly better in the country field. He had long ago adopted the ten-track lineup common to the country LPs of that era, and unlike many rock artists, he released more than one album a year.

Even his reissues seemed to connect with country radio. Along with a nicely selected second volume of the *Legendary Performer* series came the first American release of all his Sun sides in one package. Going all the way to #2 country, it was sad that the rock market didn't take to it with the same dedication.

39

It's Different Now

Covering the King

T he first Elvis Presley cover song was a slightly countrified version of "That's All Right" by none other than Marty Robbins. It's amazing today to think how influential Elvis was going all the way back to 1954, and since then numerous artists have covered items from Elvis Presley's catalogue. While the majority of these covers pale against the originals, some of Presley's more creative colleagues found something of their own in his songs.

The following are five of Elvis' contemporaries who were inspired by his lead. Some only did a few of his songs, and some continually peppered their catalogues with Presley hits, but what they all have in common is that none of them copied Elvis. Instead, they took the foundation of what Elvis laid down and built something of their own out of it.

Jerry Lee Lewis

Of any major artist with a style distinct from Presley's, Jerry Lee Lewis has likely recorded more Elvis songs than anyone else. Being on Sun may have helped bring this about, but Jerry Lee has expressed more admiration for Elvis than he has for other artists of the same era. Of course, he has at times been dismissive of Elvis, too, but that's the way Jerry Lee talks about anyone he ever considered a true competitor. He has long cited "Don't Be Cruel" as one of his favorite records, and he included it as the first track on his self-titled debut LP in 1958. He again made it the opener for his 1972 return to rock and roll, *The Killer Rocks On.*

Jerry Lee began recording Elvis songs almost as soon as he started. Sometime early into his first year on Sun (roughly anytime from late fall 1956 to the early summer of 1957), he cut Elvis' "I Love You Because" and "I Forgot to Remember to Forget" in elemental versions that differed mainly in the use of the piano as the lead instrument. Jerry Lee re-cut more polished and distinct Nashville-styled versions of both in 1961, but these early recordings show Elvis to be a formative influence.

The first Elvis record he truly made his own (and the first to actually be released) was his cover of "Mean Woman Blues" for his 1957 EP *The Great Ball of Fire.* In what was always the Jerry Lee tradition, Lewis made it barely recognizable to the original. All but rewriting it from scratch, he changed lyrics freely, put in his own fills, and made it more dangerous-sounding than Elvis already had. In short, it was a rock-and-roll classic, and it was this version upon which Roy Orbison built his hit 1963 cover.

The same early-1958 session where his sly version of "Don't Be Cruel" was cut also found Jerry Lee doing three other Elvis tunes that went unreleased for many years. It was one of Lewis' all-time best recording dates, and he transforms each song into hard, fast boogie woogie. "Hound Dog" is a speedy run-through that owes a little lyrically to Big Mama Thornton's version, but is otherwise pure rock-and-roll adrenalin.

"Jailhouse Rock" was a great vehicle for Lewis, which Elvis himself mentioned while gloating about getting it first to his friend George Klein. This rendition easily could have become the hit, as it was positively unhinged in its sheer vibrancy. It isn't any better than Elvis', but it doesn't take a back seat, either.

"Good Rockin' Tonight" isn't any less of a revelation, with Lewis taking two piano solos and incorporating "Whole Lotta Shakin'" into his middle eight. Again, it can't be said that he topped Elvis, but it's easy to see why Presley thought Lewis was going to replace him when he first was inducted into the army. In terms of raw talent and dynamism, Jerry Lee was Elvis' only serious competition.

Lewis had his ups and downs professionally, if not creatively, from the late fifties to the late sixties. In 1968, he made his comeback on vinyl as a country artist, but onstage he didn't change much, and he began to play for rock-and-roll revival crowds. One of the biggest rock-and-roll festivals took place in Toronto on September 13, 1969. John Lennon's performance is the most famous from that day, but due to lack of rehearsals, and his wife Yoko Ono's ugly screaming throughout the whole set, he paled against the fifties legends still young enough to perform with abandon.

Jerry Lee's set was basically an all-out Elvis tribute, which can be attributed to three things. First, his comparatively mellow country hits wouldn't have gone down in this setting. Second, with Chuck Berry and Little Richard on the bill, Jerry Lee wasn't going to do covers of their songs. Finally, he had seen Elvis perform a red-hot set during Presley's initial International Hotel engagement, and probably felt challenged to outdo it. It can't be said Jerry Lee eclipsed Elvis, but he damn sure gave him a run for his money.

Scorching versions of "Jailhouse Rock," "Hound Dog," "Don't Be Cruel," and "Mean Woman Blues" showed Lewis retaining a love of pure rock and roll in a way that Elvis would only match through early 1970. He also delivered a surprise by picking up the guitar and playing a version of "Mystery Train" that left the audience (in the words of his 1958 hit) "Breathless." Rock and roll had changed a lot by 1969, but Presley and Lewis were at that point still the best two performers of it as it was originally conceived.

By the mid-seventies, Jerry Lee had merged his country and rock personas on record, and one of his country hits came in early 1974 with a cover of "I'm Left, You're Right, She's Gone." Stan Kesler had been one of the co-writers,

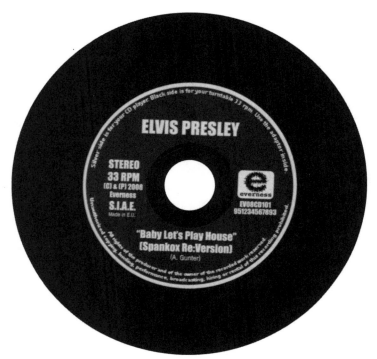

Remixing old Elvis songs is a modern way to "cover" him. This is in the curio category, being a CD on one side and vinyl on the other.

and as he was the producer of Jerry Lee's 1973 country sessions, it seemed to be a natural choice. Jerry Lee gives it the same playfulness that Presley had, but the sound is far more produced, this being 1973 Nashville as opposed to 1955 Memphis. Nonetheless, Jerry's playing and singing recalls the spirit of his and Elvis' early recordings, while at the same time the final product would fit seamlessly into the country radio of the period.

The last notable Elvis cover by Jerry Lee was cut during late 1975. "I Can Help" was a hit for its writer Billy Swan in 1974, but Jerry Lee's version is a bit looser, managing to be hard country yet still rocking. Though markedly different, it's closer in spirit to Elvis' recent version than Swan's. Jerry Lee tried it in two different tempos, and the slower version confirms that Presley's recording inspired him with his ad-lib, "Think about it, Elvis."

The misguided Killer (who in the mid-seventies was in as bad a way personally as Presley) actually did try to help Elvis the next year, but was arrested upon arrival to Graceland as he was drunk. It didn't help that, when asked by the guard about the gun he made visible on his dashboard—something he legally had to do when driving in Memphis—he flippantly replied he was going to shoot Elvis. Lewis claims to this day he was invited that evening, but his drinking (and his mouth) got him in trouble again.

The Beatles

The Beatles are the only band that ever equaled the fame of Elvis Presley. They were to the sixties what Elvis was to the fifties, and their catalogue remains one of rock and roll's finest. They cited their love for Elvis' early music on repeated occasions, and early in their career many of his songs graced their sets. With the influence of Elvis upon their first recorded composition ("In Spite of All the Danger") discussed elsewhere, let's jump ahead a few years to when the Beatles were regularly performing on BBC radio.

At the time, there were restrictions on "needle time" on English radio, due to the thought that it would reduce the number of jobs available for working musicians. From 1962 to 1965, the Beatles regularly made appearances on the BBC, and, as well as promoting their current records, they often took the opportunity to perform their favorite rock-and-roll and pop standards from their pre-fame act. Naturally, there was a fair share of Elvis covers among them, and if these aren't radical reinterpretations for the most part, they do provide a chance to directly hear how Presley influenced his most accomplished protégés.

Three out of the four BBC Elvis covers were performed on the Beatles' own 1963 radio show, *Pop Go the Beatles*. Of these, the most revamped was "I'm Gonna Sit Right Down and Cry (Over You)." Referring to the alternate U.K. release, Lennon once cited Elvis' first album among the most influential he ever heard. "I'm Gonna Sit Right Down and Cry (Over You)" was among the songs appearing on both versions, and it had been in the Beatles' set for quite some time. With Lennon dominating and McCartney in harmony, they turned it into a prime example of the Liverpool sound of the early sixties.

More in line with the American sound of the mid-fifties was their take on "That's All Right," also included on Elvis' debut U.K. LP, *Rock 'n' Roll.* Paul takes the lead and does a more than credible job of emulating Elvis. The whole band cooks, with George seeming to particularly enjoy playing the already-classic riffs. This could be called one of the Beatles' most basic covers, but it's all the better for it.

Though many of the U.K. bands of the period wouldn't have dared do Elvis' arrangement over Ray Charles', the Beatles' version of "I Got a Woman" proved they weren't at all self-conscious about their love of early rock and roll. Sounding like you better not question what he was putting across, John sang a tough lead in his lowest register. It's a fantastic rendition, and one that he equaled the next year, when they again performed the song on the radio program *Saturday Club*. What again makes the biggest impression is the Beatles' willingness to cut through the London R&B elitism and proudly carry on the rock-and-roll tradition. This was yet another song included on the *Rock 'n' Roll* album.

George Harrison was always the most keen to perform country-styled Sun covers, and his lead on "I Forgot to Remember to Forget" has a winningly earnest combination of Liverpudlian and Southern twangs. This 1964 rendition comes from an episode of the Beatles' second BBC radio series, *From Us to You.*

At a time when the Beatles were doing more of their own releases on the air, this well-chosen Elvis cover was a welcome change of pace.

James Brown

Of all of the black entertainers who came up in the fifties, James Brown was Elvis' biggest booster. Unlike those who claimed Elvis stole or copied his style, Brown always felt a kinship with a man he saw as simply another poor Southerner made good. James often made a point of defending Elvis against the rumor that he was a racist, and he spoke warmly on numerous occasions about a visit where they sang gospel together at the piano.

With his career and personal life in decline, James was hit very hard by Elvis' death. Feeling like he had to express his emotions over the loss he felt, Brown cut a version of "Love Me Tender" that is truly from the heart. It opens with a spoken section that is brief but well expressed. James' work at the time was somewhat glitzy, and this isn't an exception, but the vocal is soulful and nicely measured. The new rhythmic pattern underneath it has a vague fifties feel, yet it was still informed by Elvis' own creativity. It was a very nice gesture, and for some a revelatory one as well.

Bob Dylan

Being that he is a disciple of American music, it is no surprise that Bob Dylan is a Presley fan. Dylan was a teenager when Elvis was at his height, and in 1970 he wrote a song called "Went to See the Gypsy" about what he says was a fictional meeting with him. Most of Bob's Elvis covers either were put out without his consent on the *Dylan* LP that Columbia Records issued when he briefly left the label or appear on bootlegs. Despite that, the following are fairly easy to get, and are worthy of comment.

Dylan was a rock-and-roll fan from the start, but when he first turned professional in 1961 he was marketed strictly as a folk singer. He was a bit cagey about his love of rock and roll at first, because most of his audience and fellow folkies had a snobbery toward it. Still, his first single in 1962 was the rockabilly-infused "Mixed Up Confusion," which owed a lot to the sound of Sun Records. After it made no impact, Bob waited a few years before he tried to rock again, but an out-take from the session yielded a fine cover of "That's All Right" that made even clearer how much Bob loved the early Presley style. Of course, Dylan never could be the type of vocalist Presley was, but until heavy smoking took its toll, his delivery was artful, if not traditionally pretty.

In 1969, Dylan quit smoking for a period and his voice changed considerably. Most of his music over the next year or so was in the country-rock style that was a modern outgrowth of rockabilly. Though younger West Coast–based protagonists like the Byrds went a more traditionalist route, the acceptance of country in the rock community helped reinvigorate the careers of countless Southern artists. Johnny Cash was an early admirer of Dylan's, and during the *Nashville Skyline* sessions they loosely recorded roughly an album worth of duets. Only one track was used, but the out-takes found Bob once again pulling out "That's All Right." Johnny and Bob's duet was slipshod, but it rocked along nicely.

"Blue Moon" may not be best known as an Elvis song, but Dylan was familiar with the version included on the first Elvis album. Included on Dylan's 1970 *Self Portrait* LP, with Bob's voice in its smoothest croon, Elvis does come to mind. The arrangement isn't so sparse, being overtly country in feel, and it's not exactly Dylan's finest moment, but his attempt to sound like Presley is curiously intriguing.

What would have been a better choice for *Self Portrait* ultimately came out on the 1973 *Dylan* compilation. A minor hit single, Dylan's run-through of "A Fool Such as I" was a fun romp. Though it had also been a hit for a number of other people, this time the Elvis influence is even more pronounced. Bob again sings it in his smooth country voice, albeit with a liberal dose of Presley phrasing thrown in. Dylan rarely sounded like he was having so much fun on record, and it's a classic example of what updated rockabilly sounded like, circa 1969.

Much less worthy is a 1970 *New Morning* out-take, also included on *Dylan*, of "Can't Help Falling in Love." Bob uses his more everyday nasal voice and plays a very wheezy harmonica. It sure is different than Elvis' version, but most notably by not being all that good.

Willie Nelson

Of all the artists mentioned here, Willie Nelson was the least directly influenced by Presley. Willie was a few years older than Elvis, and most of his most overt roots were strictly country. Still, one could not be on the same label for so many years, working with some of the same musicians, producers, and arrangers, and not have something rub off. Nelson didn't directly cover Presley until after Elvis' death, and even then he showed no trace of him in his delivery. The originality Willie infused them with is probably why these two selections were among the most successful and memorable of all Presley covers.

In 1979, Willie was at the peak of his career. While his very best days as a recording artist arguably ended upon his rise to superstardom, his version of "Heartbreak Hotel," sung in duet with Leon Russell, had a good-time atmosphere. Sounding far more like something out the Hank Williams songbook, the singers trade off exuberant leads over a full fiddle section. It's not very serious, but it's so different than what Elvis did that it works wonderfully. Though it didn't cross over too strongly, Nelson and Russell took the song all the way to the top of the country charts.

"Always on My Mind" was a flip side for Elvis in the U.S., but even so it managed to climb to Top 20 country. In England, it was promoted as the top side, and was a big hit at #9. In 1981, footage of Elvis recording an alternate during a mock session was one of the key scenes in the documentary *This Is Elvis*. RCA missed a chance to reissue the song on 45 to promote the film, and in 1982 it was Willie Nelson who took it to #5 pop and #1 country. It was one of his very biggest sellers and won him a Grammy, with the song's writers—Mark James, Johnny Christopher, and Wayne Carson—scoring another two themselves.

Though the tempo and general mood of regret are similar, Willie's "Always on My Mind" is different than Elvis' in execution. Nelson was a lot older than Presley when he recorded it, so it lacks the command that Willie would have given it in years past. Yet being at a different stage of his life transformed the ballad from an emotional plea to something more like quiet resignation. Elvis sounded utterly devastated in his recording, yet there was still a feeling that if he tried hard enough, maybe he could rekindle the romance. Willie sounds no less passionate, but there is an air of self-realization that it was too late in the day to mend fences. Both versions are definitive.

40

Alone, Lonely Times

1977

While I wouldn't go so far as to say Elvis went out with a whimper instead of a bang, the last seven months of his life may be the only lengthy period where Elvis couldn't deliver one consistent performance. There were selected highlights at nearly every show, but not one of his concerts as a whole was what you could call classic. Essentially using the same format as his last tour of 1976, the set didn't evolve much over this time.

Despite these drawbacks, the year still deserves a close look, if only because the worst aspects of it have been over-emphasized so biographers can make a point about this being "The Final Curtain." By reading a majority of the articles and books on Presley covering this era, one would think Elvis was nothing but miserable, on- and offstage, unable to talk or sing with any coherence. As much as was going wrong with Presley, even a cursory glance at actual documentation of the period shows that this has been grossly exaggerated.

Studio Work

Elvis didn't record this year, but he attempted to. Outside of one or two attempts at Graceland, where Elvis ended up just talking to his musicians, the last formal studio session was going to be held in January. According to press reports and recollections, Elvis flew to Nashville with the aim of recording for the first time at the Creative Workshop studios, but on arrival he never left the hotel. This was attributed variously to illness and/or an argument with his girlfriend Ginger Alden. Even the owner of the studio, Buzz Cason, has publicly stated that Elvis didn't show up. However, according to songwriter/musician Alan Rush, this wasn't the case. Rush was sitting in the control room with percussionist Randy Cullers when Elvis walked in. Elvis did not like the size of the room, feeling it was too small, and he was also upset that an old pizza box had been left around. In order to not bring about any bad publicity for the studio, it was decided to tell the press that Elvis just wasn't up to recording.

Elvis may not have been happy about recording (or with Ginger) that day, but it makes sense that it would be the studio itself that was the problem. None of this is meant as a knock at the Creative Workshop, as a lot of artists cut quality music there. Elvis was simply booked somewhere unfamiliar that made a bad first impression. Had he given it a chance, it very well may have met his technical standards. It seems like it goes along with his state of mind at the time in that something he may have tried to overcome previously no longer seemed worth the effort. Still, it was kind of him to take the blame, so to speak, and not publicly criticize the place.

Since the fifties, Elvis had liked to record in a certain environment, and if he wasn't comfortable, he made it known—as with the soundstage sessions for *G.I. Blues* and *Loving You*. Historically, it's fairly important to know that Elvis was at least willing to check out the venue and see if it was to his liking. As it was his last visit to a studio (however brief), it does close the story of his recording career with a little more poignancy than having him just sitting depressed in his hotel room.

Live Performance

By the time Elvis was back on the road, in February, he looked terrible. Though he would improve during the tour, he never looked healthy again. Although it's faint praise, the five tours held between February and June found Elvis in better voice and somewhat better condition than he had been during the previous spring and summer. There were certain nights when Elvis was too ill to perform to even his reduced standards; the March tour had to be terminated several days early when he was felled by sheer exhaustion. Further problems occurred when the return of his intestinal issues meant that Elvis had to temporarily vacate the stage twice in May.

There's no doubt the off nights are sad, even though the gothic tragedy element has, at times, been placed out of proportion. Elvis was overweight, and the tight jumpsuits accentuated that fact, but he was not the blown-up caricature of tired legend. Though he was retaining water, it was mainly his face that reflected how seriously ill he was.

Proving he could still sing the hell out of a song that caught his interest, one of the best moments came on February 16th in Montgomery, Alabama, when he took to the piano for a stunning rendition of "Where No One Stands Alone." The band continued to provide able backing, the only major change occurring in March, when Bobby Ogdin replaced David Briggs.

Vocally, Elvis seemed breathless at times, but that doesn't mean he wasn't impressive tonally. With the exception of the final 1976 tour, vocals of top quality rarely lasted through an entire concert after 1975. Yet there was something of a recovery from 1976, because his voice itself shows less weakness on average. The really poor shows are close to his worst, but most of 1976 is less satisfying.

One can enjoy selected 1977 shows on some level because Elvis still possessed a unique talent. He did have a little fun here and there in the last year, and you can enjoy that for what it is. Still, when you go back to the early seventies, it was a different guy. Many have judged him, but how many people could be "ELVIS" and not have it affect them? Still, who doesn't wish he had been able to turn it around? Even if that meant putting his career on hold for an indefinite amount of time, fans would have understood and supported him. If nothing else, Elvis continued to be loved and successful. Sadly, his wild spending and insensitive management meant the much-needed break would never happen.

The Book

Elvis' last days can't be discussed without mentioning what became known as "the bodyguard book." In July 1976, Elvis' father fired longtime friends Red and Sonny West, partly due to the part they played in the 1974 fight in Tahoe (as well as a few other scuffles), plus a more recent employee named Dave Hebler. They claimed that they were let go because Elvis didn't like their complaining about his drug use.

While Red may have been close enough to Elvis to say something, it seems highly doubtful that Sonny or Dave would have. This is especially unlikely when one considers that Sonny was arrested for cocaine dealing in 1981. Sonny had also pressured Elvis into providing plane tickets for his wife to join the June 1976 tour. It wasn't something Elvis would normally be against, but perhaps in this case he just felt as if he was being used.

Elvis would surely have rehired Sonny and Red at least, but a chagrined Dave and the Wests hooked up with tabloid journalist Steve Dunleavy to write the book *Elvis: What Happened?* Subsequently, they would admit that Dunleavy wrote it in a way that made Elvis look like the worst person possible. However, considering his tabloid credentials, that couldn't have been any surprise. Admitting there was bitterness involved, they also stated that they hoped it would get Elvis off the pills, because he always responded to a challenge. Still, they had to have realized how hurt Elvis was that they even wrote a book—plus he naturally didn't want Lisa Marie or his fans reading a skewed account of his private life.

Still, the bottom line was that Elvis did have a drug problem, and the book did tell a decidedly distorted version of the truth. While the comments about Elvis being anti-Semitic and racist were strictly fiction, the rest of the stories did happen. They were told one-sidedly, and mostly without compassion, but they were based on the truth. For Elvis, who vacillated between severe rage and severe depression, the publication of the book only two weeks before his death put a cloud over him that wouldn't go away. Yes, there was a degree of love in the Wests' and Hebler's words, but Dunleavy even attributed much of Elvis' musical success to Red. As good a songwriter as he was, Red only wrote two of Elvis' hits, and not until well after Elvis' rise to fame.

Even more personal than the drug stories were some very private details about Elvis' marriage that no real friend would have thought to make public. To be fair, Priscilla later spoke of these things herself, and Red and Sonny were far kinder to Elvis than most who followed in their "journalistic" path after Presley's death. Also, one should remember that, if Elvis hadn't died, he would have been able to answer each and every one of their claims himself. Still, even though Presley could be thoughtless, the book by all accounts made him feel more isolated than ever during his final days.

Popularity and Impact

For all his problems, Elvis managed to be placed at #1 on the *Billboard* magazine year-end listing of top concert attractions of 1977. Even before Elvis' still-controversial death on August 16th, his records were selling decently and charting high in the country listings. The critics gave their knocks more viciously than ever, but Elvis' final single ("Way Down") and album (*Moody Blue*) were of sufficient enough quality to end his years as a record maker with some style. Of course, after his death, his records sold in the millions, giving Elvis the kind of

This boxed set was one of the many reissues quickly put together after Elvis' death. This ad attempts to pitch the release as an upmarket summary of his career.

market saturation he hadn't enjoyed since the advent of the Beatles. It is often the case that it isn't until death that people fully appreciate an artist. Even taking into account how loved Elvis was in his lifetime, no one could have guessed at the icon he would become.

Moody Blue and the *Elvis in Concert* soundtrack both made the Top 5. This would not have happened had Elvis lived, but because of his death they are still among the best-known albums he ever did. Not so popular was the *Welcome to My World* compilation. It was a fairly sloppy spring-1977 release aimed for the country market, doing well there when it came out and even better when Elvis passed away. It didn't have a chance of crossing over, but collectors had to pick it up for a few new edits and an unreleased live recording of "I Can't Stop Loving You" from the matinee June 10, 1972, Madison Square Garden show.

Like most of the posthumous albums to follow over the next seven years, *Welcome to My World* barely rose above the level of the Camden or Pickwick titles. It would take the better efforts of Joan Deary, Gregg Geller, and finally Ernst Jorgensen to put things right. Yet Elvis Presley's original catalogue should never be forgotten, and it is mainly this that his legacy should finally be judged upon.

41

You Don't Have to Face the Crowd

The CBS Special

T wo shows from Elvis' final tour in June were filmed for a new television special for CBS. The first show was mediocre, with only a few moments of radiance, but the second had many moments that show that Elvis the artist was still able to surface from time to time. In some ways, he put more of himself into what was to be known as *Elvis in Concert* than he had for *Aloha*. He seemed less distant, more emotionally invested. Of course he had declined physically, and in some ways musically, but at the same time the 1977 footage is more riveting. Even though he's not able to put on a show close to what he had during his peak years, you root for him, and he does come to life during certain segments.

Yet even bestowing this show with mild praise has been the catalyst for the most severe online arguments between one side that can't bear to see Elvis so sick and burned-out, and another side that can find some redeeming qualities in the broadcast. Both sides have good points, but both tend to get a bit extreme in their condemnation or praise. Like most things that are divisive, the truth lies somewhere in the middle.

June 19, 1977—Omaha, Nebraska

This was the first show the CBS crew filmed, and if it wasn't the worst show Elvis ever did, it comes uncomfortably close. Elvis didn't want to do the special, and even the Colonel was concerned about whether his client was up for it. However, with Elvis showing no sign of slowing down his spending, and Parker showing no sign of slowing down his gambling, they both were swayed by a generous monetary offer. There were only a few highlights this particular evening. Elvis had trouble talking, and only one song had a vocal that showed him off at his best. The song was "How Great Thou Art," on which he somehow managed to make every word ring clear and strong. The purity of his intonation as the notes are stretched out at the climax constitutes some of the most powerful vocalizing Elvis ever did.

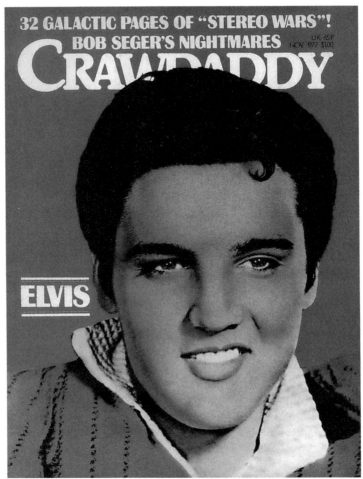

32 GALACTIC PAGES OF "STEREO WARS"!
BOB SEGER'S NIGHTMARES   NOV. 1977 $1.00   U.K. 65P

CRAWDADDY

ELVIS

In the last few years of his life, Elvis' appearance suffered. Most magazines that covered Elvis' death chose to remember the performer of twenty years before.

Other than the otherwise professionally undocumented tracks "And I Love You So" and "Fairytale," the only flashes of interest come during the introductions. The lengthy intros and band solos that were part of Elvis' show over his last three years have come in for a lot of criticism by those who have grown bored of hearing them. What is forgotten is that Elvis never intended his tours to be heard in full by the same audiences night after night. Taken in the proper context, they are actually quite interesting because of the unusual repartee Elvis and the band shared.

"Johnny B. Goode" was fun as James Burton plays lead guitar behind his head, and "Early Morning Rain," featuring John Wilkinson on acoustic guitar, was always nicely done, with close harmonies from Charlie and the Stamps. A special personal moment occurred during Elvis' intro of J. D. Sumner. As Elvis discloses how much J. D. meant to him as a youth, one cannot help but be moved by his humble display of authentic love and gratitude. He may not have been in good health, but the reports of Elvis losing his humanity or forgetting where he came from are demonstrably false.

June 21, 1977—Rapid City, South Dakota

The extent of Elvis' continued congeniality and basic kindness is made clear by footage filmed backstage at the second shoot. Presented with an award from the Sioux nation by the young Monique Brave, Elvis was gracious and genuinely moved by the gesture. Though he was dreadfully anxious about being filmed that night, that Elvis took the time to meet with this child showed a lot of character.

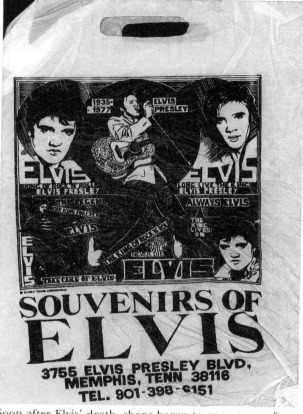

Soon after Elvis' death, shops began to open across from Graceland. This bag from a 1985 record purchase reflects the era before they were required to be "official."

Looking a bit less bloated, and with his hair properly styled, onstage that evening Elvis gave a far more lively show. Despite a quick pause to do over a line, "See See Rider" has him in solid voice, turning in a more committed version than had been heard for many a year. The highlight for rock-and-roll fans was a sly "That's All Right." Elvis has a great time with the song, providing stinging vocals and some rough-and-ready acoustic guitar.

Elvis' humor came through clearly on "Are You Lonesome Tonight?" Those who hadn't seen him perform it before have particularly misunderstood this performance as being from someone who is too stoned to remember his lines. In truth, the narration section of the song was something Elvis rarely took seriously in concerts going all the way back to 1961. In fact, a 1969 recording of "Are You

Lonesome Tonight?" with Elvis getting the giggles became a #25 hit in the U.K. upon its 45 release in 1982.

Though they aren't up to much musically, Elvis even had fun with old stand-bys like "Hound Dog" and "Jailhouse Rock." Uncommon songs like "Hawaiian Wedding Song" disprove the theory that Elvis' set was overrun with oldies, and "You Gave Me a Mountain," "My Way," "Trying to Get to You," and "Unchained Melody" were bravura vocal efforts one and all. That two didn't make the final cut of the special considerably lessened its impact. On the other hand, "Love Me" and "Teddy Bear"/"Don't Be Cruel" (included in the final cut presumably only because they had been hits) hadn't been done justice in years, and they were awful during both shows. Keeping in mind how genuinely ill Elvis was—whether it was self-inflicted or not—Rapid City was among his better shows of 1976–77.

Elvis in Concert: October 3, 1977

In documenting the final days of a career never to be equaled, *Elvis in Concert* captured an important moment of twentieth-century history. There were some alternately amusing and insightful interviews from fans, plus Vernon Presley spoke extensively to CBS both before and after his son passed away. This footage is of immense value, as it offers the fascinating viewpoint of the only person who had been through it all with Elvis.

That's not to say that this was as important as *Aloha*, nor was it made as well. The 1973 special was a polished product, and Elvis certainly looked far better, but with *Elvis in Concert* being drawn from normal shows, there is a sense of warmth here that wasn't present on *Aloha*. Though he did have breathing problems due to his condition, his voice was in better form on certain selections.

Those propagating the idea that Elvis was a slobbering dolt in his last few years are telling a plain lie. The 1977 versions of "You Gave Me a Mountain" or "How Great Thou Art" have a depth that wasn't present before. In comparing "My Way" from 1973 and 1977, Elvis was more engaged and engaging during the later recording. It even was a warranted hit.

Yes, when Elvis throws away a superb song like "Don't Be Cruel," it's almost as horrid as the mid-sixties movie songs, but there is this great artist underneath everything. When Elvis manages to let that artist out, it's something of a triumph. From the standpoint of health and well-being, the only time he seemed up to performing after 1975 was the New Year's tour of 1976. As an artist, Elvis remained compelling during select moments.

Elvis in Concert doesn't feature a performer near his prime, but he was always special. That's what some people see in this footage. Here's a guy who knows he's in poor shape but is trying to pull something out of himself. When he briefly does, it's almost heartbreaking that he couldn't pull out of his situation. He was still Elvis underneath it all, and that's what makes his death so senseless.

The Status of *Elvis in Concert* Today

The *Elvis in Concert* special has been circulated among fans since it aired, and the lion's share of both shows have been on the bootleg market for a good fifteen years. Despite the footage being fairly easy to access, Elvis Presley Enterprises won't allow anything other than short excerpts to be released officially. It is said that they want to protect his image, but to be truthful, some of the Elvis-related memorabilia they have allowed to be sold has done Presley more damage than the 1977 footage ever could. As a full release, their hesitancy is warranted. With Elvis having his own collector's label, it would be easy to quietly put out a limited DVD that wouldn't draw mainstream attention.

A Personal Observation

To conclude this chapter, I would like to share a story with the reader that perhaps explains why *Elvis in Concert* has remained important to so many.

Every time I go to Las Vegas, I make it a point to go to what was known first as the International Hotel, second as the Las Vegas Hilton, and just recently renamed the Las Vegas hotel. So many of my favorite artists played there between 1969 and 1976—Elvis, Jerry Lee Lewis, James Brown, Charlie Rich, Ike and Tina Turner, the First Edition—so it's a special place for me. Of course, considering how heavily he's marketed, compared with those performers, Elvis is the only one who still makes his presence felt in the building. It was the location of some of his best moments—and some of his worst.

On this occasion, I was in the gift shop, and a documentary called *The Great Performances* was playing. When the 1977 performance of "Unchained Melody" came on the big screen, I was compelled to watch. Being where I was, knowing the ups and downs of Elvis' life, when I saw this troubled man digging deep inside himself for a moment of transcendence, I will admit the tears flowed. In one way, you can't help but feel angry that Elvis let himself go, but I also couldn't help but feel some sympathy. I also felt a sense of pride in Elvis' continued ability to move a listener in a way few artists can ever dream of.

42

Who Are You, Who Am I?

When Elvis Isn't Elvis

Over the years, a number of records have been promoted to mislead people into believing that Elvis was the artist. With Orion being promoted almost exclusively this way, it's not too surprising that Jimmy Ellis was being used for this purpose years before he put on his mask. Yet some went far further than Shelby Singleton in putting out records that actually used Elvis' name, likeness, or nickname on the label or cover. Most of these records are based around the "Elvis is alive" rumors, but some tried to pass themselves off as unearthed vintage recordings. These are among the strangest records ever put out, and some are even good. However, not one of these is Elvis, no matter what anybody tries to tell you.

?

In late 1977, a single came out on the U.K. Sun label (distributed by Charly Records) called "Don't Cry for Christmas"/"Dr. Xmas." The artist was only shown as "?" on the label, and it came in a reproduction of the fifties Sun Records sleeve. Jimmy Ellis has been credited with this recording, but it was not him. He hadn't re-signed to the label yet, and besides, it doesn't sound anything like him. I contacted the late Shelby Singleton about this record, but he said he didn't even know of it. Charly Records themselves recorded it, releasing ads that made it seem like it could be by Elvis.

"Don't Cry for Christmas" actually sounds like it could be a black singer imitating Elvis, which itself isn't all that common. Others say it was former Elvis demo singer and U.K. star P. J. Proby. Whoever it was, it's actually pretty good. It's an over-the-top Elvis imitation, but the song is interesting, and not based on any Presley records. The "Dr. Xmas" side is a sax-infused instrumental with a decidedly fifties feel. Like all of the records found here, it tanked.

From Elvis in Phoenix!

This hoax has a whole book written on it—by one of the perpetrators, no less. In 1978, a 45 called "Tell Me Pretty Baby" was issued on the Elvis Classic label (natch) and brazenly credited to Elvis Presley. The story goes that it was recorded in early 1954, when Elvis happened to be in Phoenix and helped a local band called the Reddots record a demo. Supposedly, Reddot Pete Falco found this and sold it to one Andrew Jackson (no joke), who quickly issued it. The only problem was that Elvis had never been in the area at the time.

OK, so perhaps Falco was off on the date, but any benefit of the doubt the public was willing to give him was squashed upon playing the record. It sounded nothing like Elvis at all—a stereotypical imitation at best. The music also bore no relation to Presley's early material, coming off as a poor copy of his early RCA hits.

Vernon Presley (who gave testimony) and RCA easily put a stop to the record in court. Singer Michael Conley came clean and admitted to being the voice on the record. He claimed his manager Hal Freeman put him up to it, which

This 1978 record claimed to date from before the Sun Records sessions. In light of that, the producers were sloppy in copying a sound Elvis didn't have until he recorded for RCA in 1956. Michael Conley puts forth a very stereotypical imitation that would only convince the few who have never heard Elvis sing.

Freeman quickly denied. In the end, it was much ado about nothing, but in using Elvis' name outright, "Tell Me Pretty Baby" became somewhat notorious.

Sivle

Perhaps the strangest Elvis soundalike was Sivle. In 1981, Steve Chanzes formed an Elvis fan club called Eternally Elvis. For the most part, it was to promote a book he wrote called *Elvis Where Are You?*, which put forth the idea that Elvis had faked his death with the assistance of Charlie Hodge. Charlie eventually sued to stop the book from being sold, but by then Chanzes had introduced Sivle Nora to the world. Sivle called radio stations, produced a video where his back was to the camera, and issued an LP of Elvis songs titled *Do You Know Who I Am: Sivle Sings Again*. There also was a monologue that was planned to be an accompanying LP, but it only circulated unofficially, as Chanzes disappeared.

Sivle's singing voice had power but not much else. That said, Sivle's album was good—for a hoax. It was nine Elvis songs done more or less "unplugged," with acoustic guitar prominent. Chanzes was sure to also include the recent "I Love a Rainy Night" to prove this was a 1981 session. In a badly scripted moment, Sivle just happens to stop his rendition of "Loving You" to comment on President Reagan being shot.

It should have ended there, but Sivle's speaking voice was the best Elvis imitation ever attempted. Five years after it was recorded, the monologue tape was given to *Orion* author Gail Brewer-Giorgio, who subsequently released it with her book *Is Elvis Alive?* While Chanzes was a huckster who got little to no media attention, Gail wasn't a bad writer; she was well spoken, and she soon got the media's ear. It started a huge spate of "Elvis is alive" mania that was generally treated lightheartedly. Still, the book hit the Top 10 *New York Times* bestsellers list, and people wanted Elvis back so badly that this rumor entered the rock-and-roll lexicon permanently.

On a 1989 appearance on the Geraldo Rivera show, Gail was confronted by one David Darlock, who said he was hired by Eternally Elvis in 1981 to be Sivle. He was a psychic entertainer who claimed to be actually channeling Elvis. Actually, he came off as silly, but it was clear he was Sivle once he went into his shtick. One thing in Darlock's story that wasn't factual was when he said the original Sivle tapes and LP were given a disclaimer that indicated they were the work of a psychic channeling Elvis. Chanzes dismissed Darlock's claim, and recently tried to sell the identity of Sivle for twenty grand on eBay after canceling a book that was to tell the "real" story.

NU WAVE

NUELVIS was a singer who released a single on the ANA label in 1988 called "You Know Me"/"Dance All Night." "You Know Me" is a song written to sound like it was being sung by an Elvis who faked his death. NUELVIS was really singer Charles Alan Rowe, who later recorded a far inferior remake. "You Know Me" (a.k.a. "I'm Alive and I'm Free") was a pleasant ballad, if not exactly subtle. Being a cool fifties-styled rockabilly cut, "Dance All Night" was actually a lot more fun. Rowe has Elvis down pretty well, but it won't fool a fan.

Just Check the Spelling . . .

One of the main arguments in the "Elvis is alive" theory was that Elvis' middle name of Aron is spelled Aaron on his tombstone. Elvis actually used the second spelling in the seventies, but his legal name was Aron. In 1988, Curb Records released the single "Spelling on the Stone," which was followed by a full LP in 1989. No singer was on the label, and the title cut was again sung as if it were by an "alive" Elvis. It eventually came out that the artist was Dan Willis, but of all

Major Bill Smith released this 45 around 1987. A fake duet made with Sivle out-takes, the recording misled some longtime fans.

these records, this one got the most media attention. The reason was that Mike Curb, who owned Curb Records, is a major player in the music industry, and his label had more promotional muscle than most who put out records of this type.

The *Spelling on the Stone* LP actually isn't all that bad, with the rockers "Poor Heart," "Hit the Bricks," and "Resurrection" standing out. A monologue was included at the end by promoter Lee Stoller, who produced and wrote much of the record. He tells a fanciful story about a mystery singer coming in to his office with tapes for the LP. If nothing else, it stands as an interesting artifact of the "Elvis is alive" mania that existed in the late eighties.

Memphis and Texas Mystery

Major Bill Smith was a fairly successful Fort Worth–based producer in the sixties. He produced records like "Hey Paula!" for Paul and Paula, "Hey Baby" for Bruce Channel, and "Last Kiss" by J. Frank Wilson. In 1987, he published the first of four editions of his book *Memphis Mystery*, one of the many tomes claiming that Elvis was alive. He claimed that co-author James Wakefield Burke (a journalist who died after the first printing) knew Elvis and was told in May 1977 that Elvis would fake his death. Burke wrote three chapters, and though he never outright said what he was told, this was what was implied. Oddly enough, Burke was also respected in his field. He had a few books to his name, and had written for *Esquire*.

Around 1985, Major Bill was sent a tape of the LP Steven Chanzes put out as Sivle and also one of the monologues. Major put out 45s and a tape of the Sivle recordings overdubbed with a singer on his roster named Kelli Fenton. He credited the recordings to "The King & Kelli." Evidently he didn't have permission from Chanzes to do this, so they are essentially bootlegs. They even have bootleg sound quality, as you can tell they are taken from a dub. Most of the picture sleeves had a drawing of Elvis on the cover next to Kelli, and came out around 1987.

None of these releases is that gripping—with one exception. Sivle's recording of "Moonlight Swim" (from a *Sivle Sings Again* out-take tape that circulated in 1981) was the best recording he did, and after overdubbing Fenton to make it a duet, the Major was the first to put it out publicly. It was put on the 1993 bootleg CD *The Colonel's Collection* (featuring Kelli and all), and was widely thought to be Elvis—until the rest of the Sivle recordings surfaced.

Major Bill also released the Sivle material with musical overdubs. These 1989 tapes and singles were credited to "The King of Rock and Roll" and had a photo of someone alleged to be Elvis in 1984 on the cover. Later, it came out that the man in the picture was a friend of Muhammad Ali named Larry Kolb. The Major and many others were told it was Elvis, but the picture was from a 1984 newspaper article published when Ali got out of the hospital.

Memphis Mystery
RECORDS

Elvis is Back

The Golden Voice is
Richer, Fuller, Stronger

"If You Think You've Seen Me"   BMI   2:50
(Elvis)

B/W

"You've Lost That Loving Feeling"
(C. Weil - B. Mann - P. Spector)

Written, Recorded, and Produced By
Elvis

MM622AA&A   JUNE, 1991 RELEASE

Major Bill's final 45 was a 1991 release using the name "Elvis." It was a fun release, but it's obviously a different voice than heard on Smith's earlier issues.

In the early nineties, Major put out some tapes and at least one 1991 single credited to Elvis (first name only) called "If You Think You've Seen Me"/"You've Lost That Loving Feeling." The top side was a novelty record about seeing Elvis at Wal-Mart. These later releases were not by Sivle but by a man who contacted the Major claiming he was Elvis. Actually, there may have been more than one guy on the various recordings, but who they were is unknown.

I had been in touch with Smith at the time, and after his death in 1994 I found out that the Major did think he was in touch with Elvis and was duped out of a lot of money. Because you had to order direct from Smith, these are the rarest of these faux Elvis records, and today one feels sorry for the elderly Major, who was a tireless promoter with a good sense of humor. If nothing else, he provided yet another of the many odd stories connected to the Elvis-is-alive "underground."

Sivle Sings Again

In 2002, a Czech Elvis fan club released a boot CD of the Sivle out-takes, claiming they were private Elvis tapes. It was called *The Long Lost Home Recordings*, and very few believed it was Elvis. Of course, few knew it was Sivle, because the majority of Elvis fans don't know about him—and even fewer knew about the out-takes. *The Long Lost Home Recordings* sounds like a bad dub of a cassette, but these looser recordings are amusing. Even though he did no work before or after 1981, Sivle is the one act that won't die.

Selected Bibliography

Books

Carr, Roy, and Mick Farren. *Elvis: The Illustrated Record*. New York: Harmony Books, 1982.

Denisoff, R. Serge, and George Plasketes. *True Disbelievers*. New Brunswick, NJ: Transaction Publishers, 1995.

Guralnick, Peter. *Last Train to Memphis*. New York: Little, Brown & Company, 1994.

———. *Careless Love*. New York: Little, Brown & Company, 1999.

———, and Ernst Jorgensen. *Elvis Day by Day*. New York: Ballantine Books, 1999.

Hopkins, Jerry. *Elvis: A Biography*. New York: Simon & Schuster, 1971.

———. *Elvis: The Final Years*. New York: St. Martin's Press, 1980.

Jorgensen, Ernst. *Elvis Presley: A Life in Music*. New York: St. Martin's Press, 1998.

Lewisohn, Mark. *Complete Beatles Chronicle*. New York: Harmony Books, 1992.

Marsh, Dave. *Elvis*. New York: Rolling Stone Press, 1982.

McLafferty, Gerry. *Elvis Presley in Hollywood*. London: Robert Hale, 1989

———. *Elvis Presley: The Power and the Persecution*. London: New Millennium, 2000.

Roy, Samuel. *Elvis: Prophet of Power*. Brookline, MA: Branden, 1985.

Skar, Stein Erik. *Elvis: The Concert Years*. Norway: Flaming Star, 1997.

Smith, Major Bill. *Memphis Mystery*. Fort Worth, TX: Le Cam Publications, 1987.

Torgoff, Martin, ed. *The Complete Elvis*. New York: Delilah, 1982.

Tunzi, Joseph. *Elvis Sessions III*. Chicago: J.A.T. Publishing, 2004.

Periodicals

Elvis: The Man and His Music. http://www.nowdigthismagazine.co.uk

The Elvis Files magazine (and Erik Lorentzen books of the same title). http://elvisfiles.no

The Elvis Mag. http://www.essentialelvis.com

Websites

Elvis in Norway (an Elvis site from Norway). http://home.online.no/~ov-egela/
    indexep.html
Elvis Information Network. http://elvisinfonet.com
Elvis Presley: A Life in Books (a complete bibliography of books on Elvis Presley).
    http://vnhouten.home.xs4all.nl/intro.html
Elvis Presley in Concert. http://elvisconcerts.com
The Elvis Presley Record Research Database. http://www.elvisrecords.us
The Elvis Shop London. http://www.theelvisshoplondon.com
For Elvis CD Collectors Only. http://elvis-collectors.com
Keith Flynn's Elvis Presley Pages (a sessionography, plus other facts and figures).
    http://keithflynn.com

Index